T0244560

ZWINGLI

# ZWINGLI

## God's Armed Prophet

*Bruce Gordon*

YALE UNIVERSITY PRESS
NEW HAVEN AND LONDON

Published with assistance from the foundation established in memory of Oliver Baty
Cunningham of the Class of 1917, Yale College.

For information about this and other Yale University Press publications, please contact:
U.S. Office: sales.press@yale.edu    yalebooks.com
Europe Office: sales@yaleup.co.uk    yalebooks.co.uk

Set in Minion Pro by IDSUK (DataConnection) Ltd
Printed in Great Britain by TJ Books, Padstow, Cornwall

Library of Congress Control Number: 2021937150

ISBN 978-0-300-23597-5

A catalogue record for this book is available from the British Library.

10 9 8 7 6 5 4 3 2 1

Carlos Eire, Bill Goettler, Rainer Henrich, Christian Moser,
Steve Pincus and Neil Robertson
The Best of Friends

# CONTENTS

# ILLUSTRATIONS

## PLATES

## MAPS

# ACKNOWLEDGEMENTS

The roots of this book run deep. As a distracted undergraduate in Halifax, Canada, I randomly took a book off a shelf near my desk. It was George Potter's biography of Huldrych Zwingli. Needless to say, I had heard of neither the author nor the subject, but I quickly discovered through perusing the volume that this sixteenth-century dude was a Swiss Protestant reformer who died in battle. That had to be a good story, I imagined. Several years later, on a cold February morning, I arrived at the Institut für Schweizerische Reformationsgeschichte in Zurich with very broken German (and no Swiss dialect), where I received a warm welcome from the secretary Frau Alexandra Seger and the *Oberassistent* Heinzpeter Stucki, who listened patiently to my bumbling attempts to explain my interest in Zwingli. Heinzpeter took me to the Staatsarchiv in Irchel. He also taught me to read sixteenth-century German and handwriting, and launched me on a project that would become my doctoral dissertation. Back at the institute on Kirchgasse 9, I was given a place to work and endless encouragement. I soon came to know the editors of the Bullinger correspondence, Hans Uli Bächtold and Kurt Rüetschi, who took me to lunch at Bauschänzli and taught me a great deal, and always with a heady dose of humour. Soon, I encountered the head of the institute, Professor Fritz Büsser, a formidable figure of the old Swiss school who ended up becoming a patron, mentor, examiner of my thesis at St Andrews and, finally, a friend. I shall never forget a lunch at Le Dézaley when he recounted the great, departed scholars of the Swiss Reformation.

During my initial stay in Zurich, I rather naïvely rented a room for two months in the Niederdorf, then very much the red-light district. It was clear that the locals had little interest in the Reformation. Soon afterwards, I moved to the more congenial setting of the Studentenheim in Steinwiesstrasse. There I made some friends who would sustain my time in Switzerland. Particularly generous was Daniel Hubacher, now pastor in Bern, who invited me to his home and took me swimming in the Aare.

One of my greatest pleasures was to meet the great scholar Gottfried W. Locher, first in Scotland and then at his home near Bern. When I visited him at his apartment, he kindly invited me to put on his *Hausschuhe*, so I have briefly walked in his shoes. He patiently explained Zwingli and the Swiss Reformation to me in a way that I have never forgotten. I hope something of his wisdom has made its way into this book.

As the years passed, the institute in Zurich was both an intellectual home and a place of joy. Rainer Henrich took me to lunch, beginning a friendship that has flourished for over 30 years, with him becoming godfather to our daughter. The succession of directors, Alfred Schindler, Emidio Campi and Peter Opitz have been nothing less than supportive and generous. Emidio and Peter became dear friends, sharing their work and inviting me into their homes. I remember with great fondness Brigitta Stoll, Daniel Bolliger, Roland Diethelm, Luca Baschera, Michael Baumann, Alexandra Kess, and recently Reinhard Bodenman. I am grateful to Francisca Loetz in Zurich and Kaspar von Greyerz in Basel/Bern for their friendship and support. With affection, I am thankful for my friendship with Christian Moser, who is proof that outstanding scholarship can be combined with a wicked sense of humour. His WhatsApp messages have brightened many a day. I dedicated a book to Christian's son Sebi, my godson, and he remains deep in my heart. The pinnacle of these many years came in 2012, when I was awarded an honorary doctorate from the theological faculty at Zurich, one of the greatest moments of my life. The journey from that Monday morning in 1988 to the ceremony at Irchel has left me with an enduring love of Zurich and Switzerland, reflected not in books and articles, but in friends and family.

The roots run to Canada and Scotland. My undergraduate years at King's College, Dalhousie in Nova Scotia, transformed my life. I came under the guidance of teachers who taught me to learn languages, study philosophy (never my strong point) and history. They are mostly gone, but recently I was able to get in touch with my fellow student and dear friend, Neil Robertson and my wise teachers Henry Roper and Tom Curran. In 2019, my college gave me an honorary degree in canon law (wonderful for a Presbyterian). It was incredibly moving to be back after 40 years.

Fifteen years of teaching at St Andrews in Scotland was a once-in-a-lifetime experience. The St Andrews Reformation Studies Institute was an adventure that my friend (and best man) Andrew Pettegree and I embarked upon with nothing but a single filing cabinet; it has since become an international scholarly body. My debt to Andrew cannot be filled in these acknowledgements. We were soon joined by Bridget Heal, who has remained a friend and inspiration. Tom Scott taught me much about German and Swiss history. Occasionally, I am in contact with former students from those years – the happiest of associations from some of the best years of my life.

This year, 2020, has witnessed enormous change. A pandemic rages as I complete this manuscript, and all academic work is overshadowed by the suffering and loss of loved ones, but also by the enormous courage of those who care for the ill. One of the people we have recently lost is Peter Stephens, whose work on Zwingli has become a staple of knowledge of the reformer in the English-speaking world. His laconic humour and eccentricity will be missed. As will be Irena Backus, who was a mentor to me in so many ways. Her endless kindnesses, including invitations to dinner at her home in Geneva, inspire me to share the humaneness of learning. I remember with affection my doctoral supervisor James K. Cameron, as well as Hans Guggisberg, who hosted me in Basel. As I finish, I learn of the death of Frau Seger, who welcomed me in Zurich in 1988. Rest in peace.

When I wrote *Calvin*, Rona, Charlotte and I were about to embark on an adventure in Yale and New Haven. Now, 12 years on, I have amassed a number of debts of scholarship and of friendship. Once again, it has been all about the students, and I shall never regret my open-door policy at the Divinity School and the students who have invited me into their lives, even if some things had to be done at the last moment because of too much chatting. They have indulged this guy who talks about the sixteenth century. During my time, I have had wonderful colleagues, too many to mention. Above all, I think of Carlos Eire, whose generosity, learning and charity are a model worthy of the saints he studies. I think also of Markus Rathey (who puts me right about Luther), Joel Baden, Tisa Wenger, Ken Minkema, Harry Attridge, Melanie Ross, Joyce Mercer, Adam Eitel, Clifton Grandby, John Hare, Teresa Berger, Chloe Starr, Steve Crocco, Jennifer Herdt, Emilie

Townes and the late Lamin Sanneh. As dean, Greg Sterling has been supportive, encouraging and a friend. Also at Yale, I owe a great debt of thanks to John Rogers (our co-taught course in Britain!), Frank Griffel (with whom, in Berlin, we watched Germany win the World Cup), Larry Manley, David Quint, David Kastan, Julia Adams, Phil Gorsky, Keith Wrightson, Francesca Trivellato (now at Princeton) and Rob Nelson.

Zwingli and Luther may have died unreconciled, but two of their best scholars have taught me how to understand them, and their friendship has been a treasure: Amy Nelson Burnett and Lyndal Roper.

One of the great joys of being at Yale has been the graduate students with whom I have had the honour to work. I think of Max Scholz, Elizabeth Herman, Ryan Patrico, Dan Jones, Flynn Cratty, Brad Abromaitis, Russ Gasdia, Alexander Batson, Elizabeth Buckheit and Serena Strecker. They have taught me more than I can repay.

To the book, my overwhelming thanks goes once more to Heather McCallum at Yale, whose boundless enthusiasm and support have seen me through another sixteenth-century figure. Her short, to-the-point emails are worth framing. She kept me to my word limit! I am extremely grateful to the readers for the press, who saw an all-too-early version of the text and patiently made enormously helpful suggestions. As with *Calvin* years ago, Rachael Lonsdale expertly guided me through publication. I owe a particular debt to Philip Benedict, who influenced this book in crucial ways and whose knowledge of the Reformation has taught us all.

I realize that my thanks read like the credits from the *Ten Commandments*. I acknowledge with great joy the work and counsel of my dear friend Pierrick Hildebrand, whose own book on the Zurich covenant will arrive in due course. Pierrick rendered my Swiss German into something more comprehensible and kept me right on so many points. I will never forget a walk in Emmental, when he shared generous and thoughtful reflections on how to understand Zwingli better. Our Skype conversations are a weekly highlight, as is his model of Christian fellowship.

There are many who have read the text in part or whole, and whose feedback has been invaluable. Notable was my editor Nate Antiel, whose advice changed the direction of the book, much for the better. I thank with gratitude: Ward Holder (for friendship and a long and instructive phone call), Euan Cameron, Diarmaid MacCulloch, Alec Ryrie, Peter Marshall, Joel Harrington,

Chris Ocker, Jennifer McNutt, Paul Lim, Michael Walker, Randy Head, Kathryn Lofton, Richard Muller, David Noe, Justin Hawkins, Will Tarnasky, Bill Goettler, Colin Destache, Jamie Dunn. Russ Gasdia did wonderful work on the maps, and Pierrick Hildebrand helped procure the images.

Three people who deserve special thanks are my tireless and resourceful research assistants: Jacques Fabiunke (now back in Germany), Max Norman and Will Taransky.

While in New Haven, we have been fortunate to be part of a church community that is loving and committed to God's justice. Our friends Bill Goettler and Maria LaSala guided us for years. Now we are fortunate to have the prophetic voice of Pastor J.C. Cadwallader. If Zwingli had known that gender is no barrier to speaking God's Word, he would have been thrilled. I owe much to Dr Victoria Morrow, whom I meet weekly. I have tried to do what you suggested. I was extremely fortunate to work with Clive Liddiard at the press, whose expert copy-editing much improved the book.

At Yale, Steve Pincus was my colleague and co-conspirator. I learned from him always to ask the 'so what' question. I miss his presence here, but take great pleasure that he and Sue Stokes are flourishing in Chicago. You give us good reason to get to know the windy city. Here's to more meals.

Twelve years ago, I was able to dedicate *Calvin* to Rona, as an offering of my love. I was clear that you had taught me the meaning of our vow of 'in sickness and in health'. Little did we know that there would be more sickness, hospitals, psychiatrists and treatment. Yet, here we are, in love as much as ever. Your deep understanding of the early modern world has led me to think harder and write better. Your editing hand has made my thoughts clear and my ideas fly, even when you thought I was wrong. Every page has your wisdom. There has been nothing better than to walk around Vienna with you and learn about a vanished world.

To Charlie, your desire to change the world continues to inspire me. Here's hoping that you will soon be back in Jordan, speaking Arabic and living your passion.

Finally, it is a joy to dedicate this volume to friends who have sustained, inspired and loved me.

New Haven
December 2020

# AUTHOR'S NOTE

Where translations exist, I have made use of them, although they were checked against the originals, and extensive alterations were made to correct and update the language. Otherwise, I am responsible for the English versions of the Latin and German. I am very grateful to Pierrick Hildebrand and David Noe for their guidance. I have kept masculine pronouns for the deity, mindful that for many it jars with modern views. My intention was to remain close to sixteenth-century usage.

The nomenclature of the early Reformation is a minefield. As the term 'Protestant' is inappropriate for the years before 1529, I have preferred to designate the supporters of the Reformation 'evangelicals', although the name is highly elastic. I fully recognize that 'Zwinglian' or 'Lutheran' is almost meaningless in an age of doctrinal plurality, and so I have kept them to a minimum. I have also used 'Reformed' to reference adherents to the Swiss theological teachings, again aware that, as a group, they were hardly homogeneous. Finally, until the adult baptisms of 1525, I speak of 'radicals', and not Anabaptists. It is a loaded term, and used advisedly.

I avoid using 'Switzerland' and 'cantons', as they are a later usage, preferring the 'Swiss Confederation' and its 'Confederates' or 'states'. The Mandated Territories were those lands under joint authority of the Confederates. The Five States designates Uri, Schwyz, Unterwalden, Lucerne and Zug, all of which remained Catholic.

There is no good English translation of Zwingli's position in Zurich as *Leutpriester*, and so I have stuck with the traditional 'people's priest'. All bible passages are from the New Revised Standard Version.

# CHRONOLOGY

**1484**
1 January               Born in Wildhaus (Toggenburg)

**1494**                  Sent to study in Basel

**late 1496/early 1497**   Embarks on studies in Bern

**1498**                  Matriculates in Vienna

**1502**                  Attends University of Basel

**1504**                  Graduates bachelor of arts

**1506**
Spring               Receives master of arts degree from University of Basel
September           Becomes priest in Glarus

**1510**                  Fable of the Ox

**1513–1514**          In Italy with Glarus troops (battle of Novara)

**1515**
13 September        Battle of Marignano

**1516**                  'The Labyrinth'
                        Visits Erasmus in Basel
14 April            Moves to Benedictine Abbey at Einsiedeln

**1518**                  Elected people's priest at Grossmünster in Zurich

**1519**
1 January            Begins preaching in Grossmünster
September           Struck down by plague

**1521**

April                          Elected canon in Grossmünster chapter

**1522**

early                          Secretly marries Anna Reinhart

9 March                        Sausage meal in Froschauer's house

7–9 April                      Disputation with Bishop Hugo von
                               Hohenlandenberg's representatives

16 April                       Preached on right of Christians to eat what they want

21 July                        Disputation with monks

22–23 August                   'Apologeticus archeteles' appears

6 September                    'On the Clarity and Certainty of the Word of God'
                               published

November                       Resigns as priest to become preacher in Grossmünster

**1523**

29 January                     First disputation in Zurich

14 July                        *Exposition of the Sixty-Seven Articles* published

30 July                        'On Divine and Human Righteousness' published

29 September                   Reorganization of Grossmünster

26–28 October                  Second disputation in Zurich

17 November                    'Short Christian Instruction' published

**1524**

2 April                        Officially celebrates marriage to Anna Reinhart

June                           Removal of images from Zurich churches

November                       'Letter to Matthew Alber' on Lord's Supper

**1525**

17 January                     Disputation with radicals on baptism

21 January                     First adult baptisms

March                          *Commentary on True and False Religion* published
                               'The Shepherd' published

March–April                    Prepares Liturgy of Lord's Supper

13 April                       First Reformed Lord's Supper

27 May                         *Baptism, Rebaptism and Infant Baptism* published

19 June                        *Prophezei* opens in Grossmünster

**1526**

| | |
|---|---|
| 7 March | Council decree to execute Anabaptists |
| 19 May–9 June | Baden Disputation |

**1527**

| | |
|---|---|
| January | Formation of Christian Civic Union (alliance with Bern and Constance) |
| 5 January | Execution of Felix Manz |
| February | Schleitheim Articles |
| 31 July | *Elenchus: Refutation of the Tricks of the Anabaptists* published |

**1528**

| | |
|---|---|
| 6–26 January | Bern Disputation |
| 7 February | Reformation laws in Bern |
| 21 April | First synod in Zurich decreed |

**1529**

| | |
|---|---|
| April | Reformation in Basel |
| | Protest at Diet of Speyer |
| 22 April | Christian Alliance of Catholic states with Austrian Habsburgs |
| June | First Kappel War |
| 26 June | First Kappel Peace |
| 1–4 October | Marburg Colloquy |

**1530**

| | |
|---|---|
| July | Diet of Augsburg |
| 3 July | 'Account of the Faith' printed |
| August | Sermon on providence |
| November | Alliance of Zurich with Philipp of Hesse |

**1531**

| | |
|---|---|
| May | Renewed blockade of the Five States |
| | Folio edition of Zurich Bible |
| August | 'Exposition of Faith' prepared |
| 11 October | Zwingli's death at Second Battle of Kappel |
| 20 November | Second Kappel Peace |
| 13 December | Heinrich Bullinger succeeds Zwingli as head of Zurich Church |

1. The Holy Roman Empire and the Rhine River Valley in the Sixteenth Century.

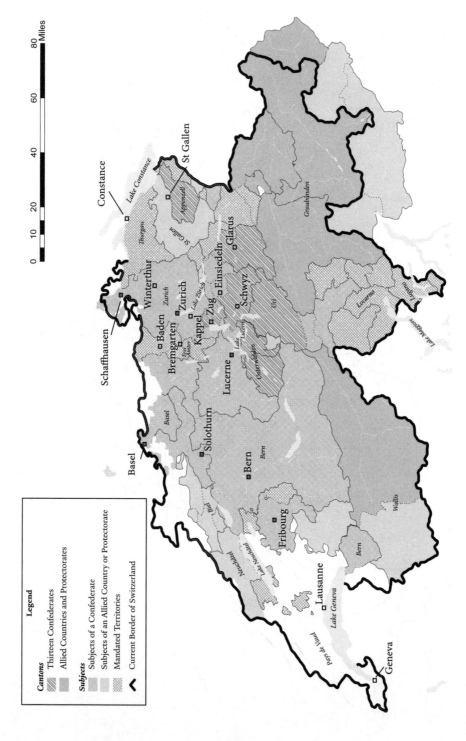

2. The Swiss Confederation in 1530.

Legend

*Cantons*
Thirteen Confederates
Allied Countries and Protectorates

*Subjects*
Subjects of a Confederate
Subjects of an Allied Country or Protectorate
Mandated Territories
Current Border of Switzerland

0 10 20 40 60 80
Miles

Constance
Lake Constance
St Gallen
Schaffhausen
Thurgau
Appenzell
St Gallen
Winterthur
Glarus
Baden
Zurich
Einsiedeln
Zug
Lake Zürich
Kappel
Schwyz
Bremgarten
Basel
Lucerne
Uri
Lake Lucerne
Unterwalden
Graubünden
Solothurn
Locarno
Bern
Lake Maggiore
Bell
Biel
Bern
Neuchâtel
Lake Neuchâtel
Fribourg
Wallis
Pays de Vaud
Lausanne
Bern
Lake Geneva
Geneva

*Hence it is that all armed prophets have conquered, and the unarmed ones have been destroyed.*

Machiavelli, *The Prince*, chapter 6

# INTRODUCTION

Those who prophesy speak to other people for their upbuilding and encouragement and consolation.

1 Corinthians 14:3

When Huldrych Zwingli died in 1531, he vanished. His body was ritually humiliated and reduced to ashes mixed with pig's blood. No funeral was held in Zurich, where disbelief took the place of commemoration. In the 12 years since Zwingli had arrived in his adopted home, Christianity had been reimagined; but at what price? A vibrant faith had been eradicated, churches stripped, opponents banished or drowned. A new reality had been created, but not the dreamed-of conversion of all of the Swiss lands to the gospel. Unyielding borders between faiths had been erected instead. Most shockingly, Zwingli had died in a war he had advocated in his preaching and military battleplans, dressed in armour, with his final words reputed to be 'They can kill the body, but not the soul.'

Huldrych Zwingli understood that violence belonged to Western Christendom and early modern society. It gave him great sorrow, but he saw its place. He railed against cruelty and injustice, but as a priest he accompanied troops to war, and as a reformer he consented to the execution of Anabaptists. He hated the sale of the young men of the impoverished Swiss lands into the mercenary service of foreign powers, which he equated with prostitution; but he saw in his valorous forefathers a folk prepared to take up arms to defend ancient liberties against predatory bishops and abbots. The problem was not the swords, but whom they served. Unlike the Florentine Dominican preacher Girolamo Savonarola, Machiavelli's 'unarmed prophet',

Zwingli never made the mistake of separating the vision of godly reform from political and military power.

Zwingli was God's armed prophet, but not simply because he fell at Kappel, cut down by Catholic soldiers. The weapons with which this visionary was armed were many. He used the pulpit to bring about radical social, political and religious change, with his words leading to the reform of care for the poor and education of young people. Faith and rule were distinct, but must never be uncoupled, as ancient Israel exemplified. Freedom existed within structures divinely given. The almighty, providential God ordains the order and hierarchy by which the people should live. Zwingli stood out among his generation of reformers for his readiness to harness Christianity's marriage to earthly authority in order to create an astonishingly bold reimagining of what the relationship between Church and society might be. He saw a new world, for which he was prepared to kill and, ultimately, die. He was not a warmonger, but he was prepared to sacrifice himself and others. Even his closest allies were deeply troubled by Zwingli's confidence: friends had warned him against military conflict, and his best friend, Leo Jud, regretted on his deathbed the war that almost ended the Reformation. The martial legacy endured. The monument to Zwingli erected in Zurich in the nineteenth century has him facing south, towards Catholic Switzerland, with Bible open and sword in hand.

Huldrych Zwingli possessed the qualities of those remarkable religious figures who, in their persons, draw together unresolved contradictions that prove to be their making; in his case, they proved also to be his downfall. To say that Zwingli was a complex person would be banal. This book explores the ways in which competing impulses and contradictory tensions became remarkably generative, fecund and destructive. Zwingli's debt to Martin Luther, who gave voice to the Protestant creed of scripture, faith and grace alone, was deep, as he acknowledged in his more generous moments. But when the two churchmen looked to the Bible, they found different truths. Zwingli's vision was not Luther's.

To reach Zwingli in a distant age, we must begin with his God. The common thread that ran through his life as priest and reformer was his perception of

God as creator – providential and, ultimately, good. Indeed, God was good-ness itself. The reformer was convinced that although God was inscrutable and his decisions unfathomable, his unconditional love for humanity had never been in question. Zwingli had influential teachers on this point: his beloved Plato spoke of the source of all things in the Good, and his mentor Desiderius Erasmus (1456–1536) taught the optimism of creation. For Zwingli, the Christian life was not a dull, self-flagellating trudge through the world. Yes, God sent hardships to test and discipline the faithful, but Zwingli delighted in describing him as joyful. Lives were constantly being trans-formed and were transforming, making the world more just. The focal point of such transformation was the Eucharist. It was Zwingli's oft-derided and misunderstood conviction that the Eucharist – a commemoration of the Lord's Supper – was primarily intended as an expression of glory and unity: as light poured through clear glass and reflected off whitewashed walls, the community at the table encountered a vision of eternity, of unity beyond time with the gathered faithful of the past, present and future. Zwingli was not a mystic, but the experience was of the presence of the Spirit.

There was a serpent in the garden. Zwingli sought to bring together temporal and spiritual authority, so that they seamlessly formed the body of Christ in the world. To do so, he tethered power and violence to magistrates and Church. Individuals and communities were constantly in a state of becoming – of striving to be – more Christ-like. But the Word, sacraments and prayer were not enough. The rod of governance was not only to correct: when necessary, the governing powers were to demonize, exclude and destroy. A man of his age, Zwingli did not accept that individuals were free to believe what they wanted. The religion of the state was the religion of its people. Zwingli quickly encountered the dispiriting reality that most people would not readily convert to the gospel. The forces of opposition to his reformation in Zurich, and to his plans for the evangelizing of the Swiss Confederation, took the form of reluctant peasants, the institutional Church and confident political authorities.

Zwingli does not allow the Reformation to rest comfortably in the modern mind, joining Luther, with his execrable views of Jews, and Calvin, with his role in the execution of Michael Servetus. In Evelyn Waugh's short novel *Helena*, the mother of Emperor Constantine asks the Christian Lactantius about the new faith in the empire and whether it will take its place alongside the old gods. Lactantius replies: 'Christianity is not that sort of religion, ma'am. It cannot share anything with anybody. Whenever it is free, it will conquer.' Zwingli inherited from medieval Christianity a powerful sense of orthodoxy and utter intolerance of heresy, but there were degrees. Ultimately these convictions led him away from his beloved Erasmus. Jews were benighted deniers of Christ, yet he found his model of Christian ministry in the rabbinic tradition of a priesthood of the educated in the service of the Word. Zwingli had an expansive view of salvation and he expected to find the virtuous figures of classical antiquity in heaven. Yet in his own time, those who rejected infant baptism deserved to be drowned in the river that flowed through Zurich.

The gospel, Zwingli believed, was not to be thwarted, and every power – spiritual and temporal – was to be conscripted into its service. The prophet of the renewed body of Christ was also the military tactician who planned the conquest of Zurich's Catholic neighbours. He joined other religious leaders of his age in understanding reformation as God's entering into human history to rescue a lost people through the renewal of his Word. His optimism was enormous, and perhaps to our eyes naïve. One does not come close to understanding Zwingli without seeing how he was utterly convinced that when exposed to the Word of God, the people would cast off idolatry and embrace the truth. He was given to overreaching confidence in himself, others and the inevitable truth of his cause.

In the pages of this book we find, however, a man who never created his own reality. Zwingli was a powerful, charismatic and flawed character who unleashed a revolution which he then struggled to lead. His was not the only narrative unfolding in Zurich: Catholics and Anabaptists also dreamed of reform and of a purified Church, and their convictions were equally unyielding. The Reformation could have taken a number of paths; and it might not have materialized at all. Further, Zwingli's friends and colleagues were never his acolytes, for their shared beliefs did not gloss over divided conceptions, perspectives and convictions. For all its compelling drama, Zwingli's life took place within a broader story and was largely reactive, responding to events over which he had no control. He did not pick many of his battles, and nor did he anticipate their outcomes.

Zwingli's Zurich was an admixture of innovation and conservation. The Reformation in Zurich, as across Europe, was built on the medieval foundations of church order, retaining the ideal that each community was focused on the parochial church and served by a cleric. It was not a liberation from a dark past. The Zurich that Zwingli entered in December 1518 was filled with processions, relics, interceding saints and the body of Christ in the hands of priests. His reformation eviscerated the Catholic doctrines and practices, and priests became pastors; but the laity still made their way to the local church to be baptized, confirmed, married and then, eventually, buried. The Reformed emphasis on the link between moral rectitude and true belief had deep roots in the medieval world, as did the violent proscription of deviant behaviour – all that polluted the communal body had to be excised.

Likewise, the Reformation took place within the magical universe of the late-medieval world, filled with malign and benign forces or spirits. Neither Zwingli nor any of his supporters denied the order or composition of the natural Ptolemaic world or humanity's place within it. The body consisted of humours determined by the movement of the stars and the elements. The forests were full of demons who could easily take the shape of a wolf or a dead grandmother. The natural world evoked awe and fear: beyond the city walls lay a dangerous world in which travel was perilous. The Reformation had no answer to plague, which continued to ravage communities, with no respect for status or wealth. Zwingli nearly died of the pest in 1519, as his future wife, Anna Reinhart, nursed him. Yet, for Zwingli, the Alpine mountains and valleys of his youth were the mirror of heaven, a land that nurtured a valorous, brave and godly people.

Nevertheless, the disruption was immense. Nothing in Luther's reforms matched the zeal with which the worship of God was spiritually and physically reconceived in Zurich. When the Reformed Lord's Supper was first celebrated in Zurich, on Maundy Thursday 1525, there was nothing to which it could be compared. Christ was no longer physically present, and the bond between the living and the dead had been severed. Symbolically, Zwingli now preached from the very spot where the high altar, the site of intercession, had once stood. The removal of altars, images, stained glass and organs was by order of the magistrates, for Zwingli envisaged a relatively seamless unity of the temporal and sacred to form a *corpus Christianum*. To his critics, this vision was a compromise with earthly power and a betrayal of the gospel. For Zwingli, the Church was the whole community, believers and unbelievers alike. Although they would be separated at the

Last Judgement, in this world they formed one visible community, subject to magistrates and prophets. To be an obedient servant of the state was to be a member of the Church, and vice versa.

In 1516, while still a priest, Zwingli had had a revelation that led him to the sufficiency of scripture alone. That encounter preceded Luther's Ninety-Five Theses, but the Swiss preacher was by no means the first Protestant. Many more miles remained to be travelled. Nevertheless, the moment was personally formative and determined a career of preaching through the books of the Bible, line by line, from start to finish. Scripture was the fullness of God's revelation to humanity, and it was also clear and perspicuous. Zwingli joined Luther in holding that the Bible interprets itself, with clearer passages throwing light on those that are thorny. As a disciple of Erasmus, he believed that knowledge of languages was key to understanding scripture, but only if the reader was guided by the Holy Spirit. Zwingli shared the enthusiasm of his day for the belief that scripture could be understood by all the faithful; but his initial impulses soon gave way to a priesthood of the learned and a didactic role for pastors. The consensus of wise prophets should hold sway. The most dramatic symbol of the new Reformed order was the creation of the *Prophezei* at the principal church in Zurich. The leading clergy gathered daily in the choir to interpret the Old Testament in Greek, Hebrew and Latin, before translating their reading into German for the faithful. There could be no more dramatic expression that the Bible was to be interpreted not by the people, but by the elite within the space of the church.

Zwingli envisaged a new form of Church, a new understanding of the sacraments and a new way of being the sacral community. That vision would ultimately become the 'Reformed tradition', often more misleadingly known as 'Calvinism', and its theology and forms of Church would find a multitude of expressions. Their origins lay in the aspirations of a peasant's son from Toggenburg. Zwingli has long been cast as a lesser man than Martin Luther and as the warm-up act for John Calvin. Neither view stands up to scrutiny. Zwingli freely admitted that Luther was the towering figure of the early Reformation, but he was no dependant. He came to his convictions about God, scripture and the Church independently of the Wittenberg doctor. He had initially believed he was in agreement with Luther, whom he read with profit, but their gazes differed. Whereas the German looked to law and gospel as the essential dynamic of the Christian life, Zwingli saw the commu-

nity as the body of Christ – fallen and deeply flawed, but capable of regeneration. If we are to speak of abiding influences, we must turn to the great
Dutch humanist Erasmus. Ultimately, Zwingli would depart from his
mentor in embracing radical reform, but to his last days he still acknowledged his debt.

In terms of their characters and thought, Zwingli and Calvin are not
simply alternatives. The Frenchman's debt to Zwingli was enormous, even if
he refused to acknowledge it. He belonged to the next generation: his conversion to evangelical Christianity came after Zwingli was dead. Calvin inherited the Reformed tradition forged in Zurich, Basel and Strasbourg, and his
great contribution was to draw it together compendiously and to deepen its
furrows. Zwingli, however, was the creative spirit. He imagined and created
a new form of Christianity grounded in the covenantal relationship between
God and humanity and founded on the positive understanding of divine law.
The shape and cadence of Reformed Christianity came from Zurich. Zwingli,
who cherished the ancient Greek lyricist Pindar and repeatedly read Plato,
was the poetic spirit of the Reformation. He loved music, created liturgy for
worship and crafted an aesthetic of the Spirit. He was the artist, while his
successor Heinrich Bullinger and Calvin in Geneva were the craftsmen.
They also inherited Zwingli's hatreds: Anabaptists, idolatry and dissent.

The onus on a biographer is to avoid over-valorizing a single individual,
casting everyone else as spear-carriers in an opera. Without apology, this
book argues that Zwingli made the Reformation in Zurich possible, and that
the networks he cultivated spread his ideas to other Swiss lands and abroad.
It fully recognizes, however, that he did not act alone and that his thought
was not entirely his own. Zwingli was undoubtedly an original thinker: he
whipped up a distinctive mixture of new and borrowed ideas to forge a
vision unlike the imaginings of his contemporaries, although he shared
many of their deepest convictions. Innovation accompanied a remarkable
ability for clarity, synthesis and polemic. Unlike Erasmus, Zwingli did not
write in the comfort and tranquillity of the study; his extraordinary volume
of writings was crafted in the fires of controversy and attack. His time was
brief: Luther lived into his sixties, and Calvin was in Geneva for almost 25
years. Zwingli was in Zurich for only 12 years and died at the age of 47. Yet,
he created a Church, and his writings and letters fill a dozen large volumes
in their critical edition.

Zwingli did not make it easy for us to engage with his texts. As for many figures of his age, his logic is now somewhat foreign in its assumptions. His theological works seem at times to operate by assertion, tautology and somewhat random proof texting. He felt absolutely no obligation to prove many of his arguments, such as God's existence, God as Trinity or the fall of humanity. The practice of infant baptism, assumed from the tradition of Western Christianity, required no explanation until challenged by the radicals. Zwingli frequently spoke of reason, but his meaning does not align with our post-Enlightenment instincts. Reason for Zwingli was embedded in creation and consonant with the will of God as revealed to humanity. This biography seeks to find him on his own ground. It is crucial for us to remember that, for all his radical theology, our subject had been a student of the medieval scholastics and believed himself an inheritor of the legacy of the church fathers.

Nineteenth-century liberal Protestants found in Zwingli the most congenial of Reformation theologians. Their case hardly bears close scrutiny, for Zwingli was no proto-liberal. True religion, the subject of his most polished theological work, was a narrow path. But he did create narratives of the freedom of a Christian, the liberated conscience and the redeemed life. Zwingli did not reject the world or human bodies. The inner working of the Spirit was expressed in outward acts. In fact, Zwingli was attacked by Catholics and Lutherans alike for not having a sufficiently robust doctrine of sin, which he famously called an 'illness'. Despite his reputation for iconoclasm and banishing church music, he possessed a heightened aesthetic that saw beauty in creation and humanity, both of which he praised in lyrical terms.

An expert showman and a brilliant tactician, Zwingli also mastered the art of communication, using the pulpit and the printing press to extraordinary effect, as he moved effortlessly between Latin and his native German. A *rusticus* brought up in the countryside, he could make the words of the gospel resonate in the narrow streets of the city and in the yards of the villages. Zwingli loved to play with language. He even played with his name, turning his baptismal 'Ulrich' into 'Huldrych', which meant in his dialect 'rich in grace'. He practised self-fashioning from the pulpit, in council chamber and on the page. In the vernacular, he evoked home and family, valleys and mountains, and the agrarian life. His language was paternalistic and most of his metaphors highly masculine, but he loved to remind the people that they stood above the angels in God's estimation. The world of antiquity was his playground: he adored Homer and the poetry of Pindar, and drew upon the comedies of Aristophanes and Terence for elegant parallels or to stick his opponents with sarcasm and mockery. He had been shaped by Erasmus' belief that the classical world could be baptized into the Christian.

Zwingli's evident charisma cut both ways. On his arrival in Zurich in 1519, he had immediately been able to weave a narrative that the corruption wrought by mercenary pensions and the abuses of the clerical class belonged to God's judgement on the world. He used the pulpit to inspire, cajole and vilify. The people had never heard anything like it, and he quickly became the principal voice within the Zurich Church, his name associated with scripture as a sole authority and with fierce social and political criticism. His preaching won him supporters, whom he convinced not only that the traditional faith was error-laden and dishonest, but also that the Bible held the promise of a better world. Admired and hated in equal measure, he was also able to cultivate contacts within the Zurich establishment, in particular with leading families who became patrons. Although his approach quickly disappointed those who sought more rapid reform or who were less persuaded that the magistrates were Christians, he would not be moved. The tactician in him understood that his evolving vision of a new Church and society would remain an illusion unless the magistrates were on board. Without their support, even from a minority of the elite within the city, the scurrilous preacher most likely would have been shown the gate of the city, or worse. The late-medieval world provided plenty of examples of the fate of unwanted preachers.

The strategist did not function at the expense of the preacher or theologian. At the heart of this book is the argument that although Zwingli's thought and actions may at times seem to be at odds, in fact they belong together – and must be addressed together. Zwingli the politician was still very much Zwingli the preacher. The Bible was always the lens through which he viewed the world. That prospect at times blinded him to political realities. His goal was to bring the people and society back to God's Word. From an early stage, he adopted the identity of a prophet, bringing scripture to the people, advising political leaders and imagining a new land governed by God's justice. Zwingli was in no doubt that he had a special calling. Yet when news of the military defeat in which he died reached Zurich on the morning of 12 October 1531, his name was spat out as that of a traitor. His successor used his first public address to defend the memory of the fallen reformer, declaring that he had been a true prophet. Many were unconvinced.

Zwingli's story has never been easy to tell. His end had all the qualities of a bad death. He had not been martyred at the hands of unrighteous persecutors, nor had he died in his bed (as would Luther and Calvin), surrounded by weeping friends. Colleagues within the Reformation movement mourned the loss of a leader of the faith, but were guarded about the circumstances. Luther was certain that his nemesis had gone to hell, having lived and died by the sword. Reviled by Catholics and Lutherans, Zwingli had become synonymous with heresy. He could not embody national or heroic sentiments within the Swiss Confederation, where he was associated with Zurich's age-old hegemonic desires. A prospective biographer was warned off the project by a close friend of Zwingli's – his subject was too controversial. John Calvin would pretend to know little about Zwingli.

By the nineteenth century, we find a reformer much transformed. The patriotic and national interests of the age reconfigured Zwingli as a founder of liberal Protestantism. He was a hero and martyr, a screen onto which Swiss identity could be projected. In the face of growing secularism, he was a reformer who could serve the confessional interests of a new age. By the end of the century, a string of commemorations had been held, a statue erected, numerous biographies and plays written or performed, and a critical edition of his works launched. Zwingli became a significant part of the resurgence of the Reformation in the English-speaking world. And in our own time, in thoroughly secular Zurich, where Catholics today outnumber Protestants (and where people of no confession outnumber both), considerable effort was made in 2019 to mark the 500th anniversary of Zwingli's arrival in the city. The reformer became the central figure in a heated debate about identity and modernity. In a post-Christian society that he could never have imagined, Zwingli still stirs the ambivalent feelings that met him at the gates of the city in 1518.

# ✣ ONE ✣

## MOUNTAIN VALLEY

The Alpine resorts created by the extraordinary feats of nineteenth-century railway construction and the chic cultures of modern-day St Moritz and Klosters are far removed from the mountainous world Huldrych Zwingli knew as a child.[1] The breath-taking elevations and verdant valleys belied a harsh struggle for existence in a world of subsistence farming subject to rapacious overlords, who were frequently prominent churchmen and religious houses. A possible escape lay in promises of money and adventure for mercenaries in the service of the king of France or the pope. The formation of the young Zwingli was dictated by a deep-rooted attachment to land and people, by the faith of his parents, by an acute sense of the depredations in God's world, and by ever-present violence.

### EARLY JOURNEYS

Ulrich Zwingli, as he was named (after his father) at his baptism, was born on 1 January 1484 in Wildhaus, an Alpine village in the Toggenburg valley. The surrounding landscape is stunning, with valleys that give way to towering mountains and open sky. Zwingli lived in the shadow of a mountain range whose seven peaks were named after the seven electors of the Holy Roman Empire. From the snow-covered heights of the neighbouring mountain of Säntis, views reach into both modern Austria and Germany. Zwingli's first biographer, his friend and colleague Oswald Myconius (1488–1562), observed that the beauty and drama of the land filled the young boy with a powerful sense of the nearness of God, drawing 'something of divine quality directly from the heavens near which he lived'.[2]

11

The farmhouse in which Zwingli was born still stands. The sturdy wooden building has a large living room on the ground level and several smaller rooms above for sleeping. The size of the house indicates that his family was relatively prosperous, people of some importance in the village. Another biographer who also knew his subject recorded that Zwingli's father came from a 'good, old family', was deeply pious and served as mayor. Attachment to the Church ran deep in his family. Zwingli's beloved uncle Bartholomäus was a priest in the church at Wildhaus – which had purchased the rights over the parish, including the ability to select the priest. His mother's cousin had been abbot of the monastery at Fischingen.

Zwingli's childhood was not the troubled one of Martin Luther. The Swiss boy was the third of 10 children – six boys and four girls. His parents seem to have lived to a reasonable age, with his father last mentioned in 1513. A letter from his brothers written in 1519 suggests that his mother, Margaretha Meili, was no longer alive.[3] We know that the two youngest brothers were dead by 1522, while his other brothers appear to have survived the vicissitudes of childhood and youth. Two joined Ulrich in becoming priests. One of the few surviving indications of Zwingli's contact with his siblings accompanies a sermon of 1522 on the Virgin Mary: in the preface, addressed to his brothers, he defended himself against accusations of immorality and warned them against the soul-destroying temptations of mercenary service.[4] His brothers appear to have embraced the Reformation, as did the abbot of St Johann, another uncle, who continued to correspond with his nephew after Zwingli had moved as a priest to Zurich in 1519 and who became a fierce advocate of reform in Toggenburg. As Zwingli tells us, his uncle loved him as if he were his own child.[5]

Zwingli's occasional references to his childhood suggest a happy youth and deep affection for his relatively prosperous family. Later in life, he would recall the goodness of God being like a father offering his son grapes from the vineyard. In one of his last letters, Zwingli wrote to a life-long friend and mentor, asking him to look after a cousin with whom he had lived as a child and who was now gravely ill.[6] Zwingli gave thanks that his parents had provided him with a Christian upbringing and had taught him to endure privation and suffering with good spirit. He once recalled:

My grandmother often told me a tale of how Peter and Jesus shared a bed together. Peter always went to bed earlier and left the Lord. Every morning the woman of the house came and clutched Peter by the hair and woke him up.[7]

No doubt he spoke from memory of sharing a bed with his brothers. Zwingli would attribute his love of his native land to stories he had been told as a child about the heroic deeds of the Swiss in their struggles against foreign rulers.

Zwingli's later writings, particularly when speaking of divine providence, remind us of his love of nature, particularly of the mountainous lands where he grew up.[8] In commenting on Psalm 104, he was moved to say of David, its author:

He portrays both the wisdom and the providence of God so that you see God as creator balancing the mountains in his mighty hand, putting each in its place, drawing out the valleys between and the cool streams in the valleys, spreading out the fields, and thrusting back the turbulent sea into its own depths, so that there may be no confusion from its unruliness. He then assigned settlers to each region, adding provision abundantly.[9]

To the end of his life, Zwingli spoke of God as a benevolent, providential deity.

Liberty and the freedom of the Christian emerge as familiar themes in Zwingli's thought, again taking us back to his years in Toggenburg. Authority over the valley had been acquired by the great monastery at St Gallen in 1468, only 16 years before Zwingli's birth. The Toggenburgers, however, were fiercely independent and jealous in guarding their rights. In the early 1490s, the abbot sent 8,000 soldiers into Toggenburg to enforce his claims over the land and Church. In Zwingli's first work, 'The Labyrinth', he made a pointed reference to the greed and ambition of the abbot, with the cleric portrayed as a bear that is 'an ugly sight' and an 'untamed animal'.[10] Zwingli's father was a passionate defender of the traditional rights of the valley inhabitants and of the independence of their Church, leading to a tradition of Swiss historians attributing Zwingli's patriotism to the experiences of his youth.[11]

Zwingli's father was determined that his young son, who demonstrated considerable aptitude, should receive a good education, which required proper instruction. He first entrusted the boy to his uncle Bartholomäus, who had left Wildhaus to serve as the priest in Weesen, some 25 kilometres away. Zwingli was extremely attached to his uncle and would remain in contact with him long after he left Weesen, regarding him as a model priest and mentor who had instilled in him the ideal of the faithful shepherd. Bartholomäus would indeed be remembered for establishing a fraternity to care for the children of labourers.[12]

Zwingli was fortunate in his educators. At the age of 10, the boy was sent to the city of Basel, much farther from home, to be taught by Gregorius Bünzli, whom the reformer would later fondly recall as an inspirational teacher. Bünzli eventually succeeded Zwingli's uncle as priest in Weesen.[13] In the university city, Zwingli was introduced to the study of Latin, music and dialectic, and his first biographer described the emergence of a remarkable student:

> He made such progress in character and letters that in the disputations, which were then customary, he carried off all the honours from all the boys and youths in the school. On this account he incurred the greatest hatred on the part of the older boys. His proficiency in music was beyond that expected of his years, as is likely to be the case with those especially gifted by nature in any art.[14]

Zwingli distinguished himself to such a degree in Basel that his teacher sent him home with a recommendation that he study with Heinrich Wölfli (1470–1532) (Latinized as Lupulus), a distinguished scholar in Bern.[15] Zwingli was fortunate to have found yet another mentor and role model, significantly a dedicated scholar of the new humanist learning who was eager for reform of the Church. Lupulus' reforming sentiments belonged solidly in the late-medieval world: he made regular pilgrimages to the Benedictine abbey at Einsiedeln and supported the indulgence preacher Bernhardin Sanson, as he traversed the diocese of Constance. Lupulus' biography of Bruder (Brother) Klaus (Niklaus von Flüe), published in 1501, may have laid the ground for Zwingli's lifelong lofty view of this saintly fifteenth-century Swiss monk, whose wisdom and guidance were held to have been crucial to establishing an earlier peace within the Confederation.[16]

Zwingli studied under Lupulus for almost two years, once more forging an enduring relationship: after Zwingli's death, Lupulus wrote a series of poems in honour of his former pupil.[17] While in Bern, young Ulrich cultivated his skills in Latin and grammar, the foundations of which had been laid in Basel; he also commenced his study of classical authors and honed his abilities in poetry and prose.[18] His musical gifts attracted particular attention. The young man, who had begun to compose his own songs, was approached by the Dominicans with an offer to join their order. Back in Basel, Bünzli got wind of this prospect and became alarmed. Together with Zwingli's father, he decided that Ulrich should be removed from Bern and should go to university.

Ulrich matriculated at the University of Vienna in 1498, at the age of 14. The events of the next two years remain somewhat mysterious. Myconius' account may have originated with Zwingli himself: he seems to have taken to the study of philosophy with relish and to have distinguished himself as a debater, but further than this we cannot go.[19] We can say that Vienna was a natural – if distant – choice for a young man from Toggenburg, for the university, the second oldest in the Holy Roman Empire (after Prague), was a major draw for gifted students from the eastern part of the Swiss Confederation.[20] In Vienna at the same time as Zwingli was his contemporary, friend and later distinguished humanist, Joachim von Watt (1484–1551), known as Vadian.[21] Vadian would play a crucial role in the Swiss Reformation, as church leader and politician.

Although we struggle to find much trace of Zwingli in Vienna, we do know a great deal about the culture in which he lived for two years. Under the patronage of Emperor Maximilian I, the university and city had become a flourishing centre of humanist learning, the study of the Greek and Roman languages, literature, philosophy and history. Most notable was Conrad Celtis (1459–1508), an extraordinary character and inspiring scholar.[22] Celtis' collection of Greek and Latin manuscripts made the imperial library, which he headed, a renowned centre of humanist learning. In 1500, Celtis published an edition of the Roman historian Tacitus' *Germania*, which he turned into a clarion call for the political and cultural renewal of Germany and freedom from papal Rome.[23]

In 1502, Zwingli returned to Basel, now to enter the university there, where he continued his study of the liberal arts; two years later he was awarded the degree of bachelor of arts.[24] He had also taken up a teaching post at the parochial school of St Martin's church, a role he relished. Years later, one of his pupils recalled with gratitude the diligence with which he had been instructed by the young Zwingli and wished he might return to the great joy of learning in those days.[25] Myconius wrote of a talented young man in love with learning and the arts:

> He mingled both joy with his studies, always of sunny disposition and agreeable in conversation to a remarkable degree ... he devoted himself to the theory and practice of all forms of musical instruments with no other purpose than to refresh his mind when wearied by long deep study.[26]

And indeed, Zwingli appears to have learned to play the lute while in Basel.[27]

The university Zwingli entered was now in a fallow period, after an age when some of the most distinguished scholars had been active in the city on the Rhine. Compared to Vienna, and later Einsiedeln, Basel offered the young student little in terms of a library. As dean of the faculty of arts, Johann Heynlin (1425–?1496) had reformed the curriculum before heading off to Paris, where he introduced the first printing press in France.[28] While in Basel, Johann Reuchlin (1455–1522) had prepared a Latin lexicon that would be a vital tool in the revival of classical Latin; he would subsequently emerge as one of the great Hebraists of his age. His lexicon was printed by Johann Amerbach (1440–1513), from a distinguished Basel family. Just as Reuchlin was departing, the young Sebastian Brant (1457–1521) had arrived in Basel from Strasbourg to study philosophy and then law.[29] Brant is best remembered as the author of the brilliant satire the *Ship of Fools* (1494).[30] This work, with its biting criticism of the Church and its excesses, was highly influential for Erasmus' *Praise of Folly*. The woodcuts for the book were possibly prepared by a young Albrecht Dürer. While in Basel, Brant had become close friends with Johann Geiler von Kaysersberg (1445–1510), considered one of the greatest preachers of his age.

Yet although the university had lost many such leading lights, their legacy remained. In particular, the city was emerging as a leader in printing. Amerbach was the first printer in the city to use Roman type, and his wealth enabled him to produce volumes of the highest quality.[31] His apprentice Johann Froben (1460–1527), who became a close friend and collaborator of

Erasmus and Hans Holbein the Younger, had already produced the first edition of the Vulgate with a printed illustration in 1495.[32]

After the completion of his philosophical studies in 1506, Zwingli turned to theology, becoming one of the few candidates for the priesthood with such an extensive education. In theology, the Basel faculty was not especially distinguished. Myconius tells us that Zwingli grew disillusioned with the scholastic positions of his teachers – something that Myconius possibly heard directly from Zwingli, although we cannot know for sure. Nevertheless, as his later theological writings would reveal, the medieval doctors did leave their mark on him. His rejection of them may simply have been later Reformation polemic, as there is no evidence that Zwingli was anything other than a diligent student of Aristotle and the medieval doctors. While his relationship with the Basel theologians remains unclear, careful research has tracked down significant influences on his spiritual and clerical formation during these years, such as the Franciscan Stephan Brulefer, a Paris scholar active in Mainz and Metz, and the ideas of Duns Scotus (1266–1308) for his thoughts on the nature of God.[33]

We have no direct evidence of a connection between Zwingli and the preacher Johann Ulrich Surgant (1450–1503), but given the relative smallness of the city, and Surgant's notoriety, there is ample scope to believe that Zwingli might have heard the older man preach.[34] Surgant was a strong proponent of clerical reform and strove to revive the spiritual life of his church, St Theodor (where Zwingli had been a pupil from 1494 to 1497), by establishing side altars and setting up a new pulpit, and by using a pilgrimage to Rome to bring back relics to the city.[35] Surgant was not a leading theological mind, but he threw himself into his dual duties of running the university and providing for the pastoral care of his congregation. His most enduring work was his *Manuale Curatorum*, dedicated to the renewal of liturgy and preaching. Printed in Basel, Augsburg and Mainz, the book was remarkably popular and the bishop of Basel declared that it should be in the library of every priest.[36] Scholars have speculated that the work was the model for Zwingli's later liturgical innovations.

By contrast, Thomas Wyttenbach's influence on Zwingli requires no conjecture. Wyttenbach arrived in Basel in 1505 and began lecturing on the *Sentences* of Peter Lombard.[37] Zwingli and his friend Leo Jud were his students. According to one biographer:

17

Zwingli studied with him [Wyttenbach] and said that he learned from him for the first time that the death of Christ was once offered for our sins, by which we have been saved. At that time, he also in Basel disputed openly against indulgences. From him [Wyttenbach] he was taught theology. The more that Zwingli studied theology the more he was drawn to the priestly office so that he could preach to the people.[38]

In the foreword to the 1539 printed edition of Zwingli's works, Jud left his own testimony to their teacher, who had died in 1526:

Alongside his rare eloquence he possessed an outstanding clarity of mind that enabled him to see and predict what others would bring forth later, such as the abuse of papal indulgences and other matters with which the pope in Rome has been able to bamboozle the silly people for hundreds of years.[39]

Wyttenbach remained in contact with Zwingli and became a strong voice in support of the Reformation. In a long letter that he wrote to Wyttenbach in 1523 (largely on the Lord's Supper), Zwingli expressed his gratitude to his 'most pious and learned' former teacher.[40]

## SWORDS AND OATHS

The processes that led to the creation of the Swiss Confederation, the land of Zwingli's birth, would boggle the mind of even the most sophisticated systems analyst. Unlike other states of the Latin West, the Confederation (*Eidgenossenschaft*) had no centre and little sense of a collective identity. It consisted of a diverse array of urban and rural territories with their own histories, cultures and institutions that formed a complex web of trade and defensive agreements which united them against traditional external enemies, such as the Austrian Habsburgs. In addition, there were the Mandated Territories, such as Thurgau and the Freie Ämter, lands jointly governed by various Confederates.

The first Confederates (*Eidgenossen*) were the Alpine regions of Uri, Schwyz and Unterwalden, which in August 1291 formed an 'Eternal Alliance' – primarily concerned with developing forms of jurisdiction and mutual defence. Only much later, in the nineteenth century, was the year 1291 recognized as the founding moment for modern Switzerland, chosen as the country prepared to mark its 600th anniversary in 1891. Previously, the genesis of the Confederation had been located in 1307 by the most influential Swiss historian of the early modern period, Aegidius Tschudi (1505–1572), in his 'Swiss Chronicle' (*Chronicon Helveticum*) of 1550.[41] The year 1307 was associated by Tschudi with the *Rütlischwur*, an oath taken by the leaders of Uri, Schwyz and Unterwalden on a meadow above the Lake of Uri. Although the historical accuracy of this event (first mentioned in 1420) has been much debated, it is entirely plausible that an oath was indeed sworn as part of a concerted action against the Habsburg overlords. The myth of William Tell had emerged among the Swiss in the late Middle Ages to bolster their claims to have resisted tyranny and thus to justify the existence of a Swiss state. Friedrich Schiller's 1804 play *Wilhelm Tell* cemented this narrative of heroic revolt for nineteenth-century patriots.[42]

During the fourteenth century, the Confederation grew to eight members, including the cities of Zurich and Bern, along with Zug and Glarus. The crucial moment for the consolidation of these alliances was the battle of Sempach in July 1386, which followed a period of growing conflict with Duke Leopold of Austria.[43] The Swiss, greatly outnumbered, gained the upper hand and broke through the Austrian lines, inflicting carnage and leaving Duke Leopold and many knights slaughtered on the field. Numbers were significant in the development of Swiss identity. Time and again, like the ancient Israelites, they defeated their numerically superior foes. The battle of Sempach came to represent the valour of the Swiss underdogs against the forces of tyranny – a struggle won by God's favour.[44] Two years later, in 1388, the fate of the Austrians was repeated with their devastating defeat at the battle of Näfels. For centuries to come – and feeding into the swelling patriotism of the nineteenth century – Sempach was recalled as a decisive moment in the formation of a Swiss identity and as the beginning of a period of military glory that would extend to the Reformation.

But the story of the Swiss Confederation in the late Middle Ages was far from a straightforward struggle with the Habsburgs. Thus, for example, when the ambitious Zurichers claimed and occupied the lands of the count of Toggenburg in the 1430s, its rival Confederates expelled the city from the Confederation. To bolster its position, Zurich made an alliance with the

Holy Roman Emperor, the Habsburg Frederick III. The forces of the Confederation defeated Zurich in 1443 and laid siege to the city. Frederick sought the support of the French king, who sent a large contingent of mercenaries to support Zurich. Although the mercenaries were victorious in 1444, the victor's losses were so heavy that the French soldiers withdrew. This extraordinarily bitter struggle, known as the Old Zurich War, was marked by one particularly notorious moment. Zurich's enemies had laid siege to the Greifensee castle, and when the garrison surrendered, all but two men were beheaded in an act of cruelty that shocked contemporaries and that survived in literary accounts by Swiss authors such as Gottfried Keller. In the end, Zurich sued for peace and was readmitted to the Confederation; but other members remained deeply suspicious of the city's motives, a bad memory revived with the Reformation.

The Swiss emerged as major players on the European stage in the fifteenth century. The ambitions of Charles the Bold (1433–1477), who dreamed of turning the wealthy duchy of Burgundy into a kingdom, greatly unsettled the Swiss.[45] Bern had not joined the recent peace with Austria and instead pursued its own aggressive policy of expansion, which brought it into conflict with the Burgundians.[46] Charles reacted militarily. However, to his great cost, he vastly underestimated his opponents, who were bolstered by support from other Swiss Confederates. Charles' infamy was confirmed when he ordered the execution of the garrison of the castle of Grandson after they had surrendered, hanging the men from trees. In March 1476, the Swiss destroyed the Burgundian army, forcing Charles to flee and to abandon both his artillery and a remarkable collection of treasures, which fell into the hands of the Bernese.[47] Worse was to follow: in June 1476, Charles was once more defeated by the Swiss and lost over a third of his army of 30,000 men, many of whom drowned or were picked off by archers as they tried to escape by swimming across a lake.[48] Charles met his own end in January 1477, when his much-diminished forces were routed. The duke's frozen, disfigured corpse was found on the ice of the river, savaged by wild animals; it was recognizable only to his personal physician.

The Burgundian wars had inaugurated the age of the Swiss soldier, acclaimed across Europe for his skill and courage.[49] The armies of the Confederation, having now humiliated both the Habsburgs and the Burgundians, acquired a reputation for invincibility, although contemporaries were already voicing concern about this taste for war.[50] Triumph came with increasing tensions. Any sense of common cause was belied by a variety of alliances and arrangements that left some of the older states feeling threatened. At a series of meetings at Stans a compromise was reached in December 1481 that established a means for conflict resolution.[51] The agreement allowed for the expansion of the Confederation, with the entry of Fribourg and Solothurn, which increased the power of the cities over the rural members.

The second half of the fifteenth century saw a dramatic rise in the number of young Swiss men entering the military service of foreign paymasters. Mountainous regions were increasingly crippled by insufficient resources to sustain growing communities, and as French and papal recruiters travelled from village to village, they found willing recruits. The numbers are staggering. The Confederation had a population of between 600,000 and 800,000 inhabitants in 1500; it has been reckoned that each year approximately 5,000 Swiss men served as mercenaries between the Burgundian wars (1474–1477) and the battle of Marignano in 1515.[52]

There was nothing romantic about the mercenary trade: half of those who left for military service are thought never to have returned. And those who did make it home were often maimed and unable to work. Additionally, opponents of the trade, Zwingli included, readily connected foreign soldiering with moral turpitude, not least prostitution and the rapid spread of sexually transmitted diseases. The pensions paid to local officials and urban patrician families were widely viewed as a corruption of older Swiss virtues of loyalty to the fatherland. This theme of a lost innocence – God's elect, the valorous people of the mountain valleys, had turned to venal rewards – was widespread long before Zwingli began his preaching. Rural communities were often decimated by attrition rates that affected the political and social dynamics of the Confederation. Thus, for example, within the towns, the deaths of leading citizens as they commanded troops in foreign campaigns created opportunities for men from less affluent backgrounds and less prominent families to advance their careers.[53]

In the figure of Hans Waldmann (1435–1489), Zurich provides us with a telling example of its ambitions to extend its influence. A military hero of the Burgundian wars who had led the Swiss troops to victory at Morat, he had advanced his chances in the world through marriage into an influential family.[54] By 1480, he was head of the guilds in Zurich, having greatly enhanced their authority over the patricians who had traditionally ruled the city. He was also deeply implicated in the mercenary business, receiving from the duke of Milan vast payment in return for political favours. Waldmann was a man of fascinating contrasts: deeply pious, he became rich from the sale of mercenaries; eager for power, he used his authority to attempt to reform the city and rural areas. Waldmann was also responsible for greatly extending the control of the magistrates over the affairs and possessions of the Church, a process by which the late-medieval Church would increasingly fall under civic authority. Arrested and tortured on accusations of corruption and sodomy, he was beheaded with a sword, a final recognition of his noble status. He died when Zwingli was only five, but his legacy was of an aggressive, aspirational Zurich that sought to dominate the Confederation.

With the Swabian War of 1499, also known as the Swiss War, the Confederates and the Habsburgs clashed for the final time, bringing a new degree of autonomy.[55] The war covered a large swathe of territory from Graubünden in the east to Constance in the Holy Roman Empire. After a series of minor skirmishes, the Swiss inflicted on the forces of the Swabian League and Emperor Maximilian I a humiliating defeat at Dornach, near Basel. Once more, the Swiss were outnumbered, but such was their skill that they succeeded in putting the imperial forces to flight, leaving Maximilian's commander Heinrich von Fürstenberg dead on the battlefield. The subsequent treaty of Basel granted further lands to the Swiss and a considerable level of autonomy, although formally the Confederation remained part of the Holy Roman Empire. Full independence would come in 1648, with the Peace of Westphalia that ended the Thirty Years' War.[56] The year 1501 did bring significant growth for the Swiss Confederation with the entry of wealthy Basel.

In the fifteenth century, Europe was only beginning to acknowledge the Swiss; and even then, the Confederation itself was not a unified, independent land. It remained a perplexing bundle of members, held together by history and agreements, but essentially composed of fiercely local identities. The Swiss had no language for a republic or for republican thought, and criticism of princes and rulers did not entail any form of political ideal.[57] The Swiss identity to which Zwingli appealed was fluid and evolving. There were few centralizing institutions. The most prominent was the Swiss Diet, to which each Confederate sent delegates. Although it had limited powers over the individual states, it oversaw the administration of shared lands and decisions about war and peace.[58] The Swiss Diet was always marked by competing interests and rivalries. In that sense, it belonged to a wider tradition of defensive leagues, like the contemporary Hansa on the Baltic or the Swabian League in southern Germany. All these associations were held together by external threats, whether political or economic, and by a desire to preserve peace and order.[59]

## FORMATION OF A PATRIOT

Huldrych Zwingli was born into a land of myths. The heroic accounts narrated by the people and written down by chroniclers were not simply fabrications or imaginary tales: they were stories by which the Swiss came to know themselves as a chosen people, with a distinctive identity. They told of the creation of the Confederation in revolt against Habsburg tyranny. By the time of Zwingli's birth in 1484, the Swiss had won a fearsome reputation for invincibility on the battlefield, having humbled a Burgundian duke, as well as the neighbouring Austrians. Zwingli was well aware of the heroes, and throughout his life he would speak reverently of the ascetic and mystic Bruder Klaus (1417–1487), later patron saint of Switzerland and canonized in 1947. Bruder Klaus stood for him among the virtuous forefathers of the Confederation, the great figures of the past. By 1479, a deacon at the great Benedictine monastery at Einsiedeln had written the first account of the Swiss, tracing their ancestry to antiquity.[60] The humanists of this generation began to speak of 'Helvetia', and its physical presence was recorded by Renaissance maps.

With its passion for the history of valorous deeds, Renaissance humanism offered ways to craft a Swiss legacy. The first history of the entire Confederation, Petermann Etterlin's *Chronicle of the Praiseworthy Confederation*, was printed in Basel in 1507, the year after Zwingli completed his studies in the city.[61] A Latin description of the 13 members of the Confederation followed seven years later, the work of the humanist Heinrich Glarean,[62] while a four-part history of the Swiss from Julius Caesar to the present day was composed by Heinrich Brennwald between 1508 and 1516.[63]

Zwingli's education led him to explore the works of Greek and Roman antiquity and to share the belief that the achievements of that golden age might be recovered.[64] Plato, Aristotle and Cicero, so far as they anticipated scripture, were guides to the proper nature of society and the cultivation of the good life. This classical wisdom fed into the history of his own people, beginning with Caesar's description of the 'Helvetii' as a Celtic tribe dwelling on the Swiss plateau. Zwingli and his humanist friends and mentors shared a passion for finding the glorious heritage of the Swiss in antiquity. It was in part from the praise of these Swiss authors for their ancient virtues and fierce resistance to foreign oppression that Zwingli acquired the language of 'fatherland'.[65]

Zwingli's love was not simply for the people of his native Toggenburg, but for the Swiss as a whole, whose mountains and valleys he knew as his fatherland. He always identified Toggenburg as his home, or *Heimat*; but above all else for him was the Swiss Confederation.[66] That would remain true until his death. Although he came to be so closely identified with Zurich, and often spoke proudly of its history and achievements, it was never his fatherland, never his primary point of reference. The Swiss people were the elect, and he spoke to them. He was Swiss, as he wrote to his fellow Confederates in 1524:

> The Confederation has never left my heart. I have always rejoiced in its fortune, and grieved in its misfortune. I therefore hope that you will look at this simple and plain writing and consider it worthy not so much because of the cleverness of the words or of the wisdom, but because of the good faith of my character.[67]

He quoted Bruder Klaus, who had declared that the Confederation could never be conquered, and then continued:

> Almighty God gave so much favour and grace to our forefathers that they freed themselves from the arbitrary nobility and lived afterwards in such a brotherly manner that they increased by example in honour and wealth.[68]

By the time he composed those words, Zwingli was already reviled by his Catholic landsmen for his apostasy and destruction of the Church. His appeal to Swiss unity was made in terms of a new vision of a Christian people that was rejected by his opponents. But his words were about his enduring conviction that the Confederation was not merely an ideal, but a reality which he served as priest and prophet, and for which he would risk his life. He was not naïve. Zwingli's love of his land and its people was tempered by his anticipation of God's terrible judgement on the Swiss for prostituting themselves, by receiving corrupting pensions and by serving as mercenaries to foreigners.

Like the ancient Israelites – a comparison Zwingli frequently made – the Swiss were God's chosen, who had sinned and were to be punished for their greed, lust and idolatry.[69] Zwingli yearned to recover the lost world of the virtuous forefathers who had embodied the singular virtues of the Swiss. Heinrich Bullinger (1504–1575) later recounted Zwingli's nostalgia:

> He showed that our forefathers were so glad about freedom and grace from God that they led God-fearing, pious and Christian lives. They gave so much care for justice that even their enemies had to admit that they were a pious and lawful people. Thanks to them, many people have often found justice who would have otherwise been without any rights. They were Christians, although they had not been rightly taught in many truths [the gospel] . . . They remained unconquered by the princes and lords because they lived honestly and innocently.[70]

Zwingli's nostalgia was for a lost age: the age of heroes could be recovered, and as a priest steeped in the Bible and the wisdom of the ancients, he sought to find the way. The history of his land was an act of remembering and forgetting, a practice he would employ with the Reformation. The recalling of a virtuous past required the eradication of unwanted memories.

## ✢ TWO ✢

# HUMANIST PRIEST

H uldrych Zwingli was rarely inclined to write about his early life. Even his voluminous correspondence suggests a pronounced reluctance to reflect on his childhood and his years as a priest. He wrote about God and salvation, the Bible, his studies, history, his land and its people, politics, war and corruption; but his early years are largely absent. He would argue with force, but it fell to others to tell his story and defend his memory. Self-effacement should not be mistaken, however, for a lack of passion: he poured himself into sermons, letters, tracts and, later, his engagement in politics.

When Zwingli went to Glarus as a priest in September 1506, its remoteness must have reminded him of his origins in Toggenburg. The small Confederate had little to offer beyond land and blood: subsistence farming and young men for mercenary recruiters. His tenure would be shaped by conflict and by the pen, for war and suffering were bound up with his intellectual growth. In Glarus we find the first indication of Zwingli the inspiring teacher, the mentor. Undaunted by the isolation, he turned his remote parish into a school for training young men who would later attend universities in Basel and Paris. But the idyllic Glarus valley also provided a brutal induction for Zwingli into the realities of Renaissance politics and warfare. The priest travelled with recruited Glarus soldiers to Italy and experienced their slaughter at first hand. His involvement in the politics of the mercenary service, with his papal sympathies, ultimately led to an acrimonious departure after 10 years.

Glarus (familiar to Zwingli as Glaris) lies on the River Linth beneath the Glärnisch, a massif of the Schwyz Alps with a peak on either side of the

Glärnischfirn glacier. In recent years, the glacier has retreated dramatically, and the town of Glarus today also bears little resemblance to the community that Zwingli knew, for its oldest parts burned to the ground in the 1860s. Glarus had joined the Swiss Confederation as a founding member. Habsburg ambitions to annex the territory were reversed in 1388 by the Glarners and their Swiss allies, in a stunning victory in which they had been reputedly outnumbered 16 to 1. Appearing through the snow and mist, a few hundred soldiers cut down a much larger force that had been taken unawares; the enemy retreated in panic, but the bridge across the Linth collapsed under their weight, drowning the army like the hapless forces of Pharaoh.

We know little of how the Glarners received their 22-year-old, remarkably well-educated but inexperienced cleric, whose accent, despite the proximity of his native Toggenburg, would have clearly marked him as an outsider. Zwingli held a master of arts degree from Basel and had begun his theological studies – a level of learning possessed by few parish priests in the region, and certainly not by his predecessor.

Zwingli's course of studies strongly suggests that he had intended to become a priest, but why he sought the position in Glarus is not known. Perhaps, it has been suggested, he wanted to be near his birthplace.[1] While many priests had little education, progress from academic studies to service in the Church was encouraged, and universities provided Rome with lists of theological candidates for consideration for benefices. Unusually, however, Zwingli was offered a benefice in Glarus before completion of his theological studies. The prodigious and ambitious young student may well have been recommended by either his uncle Bartholomäus, cleric in nearby Weesen, or his Basel tutor Gregorius Bünzli, both of whom had connections in remote Glarus. There was competition: Heinrich Göldi, a member of a good Zurich family, had been promised the benefice of Glarus in return for faithful service to the pope. Göldi received the benefice, but made it clear that he intended to be absent, as he had other livings. The Glarners wanted a resident priest, and so Zwingli was elected; but in return, he was required to compensate Göldi financially, a debt that remained until 1519, when he was called to Zurich.[2]

Zwingli was ordained by Hugo von Hohenlandenberg (1457–1532), bishop of Constance; but so little is known about his early years as a priest that we cannot be sure where or when.[3] Zwingli was not from the sprawling diocese of Constance – his native Toggenburg lay in the diocese of Chur – and he had studied in Basel, which had its own bishop, but the medieval Church was not overly concerned with such legal niceties.[4] Years later, writing to a friend in 1525, Zwingli commented that Bishop Hugo had come to regard him highly for his preaching against the indulgence peddler Bernhardin Sanson, but the provenance of this favourable view is not known.[5]

We can at least say that at some point in 1506 Zwingli was ordained. As with all candidates for the priesthood, he had first to pass through the lower orders, which he did with dispatch. The bishop likely laid on his hands in the cathedral in Constance, according to custom, but the solemnity of the service would have belied numerous contemporary concerns. Lively festivities often accompanied such occasions, and we learn from a 1516 reform mandate that Hugo was unhappy with the conduct of priests and candidates about to be ordained, who apparently formed a motley crew dressed in the clothes of peasants or in hats and cloaks favoured by the laity. His rebukes were hardly new: the Council of Vienne in 1311 had railed against clergy and monks in inappropriate clothing doing inappropriate things.[6]

Sartorial preferences may have contributed to the rampant anti-clericalism in the southern German and Swiss lands. Or it might have reflected the reality that many, if not most, clerics lived lives not much different from the faithful they served, often with 'wives' (officially proscribed as 'concubines') and children. Clerics of all stations on the ecclesiastical hierarchy had partners and children, and in the lands of the diocese of Constance priestly families were well established in local communities. Bishop Hugo was himself a father and in an established relationship. Zwingli's dear friend Leo Jud, whom he had met in Basel in 1505, and Heinrich Bullinger, who would succeed him in Zurich on his death, both had priests as fathers. Many priests farmed the land and engaged in trade and crafts to supplement their meagre livings and support their families. Zwingli, single and possibly celibate, probably dressed for his ordination as a Basel magister of arts, with beret and ring.[7]

Although Zwingli was personally unknown in Glarus, word of a sermon he had preached in nearby Rapperswil, where his cousin was a priest, may have preceded him and led to his call.[8] According to the chronicler Fridolin Bäldi, he was welcomed to his new community with a festive meal:

On St Matthew's day [21 September] 1506, mayor Kuelchly, and the leader Stucki and the whole church community received Ulrich Zwingli. On the same day there were four full tables of people together with Master Ulrich in the mayor's house and all was provided as a gift. There were many common worthy people from the valley, among whom were two mayors.[9]

His first mass then took place, not in Glarus but in his native Wildhaus nearby, on 29 September. Another celebratory meal followed.[10] Unlike Luther, who recounted quaking with fear at his first celebration of the Eucharist, Zwingli tells us nothing of his emotions that day.

## PRIEST AND WAR

A few glimpses reveal Zwingli to have been a diligent priest and scholar during his years in Glarus. He was responsible for about 1,300 souls, and his care was both spiritual and pedagogical. He founded the first Latin school in his parish, where he educated young boys, some of whom would go on to study at university. During this time Zwingli began to build his library, relying on friends to alert him to recent publications in Basel and engaging a student to bring him books from the Rhine city.[11] Zwingli had inherited a few books from his predecessor as priest, Johannes Stucki, including works by Aquinas, Josephus and Aulus Gellius.[12] Surviving notes from 1507–1508 tell us that the priest was carefully reading the Jewish historian Josephus.

In 1510, Zwingli penned an allegory in which he revealed his deep pro-papal sympathies. His fable takes place on a bucolic meadow that represented the Swiss Confederation:

There was a garden spot hedged about on one side by high mountains, on another by gurgling streams, and on which roamed, cropping the green blades of grass, a fine fat bullock of ruddy hue, with widespread horns on his rich waving coat.[13]

His fable was of an ox, representing the Confederates, beset by wily and mendacious foes. When wild animals – the leopard is the French king, the lion is the German emperor – can do nothing to harm the ox, they offer the cats (Swiss political leaders and leading families) all manner of inducements as 'rich bait'. The herdsman (the pope) reminds the ox of the wisdom of his forefathers: 'You are aware of how lively were the tried and tested virtues and faithfulness of your father and grandfather. Contemplating that, I come to warn you now not to let me find you inferior to them.'[14] The dog (the clergy) barks in joy at the herdsman's words. The lion and leopard gnash their teeth and declare war on the ox to force him to abandon the 'protecting staff' of the herdsman, who is its only hope. Crucially, for Zwingli the pope is the 'good shepherd'.

In Machiavelli's idealized view, the Swiss lived in liberty because they were simple, poor mountain people who had not been tainted by the worldliness and material wealth that had corrupted his own people. But renowned for their highly effective military manoeuvres in squares of pikeman, as well as for their slaughtering with halberds and crossbows, the Swiss were sought by popes and kings, who were more than willing to pay.[15] Machiavelli also recognized them as an invincible army, as once the Romans had had and unlike the pathetically unreliable troops on whom the Italian states relied.[16] Whatever their exceptional prowess on the battlefield, the Swiss soldiers demonstrated the usual proclivities of mercenaries, by plundering and raping their way through Italian lands, much to the horror of Pope Julius II and Cardinal Matthäus Schiner, the pope's legate to the Swiss Confederation, who had set about recruiting soldiers in the Confederation for war against the French in Italy. Schiner would later be one of Zwingli's most powerful patrons, precisely as a result of the priest's papal sympathies. In 1512, over 12,000 Swiss travelled south of the Alps under the leadership of the cardinal. The mercenaries closed ranks alongside imperial, Venetian and Spanish troops to crush the French.

The 'Account by Huldrych Zwingli of the Engagements between the French and Swiss hard by Ravenna and Pavia' was a humanist writing intended to demonstrate the priest's skills to his much-admired friend, the scholar Joachim Vadian, with whom Zwingli had studied in Vienna. The text was taken to Vadian in Vienna by Zwingli's brother Jakob, who was about to enter a monastery in the city. Zwingli relied on information provided by the Glarner soldiers who had fought in Italy and returned home. The victory of Pavia was, for the priest, the great achievement of the Swiss, revealing them as the liberators of the Church, and above all of the papacy. Their war in Italian lands was nothing other than the continuation of their struggle for freedom against the Habsburgs: it was a battle not only for the Confederation, but also for liberty itself.[17]

Zwingli's detailed treatment of politics and battles was interspersed with artful dialogue, always flattering to the Swiss, to whom he referred as 'our forces'. At one point, he related how

> some of our men swam across the Po to fix the first supports for a bridge on the farther bank. Their lancers rushed out to stop the undertaking. Meanwhile all the youthful band of brothers-in-arms being practised swimmers, runners and jumpers had thrown off their clothes and, clinging to their spears, were swimming naked across the Po to engage the enemy, who seemed to be given to them by God for constant practice in the art of war.[18]

He singled out one man from Glarus, whose skill in hunting wild beasts in the mountains enabled him to pick off a Frenchman with a single shot. Zwingli would later admonish his students to engage in both learning and physical exercise. Piety was wed to martial strength, for when Julius II wanted to reward the Swiss for their efforts, they were given 'Julius banners', beautiful silk banners that bestowed great honour on the Swiss as 'defenders of the liberties of the Church'.[19]

In 1513, at the battle of Novara, 4,000 Swiss soldiers faced a far larger renewed French army; but their strategy proved superior, not only leaving them victorious, but also providing them with considerable French booty. Zwingli experienced the campaign and battle at Novara first hand, as 'field preacher' for the forces from Glarus who had headed south to fight for the pope. He was enormously proud of these men as defenders of traditional Swiss liberties and the cause of Rome. We know little of his experience in battle. As the campaign moved toward Milan, he was with the Glarner troops in Monza, where he preached in the marketplace to the soldiers, exhorting them to remain steadfast in their support of the pope.[20]

Historians have long considered 1513 the peak of Swiss influence in Italy, marking the zenith of ventures that had brought them deep into Italian lands and made them a serious political and military player. But that year the Swiss lost a key ally in Julius II, who died in February 1513. In 1515, the new French king, Francis I (1494–1547), eagerly took up the reins of war and sent his troops back into Italian lands, this time with a mind to turn the Swiss into allies. He knew what it took: with a million crowns, promises of pensions, trade privileges and land, he divided the Swiss by winning over the men of Bern, Fribourg, Solothurn and Biel with an agreement that left the other Swiss feeling utterly betrayed. The kingdom of France would become the most crucial foreign ally of the Swiss, a position it retained until the end of the Old Regime.[21]

At the battle of Marignano, southeast of Milan, on 13 September 1515, however, those Swiss supporting the pope faced the forces of Francis I full of confidence in their invincibility. At first, that optimism was justified, as the French were pressed back. During the night, however, the French rebuilt their defensive positions, while the opposing side was weakened by hunger and cold, and depleted by desertions. Another assault the following day was repulsed by the French artillery and the Venetian cavalry, inflicting terrible losses. The battle lasted 16 hours and the carnage was great: between 5,000 and 8,000 French died, while the number of fallen Swiss was close to 10,000. In total, nearly half the soldiers at Marignano lost their lives. The Swiss fell back to Milan, soon surrendering the city and leaving Duke Massimiliano Sforza to flee. The defeat at Marignano dispelled the myth of Swiss invincibility on the battlefield.[22] A long Swiss tradition has held that Marignano marked the beginning of Swiss neutrality, a claim recently and fiercely contested.[23]

For all his praise both of Swiss bravery and of the papacy, when he returned to his parish in 1515, Zwingli was just over 30 and was deeply troubled, scarred by the brutality of war and haunted by a vision that divine judgement had fallen at Marignano on the duplicity of those who had profited from the sale of Swiss mercenaries. No longer could he hold the Swiss to be the innocent ox, for their hands were covered in blood – not least of their own countrymen – for the sake of French, German and papal reward. Further, he found that his papal sympathies were increasingly at odds with the growing Swiss sentiments toward the French.

Chastened and troubled, Zwingli turned to his pen to express his anguish, in a work entitled 'The Labyrinth'. He retold the mythical story of Theseus in the labyrinth with the Minotaur, which he slays before returning to marry Ariadne, who has aided his success. In Zwingli's morality tale, the labyrinth was the world in which humans wander without the string that saved Theseus; for without God, men and women stagger through the labyrinth unable to see the light of day, deprived of hope. The priest's tone was dark:

> The world is so full of deceit that we have no more the image of Christ than the heathen. Yea, we are worse, for the heathen do all deliberately so that repentance and misery do not come over them. We, on the other hand, in our conceit hurry all matters along thoughtlessly. Therefore, we are all in trouble.[24]

What, Zwingli asked, do Christians possess of Christ, other than his name? No one shows patience or wisdom:

> Most of all the princes have learnt nothing except to pursue their own desires. As soon as a notion enters their heads everything else must cease. When God allows peace to shine upon us, men turn into beasts.

## ASPIRING SCHOLAR

Zwingli was very attached to his parishioners in Glarus. In a marginal note to his copy of the medieval doctor Albertus Magnus, he observed that 'the people of Glarus are cheerful and like to laugh'.[25] Years later, in Zurich, he continued to be in contact with men and women from his parish, offering guidance and assistance. As a priest with several assistants, he administered the sacraments, visited the sick and instructed the children. He baptized, married and buried as a priest who took seriously his sacramental and pastoral duties. Although his years in Glarus would end in acrimony, he loved his flock, whom he described in a marginal note to a book by Erasmus as wiser than the people of Attica. He would remember them fondly during his years in Zurich.

While a student in Basel, Zwingli had been encouraged by his mentor Thomas Wyttenbach to see reading the Bible and the church fathers as essential to the study of theology.[26] This emphasis did not mean, however, that he gave up on the medieval scholastic authors. Quite the opposite. In Basel and Glarus, he pored over their texts and annotated them, and his library contained his own copies of Duns Scotus, Peter Lombard, Aquinas and Albertus. Later evidence suggests that he was, even from a young age, an outstanding Latinist, and constantly studied the classics and made notes in the margins of books to refine his knowledge. We do not know precisely when he took up Greek, but his first attempts probably came between 1510 and 1513: in 1510, he wrote to the great Swiss humanist Heinrich Löriti (known as Glarean (1488–1563)), requesting a Greek grammar;[27] and three years later, he enthused in a letter to his friend Vadian: 'I am so resolved in my intention to study Greek, no-one but God could dissuade me from this course. I do not care about glory, only about the study of the Holy Scriptures.'[28]

Zwingli was a lifelong zealous acquirer of books, and from his careful annotations in the margins we know him to have been a meticulous reader. His library in Glarus also included numerous bibles and works by Athanasius, Chrysostom, Augustine, Hilary of Poitiers and John of Damascus.[29] His study of the new nine-volume edition of Jerome was so intensive that he could note in a letter that a page was missing.[30] In addition, he possessed the complete works of the Florentine Pico della Mirandola and the influential commentary on the Psalms by the renowned French scholar Lefèvre d'Étaples, who offered a crucial path to Augustine.

As a priest in an Alpine valley, Zwingli cultivated a network of friends that gave him access to books and the newest learning. He devoured Greek and Roman authors, the works of the church fathers and the latest humanist writers. Such scholarly engagement, he believed, was a Christian vocation. During his time in Glarus, he grew to recognize, however, that all learning served the understanding of God's Word. Later, in 1522, he reflected on this experience:

> When I was younger, I gave myself overmuch to human teaching, like others of my day, and when about seven or eight years ago I under-took to devote myself entirely to the Scriptures I was always prevented by philosophy and theology. But eventually I came to the point where led by the Word and Spirit of God I saw the need to set aside all these things and to learn the doctrine of God direct from his own Word.[31]

Pastoral care and study were not Zwingli's only occupations in Glarus. As he would later freely admit, he came to enjoy the company of women and the pleasures of sex. There is nothing to suggest that his actions caused any particular scandal. Nevertheless, while quasi-clerical marriages were pretty much the norm, Zwingli seems not to have sought a permanent arrangement and to have been more promiscuous, although later he always insisted that he had been discreet. A reputation for unchastity would long outlive the Zurich reformer.

## ERASMUS

The most powerful and enduring influence on Zwingli was the Dutch humanist Desiderius Erasmus, resident in Basel. Erasmus electrified a young generation of scholars with his call for a return to the sources of the Christian faith. In particular, in 1514 he began work on a Greek edition of the New Testament, a labour that took two years.[32] Following the scholarship of Lorenzo Valla, whose annotations on the New Testament Erasmus had uncovered in a Dutch monastery, he worked with a series of manuscripts to present the Greek with a facing Latin translation and extensive notes. The *Novum Instrumentum* appeared in 1,200 copies from the press of Johannes Froben in Basel in early 1516, instantly becoming a wonder of the age.

Around 1514/1515 the priest in Glarus had begun to collect and devour works by this international champion of learning and Christian renewal. Notably, Zwingli took up Erasmus' admonition in his *Enchiridion*, or *Handbook of the Christian Knight*, to begin the study of the New Testament by reading the letters of Paul, and he filled his copy of Erasmus' work with notes and underlined key passages on the imitation of Christ and the struggle between flesh and spirit.[33] His marginal notes drew heavily on Erasmus' *Annotations* to the Greek New Testament, and he dedicated himself to writing out the Pauline epistles from that translation and committing them to memory.[34] Zwingli later recounted the profound effect of reading Erasmus' poem 'Expostulatio Jesu cum homine', published in 1514 and later translated into German by Leo Jud and printed in Zurich in 1522. The work, he said, encouraged him to doubt the intercessory role of the saints and to focus on Christ alone as 'the sole treasure of our benighted soul'.[35] In the margins of his edition of Erasmus' *Lucubrations*, Zwingli provided witness to his growing evangelical beliefs in words that may have been written as early as 1515, recording that 'today the mass of Christians worship God through certain corporeal ceremonies, whereas the piety of the mind is the most pleasing worship. For the Father seeks such worshippers as will worship Him in Spirit, since He is Spirit.'[36] It was the Greek New Testament that turned Zwingli into an Erasmian, opening him to a new understanding of Christ.[37]

In early 1516, Zwingli visited Erasmus in Basel, an encounter made possible by Heinrich Glarean (1488–1563), a Swiss humanist poet and scholar of music, who was an early patron and friend. We glean from a rather unctuous letter of gratitude, sent by Zwingli to Erasmus several months after their conversation, that he felt that he had entered the holy of holies of Christian learning. When he read Erasmus' work, he enthused to the scholar, 'I feel that I can hear your voice and I see you in your small but elegant body moving most elegantly. For you are, without flattery, my beloved – if I have not communed with you, I cannot sleep.'[38] Just as in earlier times the Spanish and Gauls had made pilgrimages to Rome, Zwingli wrote, he had now come to the centre of learning. Erasmus was, for Zwingli, the pre-eminent interpreter of Holy Scripture. In comparison to Erasmus, he insisted, he felt unimportant and unlearned.[39] Their encounter led Zwingli to commit himself with greater zeal to studying, for Erasmus had drawn him into a new world of learning and Christianity, grounded in the study of the Bible and the philosophy of Christ.[40] He read as many of Erasmus' writings as he could lay his hands on, and threw himself into accessing the Bible in the original tongues, even undertaking a self-study of Hebrew, a language the Dutchman did not possess.

The overworked Erasmus responded with brevity and restraint, but that he replied at all is significant. His words to Zwingli were warm, but not excessively so – evidently the priest had made a good impression, but little more. Erasmus cautioned Zwingli that he should not expect much of a correspondence from Basel, for he was tied down with innumerable obligations.[41] Perhaps he also dampened Zwingli's hopes by noting that, while he looked to the revival of piety and learning in the Swiss Confederation, he expected its leadership to come from Glarean.[42] Erasmus advised Zwingli to continue to work on his style, for although Minerva, the goddess of wisdom, was evidently well disposed to him, constant practice would eventually lead to a mastery of prose.[43]

Although there would not be another personal encounter, Zwingli constantly mentioned Erasmus in his correspondence. His principal contact with the Dutchman was through Beatus Rhenanus, a humanist and close friend of Erasmus in Basel.[44] By 1518, Rhenanus could describe Zwingli as an ardent follower of Erasmus' philosophy of Christ. The correspondence between Zwingli and Erasmus continued for another eight years, until it was acrimoniously ended by the Dutchman in the autumn of 1524. Zwingli never ceased to regard Erasmus as his spiritual and intellectual mentor, the inspiration for much of his theology and vision of reform.

## MENTOR AND FRIEND

Zwingli lived in communities of parishioners, pupils and scholars, surrounding himself with a broad company of people who shared his passions. Intellectually, Erasmus emerged as the model. Next to the Dutchman, the most distinguished figure was Heinrich Glarean, an esteemed friend of the Basel humanist.[45] Zwingli's first contact with Glarean was an exchange of letters while he was a priest in Glarus, with Zwingli referring to his fellow countryman as a most trusted friend.[46] Theirs was a generous friendship. While in Cologne, Glarean received a request from Zwingli for copies of the Isagoge (or Introduction) to Aristotle's 'Categories', Ptolemy's geography and a work by Pico della Mirandola; and later in Basel – so their correspondence attests – Glarean sourced many books for his friend, assuring him, for example, that if he did not have a Greek grammar, he would send him one.[47] He also advised Zwingli to be particularly warm toward the printer Froben in Basel, who could supply him with books.[48] Glarean often footed the bill for all these books himself, although their transactions indicate that Zwingli was also sending money.[49] Glarean also used his relationship with Erasmus on Zwingli's behalf – he facilitated that personal meeting with Erasmus, and we know that he encouraged the Dutchman to write to Zwingli. Where Glarean evidently understood himself as Zwingli's mentor, Zwingli joined Erasmus in investing his hopes in Glarean for a renewal of learning among the Swiss, and for their cultivation as a chosen people.

Zwingli's early letters also give us access to his developing relationship with Joachim Vadian (1484–1551), his exact contemporary and fellow student in Vienna. The son of a wealthy St Gallen patrician family, Vadian stayed on in Vienna, where at the age of 32 he became rector of the university. Like Glarean, Vadian was a poet: both men had the title of poet laureate conferred on them by Emperor Maximilian. We get a flavour of Zwingli and Vadian's friendship from an exchange from the early months of 1513. Zwingli opened with a complaint about the amount of time that had elapsed without a reply from Vadian; he then sought his friend's guidance on how to read the Isagoge to Aristotle's 'Categories' in his endeavour to learn Greek, adding that he trusted Vadian's advice in all matters of education.[50] Vadian replied with fulsome praise for Zwingli's learning, encouraging him to persevere with his writing and not, as many others had done, let his studies fall dormant. He was delighted with Zwingli's progress in Greek, he noted, as it would deepen his understanding of Latin; no one could be called learned who did not possess both languages.[51]

Zwingli's exchanges were not confined to rarefied learning. He used his friendships to find teachers for his students; the students then reciprocated by writing letters in which they reported on their progress in their studies, and frequently by expressing their gratitude to their master. The letters stand out not for references to their mentor's piety or service to the Church, but for his commitment to them, marked by expectation and enthusiasm. Little is known about many of these pupils and mentees beyond occasional references in Zwingli's correspondence; but one instance produced a distinguished Reformation career. Valentin Tschudi was born in Glarus in 1499, the son of a knight. We know that he studied Latin, and possibly Greek, with Zwingli before travelling to Vienna, and to Vadian, in 1512/1513. His studies led him also to Pavia and then to Glarean in Basel, whom he followed to Paris, staying there from 1517 to 1521. He ultimately returned to his native Glarus, where he served first as a priest and then as a pastor for over 30 years, until his death in 1555.

In a letter from July 1514, Tschudi apologized and explained that his failure to write was a sign not of indolence, but rather of the lack of messengers to carry his letters to Glarus.[52] He recounted his recent difficulties and thanked Zwingli for his generosity during his recent bout of quartan fever.[53] A sign of this kindness was a book the priest had brought his former pupil in Basel, leaving it behind with encouragement to study and not fall behind. The young Tschudi was full of praise for his former teacher, describing him as 'shrewd in reading ancient authors', surpassing all but Apollo himself.[54] He described how Glarean had gathered all his students together in his house, where they shared their resources, lived together as a community and studied Livy, Aulus Gellius and Greek; yet Tschudi remained short of means and asked Zwingli to intervene on his behalf with friends, that they might relieve his financial woes.[55]

Valentin was not the only Tschudi whom Zwingli taught and mentored. The priest also exchanged letters with Valentin's brother Peter, who had advanced sufficiently in his studies at Basel to be able to correspond in Greek with his former teacher. Peter asked Zwingli to intervene on his behalf with his father, who for some unmentioned reason was opposed to his studies.[56] A third brother, Aegidius Tschudi, would become a distinguished humanist author, Catholic nobleman and defender of the Roman Church. He wrote to Zwingli just before Easter 1517 to report that his teacher Glarean was about to leave for France, depriving him of his mentor. Worried that, without this great man, he would have to return home and would forget everything he had learned, he asked if he might study with Zwingli, with whom he did not seem to be as familiar as were his brothers Valentin and Peter.[57]

Valentin Tschudi also gives us a sense of Zwingli's manner and approach as an instructor. In a letter sent from Paris in 1517, he thanked Zwingli for his assiduity in always correcting mistakes, pushing for perfection and punishing laziness. His elegant and eloquent portrait of Zwingli suggests a learned, stern and exacting teacher, who was also caring, encouraging and humorous.[58] At times, Valentin admitted, he had grown so exasperated with the demands for practice that he had wanted to throw his writing implement at his teacher.

## EINSIEDELN AND CONVERSION

Zwingli's publicly expressed hostility toward the mercenary trade and his papal sympathies went down badly in a poor land desperately in need of the money French agents were offering. In 1515, the Swiss Confederates had concluded a pact with King Francis I, and Zwingli was on the wrong side. Although loved as a priest and teacher, his political views had caused animosity among local officials, and Zwingli knew the time had come to leave.[59] On 14 April 1516, he reluctantly agreed to depart from Glarus for the ninth-century Benedictine abbey at Einsiedeln, 15 miles across the mountains in Schwyz, a Confederate with which Zwingli had no connection, just as he had no links to the Benedictine order. He informed Vadian that his situation had changed not because he sought more pleasure or money, but because he had been driven out by the partisans of the French.[60] He did not resign his post in Glarus, taking a leave of absence instead. His position at the abbey was as a 'people's priest' (*Leutpriester*), which came with the responsibility to administer the sacraments, preach and provide pastoral care. He was to minister to local farmers and preach to the pilgrims who came to venerate the Black Madonna.[61] We know that he was well compensated for his efforts: in addition to the papal pension he was still being paid, he continued to receive money from Glarus and was remunerated by the abbey. He was also entitled to the 'confessional shilling', the fee for reading masses.[62] Much of his money, as in Glarus, went on the purchase of books. At the abbey, he was under the direct authority of the abbot. He threw himself into his new position, and in 1517 even led a group of pilgrims to distant Aachen, where they could worship at the shrine of Charlemagne.

Although he had been diligent in collecting books while in Glarus, Einsiedeln opened up new vistas for the humanist priest. He had responsibility for about 1,500 souls, but there was virtually no monastic life at the abbey, and so Zwingli could spend a great deal of time in study, working in a library that possessed thousands of texts. He continued to teach students, some of whom would fondly remember how he introduced them to Greek literature. The extant copy of his personal edition of Aristotle reflects careful and repeated reading.[63] He could now fully embrace the Erasmian vision of devoting himself to the study of scripture and of the most ancient witnesses of the faith. The works of Augustine and Jerome, both of whose writings had been produced in Basel by Erasmus, would be particularly well thumbed. The results were dramatic, as Zwingli later recorded:

> I call God to witness that I learned the essential purport of the Gospel from reading the treatises of John and Augustine and from the diligent study of Paul's epistles in the Greek, which I copied with my own hand ... This essential summary I committed to writing in such manner that many congratulated me.[64]

His efforts as a priest, scholar and mentor – first in Glarus and now in Einsiedeln – led Zwingli to a remarkable break with medieval practice. He provides few details, but he clearly had a form of conversion experience that led him to a realization that scripture was the only true authority for the Christian life. His later account of his Einsiedeln years was certainly part of a curated attempt to distance himself from Luther (an evident consequence of their hostile relations), but the early date of his conversion to the gospel offers us every reason to believe that Zwingli, through Erasmus and others, had come to his own position on the authority of the Bible.

His first move was radical: he abandoned the lectionary, the daily readings from scripture.

> Before anyone among us had heard the name of Luther, I had begun in 1516 to preach the Gospel of Christ. When I entered the pulpit, I did not preach the words from the Gospel lesson appointed for the mass that morning, but rather from the biblical text alone.[65]

He was thus aspiring to be the priest of whom Erasmus wrote. According to the learned Beatus Rhenanus, the German humanist and classical scholar, Zwingli's preaching was marked by the 'purest philosophy of Christ', carried out like the fathers of the ancient Church.[66]

We also have an account of Zwingli's preaching in Einsiedeln from the young Kaspar Hedio (1494–1522), who studied at the famous school in Pforzheim and then took a degree in theology at Basel in 1519. Hearing that Zwingli was very ill with the plague in Zurich, he recounted his early experience of having heard the Swiss preacher during a visit to Einsiedeln. Zwingli had preached a 'beautiful, learned, weighty, rich, vivid and evangelical sermon in a manner that renewed the power of the old theologians' and, Hedio continued, 'this sermon so inflamed me that I was filled with the greatest inward love for Zwingli, and looked up to him in wonder.'[67]

In 1523, Zwingli wrote of an undated experience in which he found relief for his conscience in the Lord's Prayer. The evidence suggests Einsiedeln as the setting. In the petition 'forgive us our trespasses, as we forgive those who trespass against us', Zwingli described himself as reaching a mountain so great that he stepped back. What does it mean for God to forgive us as we forgive others? In great anxiety and self-doubt, he surrendered his troubled conscience to God, crying out: 'Lord I must not presume that you should forgive me according to my own forgiveness. Lord I am an imprisoned person. Forgive me, Lord, forgive.'[68] He continued to babble, he wrote, until

'I stood so utterly exposed in the very prayer that God had commanded me.' He meditated on a psalm, but it brought greater accusation, for his conscience told him that he was self-satisfied that he had taken hold of the Spirit. If he was to find relief, it would be in learning what it meant to be forgiven and then to forgive others. That was the heart of the matter.[69]

## SINS OF THE FLESH

The celebrated priest and preacher was pursued by gossip. In both Glarus and Einsiedeln, Zwingli was sexually active – even highly active. Though in itself that was hardly remarkable. Bullinger was to write many years later that there had been plenty of stories about the priest's relationships; and Zwingli later admitted to Bishop Hugo that he had not been celibate.[70] His sexual encounters only became an issue, however, in 1518, when he was being considered for an appointment as a priest in Zurich.

In response to the accusations of frequent fornication, Zwingli wrote a letter dated 3 December 1518 to Heinrich Utinger in Zurich, an early supporter of church reform.[71] Zwingli rejected the suggestion that he had violated the daughter of a leading citizen in Einsiedeln, but he acknowledged that his relationship with another woman, the daughter of a barber, had not been chaste and he was concerned that he had made her pregnant. Apparently thinking it vindication, he claimed that she had not been a virgin before he slept with her, and her reputation was such that no one blamed him for having sex with her. When she discovered herself to be pregnant, she had left Einsiedeln for Zurich, but Zwingli offered no more information about her whereabouts or condition. It is tempting to wonder whether the newly arrived priest ever encountered the woman or her (their) child in the city. Zwingli's response was a mixture of victimhood and tortuous logic: he insisted that he had never slept with a married woman, a virgin or a nun; he did not mention prostitutes, on whom the rumours focused. He had always been discreet in both Glarus and Einsiedeln. The admission was part confession and part excuse, salted with a self-deprecating biblical line: 'A dog returns to its vomit' and 'A sow that is washed returns to her wallowing in the mud' (2 Peter 2:22).[72]

Years later, in Zurich, Zwingli would publicly acknowledge his conduct in print on two more occasions. In a sermon from 1522 on the Virgin Mary that was addressed to his brothers, he confessed that, as a priest, he had been beset by 'pride', 'gluttony', 'impurity' and other fleshly sins. Therefore, he wrote,

> most beloved brothers, if you are told something about me which you feel ashamed of, think from what motive or intention this comes. If you are told that I do sin with pride, gluttony or unchastity, believe it with ease, as I am sadly subdued to these and other vices. However, if you are told that I give wrong teaching for the sake of money, whatever the sum they swear it is, do not believe it. For I am not bound to any lord on earth for a single penny.[73]

A direct reference, without details, is also found in his 1522 petition to Bishop Hugo von Hohenlandenberg for priests to be released from the vow of chastity. Zwingli makes the well-founded observation that few priests had kept to that vow, and he hardly concealed his own experience:

> We, then, having tried with little enough success, alas, to obey the law ... have discovered that the gift has been denied unto us. We have meditated long within ourselves how we might remedy our ill-starred attempts at chastity.[74]

Although he would be the first reformer to marry, nothing Zwingli wrote or said suggests a particularly high view of women. His wife, Anna Reinhart (1484–1538), remained largely invisible, the model wife and mother; and when the religious houses were ultimately closed, Zwingli was clear that nuns were to make themselves useful and marry. We find nothing akin to Luther's passion for his beloved Katharina.

## ZURICH

At the Benedictine abbey, the priest had enjoyed the support and admiration of the administrator Diebold von Geroldseck, whom he described as not learned, but an advocate of study. As a preacher in Einsiedeln, however, Zwingli also attracted attention further afield. The Zurich *Bürgermeister* Marx Röist met the priest while on pilgrimage to the Black Madonna. In

October 1517, Zwingli declined an invitation from the town of Winterthur to be city preacher and head of the school, stating that he still had unfinished business in Glarus.[75] The priest's reputation was spreading: in 1518, the papal legate Antonio Pucci wrote to Zwingli that there was no one who would not 'praise your learning to the heavens'.[76] That year a more attractive possibility arose with the prospect of moving to Zurich, a city with which he had growing connections, fostered by its ties with Einsiedeln. On visiting the city, he made it very clear that he was open to an invitation.[77]

In October, his friend Oswald Myconius wrote, encouraging him to apply for a position in the chapter at the Grossmünster, the leading church in the city.[78] Zwingli was by no means passive in the matter: he bombarded Myconius, who taught at the church, with questions and requests, finding out who the other candidates were and beseeching him to speak on his behalf. His pride was at stake: Zwingli insisted that he would be mortified if he, a learned Swiss, was beaten to the post by some 'flatulent and windy Swabian'.[79] Myconius played the roles of adviser and confidant, calming Zwingli about his prospects for the position, but warning him of the major impediment arising from the rumours of his sexual misconduct. The outcome was his confessional missive to Utinger. Zwingli received several supportive letters, including one from the secretary to Cardinal Schiner, who was still active for the papal cause.[80] In Zurich, the influential humanist canon Konrad Hofmann declared himself satisfied. Zwingli's election to the position of people's priest followed on 11 December.

‡ THREE ‡

‡

# DISRUPTIVE

## 1519–1522

The city in which Zwingli arrived at the end of 1518 was not especially remarkable. Nor was it an obvious place for a religious revolution. A member of the Confederation since 1351, Zurich was of middling size, with some 6,000 inhabitants, well placed on the trade routes that led south through the Alps to Italy and north toward the Rhine. Located where the River Limmat meets a large lake, Zurich was a city of trade, pre-eminently in textiles, but it also engaged in the exchange of iron ore from the northeast of the Confederation and of salt, grain and manufactured goods obtained through Basel.[1] Once the centre of a flourishing silk industry, by the early sixteenth century the city's economy was largely local, dependent on cattle and agriculture. In 1518, the situation was not good: the economy was languishing and the rural people were suffering from the collapse of markets. There was considerable social unrest, and the mercenary trade was widely blamed for the economic woes. All this served to prepare an audience for Zwingli's message.

Zurich was not the seat of a bishop, did not possess a university like Basel or Wittenberg, and had nothing to rival the great banking and merchant houses of Augsburg and Nuremberg. Nevertheless, next to Bern it was the most powerful Swiss Confederate, traditionally exercising considerable influence in the eastern lands. Much of its power came from its large rural territory, which extended along the Lake of Zurich toward the Alps, giving a total population of around 60,000. It was from the land that it drew its soldiers, tithes and agrarian goods. Geography offered clear advantages: the bishop of Constance, its spiritual overlord, was a distant figure with nominal influence; this allowed the magistrates gradually to acquire control over the affairs of their churches, against the bishop's will. By the time Zwingli arrived in Zurich, the civic rulers already controlled much of the religious life of the city and its rural areas. Furthermore, Zurich lacked rivals in the eastern part of the Swiss Confederation, enabling the city to expand its influence and act on long-held hegemonic aspirations that unsettled its neighbours.

The diocese of Constance sprawled across the lands of southern Germany and the Swiss Confederation, and its bishop was a prince of the Holy Roman Empire. In the late fifteenth century, an agreement had been struck that gave local churches a high degree of autonomy in return for the payment of dues. Within the city of Zurich, there were about 200 clergy, the most prominent of whom had strong links to the leading families. The economic depredations in Zurich, however, had left many priests and monks in poverty. At the same time, the ruling magistrates succeeded in obtaining control over appointments to clerical positions in the city, including to the principal church, the Grossmünster. The magistrates were able to intervene in the affairs of the churches and monasteries, often resolving disputes and choosing candidates for positions. On the whole, they tended to favour candidates from Zurich.

The city was ruled by the Large and Small Councils.[2] The former was made up of 212 men elected from the 12 guilds, which included the butchers, tanners, printers, vintners, tailors and merchants. The Small Council was charged with running the daily affairs of the city; its 24 members, all Zurich born and resident, were also members of the Large Council. Presiding were the two *Bürgermeisters*, who took it in turns to serve for six months and who chaired the two councils. Along with the *Bürgermeisters*, the *Obristmeister* (master of the guilds) was especially influential within the city. When key decisions regarding affairs of the state and Church were imminent, the councils appointed members to prepare and present the necessary material. The election of the same families and members of the guilds created considerable continuity in the make-up of these advisers.

Despite the fixed forms of government, the political and social world in Zurich was highly dynamic. The leading families of Röist, Grebel, Göldli, Bonstetten, Landenberg and others – some of which belonged to the nobility – enjoyed enormous prestige and continued to provide many of the civic leaders.[3] Experience counted for a lot in political life, and most political players were in their forties or fifties; it was highly unusual for a young person to exercise influence. Substantial power lay with the Constabulary, a body of 18 of the most socially elite and economically powerful men, who largely led the city on foreign affairs. However, by the time Zwingli arrived in Zurich, the Constabulary was in decline, as artisans of the emerging craft guilds were starting to wrest power from the old families. Wealth and status were not the only keys to political power: men rose from the lesser guilds and families, making their way through connections and force of personality. Nevertheless, most of the leading magistrates continued to be members of old families and of the influential guilds, such as those of Meisen and Saffran.

We know that Marx Röist (1454–1524), who served as *Bürgermeister* from 1505 to 1523 and who had visited Zwingli in Einsiedeln, and his son Diethelm were particular patrons and defenders of Zwingli, using their considerable influence and connections to support his preaching and reformist convictions. The records allow us, however, few glimpses into the relationships that developed between the new preacher and the powerful families and guild members, although they were undoubtedly foundational for later reforms within the city. Zwingli appears to have drawn his supporters mainly from within the Large Council, which included all the guilds, and this exacerbated the conflict between the two councils. For the most part, the Small Council was dominated by noble families opposed to Zwingli, although a significant minority did sympathize with the reforms. It is impossible to know exactly who supported Zwingli and who opposed him. However, since the city was mostly governed by older men, what we can say is that his sympathizers did not necessarily represent the younger generation; rather, they came from the establishment.[4]

Following the battles of Novara and Marignano, opposition to both French mercenary recruitment and pensions (paid by foreign agents in return for political support and the flow of mercenaries) was growing in Zurich. The rising artisan class deeply resented the flow of such pensions into the pockets of the noble families, providing them not only with income, but also with military careers for their sons. Yet the monies from France, Rome and the Austrians also provided employment for young men from the lower classes, who struggled to make a living in the city and on the land. At the same time, concerns were growing over French influence in the Swiss

Confederation, where almost all the states except Zurich were aligned with the French king. For both political and moral reasons, well before Zwingli began to preach, there were already many critics of the system, who regarded the taking of pensions as unpatriotic.

The feuding in Zurich between parties played a significant role in Zwingli's call to the Grossmünster – and in the opposition that awaited him. Many patrician families benefited from the existing situation, in which they both received pensions and accrued income from the canonry of the Grossmünster, to which they had close family relations. The election of Zwingli, a known opponent of pensions and the mercenary service, was a reversal for them. They were defeated by the anti-French party that had brought the priest to the city, but they remained a powerful opposition.

Outside the walls of the city, further unrest was fostered by residual resentment among rural subjects of their urban overlords. In comparison to their peers in German lands, Swiss peasants had traditionally enjoyed greater autonomy thanks to their traditional rights.[5] Nevertheless, these claims clashed with the desires of civic rulers and religious institutions to enhance economic profits. There was a long history of resistance in the countryside, and in 1515 peasant forces attacked the city of Zurich, marauding and looting in protest at corrupt politicians.[6] Fortune, however, did not favour the peasants, and the Reformation would only enhance the growing control of the rural areas by the urban rulers through coinage, custom tolls, required labour and taxation administered by officials sent out from the city.[7] Zwingli's initial sympathies for the plight of the peasants, with whom he identified, even though his own family had been prosperous, quickly faded, as he embraced the power of the urban elites as his means to reform.

Zurich society was also military, organized into bands armed with pikes, halberds, crossbows and swords. Service was compulsory for men of the city and its territories, and the Swiss mercenary armies ensured that Zurich could draw on plenty of martial experience. Zurich had no standing army: whenever war loomed, an officer (often a leading citizen) was appointed to raise troops. The men received no salary: the army was to live off the land it occupied and the booty it acquired. The arts of warfare were central to the life of the community, with marksmanship and combat skills regularly rehearsed in festive shooting competitions between the guilds. The young Zwingli had been trained in the use of arms, which served him all his days.

## PEOPLE'S PRIEST

On 11 December 1518, the 34-year-old priest and preacher from Einsiedeln was elected to the post of 'people's priest' (*Leutpriester*) at the Grossmünster, continuing many of the duties he had performed at the abbey: preaching, celebrating mass and providing pastoral ministrations. The decision was by no means unanimous, with 17 canons voting in favour and 7 against. Zwingli's hostility to mercenary service and his pro-papal sympathies were well known, making him a controversial candidate in a city where those French pensions lined the pockets of influential families. Nevertheless, hopes ran high for this celebrated preacher, scholar and patriot.

Founded in the eighth century, the Grossmünster was the most prominent ecclesiastical foundation in Zurich. The church was dedicated to the saints Felix and Regula, whose relics resided beneath the high altar, a source of civic pride and identity. The city also had a long association with Charlemagne, whose image appeared on the seal of the Grossmünster. The chapter of the church consisted of 24 canons, who traditionally came from leading families and resided on church property. They were not, however, without worldly interests, deriving income from a plurality of church offices, familial lands and titles.

Zwingli's office placed in his hands the care of souls, a role for which he was well prepared as a university-trained priest with years of pastoral experience. In Zurich, those who held this office had normally studied at a university.[8] Alongside the people's priest were the deacons and chaplains, who assisted in the sacramental life of the church. As among the guilds, there was considerable internal tension within the church, as the secular and regular clergy quarrelled over rights and privileges – not least over providing pastoral care and entitlement to income for saying masses and burying the dead. Typical of the age, the laity responded with harsh criticism, and anti-clerical sentiment was rife among the faithful. Nevertheless, in December 1518, Zwingli would have encountered in Zurich a world of traditional devotion: a liturgical year full of saints' days, processions, commemorative masses and the veneration of relics.

### 'CALL MY FLOCK'

Zwingli the priest was to preach to those assembled in the Grossmünster. Like all medieval cities, Zurich was awash with preachers declaiming from pulpits and on street corners.[9] Most of the leading cities of the German Empire had established preacherships in their principal churches for prominent clergymen.[10] Church festivals and the liturgical seasons of Advent and Lent were marked by sermons by well-known clerics, who could dazzle with their rhetorical skills. That Zwingli was called to preach in Zurich was not in itself remarkable: it was what he said that was electrifying. Medieval preaching was full of exempla and familiar accounts of sin and virtue, but Zwingli presented to his listeners the full drama of the gospel story, from the opening genealogies of Matthew to Christ's Great Commission.

On Sunday, 1 January 1519, the newly arrived priest entered the pulpit in the Grossmünster to preach on his beloved Gospel of Matthew, having resigned his living in Glarus and having delivered his last sermon in the Benedictine abbey at Einsiedeln. Zwingli had informed the canons of his plan to abandon the set readings of the lectionary and to preach from the beginning of the gospel to its conclusion, as he had done in Einsiedeln.[11] Through the cold weeks of January and February, each Sunday Zwingli took up where he had left off in the previous sermon, to continue the journey through the lives of the patriarchs, prophets, Christ, the Apostles and the first Christians.[12] The priest who stood before the people was a dedicated follower of Erasmus, passionately committed to putting Christ before the people by bringing them to the gospel. The conviction of the power and accessibility of the Word, set out by his mentor in the preface to the Greek New Testament, had become Zwingli's agenda.[13] Zwingli's later adoption of Matthew 11:28–30 as his motto – 'Come to me, all you who are weary and burdened, and I will give you rest. Take my yoke upon you and learn from me, for I am gentle and humble in heart, and you will find rest for your souls. For my yoke is easy and my burden is light' – was an expression of his spiritual indebtedness to Erasmus.[14]

In the years immediately following his appointment in Zurich, Zwingli attended to all his duties as a priest by hearing confession, celebrating mass and participating in festive processions; but it was his preaching that drew most attention. He had made a name for himself with sermons to pilgrims in Einsiedeln, and now he turned to the crowds gathered in the Grossmünster to speak very plainly. 'I have not,' he later remarked, 'used any false nostrums or tricks or exhortations, but in simple words and terms native to the Swiss I have drawn them to the recognition of their troubles, having learned this from Christ himself, who began his own preaching with it.'[15] He was convinced that men and women needed to be brought to a visceral awareness of their sins and of the pressing need for repentance. His purpose was clear: 'to call my flock absolutely away, as far as I can, from hope in any created being to the one true God and Jesus his only begotten Son, our Lord. He that trusts in him shall never die.'[16] Renewal in Christ healed both the inner person and the society in which that person lived.

Every word of the gospel was good news – not just the highlights that the lectionary offered. Zwingli preached the direct application of the scriptural message, with the lives of biblical characters immediately applied to the circumstances of his audience, including the injustices of power and the corrupting of the body by the infection of sin. They heard words of correction, and of rebuke, but they also learned of a better Christian world. According to his friends, Zwingli did not possess a particularly strong voice, but he did employ a heightened sense of the dramatic that befitted a poet and lover of classical literature. He preached extemporaneously, without a text, but with the Bible open before him. Plainly and passionately – clearly too plainly for some – he expounded the scriptures, always keeping his eye on the society in which he now lived, not hesitating to name from the pulpit those who neglected or corrupted their spiritual or political offices.

The new priest took aim at medieval practices that he regarded as unscriptural. Both his reading of Erasmus and his conversion in Einsiedeln had led him to doubt the intercessory powers of the saints and of Mary, mother of Christ.[17] It was his first major break with medieval devotion. The people were warned against praying to Mary and use of the rosary, as well as against the veneration of saints. He put himself in dangerous territory by attacking a deeply popular expression of faith. In his sermons, apocryphal stories of saints were dismissed – including those of Felix and Regula, the patrons of Zurich. Some canons in the Grossmünster chapter were already alarmed in 1519 by Zwingli's open support for Martin Luther, whom the Church was seeking to excommunicate and who was being attacked by the theological faculties in Louvain and Cologne. The dual question of when Zwingli began to read the Wittenberg reformer and the extent of the influence of the doctor's writings on him remains unresolved, but by the end of his first year in Zurich the Swiss priest was defending the German's attack on the papacy.[18] Monks and religious houses were a particular object of

Zwingli's attacks: he railed against their indolence and immorality, telling the people that in his role as confessor at the Benedictine house in Einsiedeln he had heard litanies of their transgressions.

Zwingli had in his sights the selling of indulgences, no less an issue in Swiss lands than in Luther's Saxony. The Franciscan preacher Bernhardin Sanson, whom Zwingli had first encountered in Einsiedeln, arrived in Zurich in January 1519, selling assurances of relief for the dead that would assuage the anxieties of both rich and poor.[19] Following Zwingli's advice, the Zurich (Large) Council refused to admit Sanson to the city, while the bishop of Constance was clear that he did not sanction the indulgence seller, whom he regarded as depriving him of much-needed revenue. It was less the idea of indulgences that infuriated Zwingli than the Franciscan's taking coins from people who had no idea what they were doing, a clear echo of Martin Luther's response to Johann Tetzel. The papacy, allied with the Swiss and a major employer of mercenaries, did not want another fight along the lines of the events in Wittenberg, and Sanson was recalled to Rome. Zwingli's protest had been well received by the reform-minded bishop of Constance and Pope Leo X, and he remained on close terms with the bishop's adviser, Johannes Fabri (1478–1541), with whom he continued to correspond until as late as October 1520.[20] Their connection is all the more intriguing in light of Fabri's prominent role in the process against Luther.

Canon Konrad Hofmann (1454–1525) had supported the priest's appointment, but the unfiltered attacks on abuses in Church and society proved too much to stomach, even for a reform-minded cleric.[21] In 1522, he provided a sense of Zwingli's outrages, and his complaint offers us the best evidence of what the people's priest was preaching. In sermons on the gospels and epistles, he held the lives of the people, clergy and magistrates up to the standard of the Bible. For Hofmann, however, Zwingli's intentions were subversive.[22] The canon charged the priest with demeaning the fathers of the Church and declaring that ecclesiastical laws had no validity, since Zwingli argued that the laws of the Church should be submitted to the judgement of scripture. He attacked the morals of the clergy, denied purgatory, rejected veneration of the saints as having no biblical warrant, and assured the faithful that unbaptized babies were not damned. Perhaps most controversially, Zwingli declared that the pious Swiss Confederates should refuse to serve any foreign prince, whether the French king, the German emperor or the pope. According to Hofmann, the preacher brought not good news, but spite and polemic, and was dividing the community.[23] Hofmann and Zwingli agreed that Church and society should be reformed, but they parted company on the nature of true faith. The senior canon believed that the Church was to be restored and improved, while Zwingli was openly advocating binding reform of the Church with social and political questions.

Zwingli's sermons had an immediate effect. His attack on the morals of the clergy also brought into the line of fire the patrician families of the city, with whom the senior clerics were closely connected. These families formed the core of the Small Council, where resistance to Zwingli was most pronounced. Hofmann's objections represented not only the clerical elite, but also families of the noble and merchant class. But matters went further. Zwingli's attack on religious houses also cut close to the bone: the monasteries of the city and rural areas were occupied, and often led, by members of the leading families, which depended on these offices for a rich seam of income. Zwingli posed a danger to this class beyond the purely religious, for his attack on the mercenary service and pensions also made public the simmering dispute over mercenary service and the receipt of pensions from France and Rome. His incendiary preaching threatened many in the higher echelons of Zurich society, and through Hofmann their displeasure was voiced.[24] Bullinger recounted how Zwingli's preaching against pensions and mercenaries stirred up fierce opposition, and he was branded a heretic by prominent Zurichers. These people, Bullinger added balefully, had not previously been interested in religion, but had been outraged by the threat to their pockets. The matter was not about the faith, Bullinger concluded, but about the purse.[25]

Zwingli, however, was not an easy target. He had been brought to the city by the anti-French faction in Zurich, including the Röist family, and he held their support. The people's priest had influential supporters, such as Cardinal Schiner, who saw him as an important player in the papal campaign against the king of France. Schiner, who had good relations with Zurich, was a powerful backer of the priest, though he would die before Zwingli came to espouse his more radical reforms.[26] In 1520, Zwingli was still seen as loyal to Rome (from which he continued to receive a pension), and that insulated him against criticism. Inside the city, his preaching led to the formation of a circle of friends who shared his attachment to scripture, his evident patriotism and his attacks on the clergy.[27] In the years 1519–1520, Zwingli still separated the corruption of the Church from any attack on Rome (in contrast to Luther, who was excommunicated in January 1521), and also made clear that religious change involved the civic magistrates, who were responsible for the spiritual health of the community. Rome's need for Zurich provided the crucial space for Zwingli to preach.

Although he preached on highly sensitive subjects, in his first few years in Zurich Zwingli did not much engage in either domestic or foreign politics. He showed little interest in becoming involved in the governing of the city. His focus was elsewhere: promoting his Erasmian pacifism, with its rejection of military conflict. Zurich must be armed, he argued, but only in order to maintain a policy of neutrality. He opposed all martial alliances, a position that must have disappointed even his supporters. Zurich was an ambitious city that looked to extend its influence over the eastern part of the Swiss Confederation, and to do so would require force. When Zwingli preached in 1521 against an alliance with the papacy, he was largely ignored.[28]

He had his critics, and Zwingli knew it, writing to Myconius that 'if I should please men, as Paul says, I would not be a servant of Christ'.[29] In November 1519, he further remarked to Myconius that he had to defend himself from accusations that he was an agent of Cardinal Schiner, the pope's representative.[30] He acknowledged that his reputation was spreading in Swiss lands, and enjoined Myconius to defend him. Zwingli boasted that his success had been remarkable and that there were many who had been won over to the gospel: 'For we are not alone: at Zurich more than two thousand children and adults are already sucking spiritual milk, and will soon be ready for solid food, while others starve.'[31] By the priest's perhaps optimistic reckoning, almost a third of the city supported his preaching. Zwingli's allusion to milk and solid food referred to the fifth chapter of Hebrews and provides us with a glimpse of how he saw his ministry: although his statements could be brusque, his goal was to move the people gently toward God's Word.

Sensitive to the question of pensions, Zwingli relinquished his pension from the papacy at some point during 1520. The move may have had something to do with the Luther case in Germany, where the Wittenberg reformer was being excommunicated by Rome. In Zurich and the Swiss Confederation,

Zwingli's preaching was being termed 'Lutheran', and he was seen as sympathetic to the German, an association that made the Zurich Council nervous. Accusations of heresy imperilled commercial activity and stirred up social unrest, and pressure was brought to bear on the Swiss Diet to enforce the condemnation of Luther. It was crucial to demonstrate that Zwingli was not a supporter of Luther, and a civic mandate was issued to offer that fig leaf – whatever the truth.[32]

Yet the combination of influential supporters and the papacy's unwillingness to alienate Zurich led to further advances. Zwingli had been careful never to cast his preaching as a threat to the magistrates, but rather to present an open invitation for them to lead reform. Furthermore, the growing number of his supporters gave him influence among the political leaders. Dividends came in the autumn of 1520, when the Council supported his preaching from the Bible, clearly asserting its right to decide on the matter of religion. The magistrates waded deeper into the waters of reform. Singing of the Ave Maria ceased in the Grossmünster – an evident sign of Zwingli's influence – and the monetary resources for the devotion were redirected to the city's hospitals.[33]

## 'DEATH IS AT THE DOOR'

In 1519, the chronicler Johannes Stumpf recorded the onslaught of plague: 'At this time a swift and horrible pestilence reigned in all German countries and also affected a remarkable number of people within the states of the Confederation in a short time.'[34] In Schaffhausen, out of a population of approximately 4,000 souls, the city lost 3,000. Zurich lost about a third of its inhabitants. As the shadow of death was cast over the urban and rural areas, Zwingli was at the baths in Pfäfers in the mountains, near Bad Ragaz – today the site of a famous psychiatric clinic. On hearing the news, he hurried to Zurich, believing it his duty as a priest to be with the people in their suffering and final hours. Plague was no respecter of sacred office, and in September Zwingli was struck down. Friends and family had a strong presentiment of the priest's impending death. We know from a letter that by 6 November the Zurich preacher was recovering, but he still needed to convalesce through the winter and into 1520.[35] In response to his near-death experience, he composed his 'Plague Song', an astonishingly moving account of despair, resignation and recovery, and a hymn to the Christian's dependence on the goodness of God.

Composed for solo voice and sung during Zwingli's life in household worship, the text reveals a Christ-centred spirituality rooted in scripture, with few traces of traditional religion and no reference to either Church or sacraments:

Help, Lord God, help
In this trouble.
I think Death is at the door.
Stand before me, Christ;
for You have overcome him.
To You I cry.[36]

The opening petition was neither to Mary nor to the saints, but to 'Lord God' and his son, Christ, who alone protects as mediator. Alluding to Romans 9:21 – where Paul asks: 'Does not the potter have the right to make out of the same lump of clay some pottery for special purposes and some for common use?' – Zwingli declared: 'Your vessel am I; To make or break altogether. For, if You take away my spirit from this earth, You do it that nothing shall be worse for me.' God's chosen are wholly dependent on him as the creator of the vessel. The disease laid waste to the body, creating unbearable pain and putting to flight all trust in human effort:

Console me, Lord God, console me.
Pain and fear seize
my soul and body.
Come to me then,
with Your grace, O my only
consolation.
It will surely save
everyone, who
his heart's desire
and hope sets
On You . . .

In the midst of agony, the tongue cannot speak and resistance to the ravages of the devil is no longer possible. Only God's abiding presence could bring relief. His divine love alone brings healing: 'Sound, Lord God, sound! I think I am already coming back.' Restored by Christ the physician, and consoled by the God who does not abandon, the sufferer finds the afflictions of body and soul overcome. For this there can be only one response – thanksgiving:

> Yes, if it please You,
> that no spark of sin
> rule me longer on earth.
> Then my lips must
> Your praise and teaching
> proclaim more
> than ever before,
> However it may go,
> in simplicity and with no danger.

The 'Plague Song' has long remained something of a mystery, as it cannot be dated with any certainty: scholarly speculation has placed its origins between late 1519 and 1525, the year of the Reformation in Zurich.[37] Whatever its dating, the song reflected the state of Zwingli's soul in 1520, once he had emerged from imminent death. The stirring, affective language was wholly in line with his 1516 conversion to the gospel, for it was in biblical words that he found expression for his song of mercy and redemption. The unanticipated recovery was God's purpose, and Zwingli was his agent; his lips were to 'praise and teach'. The mortal body must die, yet the promise of eternal life brings strength, notwithstanding the 'spite and boasting' of the world. Without God's grace in Christ 'nothing can be perfect'. Zwingli drew no connection between bodily health and spiritual blessings, for he was firmly persuaded that he would die and enter bliss; but his recovery convinced him that he had survived for God's service, his prophetic office in Zurich.

## WHEAT AND THE TARES

By the summer of 1520, the intensity of Zwingli's focus on Christ alone, together with his growing concern about the failure of anticipated church reform, had found darker expression. The 'Plague Song' was Zwingli's plaintive call for divine intervention from an abyss of extreme anxiety and spiritual despair. He had survived, and for a purpose; but he awoke to an unrepentant world. In March 1520, Zwingli wrote to Myconius a lengthy letter about God's angels, to whom he attributed divine healing from the plague. After speaking of how Origen, Jerome and Augustine accounted for the good and fallen angels, Zwingli observed that it pleased God to demonstrate his love and care to the faithful through the appearance of his messengers. Myconius replied that he was much pained by the constant attacks on Zwingli, observing that perhaps it was on account of the wine he was drinking in Zurich that his friend's voice, once so weak, now thundered through the Confederation.[38]

In 1520, Zwingli wrote of the powers of the world arrayed against renewal and learning, forming the 'constant enemy of the truth that itself cannot be conquered'. Were Zwingli's words a spiritual groan or a battle cry? His language was unambiguous:

> I say all this in order to hasten the battle that is already under way and hurries towards its end, to win for Christ as many soldiers as possible who will then fight boldly for him. Admonish them long and hard, so that the more cruelly they are persecuted, the less shamefully they will respond. For this I will tell you plainly: just as the Church was born through blood, only through blood can she be renewed.[39]

It would take many personifications of Hercules to cleanse the Augean stables, and for their labours they would be persecuted. Zwingli referenced Luther as a prime example of those who would be handled unjustly, and declared his own readiness to die for the faith. Persecution is the fire spoken of by Jesus: it tests the faithful and proves their perseverance. Zwingli's pessimism reflected a significant theological shift away from sanguine hopes invested in the revival of learning as the key to the renewal of piety and toward a more radical trust in the will of God acting through Christ.[40] It was also the beginning of his martial language.

Drawing on the parable of the wheat and tares found in Matthew 13, he had begun to understand the world in terms of supporters and opponents of

Christ. His interpretation of the parable, drawn from Augustine, saw the Church as a mixed body of believers and unbelievers – the wheat and tares – who would be separated only by God's judgement at the end of time. Indeed, the role of Augustine, whose works Zwingli read carefully in Einsiedeln and Zurich, was crucial. Zwingli possessed the 1506 complete edition, produced in Basel, and his marginal notes are an invaluable source on his developing thought. Through his reading of the North African father's *City of God*, Zwingli came to think of history as the ongoing struggle between good and evil, a reality played out in the lives of the faithful. Augustine also instructed him in the role of law in the life of the justified Christian. Zwingli rarely named his intellectual mentors, but later, in 1527, he recalled the transforming influence of Augustine's commentary on John.[41]

While we have no evidence that Martin Luther influenced Zwingli directly, the latter certainly regarded Luther as a supporter of the humanist vision of church reform, and saw the fierce attacks on the German as a threat to the renewal of Christ, the gospel and true learning. In other words, he had seen Luther through the lens of Erasmus. That would begin to change in the summer of 1520, when the papal bull *Exsurge domine* appeared, threatening Luther with excommunication. Zwingli was now persuaded that Rome was the enemy of reform. And if Rome persecuted Luther, might he be next?[42]

No bolts from the blue, but rather a confluence of forces brought a turning point in the second half of 1520. The dangers posed to hoped-for reforms by the Luther case, a growing pessimism about the willingness of the Church to effect change, and his reading of Augustine all moved Zwingli toward a more radical assessment of the world around him. The battle for the gospel pitted the forces of Christ against darkness; God alone was the author of change; and little was to be expected of human efforts. The great Dutchman remained the towering influence, but Zwingli's perspective had shifted. His focus was now on an all-powerful God leading the renewal of the Church in this world, which would remain mired in conflict with darkness until the end of time. For the rest of his life, Zwingli would view the gospel in terms of a seismic Pauline struggle between light and darkness. The opponents would vary – from Rome to the Habsburgs and Luther; but the conviction never ebbed.

## FEEDING THE POOR

From his days in Glarus, Zwingli was well aware that mercenary service often left survivors unable to work and in penury, and villages and towns full of widows and fatherless children. Additionally, begging was everywhere in the fetid conditions of the cities. In drawing attention in his sermons to the most vulnerable in society, Zwingli was directly entering into another already disputed matter: who should tend to the poor? Traditionally, the religious houses, guilds and hospitals had cared for those suffering most; but in a mandate of September 1520, the Zurich magistrates took matters into their own hands by establishing their own system of poor relief, a position that Zwingli supported, but by no means initiated.[43] He justified from the pulpit the intentions of the rulers. The mandate enhanced the control of the ruling Council over the ecclesiastical affairs of the city, but the policy also changed. The decree distinguished between two types of poor: those who genuinely suffered 'through fire, war, crop failure, drought or a variety of illnesses' and those who simply were lazy and indolent.[44] In other words, the magistrates separated the deserving and undeserving poor. Begging was permitted, but the community was to provide for the destitute through common collections, taken at the door of the city's churches by 'worthy, pious women'.[45] Central to the question of destitution and poverty was the burden of the tithe, to which we shall return. The poor loomed large in the reforming impulses of Zwingli and his earliest supporters. The wealth represented by the Grossmünster and other civic churches, along with the religious houses, was an affront to the teaching of gospel. Care for the destitute, fired by sermons decrying injustice, would lead to iconoclastic attacks on the symbols of Catholic worship. Poor relief was a mark of a renewed society.

## FRANCE AND ROME

An early sign that Zwingli was winning influential supporters within the city came on 29 April 1521, when he was elected to a canonry in the Grossmünster, on the death of an elderly incumbent. He now belonged to the leading clerical body in Zurich. Additionally, the position bestowed citizenship of the city. Zwingli's election confirmed the esteem in which he was held by influential clerics in the city, and from the Grossmünster a circle of humanist-minded friends had begun to form, including Erasmus Schmid, Heinrich Engelhart (people's priest in the Fraumünster) and Heinrich Utinger, with whom Zwingli had corresponded and who became godfather to Zwingli's first child.

In May 1521, Zurich refused to join the alliance with France that had been concluded by the rest of the Confederation. The Swiss had signed an agreement by which they would provide between 6,000 and 16,000 mercenaries, in return for payment of 25,000 crowns.[46] Zwingli was not the principal force behind the rejection, but he gave it his full support. The refusal to join France stemmed from stiff political resistance within the city, where Zwingli was a significant but not singular voice. His views were not so much against France, but against all forms of mercenary service and foreign wars.

Not only did the magistrates reject the French alliance, but they forbade Zurichers from service in any foreign army. This was also bad news for Rome, with which they had had an agreement since 1515. The city was politically isolated by the decision, and the opprobrium of the fellow Confederates was fierce. Although anti-mercenary sentiments were to be found throughout the Confederation, the opportunity was a lifeline for many of the members, especially the poorer central ones. This reality was never accepted by Zwingli. The intertwining of calls to end the profitable trade in soldiers with calls for gospel religion was creating a new dynamic. Those who had most to gain from mercenary service were hardened against the evangelical reforms led by Zwingli, while in Zurich, the rejection of the French alliance was the first sign that religious reforms in the city were beginning to determine external affairs. Yet the connection with Rome had served the evangelical cause well in the city: the papacy was unwilling to move directly against Zwingli and his allies while it still needed Zurich's force. The effect of the new policy was powerful: in January 1522, the Council forbade the receipt of pensions and participation in mercenary recruitment on pain of fines and banishment.[47] Those who persisted could lose their citizenship. With Zwingli's continued support from the pulpit and in print, the magistrates maintained the pressure on supporters of the financial and military arrangements until, by the late 1520s, they were largely suppressed.[48]

One of the most remarkable transitions that Zwingli made in his first years was from partisan of Rome to opponent of the papacy. No doubt the

Luther case had influenced his sentiments, but he was also appalled by Rome's cynical politics. At first, he had tried to separate his attacks on the Catholic faith and clergy from his attitude to Rome itself. But by 1522, that effort had come to an end. And Zurich was done with the pope, whose refusal to pay for the city's soldiers he received stirred anti-papal sentiments in the city that greatly aided Zwingli and his followers. Zurich recalled its troops in January and issued a mandate forbidding any further service. It would be the last time Zurich sent its soldiers to serve a foreign master. Rome was no longer a significant player in events in Zurich, and Zwingli's reforms now depended on the good will of the magistrates.

Rome needed Zurich's military support, but it also wanted to be rid of Zwingli, whose preaching was increasingly becoming an irritant. Efforts were made to discredit him with accusations that he had been more a papal agent than a loyal Swiss. Those hostile to him within Zurich were in close contact with Catholic leaders in Lucerne, Basel and Bern, and numerous plans were hatched to force his expulsion from the city by traducing his name. More draconian methods were also envisaged. In January 1522, the Council heard the case of Kärli Köchli, a dishwasher at the Dominican house, who boasted in a tavern while drunk that he had come to Zurich to kill Zwingli. The Council took the threat (not the first) seriously, and Zwingli was provided with an armed guard.[49]

## STAGED PROVOCATION

As soon as Zwingli arrived in Zurich, he sought out the company of others. He became part of a circle of friends committed to reading Greek works, such as Homer and the tragedies, as well as the New Testament. A network of friends and supporters took shape, encouraged by the preaching, as well as by the flow of new ideas into the city from the printing world of Basel. His advocacy of the Bible spurred groups of laymen and women to meet in homes to read scripture, pray and sing.[50] For the most part, these gatherings were independent of the clergy, led by educated laymen known as 'readers'.[51] The lay members were moved by Zwingli's preaching, but they also formu- lated their own ideas. From these early groups would emerge figures such as Konrad Grebel and Felix Manz, who became friends, but were later bitter opponents of Zwingli. Many of these men belonged to a younger generation.

Christoph Froschauer (1490–1564), originally from Bavaria, had arrived in Zurich in 1515/1516, becoming a citizen in 1519; and at an early stage he was already printing both the works of Luther and the German translations of Erasmus' biblical paraphrases.[52] His home became one such meeting place.

A group of some 12 friends, including Zwingli, met on 9 March 1522 in Froschauer's house. That they gathered was not remarkable; but what they ate changed the reform cause – they sat down to a meal of sausages in Lent. The event was not the first flagrant breach of the Church's rules on abstinence from meat during the penitential season, for earlier the same day a small group had assembled at the house of Hans Kloter to eat soup with wine, bread and eggs. That gathering, which included members of the city's Large Council, had then moved to Froschauer's home, where the printer's wife, Elsie Flammer, had prepared sausages. At this point, Zwingli and others joined the company.[53] The presence of a canon of the Grossmünster offered a degree of unofficial sanction of the flouting of the church laws.

Although Zwingli sat with the others, he did not eat the meat. Why he did not is not entirely clear, but his abstinence cannot be attributed to either timidity or fear of controversy. He was fully aware of the implications and that his presence would ensure scandal. The sausage-eating incident was no private matter. It was a well-staged provocation, intended to turn Zwingli's preaching into action by flaunting unbiblical practices. It did not matter whether Zwingli ate the sausages or not: he was fully complicit, encouraging the breaking of the Lenten fast.

The desired effect was immediate. Senior church officials were appalled and called for the offenders to be punished, while sympathizers were emboldened to hold their own meals. The choice of breaking Lenten strictures by eating was not coincidental; food was closely connected to the associated matter of poor relief. The magistrates, some of whom had been present, were not much inclined to act. A half-hearted investigation led to no further action. As host of the meal, the printer Froschauer appeared before the magistrates to claim that

> I believe the Holy Scriptures, which say that a Christian life is not dependent upon food or drink. Indeed, it is not dependent on external works, but only on true faith, trust, and love so that we may all live simply, friendlily, justly and truly with one another.[54]

The printer's words were those of Zwingli, certainly heard from the pulpit and likely at the table during the meal. A couple of weeks later, the priest preached on the freedom of Christians to eat what they wished. His sermon was a public justification of fast-breaking. He defended the actions of the fast-breakers, portraying them as honest Christian men.[55] Referring to Paul's arguments as to whether the ancient Christians should have eaten food consecrated to pagan idols, Zwingli came to the crux of the matter: in terms of the faith,

> food is neither good nor bad in itself . . . but it is necessary and therefore truly good. And it can never become bad, except as it is used immoderately; for a certain time does not make it bad, but rather the abuse of men when they use it without moderation and belief.[56]

A printed version of Zwingli's sermon appeared in April 1522, offering his first major statement on the freedom of the Christian conscience and echoing the teaching of Martin Luther.[57] It also marked a further step away from Erasmus, who had also criticized fasting: unlike his mentor, who suggested that reform should be in the hands of church leaders, Zwingli advocated that the magistrates should ban fasting, and that no Christian was bound to the unscriptural practice. Zwingli had deftly woven together social reform and Christian freedom, while attacking the Church for encroaching on the liberty promised by the gospel.

By pouring oil on the fire, Zwingli sought to draw the reluctant magistrates into the quarrel. He must have been satisfied. His opponents responded quickly: some spoke of Zwingli as a heretic who should be driven from the city, while others claimed that he brought only 'hate' and 'jealousy'.[58] The Council appointed a commission, which consisted of Zwingli, together with Felix Fry, dean of the Grossmünster chapter, and two other priests. That he was appointed to investigate himself was a sign of his secure position. The outcome was a partial victory: while the fast was deemed not biblical, it was to be continued in the interests of preserving peace in the city.[59] The instigators of the provocation were not to be punished, but were instead admonished to go to their confessors. Having dismissed the saints as intercessors, Zwingli had now opened another crack in the wall of medieval piety. The sausage incident was the first clear evidence of growing support for reform among the laity, as well as among some clergy and politicians.

The Council's appointment of Zwingli to the commission and its unwillingness to punish the fast-breakers were all the more remarkable as the church hierarchy had not been idle. Even before Zwingli's sermon was printed, the bishop of Constance had sent an investigative delegation to Zurich, where it remained from 7 to 9 April 1522, holding meetings with various ecclesiastical and civic leaders. Zwingli prepared a written account of the discussions.[60] The delegation understood the delicacy of the matter and wished to express the bishop's displeasure, while not offending the Zurich magistrates. Those magistrates, however, were not united. Many, particularly those on the Small Council, wanted Zwingli to have no role in the discussions and for him to be punished for insolence.[61] For his part, the priest lobbied hard to meet the delegation and explain his views; in the end, his supporters on the Large Council made this possible.

For the first time, as Zwingli described it to a friend, he had been on an equal footing with the bishop's authorities. The magistrates had given him a new status, as well as a stage for his convictions. He offered a rather wry account:

His [the bishop's representative's] whole speech was violent and full of rage and arrogance, though he took pains to hide the fact that he had any quarrel with me. For he avoided mentioning my name as scrupulously as if it were sacred, though meanwhile there was nothing that he didn't say against me. When the tragedian had finished shrieking out his part, I stepped forward, feeling that it was unbecoming and disgraceful to allow a speech which might do so much damage to go unrebutted, especially as I saw from their sighs and their pale and silent faces that some of the feebler priests who had recently been won for Christ had been troubled by the tirade.[62]

In contrast to the histrionics of the bishop's man, Zwingli portrayed himself as a humble priest:

'My Lord suffragan' (and in this I made an indiscreet and ignorant enough blunder; for they tell me I should have said 'most merciful Lord', but being unskilled in polished ways I take hold like a clodhopper) 'and fellow-ecclesiastics', I said, 'wait, I pray, until I make explanation in my own behalf.'

The conscious self-deprecation could not hide a confidence that enabled him to speak to the officials of the true ancient faith as a prophet calling for reform. He declaimed with conviction and attacked his enemies, an assault leavened with humour: his opponents, he observed, were able to 'see how clearly I handled the sacred writings'. He concluded the letter with a marvellous self-assessment: 'These are the wounds I received and inflicted in the assembly of the ecclesiastics and councillors; these the means with which I ran to the aid of the feeble.'

Bishop Hugo von Hohenlandenberg, friend of Erasmus and himself an advocate of reform, was deeply troubled by what was transpiring in Zurich, and he remained resolved not to allow the heresy that was engulfing German lands to spread to his diocese. He wrote to the Grossmünster chapter, citing reports that

> all through Germany people of Christ cry out day and night that they have been wrongfully oppressed until now by the heads of the Church with hard and burdensome regulations, observances, and ceremonials, and as a result such persons are attempting with all their might to cast off and do away with such ceremonials.[63]

He cautioned Zwingli to 'abide in the unity of Holy Mother Church and in obedience to those set over you, and not to cast away hastily the ceremonies of the Church introduced by our forefathers'.[64] On 9 May, he wrote to his whole diocese that the faithful were to stand by the teachings and practices of the Church. The statement reached Zurich on 24 May and proved a catalyst for Zwingli's increasingly bold statements – not only about fasting, but now also about clerical celibacy. And with the arrival in Zurich of his close friend Leo Jud, who had become people's priest in the city church of Saint Peter, Zwingli now had a powerful ally.

## TESTED PATIENCE

Zwingli was playing a complex game in which he attempted to balance provocation with tact. Although driven by his theological views and profound convictions, he knew that rash action could be disastrous. In many respects he was struggling with his own impulses, which were to attack. His opponents were not simply corrupt and venal. The tensions instead surrounded a clash of views of reform: was change to come from within the institution or be pressed from without? Zwingli wrote to Jud in May 1522 that one must do less than one wants in order to achieve a greater result.[65] Zwingli was by no means the only advocate of reforming the Church. Many of his colleagues were passionate about change, while at the same time disturbed and even angered by his assault on traditional piety and authority. Zwingli's radical teaching inspired many of his followers; but as he fully understood, their zeal posed a considerable risk. Even though the Council had backed him several times, moving towards his position on the authority of scripture and the role of the magistrates in making decisions concerning the religious life of the city, the situation was precarious – and he knew it.

The Lenten protest and its largely favourable resolution emboldened Zwingli and his followers. In May, a group of Zwingli's colleagues, many of whom had eaten the sausages, met at the home of patrician Konrad Grebel to plan an event to honour the reformer, who was returning from the baths at Baden, where he had undertaken a cure.[66] Some 300–500 people were to be invited to an event intended less as a social gathering than as an expression of support for Zwingli, putting pressure on the magistrates to resist efforts by the bishop to quash the reforms. The size of the proposed assembly made the Council nervous, and the occasion was forbidden. The magistrates were concerned that the gathering would only encourage Zurich's enemies to claim that the reforms were politically subversive. It is not clear whether Zwingli had any role in the plans, or even knew of them, but undoubtedly he was to be the centre of attention. The organizers' purpose was to put pressure on the rulers to act with great speed in bringing about reform. Their impatience bordered on hostility, as Grebel articulated:

> The Devil not only sits in the chambers, but he also sits among my lords. For one sits among my lords who has said, 'the gospel should be preached in a cow's ass'. And insofar as the lords do not allow the gospel to progress further, they will be destroyed.[67]

Grebel's remarks suggest that, by the summer of 1522, some of Zwingli's supporters were growing suspicious of his close alliance with the guilds and magistrates.

By June 1522, the priest's increasingly vociferous critique of the venera-tion of saints was leading supporters to dare to interrupt the sermons of other priests and monks with catcalls. Grebel took the lead, but Zwingli himself shouted down a Franciscan preacher from Avignon, François Lambert, when the latter spoke in the Fraumünster: in the middle of Lambert's sermon on Mary and the saints, Zwingli called out 'Brother, you are in error!' The overt offensiveness was a conscious strategy to force a public debate and keep up the pressure on the magistrates, and it succeeded.

A disputation was held in the city among the leading ecclesiastical figures to consider the preaching of the mendicants. The result was gratifying for Zwingli and his supporters. The Large Council issued a mandate declaring that the friars were to preach from scripture along the lines set down by the priest, abandoning the scholastic teachers.[68] This time a delegation of magis-trates had not only intervened directly in church matters, but had also ventured a judgement on a theological question. Their decree was limited to the mendicants, and was not a full endorsement of Zwingli's preaching as normative for the Zurich Church, but the direction of events was evident. Zwingli had set the agenda for scriptural preaching, and his name was unmistakably identified with the evangelical cause. The Council, although divided on the question of Zwingli, had no desire to fall in step with the bishop, whose authority it had for years only nominally acknowledged. Zwingli's first victory was in persuading Zurich's rulers that questions of religion were in their hands and could be resolved locally. In an ensuing debate with Lambert over images in the Church, which took place before the *Bürgermeister* Marx Röist and senior officials, Zwingli made an aston-ishing statement: 'In this city of Zurich I am bishop and priest.'[69]

## MARRIAGE

By early July 1522, priestly celibacy had become the next point of conflict. For Zwingli, who openly admitted that he had not abstained from sex while in Glarus and Einsiedeln, the matter was deeply personal. More importantly, at some point in early 1522 he had secretly married Anna Reinhart, a young widow who had tended him when he nearly died of plague.[70] To what extent they were able to keep their marriage hidden in crowded Zurich is not known, but Zwingli told only a few close friends. Anna was the daughter of an innkeeper in Zurich and had married Hans Meyer von Knonau against the wishes of the bridegroom's father, who had cut him off from his inheritance. Knonau had died in 1517, leaving Anna with three children, one of whom, Gerold, was very close to Zwingli (and would die with his stepfather at the battle of Kappel in 1531). For a priest to cohabit with a woman was hardly unusual, but Zwingli and Anna claimed to be married, and that was another matter. They would not officially celebrate their marriage until April 1524, three months before the birth of their first child. Zwingli was the first of the Reformation leaders to marry – three years before Luther.

What took the edge off the demand for clerical marriage was the reality that throughout the German-speaking lands, and perhaps particularly in the diocese of Constance, the cohabitation of priests with women was almost universally accepted, even if the derogatory term 'priest whore' was widely used.[71] Formally, church law had long proscribed what was in fact the reality. It has been reckoned that by the early 1520s there were about 1,300 children of priests in the diocese, and for each one the bishop collected money, known as a cradle tax, in order that they might be baptized and made legitimate.[72]

Together with 10 other priests, on 2 July 1522 Zwingli signed a petition requesting the abolition of celibacy, on the grounds that there was no basis in scripture for this manifestly unsustainable burden on the clergy.[73] The petition presented was carefully timed for maximum impact, appearing in Latin and German to reach a wide audience beyond Zurich.[74] Ever the tactician, Zwingli was learning the possibilities of printed media, as had Luther, and was mastering the benefits of striking first, to put his opponents on the defensive. The German edition came off the press only two weeks after the Latin original, signalling Zwingli's intention to carry out this fight in public.[75] The German version, with the title 'Friendly Request and Admonition Addressed to the Confederates', was addressed to the Swiss Confederates, not the bishop, and sought to remove the celibacy debate from the ecclesiastical hierarchy and place it in the hands of sympathetic temporal rulers. Zwingli framed the argument along lines similar to Luther's 'Letter to the German Nobility' of 1520, by encouraging the magistrates to embrace church reform and free priests from burdened consciences.

The 'Friendly Request' broadened the vision of reform. Christian freedom was released from human rules and regulations that deadened the spirit of the Word. It was God's will that men and women should marry and not allow their sexual appetites free rein, an inevitable consequence of forcing clergy to abstain from licit, divinely sanctioned sexual relations.[76] Celibacy could not be the marker of priestly identity as members of a higher spiritual order, superior to the laity. Marriage was the natural order: 'If we run through the whole of the New Testament, we find nowhere anything that favours free concubinage, but everything in approval of marriage.'[77] Bishop Hugo von Hohenlandenberg was not to be moved, and in early August 1522 he issued a mandate requiring the Zurich Council to proceed against the agitators. His request fell on deaf ears, but it was clear that Zwingli was reaching beyond the city to a wider audience in the Confederation.

## 'IT WILL KILL US'

Although the benches of the Large Council held considerable support for Zwingli, external affairs and prudence dictated caution. Zwingli had lent his voice in Zurich to those opposed to an alliance with France, but the city was isolated as the Swiss Confederates joined the French king. The result was disaster for the Confederates. In the spring of 1522, as Zwingli was engaging in his first open debates, the French army with its Swiss mercenaries was decisively defeated at the battle of Bicocca by imperial and papal forces. Having nearly revolted because they had not been paid by their French employers, the Swiss had launched into battle only to be slaughtered by cannon fire as they sank into a quagmire. The traditional formations of pikemen proved ineffective against heavy artillery and Spanish arquebuses. The surviving Swiss soldiers turned tail and fled home, far from their glory days on Renaissance battlefields.[78]

Deep resentment at the supposed mendacity of their French masters led to renewed debate about the willingness of the Swiss to serve the king. Two days before the issue was discussed at a local assembly in Schwyz on 18 May, Zwingli had written to the Confederates. He spoke with a prophetic, patriotic voice warning of divine judgement. Moral decay and devastation of the land were the consequences of the people's departure from the virtues of their forefathers, he insisted.[79] The piety of the traditional Swiss, who had stood with God the creator and his son, Jesus Christ, contrasted starkly with the rapacious immorality manifested in mercenary service and pensions. The perils of foreign alliances for the Swiss were incalculable. Above all, war brought God's opprobrium upon the people of the Confederation and endangered the Swiss alliance itself. 'Protect yourselves from the money of foreign leaders!', warned Zwingli. 'It will kill us.'[80] He gave no quarter to the crucial economic role that mercenary service played in the mountainous Confederates.[81]

Zwingli interwove divine promise with the innate virtues of his kinsmen, a glorious past written in the annals of history. Quoting Paul (Romans 8:31) – 'If God is for us, who can be against us?' – he linked the natural defences of his land with God's protection: 'The Rhine is now our border security . . . Think on the earlier Swiss Confederation, think of how God helped our honest forefathers in the same way that he had the Israelites.'[82] Zwingli's warning to the Schwyzer was no pacifist tract. War in defence of the fatherland was wholly justified, as it had been in the Old Testament. The banishment of mercenary service and pensions was essential to the renewal of the whole of society.

Zwingli's brutal and coruscating 'Apologeticus archeteles' appeared in August 1522, as his 'first and last word'. Heinrich Bullinger would later record that the work summarized what Zwingli had been preaching since his arrival in 1519.[83] The text was polemical and artful, coloured at moments with humour, and remains one of Zwingli's most compelling cases for evangelical reform. Penned in haste, it assumed the tone of offended honour and righteous indignation following the episcopal investigation of the reform movement in Zurich.

Are you mightier than God, Zwingli mocked his Catholic opponents, wiser than God,

> or just so stupid, that you think you are going to persuade consciences free in Christ not to regard as lawful what they know is lawful by the divine law, even though you shout about it till you are hoarse?

Switching metaphors, he threatened:

> I shall certainly not spare your names but shall challenge you by name to single combat as Menelaos challenged Paris, and if you scorn me so far as to refuse to come forth, I will proclaim your reluctance to the whole world.[84]

Once more the prophet saw the need to enter into battle.

Zwingli, in his own estimation, stood for the pure preaching of the gospel, at one moment a Peter, then a Paul, enabled by the Spirit to separate biblical truth from the inventions and pretensions of human fantasy. He pleaded in the dock as a man wronged by his opponents, traduced by those unable to see the truth of the gospel. The Zurich priest did not recoil from advising the bishop on how to do his job:

> You should therefore be wary and wise, and pray to the Lord to guide your path, and, to make an end finally, you should take it in good part if something be taken from you to be added to Christ. For thus you will make the House of Hohenlandenberg most illustrious and your own soul most acceptable to Christ.[85]

Against the sophistication of the episcopal court with its misconceived nostrums, Zwingli enjoyed fashioning a humble, rural background, as a *rusticus* or country bumpkin who was 'preaching the gospel with such energy and risk of harm'.[86] Having earlier spoken with the words of the exilic prophet Ezekiel, Zwingli shifted his self-portrayal to the prophets Amos and John the Baptist, outsiders and men of the people. Erasmus had predicted how the simple of faith would confound the doctors and bishops. Zwingli was extremely proud of his Toggenburg heritage and frequently referred to the virtues of the mountain peoples. It should be no surprise that God would raise up a prophet from among them to strip away the hierarchical pretensions of his accusers, who for all their privileges raged against the wind 'urging the unity of the Church, when your words breathe nothing but rebellion, uproar, war, destruction and whatever belongs to it'. Zwingli rightly sensed that 'it is absolutely clear that you [Bishop Hugo] are aiming at me alone'.[87] And in response to the bishop's accusations, he asserted his prophetic calling: 'God spoke by my mouth when I was setting forth His Word.'[88]

Both parties – Zwingli and Bishop Hugo – claimed the other was of a different and deceitful spirit, employing God's words to their own ends. Zwingli's accusatory words of wilful distortion of scripture could have been hurled back at him by his opponents: 'Therefore if I have anywhere handled the scriptures improperly, you ought to have pointed that out. That you have never done.' Zwingli repeatedly asserted that he had 'handled the scriptures according to Christ's intentions' and that the bishop's men should yield to his views. Otherwise, their perdition was certain. And with further mockery, he promised them the fate that had befallen Julius Caesar:

> when he saw that he could not escape death, he took care to gather the edge of his garment about him that he might fall in a suitable manner. So should you, now that you see ceremonials tottering and almost ready to fall, strive to cause them to fall as fitly as possible – that is, not let them hold on so obstinately.[89]

The 'Apologeticus archeteles' bore no message of rapprochement. A boundary had been crossed and Zwingli recognized that return would require full recantation. By 1522, he had separated himself from the church hierarchy and the papacy – and increasingly also from his beloved Erasmus, whose conciliatory language he had set aside. He stood charged with heresy and was unrepentant. In the eyes of his opponents, the rulers of Zurich were complicit in Zwingli's errors, and thereby placed the Confederation in great danger. The demands for reform went beyond anything Bishop Hugo of Constance could possibly accept; there was no path to reconciliation.

Zwingli sent the text to Erasmus in the hopeful expectation of approval, but the Dutchman was in a difficult place. He had sought to improve his relations with Bishop Hugo, who was not averse to church reform. Erasmus stayed up all night to respond and had a warning:

> I beseech you by the glory of the gospel – which I know you have at heart above all else, as all of us are bound to do who are enlisted under Christ's name – if you publish anything in the future, it is a serious task, and you must take it seriously. Do not forget modesty and the prudence demanded by the gospel. Consult scholarly friends before you issue anything to the public. I fear that defence of yours may land you in great peril, and even do harm to the Church. In the little I have read there was much on which I wanted to see you put right. I do not doubt that with your second sense you will take this in good part; for I write with the warmest affection for you, and late at night. Farewell.[90]

Zwingli the provocateur was the recipient of considerable abuse, and it was taking its toll. In August he reflected to Oswald Myconius: 'If I did not rightly see that the Lord watches over the city, I would have long ago abandoned the rudder.'[91]

The following spring, Zwingli shared a similar reflection with two other friends. To Johannes Oecolampadius in Basel he defended himself:

> I have no fear, as I know full well what sort of irreproachable life I have led ... Zwingli has done nothing for which he must render account and from which he would not be set free by an honourable judge.[92]

To Berchtold Haller in Bern he pleaded his case: 'I do not gainsay that weak men here and there insult me when they unworthily pounce, when I believe that I have done the best I could and deserved the best.'[93]

## FRIENDSHIPS

From his early days in Basel, when he sat on a bench alongside Leo Jud listening to Thomas Wyttenbach, the teacher he claimed had introduced him to the power of the gospel, Zwingli had loved his friends and was deeply loyal to them.[94] They reciprocated his affection and trust. His concept of friendship was rooted in a theology of divine human reconciliation, manifested in God's will. Friendship formed part of the order of creation. There had been friendship among humanity's first parents in the garden, and it was a casualty of the fall. Christ offers humanity true friendship: 'being human, he promises friendship and intimacy, which is the common bond of relationship. What then can he refuse who is a brother and sharer of our weakness?'[95]

A poignant expression of Zwingli's ideal of friendship is located in his 1523 dedication of 'On Divine and Human Righteousness' to Niklaus von Wattenwyl, dean of the Bern Münster. 'That I, dear brother,' Zwingli wrote,

> am so bold as to address you in an open letter, although I have no particular friendship with you before this, comes simply from one Christ who makes us brothers and members of one body. For as the

heathen have it in a proverb, 'The good join with the good unsolic-
ited', so also a Christian has every right to seek the friendship of other
Christians since they are of one God, one baptism, and one faith; one
God and Father of all, who is above all and through all and in all.
(Ephesians 4:5)[96]

In reality, friendship was difficult to maintain in light of the pressing daily
demands. In December 1525, Zwingli wrote to the anxious Ambrosius
Blarer (1492–1564) in Constance, offering a striking (if somewhat harsh)
view of his understanding of their friendship. He acknowledged Blarer's
complaint that he had written two letters to the Zurich reformer without a
response. Zwingli believed that he had written back, but it was possible that
he had 'deceived himself' and had formulated in his head what he would say
without actually putting pen to paper. Many letters had to be written in
great haste, and so Blarer should not take it amiss if a mistake had been
made, particularly as Zwingli was constantly overwhelmed by work and
unrest. Friendship entailed commitment to the gospel modelled by the
disciples of Christ.

> For I am not in the habit to seek friends casually. I note whether they
> have the same faith as I proclaim it. I do not seek to become their
> personal friends. I know that I am dear to them when I without deceit
> declare the truth. More than sufficient for me is the reward of the
> Spirit. As soon as I see that one is in possession of the Spirit that is
> friendship enough for me. So I need you only out of faith in Christ to
> judge your work and then I am certain that I am your friend and you
> are mine.[97]

The most difficult friendships to assess existed between those who lived
in the same place and had no reason to commit their sentiments to paper.
Without doubt, Leo Jud was Zwingli's dearest friend, supporter and
colleague, but because they lived side by side and did not correspond, we
have relatively little information about their interactions.[98] Unlike Zwingli,
Jud was not Swiss. The son of a priest, he was born as Leo Keller in Guémar
in Alsace and was a pupil at the famous Latin school in Sélestat, a centre of
humanist learning. He was two years older than his friend, whom he had

met in 1505 during their student days in Basel. In addition to the study of the arts for his baccalaureate, Jud also trained as an apothecary.

When Zwingli was called to Zurich at the very end of 1518, Jud was summoned to Einsiedeln as his replacement. A gifted linguist and committed humanist, he used his time in the monastery to begin translating the works of Erasmus into German.[99] In time, he would become known as one of the leading voices of the Dutch scholar in the vernacular.[100] In 1521, he published his translation of Erasmus' *Education of a Christian Prince*.

Jud's growing attachment to Zwingli's circle deepened with his close working relationship with Froschauer and the esteem in which his translations were held. He soon expressed the wish to go to Zurich permanently. In May 1522, not long after the sausage incident, Zwingli invited Jud to preach in the church of St Peter in Zurich.[101] His purpose was clear. St Peter's was one of the most prominent pulpits in the city, and Zwingli would naturally have been delighted to have a friend, supporter and talented preacher hold the position. Jud gave a sermon on that Sunday and then stayed in the city for a week, during which he preached several times. On Zwingli's recommendation he was formally elected to the post in June. Zwingli wrote to Myconius that 'soon will also the Leo, the lion with the mighty voice and righteous heart arrive: small in stature but great in valour'.[102] Jud took up his position in Zurich at St Peter's in February 1523, and continued his translation work with more editions of Erasmus, Luther and Zwingli.[103] Jud possessed neither an original nor a powerful theological mind: his long years in Zurich were committed to preaching and preparing educational and devotional works for the laity in their language.

Jud wrote letters for Zwingli and often read and summarized books when the reformer was pressed for time. When Zwingli left for Marburg in 1529, Jud preached for him in the Grossmünster. He was also Zwingli's editor and translator. As often as he could be, he was present when Zwingli preached, and he worked to edit the biblical commentaries – both those published during Zwingli's lifetime and those that came out posthumously. Although Zwingli wrote in the vernacular when the situation demanded, it was Jud who translated his major Latin works into German. The two men appear to have worked together on these translations in Jud's house.[104] Scholars have noted that Jud's translations were more than faithful renderings of the original and often brought greater clarity to Zwingli's ideas.[105]

Jud would share Zwingli's call to arms and the necessity for military action against the Catholic Confederates. On his deathbed, however, he regretted that enthusiasm. Four days before his death in 1542, Jud gave a remarkable confession, seeking God's forgiveness:

> Protect yourselves from war. Do not be driven by lust for war. Work for the maintenance of peace. It is fitting for Christians and above all the shepherds [pastors] to show humility, not thirst for revenge. Regrettably, I rode to war in time, a great evil. Therefore, I cry out to God that he might have mercy on me and forgive me. Remember forever the unfortunate consequences of this war.[106]

Where Leo Jud might serve as Zwingli's loyal lieutenant, Johannes Oecolampadius (1482–1531), the reformer of Basel, emerged in many respects as Zwingli's theological better.[107] He certainly could command greater respect from Luther and Melanchthon. Two years older than Zwingli, Oecolampadius served as a preacher in his native Weinsberg, in southern Germany, before making extended stays in Tübingen, Heidelberg and Basel to deepen his knowledge of Hebrew, Greek and theology. While in Basel in 1516, he worked for the printer Froben on Erasmus' 1516 Greek New Testament, the *Novum Instrumentum*. A gifted linguist, he undertook the translation of a number of the Greek church fathers into Latin. In 1518, he became a doctor of theology in Basel; thus, compared to Zwingli, Oecolampadius possessed better theological credentials.

The extensive correspondence between the two men, whose friendship began in 1522, tells the story of the Swiss Reformation in the 1520s. They had different temperaments:[108] Zwingli could be impulsive and thrived on controversy, while the soft-spoken Oecolampadius proved a canny politician, who struggled in the polemical heat of the period. However unjustly, Oecolampadius is nowadays barely remembered, and virtually none of his extensive works in Latin have been translated into modern languages; yet in his day, he was much admired by scholars across the confessional divide, including Philipp Melanchthon (1497–1560), whom he met in Marburg and with whom he corresponded. John Calvin, who rarely had a kind word for Zwingli, deeply admired Oecolampadius' biblical commentaries.[109]

The relationship between Zwingli and Oecolampadius is fascinating because, as they themselves understood well, they each possessed qualities lacking in the other.[110] Zwingli greatly admired and relied on Oecolampadius' theological abilities, as well as his high reputation. The reformer of Basel, in turn, acknowledged Zwingli as the leader of the Swiss Reformation, frequently consulted him on a wide range of questions, and relied on his strength and fortitude. Many letters survive from an active correspondence that often saw the two men writing to one another several times a month. They discussed all the major events of their period, devised strategies, read each other's works, and commended students, clerics and lay persons to one another. When their correspondence was printed posthumously, in 1536 in Zurich, it caused outrage in Lutheran circles, because it revealed the attitudes of these two leading figures on Luther, doctrine and politics. No subject of the Reformation in their time was not discussed in detail.

Oecolampadius opened their exchange, sending a letter in December 1522:

> Do not wonder, good Zwingli, when I have the personal honour of making your acquaintance through a friendly letter. You may take this offer to the glory of your virtue and personal wellbeing, to the glory of Christ, this gift as precious balm to flow over you. Those who seek good things feel themselves compelled not only to love the man but also to seek his friendship.[111]

Quoting from Pliny's *Natural History*, Oecolampadius told Zwingli that he and his circle should heed for themselves what the Romans said about panthers – with their scent they draw others to them. He admitted that he had no particular purpose in writing to Zwingli, other than to wish him well, which he did most heartily, and to celebrate a man so beloved by others. Who could not love one who 'undertook Christ's work with such zeal' and erected a wall for the protection of the house of Israel? Zwingli was a 'devotee of true religion'. Oecolampadius poured forth his admiration:

> I beseech God that he ever more grant you great treasures of strength and zeal, and make you ever more fruitful, that I will with joy always

hear through good reports of you and your efforts to the glory of the Gospel of Christ.

Zwingli's reply, written in early January 1523, expressed his surprise at such flattery and offered the modest response that it was not he, but Christ who was the hero. Nevertheless, he was clearly thrilled by this new contact with a scholar of whom he knew. Oecolampadius, he wrote, was equally praised as a humanist and as a Christian, two virtuous roles that flowed together and were inseparable. He welcomed the possibility of a friendship grounded in learning and commitment to the gospel. 'Let us now and ever discuss the matters demanded to serve the heavenly doctrine.'[112] Zwingli concluded by saying that the courier of the letter would report more fully on events in Zurich concerning an upcoming disputation: there was a rumour, he reported, that Johannes Fabri, the vicar general of Constance, might be coming to Zurich. Zwingli hoped this news was true, as it would deprive the pope and bishop of their claims to victory.

Zwingli was never a singular figure. He lived in a family and community, and among a web of friends spread across Europe. In Zurich, he moved in circles of friends who met in homes, reading scripture and discussing reform. Although decisive and confident in his own judgement, his work as a reformer was rarely solitary. His personality and charisma dominated those around him and were key to many of his successes. Like Luther and Melanchthon, he recognized talents in others that he lacked. He was also thoroughly Swiss in his communal view of friendship, Church and society. Despite their evident affection, Zwingli could easily confound and confuse even those closest to him. He could make them laugh and cause them to shake their heads. His confidence in his calling made him a challenging friend.

## THE WORD

Zwingli's deep and abiding attachment to Erasmus found expression in 1521 in a pamphlet entitled the 'Description of the Godly Mill' that he helped to prepare with Martin Seger from Graubünden.[113] According to Zwingli, he received the image from the layman and was deeply impressed, asking one Martin Füssli to compose verses to accompany it. 'My only contribution,' Zwingli observed to Myconius, was to point out to him most of the references in Holy Scripture, which he diligently examined and then proceeded to show me the poem. It pleased me exceptionally with its simple, easily understood language: and because it was to sound authentically Swiss, it was printed quickly and without rewriting or improvements. I designed the look of the pamphlet with him: the first verse and the title are mine, nothing else.[114]

Füssli, Zwingli added, often stood beside him when he preached. Christ is represented as the miller, pouring his Word between the millstones. Erasmus is his humble aide, who puts the flour into sacks (his Greek New Testament) and passes it to Luther, who is the baker preparing the bread (Bibles). The other assistant, who distributes the bread to the people (God's Word), may well be Zwingli himself. The pamphlet became one of the most famous images of the Zurich Reformation, expressing the evangelical hopes of its early years.

Zwingli's publishing frenzy during the summer of 1522 continued with 'On the Clarity and Certainty of the Word of God', which Froschauer produced on 6 September. This text, too, was a reworked and expanded sermon, which in this instance had been preached in the Dominican convent at Oetenbach. It was a sign of Zwingli's growing influence that the Council appointed him to preach at the religious house, a duty formerly reserved for Dominicans. The sermon addressed the question on which Zwingli and the bishop's examiners could find no common ground – how was the Bible to be interpreted? The published work was Zwingli's fullest exploration to date of that issue, and his overarching argument was arrestingly bold: scripture, the source of all wisdom, could only be grasped by those led by the Holy Spirit. Without that Spirit, nothing availed – neither tradition nor the teachings of the ancient fathers – and the Bible was mere words. But God calls men and women to something more: 'We are made in the image of God and that image is implanted within us in order that it may enjoy the closest possible relationship with its maker and creator.'[115] To love God is akin to drinking 'strong wine'. To the healthy, Zwingli wrote,

it tastes excellent. It makes him merry and strengthens him and warms his blood. But if there is someone who is sick of a disease or fever, he cannot even taste it, let alone drink it, and he marvels that the healthy are able to do so. This is due not to any defect in the wine, but to the sickness.[116]

The Word of God is absolutely clear, because it is God speaking to humanity.[117] In truth, it is nothing other than God himself. The faithful receive the Word through the Spirit, an interior illumination that leads to Christ.[118] Even the difficult or 'dark' passages, which might seem contradictory or unclear, feed the faithful, inspiring men and women to hear more, to delve deeper. Zwingli saw the reception of the Word as a deeply communal activity: the Church knows when it is being fed. Certainty lies in the Bible itself, the work of Spirit, and requires no external verification.

Zwingli's interest was not in damnation, but in salvation, and he was remarkably sanguine about how those in the Spirit might be certain of God's will. He was totally confident that it was the divine purpose to save:

If you ask further, how can I be taught of him so that I know with certainty that this or that doctrine is according to his will? There is just one answer: ask of him and he will give you all that is needed, for he knows what is needed far better than you do yourself.[119]

The tract has a rare autobiographical quality, offering us insights into his conversion:

Again, I know for certain that God teaches me because I have experienced the fact of it, and to prevent misunderstanding this is what I mean when I say that I know for certain that God teaches me. When I was younger, I gave myself overmuch to human teaching, like others of my day, and when about seven or eight years ago I undertook to devote myself entirely to the Scriptures I was always prevented by philosophy and theology.[120]

'On the Clarity and Certainty of the Word of God' did not please Erasmus, to whom Zwingli had sent the text. While both held to scripture as the foundation of the Christian life, their approaches differed in significant ways. For the Dutchman, Zwingli's emphasis on the perspicuity of the Bible was troubling, if not arrogant. Both men recognized that scripture was difficult, obscure and even contradictory in places; but whereas Zwingli looked to the text interpreting itself, Erasmus advocated humility.

The Zurich preacher was deeply concerned by the growing row between Erasmus and Luther. For Zwingli, they were titans. He described them as Odysseus and warlike Ajax, struggling for the arms of Achilles. He declared his love for both and was desperate that they should be reconciled.[121] Although Zwingli had moved away from the Dutchman, he was loath to voice criticism.

In 'On the Clarity', Zwingli offered another glimpse into his experience of coming to the gospel during his years in Glarus and Einsiedeln:

> But eventually I came to the point where, led by the Word and Spirit of God, I saw the need to set aside all these things and to learn the doctrine of God directly from his own Word. Then I began to ask God for light and the Scriptures became far clearer to me – even though I read nothing else – than if I had studied many commentators and expositors. Note that that is always a sure sign of God's leading, for I could never have reached that point by my own feeble understanding.[122]

Just over a week after the publication of 'On the Clarity and Certainty of the Word of God', Zwingli printed another sermon, this time on the perpetual virginity of Mary.[123] Dedicated to close friends and relatives, the work was both martial and autobiographical. He opened with his continued praise of the virtue of the hardworking, pious peasantry, who are the true Swiss. Those who hold to that patrimony are God's chosen; those who prostitute themselves for war are the damned:

> As long as I hear that you live from the work of your hands, as is your custom, I am pleased and confident that you preserve your lineage from which you are born, that is from Adam. As long as I hear that some of you take up war for money and thereby kill your body, and let the Devil lead your soul into eternal prison, so do I mourn that you depart from the community of the pious inheritance of the peasants and workers and are led into robbery and murder. How is it any

different to serve a foreign lord in war for money than to commit robbery and murder?[124]

For Zwingli, the peasants represented the best of both Christianity and the Swiss. Their hard, honest labours stood in contrast to the mendacity of the wealthy urban families that lined their pockets with money from foreign pensions. Mindful of his own background, he associated himself with those true faithful who lived close to the land and embodied the virtues of their Swiss forefathers. 'Those, however, who go to war, I am certain of their sorrow and the damnation of their souls. May God grant them a right disposition that they never more do this kind of thing as they had promised.'

By this point, Zwingli had an impressive list of rejected Catholic practices: he had denied the obligation to fast, denounced celibacy, questioned the intercession of the saints and snubbed the church hierarchy. Now he took aim at the cult of the Mother of God, essential to medieval popular piety. Zwingli had a strong personal attachment to Mary, but he believed that her role for Christians was gravely distorted. She was not a mediator, but a model for the faithful.[125] Any attribution to her of intercession necessarily diminished the crucifixion and resurrection of her son. She was present at the crucifixion, an enduring testimony to her unfailing faithfulness. God himself had placed her above the saints and angels; her prayer from the innermost part of the heart was an example to all of how to speak to God. She alone had responded: 'Here am I, the servant of the Lord; let it be with me according to your Word.' It was right to offer praise in the 'Hail Mary', but without expectation that it would bring merit or reward.

Zwingli's seeming demotion of the Mother of God was, for his opponents, unequivocal evidence of his heresy, and he was forced onto the defensive:

This passage in the Gospel of Matthew I have, therefore, interpreted with such zeal that all those who everywhere put words in my mouth and speak falsely and dishonourably about me claim that I have preached the following: that Mary was a silly and stupid woman. Further, that I have dirtied her purity and profaned it, which is badly thought of me. I can swear that such nonsense about the holy Mother of God was never my intention.[126]

In the middle of the sermon, he made an extraordinary confession to his friends and relatives. Not only had he been accused of preaching against Mary and traducing her name, but he had endured numerous charges of having fathered illegitimate children, wandered the streets at night and received money from foreign rulers. Zwingli was not imagining these rumours. They had been widely circulated through Swiss lands, repeated, for example, in Chur by a wealthy Zurich statesman.[127] Past promiscuity continued to haunt him. The priest was so deeply troubled by the accusations that in the sermon he robustly defended himself:

> I decided not to give an answer to this provocation or false news about how many children I have fathered in this year or the money I have received from princes and lords. Although I have not answered these rumours, I could not permit these shameful insults about me to be believed. Each can say what he wants about my moral integrity, may God forgive him, but I will no more tolerate blasphemy.[128]

The connection was clear. Zwingli linked the accusations that he had made Mary a whore with the charges made against his own sexual licence. Neither was true, and by implication both he and Mary were models of faith.

## PRIEST TO PREACHER

Zwingli's sermons and writings spoke to specific moments and occasions, often responding to charges of heresy or misconduct. Additionally, however, he kept a weather eye on the wider European stage, on those events beyond the Swiss border that were determining the fate of Christ's Church and potentially threatening the Confederation. He followed with care how popes and rulers struggled to find unity against the spread of heresy. Luther's nemesis, Leo X, died suddenly in December 1521, unleashing a fierce struggle for control of the papal throne between French and imperial parties. The new pope, Hadrian VI (1459–1523), once Erasmus' teacher, proved no puppet of Emperor Charles V (1500–1558), and committed himself to restoring peace among the Christian rulers, in order to launch a crusade against the Turks, reform the Church and extirpate heresy. Unlike his predecessor, Hadrian was more willing to accept that the Church had at times erred. A penitent Martin Luther would be accepted back into the fold. However, as Eamon Duffy has astutely stated: 'Nothing in Hadrian's response suggests any grasp of the real power of Luther's message, the evangelical fervour and the sense of the radical and blessed simplification of religious life which it offered.'[129]

Charles V had convened the Diet of Nuremberg to face the Turkish and Lutheran threats, mindful of the fact that he needed the support of the German princes against the enemy in the east. The Swiss had no representatives or any voice at the sessions, but Zwingli was moved in November 1522 to write a submission to the delegates, who probably never saw it.[130] He offered his most fulsome praise of Martin Luther as a man of the greatest integrity and learning, who was to be protected at all costs.[131] The Reformation would be lost without him. Taking up a theme to which he would return in later years, Zwingli rejected the idea that those who preached the gospel should be known as 'Lutherans'. The renewal of God's Word was through following Christ, not any man. Nevertheless, the movement for reform was greatly threatened by any alliance between Charles V and Francis I, who were committed not to a crusade against the Turks, but to the suppression of the gospel. The only real victor would be the pope, whose claims to reform the Church could and should be dismissed as false.

Although Zwingli's reputation as a heretic was rapidly spreading across the Swiss lands and abroad, the city of Zurich remained in the Catholic Church and the traditional services continued to be celebrated. The mass, processions and holy days still marked the rhythm of the faith. Zwingli, however, knew that he could no longer in good conscience perform his duties within a Church whose central tenets he no longer believed. In November 1522, he resigned his living as a secular priest and ceased his duties, although he continued to preach. His official status in the Grossmünster was not clear. It was evident that his change of position had the support of the magistrates, who had given their permission. Zwingli was now *the* preacher in the city. His sermons were reaching audiences beyond the city, winning followers who echoed his views in urban and rural churches. At sessions of the Swiss Diet held in Baden in late November and early December, resolutions were passed calling for the prohibition of the 'new learning'.[132]

The magistrates of Zurich were fully aware of the accusations that the city was a nest of 'Lutheran' heresy. At the same time, many leading figures were proud of the distinguished humanist, whose knowledge of scripture and the classics in Greek, Latin and Hebrew could not be rivalled in Swiss lands, except by the great Erasmus in Basel (who, however, was unable to read the Old Testament in its original language). There was no doubt that Zwingli was a committed patriot and defender of his homeland, whose call for the renewal of the faith went hand in hand with outrage at the injustices inflicted on his people. The priest had also proved himself a canny adviser on politics, and well aware of events in the Confederation and Empire.

Zwingli's repudiation of the authority of the bishop of Constance was joined by an appeal to the people of Schwyz to follow Zurich and abolish the receipt of pensions as an abomination in the sight of God. A particular flash-point was the Mandated Territories, jointly administered by the Confederates, where the evangelical preaching was making inroads. The Zurich Council demonstrated a willingness to defend those preachers charged with heresy against any trial in the episcopal courts, preventing the accused from facing ecclesiastical punishment. This move led to complaints to the Swiss Diet, which in the summer of 1522 issued an unequivocal condemnation of the innovations in Zurich. The rebuke was renewed in December, when the Confederates were warned not to foster the 'new teachings', and Basel and Zurich were counselled to watch over what was printed in their cities.[133]

By the end of 1522, and no longer a mass priest, Zwingli occupied no particular position of authority within the Church or city, beyond being the preacher in the Grossmünster; his power in Zurich derived not from high office, but from the pulpit, his pen and his personal contacts. Above all, he continued to exhibit a tireless charisma, a force of character that showed no want of boldness or willingness to take on his superiors. To put it baldly, he was equally admired and reviled. The sausage meal had demonstrated his willingness to stage a controversy and force public debate, in which he sought to dictate the terms. As we shall see, however, his supporters did not speak with one voice. He was married and had turned his face against epis-copal authority and the legal claims of the Church. Such was his sense of biblical and moral authority that he felt empowered to advise his fellow Confederates on religion and politics. Combative and aggressive, his language, both personal and public, tended to the martial and confronta-tional. He did not doubt that he led the forces of traditional Swiss peasant virtue against foreign corruption, that God had appointed him to restore both the Church and his homeland – two responsibilities between which he drew little distinction.

The events of 1522 had clearly demonstrated that the reforming instincts of Zwingli were not those of Bishop Hugo or Erasmus. The preacher expected nothing from Rome. The church hierarchy had no desire to sanction gospel preaching, lift restrictions on eating, or abolish clerical celibacy. Nothing that Zwingli and his supporters had advocated had found any purchase with the higher ecclesiastical powers: their arguments had been met only with denunciations and condemnation. They were 'Lutherans', to be suppressed as quickly as possible.

Nevertheless, Zwingli knew that he had influential supporters among both the clergy and laity in the city. If there was to be a breakthrough for the reforms, however, he had to win the backing of his political masters. But he was being pulled in different directions. He had continually invoked the rural peasants and the dwellers of the valleys as the authentic embodiment of patriotic Swiss Christianity, but he knew that his path relied on the support of the urban rulers whose interests did not always align with his own convictions. The seeds of accommodation were laid. If reform was to be raised beyond a series of oppositional claims against the Catholic Church, Zwingli knew that his principles for a new order urgently needed to be set out with clarity and force, offering politicians and the faithful a vision of how a reformed Church might look. As his engagement with the bishop's commissioners had demonstrated, he relished stating his case publicly in debate. The wary magistrates had made it clear that they were prepared to make decisions on religious matters, but just how far they were prepared to go remained uncertain. Their willingness had to be channelled, empowering the rulers to determine the course of church affairs in the city, but guided by the former priest. Zwingli was fully aware that he was supported by a slender majority, mostly guildsmen in the Large Council. His tactic was to draw his opponents into open debate on terms that would ensure the victory of the gospel. He pushed for a public disputation on the nature of the Christian faith – a debate that could be resolved in Zurich, not Constance or Rome. The door to a new order was opening. It was to be Zwingli's moment.

✤ FOUR ✤

✤

# DIVERGENT VISIONS

## 1523–1524

Zwingli was the ringleader, the public voice of change, but by no means did he act alone. The sausage incident had demonstrated that he was part of a circle of clergy, guildsmen and politicians. Many were personally close, such as Leo Jud and his printer Christoph Froschauer, bound together by a vision of reform. Jud was a powerful preacher, deeply influenced by Erasmus, but – like Zwingli – was committed to action. Froschauer provided Zwingli with access to a well-equipped printing house that was networked across the German-speaking lands. Yet, Zwingli's plans would in time diverge from those who were looking for a more purified church.

Magistrates like Röist were drawn to gospel preaching, and the appeal of the preachers' message lay in their ability to convince listeners that the Bible alone was authoritative. Well-disposed contemporaries, including his students, spoke of Zwingli's personal charm, warmth and wit; and in the early modern city, charisma was a significant factor in politics. By no means all, however, were persuaded, and opposition remained fierce; but by the end of 1522, supporters were to be found across the Council and guild halls. All were fully aware of the dangers of rash or precipitate deeds, and the magistrates – mindful that events in Zurich were raising alarm across the Confederation – were concerned that religion should not become a source of unrest beyond their control. As Christian rulers had long known, accusations of heresy went beyond the Church to threaten commercial and political stability. Many welcomed Zwingli's advocacy of greater control over the Church and his attack on the corruption of pensions from foreigners, so long as the preacher presented a new Christian society based on law, order and moral conduct.

The summer and autumn of 1522 had seen the door close on agreement between the reform-minded in Zurich and the bishop's court in Constance. The conflict was not between advocates of reform and recalcitrant opponents: Erasmus had good reason to believe that Bishop Hugo was committed to addressing problems within the Church in Constance. Bishop Hugo attempted to use his authority to censure priests in the diocese who had followed Zwingli's lead and spoken against the veneration of saints and images, but his efforts proved fruitless, given his dependence on the cooperation of the rulers of Zurich.[1] And Zwingli had gone well beyond the traditional reform language that had swirled through the late-medieval Church, dividing him from Johannes Fabri, the vicar general of Constance, an erstwhile friend who had been active in the Luther case. When, in 1522, Erasmus put down his copy of the 'Apologeticus archeteles' with a deep sigh, it was a clear indication that the Zurich priest had also moved away from his mentor, by abandoning the unity of a wounded Church. Two years later, their relationship would be over.

## DISPUTATION

The last months of 1522 saw Zurich in a state of turmoil, unsettled by inner conflicts and external threats, yet Zwingli's position in Zurich was bolstered by the willingness of the *Bürgermeister* and Council to stage a disputation in the city concerning the reform of religion. The preacher was pushing hard to align his vision of change with political support, the only possible way forward if he did not wish to share the fate of so many John the Baptists before him. A disputation was his most audacious move, a calculated plan to push religious change into the public square. The disputations that emerged in the early Reformation were not intended as open debates, but as a means by which one side might demonstrate its superiority.[2]

At Zwingli's request, on 3 January 1523, the Zurich Council invited its bishop to assemble with local clergy and laity to debate religion before the gathered magistrates of the city. There were no precedents for such a meeting, and no one could know what to expect: theology and governance of the Church were being removed from the episcopal courts and the universities and placed in the city hall.[3] The idea that the magistrates, clergy and laity should be present for a debate on theological questions, carried out in German no less, was astonishing. There was no script.

In persuading the Zurich Council to stage the debate, Zwingli had effectively cornered his nemesis, the bishop of Constance.[4] Without doubt, the very suggestion of a public disputation on church doctrine and discipline was an affront to the noble, mild-mannered bishop, who had been invited as a participant, not to preside. Although Bishop Hugo had no intention of gracing the event with his presence, and thereby lending dignity to a meeting he repudiated, he was canny enough to recognize the folly of leaving matters in the hands of the Zurich authorities. Prudence dictated that a delegation from Constance should be present; but it would attend to observe, for to participate in any manner might bestow an acknowledgement of authority.

Like Albrecht Dürer, with his famous rhinoceros, the magistrates were drawing something they had never seen. The results were equally remarkable. Invitations were spread far and wide across the Confederation, although only a few people responded, and the bishop of Basel demurred, fearing that the sessions might become disorderly. No Catholic authority was willing to recognize what was transpiring in Zurich. The magistrates did insist, however, that all the clergy from the city and its rural lands attend. The terms of the disputation were radical and a break with the medieval Church: no appeal was to be made to church tradition. As Luther had stood before Emperor Charles V at Worms in 1521 to declare that he would recant only if proved in error by scripture, so now in Zurich the Bible was to be the sole standard. With one stroke, Zwingli had hamstrung his opponents.

The extraordinary occasion, now known as the 'First Zurich Disputation', took place on 29 January 1523.[5] The one-day session was chaired by *Bürgermeister* Marx Röist, a crucial Zwingli ally, who delivered the opening address. The Large Council, before which the disputants appeared, principally comprised the leaders of the handworkers, small traders and merchants, whose voices were strengthening in the city.[6] More than 600 people attended, with some coming from across the Swiss Confederation, although not nearly as many as Zwingli had hoped.

Zwingli was not the only speaker, but he was the writer, director and performer. He had prepared 67 articles that summarized his preaching, drawing them up with considerable speed. In the first 16 articles, he laid out his position on the Bible and faith. Articles 17 to 33 dealt with a long list of abuses and supposedly false teachings in the Catholic Church, including the mass, good works, the saints, the papacy and the marriage of clergy. In articles 34 to 67, the preacher addressed temporal authority, prayer, forgiveness of sins, purgatory and the priesthood.

Now, standing with the Latin Bible, Erasmus' Greek New Testament and the Hebrew Bible open before him, Zwingli took on all comers, as he moved quickly from text to text to summon passages with impressive recall. The scope of his ambitions was arresting, and the full expanse of his thinking, as it had evolved over the previous year, was laid out in German for a lay audience. Zwingli rejected the authority of the institutional Church, declaring Christ the sole authority. And Christ was revealed through God's Word, the Bible. The audience heard a wholesale reorientation of order and authority, a new vision of the Church.[7] In the eighth and fiftieth articles, Zwingli made it clear that the Church as an institution could not serve as the mediator of the sacred. That role fell not to priests, bishops or councils, but to the Holy Spirit acting through the gospel. The whole disputation was about Church and community under the direct rule of the Spirit. The faithful alone, those elect of God, form the true Church, an invisible body known only to God and dispersed through the ages and the world. The parish community is the visible manifestation of that holy body, but unlike the invisible Church it remains a living, breathing mixture of the faithful and unfaithful, who rub shoulders in this world.

The bishop's party largely sat glumly enduring Zwingli's heresies. Their hands tied and with no mandate to intervene, they had little to offer by way of counterarguments.[8] Johannes Fabri was not, however, entirely silent, and this formidable, experienced and gifted polemicist was well prepared to defend the Catholic Church.[9] Thus, for example, he quickly scored against Zwingli by pointing out that Zurich, as one small part of the Catholic community, had no right to set itself at odds with the rest of the Church. He also argued that without the guidance of tradition, the faithful could easily be led into error, for the devil could speak with the words of scripture. Another intervention addressed clerical marriage; he likely knew full well that Zwingli himself was married. No priest had been married in the Church for over a thousand years, Fabri argued, so what right had Zurich to reverse this tradition? Once again, an effective point was made, only to be dismissed by the preacher as mere sophistry.[10] Although Zwingli was eager to demonstrate his grasp of scripture, and clearly relished the cut and thrust, in truth he was stabbing at a lame animal. The Catholic party had no chance. The process was rigged. The Catholics would never forget the ritual humiliation, and three years later, in Baden, would exact their revenge.

The event was cut short by hunger. Possibly having heard enough, the presiding magistrates retired to lunch. When they returned, they were ready to deliver their verdict. How they had reached their assessment is not known.[11] After a morning of mostly listening to Zwingli, with the occasional response from Fabri, the rulers declared themselves content with the preaching of the gospel, and the priests of the rural areas were ordered to follow Zwingli's model, with sermons from scripture alone. All accusations of heresy were set aside. Zwingli had the magistrates' support, or at least enough of them on the Large Council. The Council would preserve its authority over public worship and would decide what constituted Bible-based preaching.[12]

Zwingli had persuaded the rulers of Zurich to take religion into their own hands and, against the counsel of their bishop, to make an unequivocal statement on the nature of the Christian faith by openly accepting that preaching meant interpreting the Bible alone.[13] That pronouncement made the day a turning point in the Reformation: though not yet formally created, Reformed Christianity had essentially been conceived. Furthermore, Zwingli was granted a licence to proceed without challenge, and the clergy of the city and rural areas were to follow his example. The Reformation had not yet occurred: the Council had sanctioned 'Bible preaching' without committing itself to either any specific doctrines or any agenda of church reform.[14]

Nonetheless, the reformer had staged a revolution and laid the foundation for a new church order, in which magistrates and clerics would share authority. Zwingli had argued that the gathering, as the community in Zurich, was a manifestation of the universal Church and could, therefore, make decisions about doctrine and practice.[15] There was no need to rely on distant hierarchies: it was in the magistrates' hands to reform Church and community according to the gospel. This was the point made by Luther in his letter to the German princes in 1520: Zwingli was now enacting it. Indeed, Church and community were one. The rulers themselves had brought about this moment, following Zwingli's argument that they, not the bishop, were the guardians of true religion. The preacher had delivered the faith into their hands and was handsomely rewarded with the right to preach what he wanted. The bishop's representatives could only protest and grumble, but they had been irrelevant in this staged performance, playing their part by providing symbolic resistance.

Zwingli's status among Catholics as arch-heretic was now confirmed. In Lucerne a picture of him was burnt during carnival festivities, to which he responded in a letter to friends that he had never felt calmer in the face of such hateful conduct. Indeed, he wrote,

> it brings great joy to me that I have been found worthy to suffer humiliation for the sake of Christ. The matter is hard to believe, but God be thanked that never before have I so patiently borne such loathsomeness. This should encourage you that Christ never abandons his own.[16]

By his own account, Zwingli laboured day and night after the disputation to prepare a vast commentary on the 67 articles and turn them into a coherent statement of doctrine. In part driven by fierce criticism from Fabri, Zwingli worked from early February to mid-June 1523, writing in German, the language of the disputation.[17] He dedicated his *Exposition of the Sixty-Seven Articles* to the people of Glarus, his former parishioners, stating that he sought to prove to friend and foe alike, and above all to Fabri, that the disputation articles had been wholly grounded in scripture.[18] Zwingli did not hesitate to claim that 'these conclusions contain nearly all of the greatest points of controversy that are being debated in our time'.[19] In many respects he was correct, but his labours only fuelled those debates. Johannes Oecolampadius in Basel and Berchtold Haller (1492–1536) in Bern wrote with encouragement, while Bishop Hugo referred to this little book as full of Zwingli's errors and seductive doctrines.[20]

The *Exposition of the Sixty-Seven Articles*, which appeared from Froschauer's press on 14 July 1523, was essentially a careful expansion of what Zwingli had argued before the magistrates, but set out in greater detail and deepened by a forest of references to the Bible and the church fathers. Zwingli was offering a full statement of his theological convictions, with an emphasis on the providential power of God, salvation through Christ and the role of the magistrates in governing the Church. The Church was not the ecclesiastical hierarchy of Rome, but the gathered faithful in one place, led by the Spirit. Moving through the individual topics (or loci) of the debate as Zwingli had determined them, the text built on the 'Apologeticus archeteles' and on 'On the Clarity and Certainty of the Word of God', published the previous summer and autumn, and laid the foundation for his greatest work, *A Commentary on True and False Religion*, which would follow two years later. More apologetic than elegant, the writing in the *Exposition* is often discursive, almost homiletic, as Zwingli moves back and forth through his primary claims. The arc of all those claims was that the gospel is the foundation of the faith, for 'according to the words of Paul, in Romans chapter one, the gospel is nothing but the power of God for the salvation of all believers'.[21]

The enemy was identified as the papists, a pejorative tag Zwingli applied with care. The Zurich preacher judiciously did not explicitly place himself outside the Roman Church, but employed the term 'papist' to identify those who embodied false religion through their adherence to tradition and ecclesiastical authority above the Word of God.[22] It was a highly effective rhetorical manoeuvre. Nevertheless, the choice of the term 'papist' was a turning point in the life of a man who had for so long advocated for the papal cause.

## ERSTWHILE FRIENDS

Like Luther, Zwingli insisted on correct and binding interpretations of scripture. Fidelity to God's Word required the reform of Church and society. Inaction was not an option.[23] At the same time, Zwingli was a student of Erasmus and was fully aware that the Bible contains plenty of passages that elude straightforward or singular interpretation. His goal in preaching was to place the Gospel of Christ before the people, in order that they might be transformed. There was nothing more urgent. But how was a community to live faithfully in matters where the Bible was not explicit? Having rejected the role of the hierarchy as interpreters of scripture, Zwingli had to determine what approach needed to be taken in bringing about change. Was, for example, all that was not proscribed by scripture to be retained? Or was the opposite true – anything not testified to by scripture should be removed? The question was both crucial and divisive. The events of 1522/1523 took place in a city that was still officially Catholic. There was a profound disconnect between the preaching advocated by Zwingli and his supporters and the official sacramental cult in the city's churches. Most strikingly, Zwingli had declared the mass incompatible with scripture, but the contrast between his words and the daily experiences of the faithful in worship was arrestingly evident in every church, whether in the Grossmünster or in rural parishes. Zwingli had written in the articles about the idolatry of images and the seduction of men and women by sensory experiences – whether statues or incense – that filled houses of worship. Yet his gospel sermons, with their demands for the purification of the cult, were delivered in churches filled with altars and paintings, the material fabric of the medieval Church.

Zwingli's calls for the cleansing of the temples did not go unheeded. Wilhelm Reublin at Witikon and Andreas Castelberger preached and led private discussions of biblical texts among lay people and were vociferous critics of images, the mass and traditional forms of piety, such as relics, veneration of saints and processions. Reublin had come to Zurich in 1522 from Basel, having being expelled from the city after preaching radical reforms to large crowds. Castelberger had been deeply influenced by Erasmus' pacifism and was strongly drawn to Zwingli's attack on the mercenary service. As a colporteur, Castelberger had travelled through the Swiss lands distributing radical religious literature, and provided Zwingli with a number of pro-reform tracts. A friend left an account of Castelberger's passion:

Andreas said much about war, how the divine teaching was so violently against it and how sinful it was. He expressed the opinion that someone who could live from his own paternal inheritance and go to war, receive money and kill decent people who had never done him any harm and seize their property – such a warrior is a murderer before God and evangelical teaching and no better than he who murders or steals out of poverty.[24]

Castelberger, a bookseller who brought evangelical pamphlets from Basel and the Empire to Zurich, supplied the growing circle of radicals with literature.[25] Lamed by an injury, he was known as 'limping Andreas'.[26] Castelberger's circle read the Bible as condemning social inequality and economic exploitation, arguing that anyone who benefited from the goods and labour of others was no better 'than a thief and murderer'.

Reublin, Castelberger and Grebel were just as passionate as Zwingli about reform, but they were not prepared simply to do his bidding. Indeed, they voiced their convictions with greater ardour, pushing for more rapid and radical change, as they were alarmed by the growing distance between words and deeds. They were also in close contact with men and women in the rural areas who were increasingly drawn to the gospel as crucial to their protests against economic oppression. Two paths opened up: on the one hand, there was Zwingli's careful management of the magistrates and his attempts to nurse the lay people towards change; on the other hand, there were the demands of his colleagues to press the purity of the gospel and to remove all that stood in its way.

## RIGHTEOUSNESS

During the summer of 1523, as the *Exposition of the Sixty-Seven Articles* was printed, rural unrest brought back to the fore the issue of the tithe, a long-standing grievance.[27] Communities in the rural areas were raising complaints about the burden owed to urban elites, including churches.[28] Reublin, who preached in the Fraumünster and became pastor in Witikon, incited the peasants to refuse to pay the tithe and railed against the immorality and corruption of the magistrates and patricians.[29] Resistance to the tithe went hand in hand with withering attacks on the high-living clergy and their excesses. Anti-clericalism was integral to social grievances. While the Council refused to remove the tithe, the attack on the clergy was not thought to be without merit, and in September 1523 reform of the Grossmünster chapter was introduced to improve standards.[30] The number of clergy was reduced and finances were reorganized to devote money to education. Zwingli was appointed by the Council to serve as principal of the school, enabling him to begin to implement Erasmian-influenced education.[31]

In 1520, Zwingli had initially been sympathetic, arguing that the tithe was not sanctioned in the Bible and might be abolished.[32] But as resistance to the tithe grew in rural areas during 1522–1523 and was supported by men such as Grebel and Reublin, he shifted ground. He addressed the tithe in a sermon on the feast of St John the Baptist, printed in 64 octavo pages in July 1523 with the title 'On Divine and Human Righteousness' (see chapter 3).[33] The sermon ranged across various topics, as Zwingli sought to take stock of where reform demands were now headed. The work was dedicated to Niklaus von Wattenwyl, provost in Bern, a sign that Zwingli was reaching out to the most powerful of the Swiss Confederates. He set out in bold prose his conception of the Bible as the foundation for a just, Christian society, while defending his position as a social critic.

There were two forms of righteousness:

Measured by divine righteousness, we are all fools or knaves. Since our iniquity is known to God alone, that one God judges us through his grace if we believe that he died and made payment for us out of his compassion. Measured by human righteousness, we are often found to be righteous, though we are truly knaves in God's sight. But one who is found by human righteousness to be not only a knave in God's sight but a known sinner is turned over to the one who judges transgressors, namely the magistrate or judge.[34]

Human righteousness kept people obedient to the laws of the land, yet it had absolutely no effect on a person's standing before God. Such order and submission to authority preserved the conditions under which true religion might flourish through the preaching of the Word. Ministers of the Word must preach freely – that was their duty – and the magistrates were not to interfere. Quoting the words of Ovid, Zwingli made clear that magistrates had no claim over faith: 'Caesar has not been able to control my heart or take away from me the gifts of the heart.'[35] Human righteousness, which Zwingli called a 'poor and feeble righteousness', had no call upon the divine. In contrast:

divine righteousness ought to be revealed and preached unceasingly to all people and one should rather risk life and limb than allow anyone to frighten us off such preaching and proclamation, as Christ often commanded ... We hear that everyone is bid to seek divine righteousness, which means unceasingly, in keeping with his will, to strive after innocence until we reach the measure of Christ, and that we should never be satisfied with being considered good according to human righteousness.[36]

Zwingli's position on tithes was sympathetic and subtle. He had not simply reversed his earlier objection to the burden as unbiblical. He concurred with the peasants that it was oppressive and frequently unjust. It ran counter to divine righteousness, as did ownership of property. Quite simply, there was nothing in scripture to justify either. But should the tithe be abolished? On this question, Zwingli offered both a remedy and an argument for the status quo. The large and small tithes belonged to human righteousness, the necessary structures of society for commerce and community.[37] Because they were necessary, they should remain, but justly. The tithe was not a licence for excess or exploitation. Human righteousness must be made to conform to divine righteousness as far as possible, an ongoing demand laid on rulers:

> whoever then should not willingly render the tithe, in opposition to this common agreement of the authorities would therefore go beyond what was granted him in an upright, straight-forward purchase which the authorities considered to be right and legal. Such a person would then resist the authorities, and whoever resists the authorities opposes God, as we have shown earlier.[38]

Zwingli's sermon on divine and human righteousness tied reform to established political order, further splintering a movement in which there was no consensus on how Christian the magistrates were. Reublin saw the defence of the tithe as a betrayal, and Konrad Grebel wrote to his brother-in-law Vadian that 'the people of our world of Zurich are doing everything tyrannically and like the Turk in this matter of the tithe'.[39]

## EDUCATION

Having been made head of the Grossmünster school, Zwingli threw himself into reforming education. His commitment was personal. In the summer of 1523, having returned from taking a cure at the baths, he dedicated to his beloved 14-year-old stepson Gerold a small book entitled *Of the Education of the Youth*. Zwingli had been committed to the teaching of boys from his first days as a priest in Glarus. The text was less a concrete plan for educating pupils than a vigorous expression of Zwingli's belief in the transformative power of learning. The beginning point of true education was piety, knowledge of God's providence, humanity's fall and the gift of reconciliation in Christ. For the Zurich preacher, the propagation of the gospel depended on a new generation both steeped in the Word of God and equipped with a classical education.

Zwingli aligned education with faith. True enlightenment is a gift of the Spirit, and ancient languages are the foundation:

> There is no better way to preserve the order of the soul than to pore over the Word of God day and night [Psalm 1:2]. This labour cannot be performed until one has mastered the languages of Hebrew and Greek, for without the first the Old Testament and the second the New cannot be properly understood.[40]

Learning is not measured merely in terms of the acquisition of knowledge, but is to be experienced as the transformation of body and soul. Pupils should take regular and rigorous physical exercise and cultivate friendships, as well as the mind, through play:

> I recommend the playing of games with one's contemporaries, but only those that contribute to education and building of one's body: educational games and playing with numbers, such as those for learning arithmetic, or physical games of attack and defence, or of attack and ambush as in chess. Such games teach one not to overlook anything. All such things, however, should be done in moderation. There are those who abandon their duties to devote themselves to play. I say that games should be played in spare time and alongside one's studies. Playing with dice and cards I reject.[41]

Zwingli's fondness for making music and engaging in conversation with friends inflected his belief that education was linked to friendship, a sacred bond in which all are equal through mutual sharing.

Zwingli closed with an admonition to Gerold: 'Use your youth! The years fly by with swift feet and later years are rarely as wonderful as the earlier.' His beloved stepson was to have little time beyond his youth, for at the age of 22 he died alongside his stepfather at the battle of Kappel.[42]

## THE MASS

By the end of 1522, when he resigned his office as priest to become a city preacher, Zwingli had already stopped celebrating mass, which he regarded as idolatrous. Most offensive in his eyes was the belief that on the altar of a church the priest repeated the sacrifice of Christ on the cross. For Zwingli, that belief contradicted the biblical message that Christ died for the sins of the faithful, was resurrected and ascended to heaven. His sacrifice, once offered, was full and perfect and need not be repeated in a human form of worship. Precisely because Christ is in heaven, the bread and wine could not truly be his flesh and blood. Zwingli denied the central teaching of the medieval Church, the doctrine of transubstantiation, in which at the moment of consecration Christ was physically present in the church.

Zwingli understood that he could not rush to demand that the Council abolish the mass. The city was divided and his support among the magistrates remained partial. Nevertheless, reform of worship was advanced, and during the summer of 1523 Leo Jud, pastor in St Peter's church, published in a small pamphlet a vernacular baptismal rite for children.[43] The liturgy followed Luther's *German Baptismal Book* of the same year.[44] Children were to be baptized in a service conducted in the vernacular, and certain traditional elements were to be omitted, such as the exorcism of the demonic forces. Nevertheless, Jud had preserved a number of traditional practices, including the double signing with the cross and the placing of salt in the child's mouth.[45] On 10 August 1523, the first child was baptized according to Jud's new liturgy.

The cautious changes in the new baptismal service were mirrored in Zwingli's first attempt to provide a new order of worship for the mass, known as 'On the Canon of the Mass', which was followed in October by a more detailed apology.[46] The liturgy was written in haste over four days, as Zwingli raced to meet the deadline set by Froschauer in order for the printed text to reach the Frankfurt book fair. Despite the rush, Zwingli wrote in his preface that he had been thinking about liturgical reform since his days as a priest in Glarus, when he had begun to study with care the missals, the liturgical books containing all instructions and texts necessary for the celebration of mass throughout the year.

His studies had led to the conviction that the Catholic mass was not an ancient rite; it was, he held, of more recent provenance, having been improvised over the centuries. In other words, the missals indicated that the liturgy had evolved and did not come from one ancient source.[47] In the twentieth article of his *Exposition*, Zwingli had derided the antiquity of the mass and its liturgy, rejecting claims that it could be justified on the grounds of history:

> It is likely that this canon which we have now is of too recent origin for any of the earlier prelates, such as Ambrose, to have made additions to it, and it is manifestly nothing but a collection of various prayers which men who were pious enough but not overly learned had put up publicly or privately.[48]

It was not, consequently, an inviolable sacred inheritance.

'I am not going to bring forward,' Zwingli proposed, 'anything that is not adapted to the norm of the divine word, and this I want to understand as applying to the Canon I am going to offer.'[49] His proposed changes managed to be both modest and radical. For the most part, he kept the order and structure of the mass, while at the same time eviscerating it: gone was the consecration of the bread and wine into the body and blood. In its place was a simple order in the middle of the service for the elements to be received by the faithful. He also moved the Lord's Prayer from its traditional location between the canon and communion to the opening of the service, claiming that the dominical prayer was 'the best expression that God is received in the sacrifice of praise and appeal'.[50] Zwingli's intention was to replace the mass with a liturgy in which the Word would be preached and the Lord's Supper celebrated. The reform of liturgy was a significant step in Zwingli's rejection of tradition as authority in the Church. He was beginning to relish having a free hand to create something new: an order of worship that expressed what he saw as the biblical message of repentance and thanksgiving in the Spirit.

## IDOLS

God is Spirit, Zwingli preached, and should be worshipped in Spirit. The altars and images that filled the churches were manifestations of the idolatry of human attempts to capture the divine, to render the transcendent in material form. Instead of hearing the Word of God, the people were taught to worship statues and relics, just as they had turned for aid to the saints, and not to Christ. Zwingli's message was of a direct encounter of the faithful with God, wholly unmediated by the material. The preacher's rejection of transubstantiation was a denial that God in Christ could be physically present in the world. The second commandment of Moses forbade any graven images of what is in heaven above. There could be no possibility of true worship without a cleansing of the temples. Zwingli was adamant on this point and his supporters were moved to action, fired by both zeal for the gospel and hatred for the clergy. Their goal was not in question, but the timing was crucial. Reform for Zwingli had to follow the lead of the magistrates, who would not tolerate wanton destruction of the churches. Iconoclasm remained a capital offence in Zurich.

Leo Jud emerged as a key figure in the discussions, and preached in his church of St Peter's on 1 September 1523 in favour of the removal of images; but there was little consensus among reformers and politicians on how to proceed.[51] It was one thing to object to images on spiritual grounds, but quite another to engage in unbridled and illegal desecration. The magistrates were not prepared to tolerate vandalism, and damage to churches and religious symbols was severely punished. Forced to bide his time, Zwingli was in a bind. Sermons from the pulpits of Zurich denouncing idolatry incited lay people to act against the material fabric of the medieval churches in which they prayed, but the magistrates had not approved the radical removals he was advocating.

Events forced Zwingli's hand. During the autumn of 1523, the first spontaneous acts of iconoclasm took place in Zurich and the rural areas. An assistant at the church of St Peter's was hauled before the Council and charged with destroying an altar. His defence, which echoed Zwingli and Jud, was that the money should be redirected to the poor. Likewise, an altar in the Fraumünster was attacked, and the perpetrators thrown in prison. Another three men broke into the Fraumünster, sprinkled each other with holy water, and destroyed lamps in the chapel in the name of rejecting idolatry. Two weeks later, and more spectacularly, Klaus Hottinger pulled down the large crucifix that stood at the crossroads outside the city at Stadelhofen.[52] At his trial, he claimed that he wanted to sell the wood to provide for the poor. For his efforts, he was banned from the city; he was beheaded in Catholic Lucerne four months later for his radical sentiments. The destruction of images was not only a subject for sermons: trial records show that it was hotly debated in guild halls, taverns and homes.[53] The Council would not tolerate wanton violence and cracked down on the perpetrators with fines and imprisonment. The question of religious images presented Zwingli and his comrades with the first great challenge of how to realize change. How could reform be implemented without unleashing chaos?

Jud's sermon certainly played a role, but so did a tract by Ludwig Hätzer (1500–1529) with the title 'How One Should Conduct Oneself with Idols and Images'.[54] Hätzer was chaplain in the nearby village of Wädenswil and belonged to the circle around Zwingli.[55] His views were uncompromising: 'Let all Christians strive diligently to do away with idols without hesitation before God visits them with that punishment which he is accustomed to send to all those who do not follow his word.' Hätzer would soon part ways with his erstwhile friend and become a founder of the Anabaptist movement, a conviction for which he was beheaded in 1529.

The religious objects in the churches were seen by many as images of economic oppression. Several of Zwingli's supporters argued that devotional items donated to the churches should not be used for the decoration or ornamentation of the places of worship; rather, they belonged to the poor, who are the true image of God. The false images should be redeemed by being turned into resources for poor relief.[56] In the century before the Reformation, the Zurich rural areas had doubled in population, from about 25,000 to 60,000, with the result that by the early 1520s hunger afflicted many of the peasants beyond the walls of the city. Deprivation had heightened the resentment of the tithe. The plight of those suffering could not be separated from an assault on the privileges and wealth of the Church. Frequently, the attacks on the images were closely connected to demands for relief from feudal dues.[57]

The Zurich magistrates were in a seemingly impossible situation. Preaching and iconoclasm were disrupting the peace and stability of the city, which was their overriding concern. They had sanctioned the preaching, but were punishing the vandals. In rural areas, traditional grievances were being cast in terms of religious freedom. Beyond the city walls, the Catholic Confederates were growing so hostile that rumours spread of an attack on Zurich. Such was the concern of the magistrates that when the Grossmünster was reformed, some of the resources had been invested in strengthening the city's defences. To deal with the unrest in the city, the magistrates appointed a committee of politicians, laymen and clerics to make recommendations about how to proceed with images in the churches.[58] Its recommendation was for a second disputation 'to discuss and help find a decision of Holy Scripture of the Old and New Testaments concerning images and the mass'.[59]

The magistrates consented and ordered a disputation that would address images and the mass, to take place from 26 to 28 October 1523.[60] Invitations were sent to the bishop of Constance, as well as to other leading Catholic ecclesiastics, the university of Basel and prominent scholars. This time, neither Constance nor any other leading Catholic churchmen attended. The event was mostly made up of politicians, guild members and clerics from Zurich. Over 900 people attended, a third of whom were clergy. Leo Jud was to lead on the first day, which would address images, while Zwingli presided over the next two days, with discussion of the mass.[61]

The second disputation was not as well orchestrated as the first, but it did not need to be, for there was hardly any opposition from the church hierarchy. Jud and Zwingli argued vigorously that 'images should not be endured, for with all that God had forbidden there could be no compromise'.[62] The results, however, were mixed. There was division with the reform party about how quickly the images should be removed, and such disagreement displeased the magistrates, who declared that no one should remove anything from the churches without their permission. The second disputation, like the first, faced the question of legitimacy, as the Catholic Konrad Hofmann protested. Nevertheless, the principle of independence established at the first was upheld – that the local church could preside in matters of faith.[63] When Konrad Grebel rose to ask what should be done about the mass, Zwingli replied that the Council would decide. Simon Stumpf, a local priest, shouted out provocatively: 'Master Huldrych ... you have no authority to place the decision in the hands of my lords, for the decision has already been made by the Spirit of God!'[64]

Martin Steinlin of Schaffhausen was the lone voice in support of traditional Catholic understanding of the sacrament, for which he was censured.[65] Among the wider body of clerics, the thrust of the argument, following Zwingli's lead, was repudiation of any idea that the salvific death of Christ could in any way be repeated on the altar. Further, prayers for the dead were denounced as having no scriptural warrant. The reformers argued that the laity were to receive both the bread and the wine, rejecting the medieval practice by which men and women received only the Eucharistic wafer. The Lord's Supper was to be celebrated in the language of the people, and priests were not to adorn themselves with vestments. How exactly the people were to receive the elements was deemed a matter for local churches to decide.

The disputation cast in sharp relief the growing divisions within the reform party. Zwingli was largely in sympathy with Konrad Grebel and Simon Stumpf on the mass and images, but he had an entirely different approach to how scripture should be read and its commands implemented. All should be done in due order, not according to the immediate, individual biblical interpretation. Two distinct visions were at odds: that of the magistrates, working together with the clergy to introduce reform in time; and that of local congregations as the source of authority. Who was the legitimate bearer of reform?[66]

In late 1523, Zwingli and Jud met Konrad Grebel (1498–1526), Simon Stumpf and Felix Manz (1498–1527) at a gathering, of which we have no record beyond a report in Zwingli's own hand, written some four years later. This account defended his support for the Council's determination to stop acts of iconoclasm.[67] In Zwingli's telling, Stumpf, Manz and Grebel had wanted to establish a separate church of believers that had nothing to do with the civil government. Their church would contain only 'upright, Christian people' who lived lives of moral rectitude without need of 'interest or other usury'. Stumpf, Zwingli claimed, had once told him that priests should be 'struck dead', and that the people should not have to pay interest and tithes. Further, Grebel and Stumpf had claimed more than once that 'all things must be held in common'. Felix Manz had demanded that no one should be admitted into the Church unless they knew themselves to be 'without sin'.[68]

Zwingli's account was hostile and unsympathetic, as he sought to present the radicals as seditious and a threat to the true Christian state. He summarized their argument for a separate Church of the holy:

> They begged us to make a declaration to this effect: Those who want to follow Christ should stand on our side. They promised also that our forces would be far superior to the army of unbelievers. Next the Church of the devoted itself was to appoint its own council from the devoutly prayerful.[69]

His hostility was reciprocated. After the meeting, Konrad Grebel responded: 'Whoever thinks, believes or declares that Zwingli acts according to the duty of a shepherd thinks, believes and declares wickedly.'[70] Zwingli, he added for good measure, was one of the 'tonsured monsters'.

The lack of consensus among the reformers demonstrated at the second disputation was reflected in the words of one chronicler, who recorded that 'the pastors in the Zurich countryside were not of one mind in doctrine, and some did not gladly receive the restoration of evangelical truth and apostolic teaching'.[71] The Council looked to Zwingli to provide a concise statement of the new faith, and his response, 'A Short Christian Instruction', was published as an official mandate on 17 November 1523. The mandate demonstrated the high level of support on the Council for Zwingli's teaching, instructing the people of Zurich to 'let the evangelical scriptures declared therein be thoroughly and diligently reflected on in their original form'. It was the first confessional statement of the Zurich Reformation.

The purpose of the 'Short Christian Instruction' was didactic, to serve as a resource for pastors with little idea of what they were doing and what was going on around them. Having rehearsed the key topics of the faith, and having provided the pastors with the relevant passages in scripture for consultation, Zwingli ended with guidance on how reform should be introduced. He argued once more against the mass, before turning to what he named as 'good ways to abolish the abuses'. Charity was the rule, and pastors should look kindly upon the mass priests who had not accepted the evangelical faith. They were not responsible for the errors they committed, and therefore were not to be punished. As Zwingli wrote:

> Let all the people be admonished to let them depart in peace as they came. For the majority of them are so old that they cannot any longer be set to work. And no Christian should destroy the work of God on account of the Supper, as Romans 14:20 says. Where some behave so indecently, that is with an opposition that lacks foundation in the Word of God, then nobody should act against them. Rather, leave them for the government, which will handle them as is fitting.[72]

Despite Zwingli's efforts to bring clarity, much remained uncertain. The magistrates adjured the clergy and people to follow the Bible and the evangelical teaching, but were not prepared to abolish the mass or have images removed from the churches. The church clerics were divided. Numerous priests in the Grossmünster, following Zwingli's example, refused to celebrate the mass. One who did, a Johannes Widmer, was denounced as a 'butcher of God'. The members of the Grossmünster chapter swore before the Council that liturgical books were being damaged, stolen and even thrown into the river.[73] At the same time, the reform movement had split over the pace and extent of change, and did not speak with one voice. Another mandate was issued on Sunday, 13 December, to be read from the pulpits of the three major churches in the city, threatening to punish those who took it upon themselves to damage church property.[74] The mandate declared that the magistrates themselves would determine how to proceed in the matter of the mass and images. A commission that included Zwingli and Jud advised the Council that the mass should be abolished and replaced by an evangelical service, but out of respect for weaker brethren this change should be made slowly.[75]

The city remained in no-man's-land, caught between traditional and evangelical forms of worship. The Large Council, where Zwingli's supporters predominated, was clear that scripture alone could be the only yardstick for determining matters of religion. Those who dissented from the new order were to appear before the magistrates to argue their case, but on the basis of the Bible alone. The Council agreed that images should be dealt with as recommended, but was in a quandary on the mass. Mindful of Zurich's precarious position within the Confederation, the Council decided that Zwingli's 'Short Christian Instruction' should be sent to the bishop of Constance and the other Swiss Confederates as an official statement of the city of Zurich.[76] Konrad Hofmann, Zwingli's leading Catholic opponent, took the opportunity to appear before the Council, presenting several articles against the evangelical party, but he made no headway.[77] Two weeks later, the magistrates declared that he and other Catholics could believe what they wanted, but should they speak or act against the Council's mandates, they would be stripped of their benefices.[78] Catholic resistance in the city was by no means vanquished, but it was being worn down. By early 1524, evident signs of change had appeared in the city: mass was celebrated less frequently, and Candlemas was not marked that January with its usual festive processions of lights. Later, in Lent the faithful did not observe Palm Sunday with the traditional palms and relics, and there was no creeping to the cross on Good Friday. The altar triptychs were kept closed.[79] In Holy Week, Zwingli suggested that the people gather outside the churches to hear sermons on the Penitential Psalms, with money collected for the care of the poor.

Catholics were put on the back foot by the growing support for the reform party among the Zurich magistrates; but beyond the city, the sky was darkening. The Confederate states of Schwyz, Unterwalden, Lucerne, Uri and Zug began to prepare to take action against Zurich, meeting regularly to draw up plans. It was at this point that the Five States, as they became known, formed a bloc within the Confederation, united against Zurich and its precipitate and provocative shedding of traditional religion. The 'Short Christian Instruction' of late 1523 had been Zurich's confirmation that it had abandoned Catholic doctrine; and although the official break with Rome was yet to come, heresy had prevailed, stirring other Confederates to action.

### 'THE SHEPHERD'

On the morning of the last day of the second disputation, Zwingli delivered a sermon in which he wholly reimagined the Christian pastorate, in contrast to the Catholic priesthood. From his denial of the mass, it could only follow that he would strip the clergy of their sacrificial role. Zwingli provided a rich and evocative picture of both how the faithful were to encounter the Word of God and how the Christian community should look. Although he had been encouraged to have the sermon printed immediately, the reformer was not able to revise and publish the text until late March 1524. By that point, the combined opposition of the bishop of Constance, the Catholic Confederates and the Imperial Diet was consolidating against Zurich. As a result of the enormous pressure from hostile parties, and on account of the difficult social and economic conditions, above all among the rural populace, Zwingli reworked his text by drawing on a wide range of examples from daily life to illustrate his case for gospel-based church offices. He entitled the work 'The Shepherd'.[80]

Zwingli dedicated the work to the pastor Jakob Schurtanner in Appenzell, citing him as a 'true shepherd of God'. The 72-page quarto book was printed by Froschauer and included an engraving of an image by Hans Holbein depicting Christ with his disciples and accompanied by the scriptural text from Matthew – 'Come to me all you that are weary and are carrying heavy burdens and I will give you rest.' The Holbein image would be found in most of Zwingli's subsequent works printed by Froschauer. He had written 'The Shepherd' in German with an intended readership of non-latinate clergy and literate laity; only later was it translated into Latin. The book was an immediate success, quickly spreading across the Swiss and German lands. As early as July 1524, the great French scholar Jacques Lefèvre d'Étaples was in possession of a copy. In 1513, Lefèvre d'Étaples had edited *The Shepherd of Hermas* the popular early Christian text from the first or second century, from which Zwingli had taken his title. An English translation with the title *The ymage of both pastoures, set forthe by that mooste famous clerck, Huldrych Zwinglius*, published in London in 1550, proved highly popular in Elizabethan England.[81] The printer described the work as a 'most fruitefull and necessary boke'.

In his letter of dedication to Schurtanner, Zwingli remained convinced of the special calling of the Swiss to the gospel. Rejoicing in the news that the people of Appenzell had received the Word of God through the labours of his friend, Zwingli portrayed the inhabitants as the best of the Swiss: people of the land, faithful and free from the corruption of the city. For the particular qualities of the Swiss, Zwingli once more invoked the patriotic story of Bruder Klaus:

Rather their [the Appenzellers'] unspoiled behaviour still shows us something of the qualities of the Confederation. When the Word of God comes to them, it will create a wonderfully pious and God-fearing people, and will do away with the selfishness which Bruder Klaus of Unterwalden prophesied would be so detrimental. Where the selfishness is not done away with, no government can continue. Although some are of a different opinion, nothing other than the Word of God has done away with the mercenary service with foreign lords in Zurich city and territory.[82]

The heart of the life and teaching of the evangelical pastor was the proclamation of the Word of God. The transforming of the gospel message raised the common person (*der gemeine Mann*) as well as the community to recognize the powers of spiritual oppression and to find divine emancipation. The Word of God was causing reformation and was unstoppable. Christ was the model of the good pastor in his harmony of life and learning, of prophecy and pastoral love. To imitate Christ, each pastor had to break with Catholic superstition, proclaim the gospel, deny himself and bear the cross. To preach the gospel was to teach people of the misery of the human condition, reconciliation through mercy and the Christian life. One must be fearless in trusting God and never shrink from battling the enemies of faith. Love must replace law.

> Christ presented us with a true model. For when he saw the hypocrisy and avarice of the priests among the Jewish people as a cause for all the people straying from God and that they were held captive in the priests' avarice, statutes and wilfulness, he attacked nothing more vigorously than the hypocrisy and avarice. He had great sympathy with the misled people in that they were robbed of the Word of God and had no fatherly shepherds.[83]

Zwingli claimed that his model for the pastor was Christ, but his argument was more complex. His vision of the pastoral office drew upon the traditional role of the medieval priest that he had himself performed as people's priest: preaching, administering the sacraments and caring for the people. Although the sacral nature of the priesthood was denied, the faithful still required pastors and were dependent on them to provide the right interpretation of scripture and to minister to their pastoral needs. But Zwingli had another model – one that he would never have publicly claimed: the Jewish rabbi as learned teacher. Zwingli's enthusiasm for Hebrew and the Old Testament, and his engagement with Jewish teachers offered him a way of thinking about the pastor as engaged in study and with knowledge of both languages and profane and sacred literature. Zwingli's pastor was to be learned, married and an advocate of God's Word, in imitation of the Old Testament prophets and of Christ the shepherd.

## MUSIC

Among the leading reformers of the sixteenth century, Zwingli appears to have been a particularly talented musician. All his contemporary biographers, from Oswald Myconius to Heinrich Bullinger, refer to his gifts in playing the lute, among other instruments, and in singing. As befitted an avid reader of Plato, Zwingli loved the harmony of music, which he saw as embedded in the order of nature. Indeed, his preaching voice was much admired for the way in which he could modulate his tones and project pastoral images drawn from nature. His musical achievements, his friends recorded, were recognized when he was a boy in Toggenburg and cultivated by his uncle Bartholomäus. Later, Zwingli received vocal and instrumental instruction in Bern from Arnold Geering and the Münster cantor Bartholomäus Gottfried Frank. The education continued in Vienna, where Zwingli studied the arts with the great German humanist Conrad Celtis, who had set the Odes of Horace to music. Bullinger tells us that when the young student went to Basel, his knowledge of the quadrivium, which included music, was deepened by his young teacher Gregorius Bünzli.[84] During his stay in Basel, Zwingli mastered several instruments. In Bullinger's eyes, his ability to make music was very much part of a character that relished humour and wit, and one that loved to perform. While he was in Glarus, he became good friends with the distinguished music theorist Heinrich Glarean. The chronicler Bernard Wyss was admiring:

I never heard of anyone who was so learned in the art of music – that is singing and every instrument like the lute, the harp, the violin, the Abögli [a small stringed instrument], the pipe, the whistle like a good Confederate, the trumpet marine, the dulcimer, the cornett and the horn anything other you can think of – any [instrument] as soon as he took it in the hand and was so talented, as written before.[85]

To his supporters, Zwingli's love of music reflected the very best of his engaging and charismatic personality. It also spoke to his poetic nature. Bullinger observed that 'he practised music with joy, including flute, which he did with modesty'.[86] His opponents, in contrast, portrayed him as a buffoon or fool. The Catholic chronicler Hans Salat (1498–1561) spoke of him as 'engaging in all manner of frivolity, including playing drums, flute, lute and harp' and called him an 'entertainer'. Thomas Murner despised Zwingli as 'a fiddler of the holy Gospels and a lute player of the Old and New Testaments'.[87]

At the first disputation in Zurich, the leader of the bishop's party, Johannes Fabri, had accused Zwingli of replacing the organ with fiddles and flutes, to which the preacher sarcastically replied:

You reproach me also, dear Fabri, [for playing] court lute, violin and pipe. I say, however, that I cannot [play] anything on the court lute. You know without doubt better about it; I do not know what kind of music it is. However, I learned once to play lute, violin and other instruments. I will keep silent with regard to children, for you are no doubt too holy for such amusement and other things. Therefore, you should know that David was a very good harp player, who calmed his own ... Your greed for honour and glory, indeed for money and blood, would vanish if you would dwell in the sound of the celestial court.[88]

Zwingli arranged for the creation of a music school in the former Franciscan monastery, and as teacher he recruited the young Hans Vogler from St Gallen. Vogler lived in Zwingli's home, adding to the circle of musicians, including Leo Jud, who performed and sang together. In 1528, Zwingli ordered two violins from Bern, although he does not seem to have received them. They may have been intended to be played at the musical performances that were staged in Zurich during Zwingli's time and in which he took a leading role. In 1529, the play *The Rich Man and Poor Lazarus* was performed with musical and voice accompaniment, while in January 1531 Aristophanes' *Ploutos* was staged, with music composed by Zwingli.[89]

The evidence suggests that Zwingli was an active composer, although many of his creations have been lost. We know that his friend Wolfgang Capito (1478–1541) wrote from Strasbourg, asking that the reformer send him more of his songs – by which he meant not only the tunes, but also the texts.[90] Capito already had some of Zwingli's music in his possession, most likely pieces for multiple voices. Influences and possible attributions can also be detected. Zwingli's use of folk melodies for his setting of Psalm 69 was replicated by Jud, and striking similarities exist between psalms traditionally credited to Leo Jud and Zwingli's three surviving songs.[91] These three extant works by Zwingli the composer, singer and accompanist are his 'Plague Song' of 1519, his setting of Psalm 69 of 1525 and the 'Kappel Song' of 1529. The genesis of the last of these is explained by Heinrich Bullinger: 'Zwingli endured great danger in this war . . . therefore in sorrow and fear he composed the following song':

Lord, hold the carriage yourself,
or soon the ride will go astray.
That would bring joy to the adversary,
who despises you beyond measure.
God lift up the glory of your name,
fight and punish the fierceness of the wicked,
awaken the sheep by your voice,
[the ones] who love you most deeply.
Help that all bitterness might depart, O Lord,
and that the old faithfulness might be restored and renewed,
so that we can eternally praise you.[92]

Zwingli had taken the old Swiss tradition of battle songs (such as those sung by soldiers before Novara in 1513) and spiritualized it for the battle of faith. He was a craftsman of words, and wrote tracts and expositions feverishly; but his most intimate expressions of faith and hope came in poetry and music. In the pulpit, before the Council, in making music with friends and staging plays Zwingli was a performer, and Zurich was his stage.

## END OF THE ROAD: ERASMUS

Despite their differences over reform of the Church and the Zurich reformer's vilification by Catholic opponents, Zwingli and Erasmus had continued their correspondence. Their relationship was severely strained by the German knight Ulrich von Hutten (1488–1523), an avowed supporter of Luther and an outspoken German patriot.[93] Erasmus, formerly Hutten's patron, turned against him when it became clear that Hutten's violent claims for reform brought the threat of revolt. Erasmus acrimoniously broke with Hutten and would not receive him when the imperial knight, stricken with syphilis, came to Basel in 1523. Hutten published a pamphlet in which he bitterly insulted Erasmus as immorally faint-hearted for abandoning church reform. Near death, he was offered refuge by Zwingli, who enabled him to live on the island of Ufenau in Lake Zurich from May 1523 until his death in August that same year.

Zwingli's harbouring of Erasmus' enemy was long thought to have been the final straw that broke their relationship; but such was not the case.

Erasmus certainly rebuked the Zurich reformer, but undaunted, Zwingli kept sending him letters. In the month in which Hutten died, Erasmus wrote defending himself against criticism from Zurich. In correspondence now lost, Zwingli had apparently referred to the Dutchman as a 'vacillator'. Erasmus conceded that he had sought compromise, but never at the expense of the gospel.

The problem was Zwingli's support for Luther. When the German reformer warned Oecolampadius in Basel that Erasmus was not to be trusted in matters of the Spirit, the Dutchman turned to Zwingli to ask what spirit Luther had in mind.[94] He was evidently disappointed by the reply. Their exchange is lost, but clearly over the course of 1524, as Erasmus' conflict with Luther boiled over, his relationship with Zwingli came to an end. Erasmus complained to Philipp Melanchthon in September 1524 that Zwingli had responded to his admonitions with contempt.[95] The relationship so desperately sought by the priest in Glarus in 1516 was slipping away. Four years later, Zwingli reflected on how presciently Erasmus had warned him against Luther. 'Now I realize how prudent Erasmus' admonitions were,' he wrote.

> My eyes have been opened – but too late. For, by being too outspoken in my defence of one man, I offended the other more than I supposed. How stupid I was! Therefore, I imprudently turned the one [Erasmus] into my prudent enemy for the sake of a man [Luther] who is less conciliatory and less likely to be a friend than the one against whom I defended him.[96]

Zwingli never relinquished his reverence for Erasmus, but they had diverged over how the revival of the classical world might serve the faith. The two men were of strikingly different temperaments. Zwingli's apparent desire to employ humanist learning to tear down the Church and create a new order horrified the Dutchman. Once Zwingli embarked on transforming Christianity, their relationship was doomed.

## ✤ FIVE ✤
✤

# REFORMATION

In the opening months of 1524, Zurich's suspected parting from the Catholic Church on account of heresy hardened the opposition from fellow Confederates, notably the Five States (Uri, Schwyz, Unterwalden, Zug and Lucerne). The cities of Basel, Bern and Schaffhausen were more circumspect, as they also had active reform movements for which there was sympathy among their magistrates. The Five States sent a delegation to Zurich in late February to protest about the religious changes within the city, but it returned unsatisfied. Implacable hostility led the Swiss Diet, meeting in Lucerne on 20 April 1524, to rebuke the Zurich Council for tolerating and abetting attacks on the Catholic Church. The Diet would stand by the 'faith of our forefathers', a contested patrimony claimed equally by Zwingli and his opponents.

The spring of 1524 brought a shift in Zwingli's attitude towards the Confederation. From his arrival in Zurich in 1519, he had largely espoused an Erasmian pacificism, hostile to mercenary service, pensions and foreign alliances, and reluctant to link religion and war. Hostility, however, was moving beyond words. The opposition of the Five States and the decision of the Diet at Regensburg to enforce the Edict of Worms against heretics, of which Zwingli was one, moved the preacher towards the acceptance of force.[1] His dedication of his *Commentary on True and False Religion* to Francis I in the spring of 1525 was an expression of hope that French support would overcome resistance to the Reformation.

Although as preacher in the Grossmünster he had no official political role, Zwingli increasingly spoke on behalf of the city. As part of Zurich's tactics of aggressive defence, the reformer prepared his 'Friendly and Earnest

Admonition to the Swiss',[2] which appeared on 2 May 1524, as the Catholics were consolidating their position against him and the city. So reviled was the name Huldrych Zwingli that the 'Admonition' appeared anonymously.

Addressing his fellow countrymen, Zwingli returned once more to the theme of lost virtue, contrasting the conduct of contemporary Swiss with the valour of their forefathers.[3] While past generations had struggled to defeat the rapacious nobility, tilled the hard soil and liberated themselves from foreign masters, all that could be seen now was the squandering of their inheritance.[4] Most execrable were those who received pensions – their hands were stained with blood. The consequences for the fatherland were all too evident: strife, godlessness and the imperilment of the Swiss Confederation.[5] The 'pure' Word of God, when freely preached, demanded repentance and abandonment of self-interest. The restoration of true Christianity would recover a heroic past. In truth, it would do more, for despite their piety and vitality, the forefathers had lived under the shadow of the falsehoods and idolatry of the Catholic Church. Now that the Word once more shone, the traditional virtues of the Swiss would flourish in the light of Christ. Faith and patriotism were mutually sustaining. Zwingli's opponents were left unmoved, no doubt fully aware of who had actually written this anonymous tract.

## CLEANSING THE TEMPLES

The hesitation of the magistrates to act against the mass and images in the churches fostered an atmosphere of tense uncertainty in Zurich. In January, rural unrest directed against the hated tithe and burdensome obligations reached such a pitch that, alarmed the city might be attacked, the Council ordered the walls reinforced.[6] Those who sought the stripping of sacred spaces were frustrated and angered by what they saw as a lack of leadership and determination, but the civic rulers were in no mood to be pushed into rash action. They were primarily concerned about order in the city and rural areas, and in May a seven-point mandate was released prohibiting a range of widespread activities, including dancing – except at weddings – drunkenness, elaborate clothing, and the firing of arms by young men.[7] Among the punishable offences was iconoclasm. The fabric of the Church was not to be touched.

Nevertheless, sporadic acts of desecration continued in both the city and rural areas, and preachers such as Wilhelm Reublin connected iconoclasm with aid to the poor. On the Monday after Pentecost, a commission was created, including Zwingli, to consider how to proceed. The magistrates were growing more inclined to move, and by the end of May a report was delivered that offered a bold plan.[8] Reformation was to be implemented through the removal of images from churches and the institution of an evangelical Lord's Supper. By 8 June, the divided Council had agreed that images in churches were contrary to the Bible, but the cleansing was to be carried out in an orderly manner and in charity: 'with love, without anger or divisiveness, since such images originated among Christians many hundred years ago and not long after the holy apostles and the son of Christ'.[9] Those citizens in Zurich who had commissioned devotional items had eight days in which to collect and take them home, where they could remain in private.[10] No new images were to be commissioned, and sculptors who took on new orders would be fined.

The magistrates' concern was to head off random iconoclasm and staunch the flow of violent language from the pulpits and in the streets and taverns. They were determined to demonstrate to their opponents that chaos had not broken out in Zurich: reform would be peaceful. Such caution, however, was revised with the deaths in mid-June of two crucial supporters of Zwingli who had advocated prudence and restraint: *Bürgermeister* Felix Schmied and Marx Röist. Röist had been Zwingli's most significant supporter, and with his death opposition to more draconian measures in dealing with images was removed.[11] Immediately, indeed on the very day of his death, the Council passed a much more robust edict, determining

> to do away with the images or idols in all places where they are worshipped, so that many turn themselves from the idols entirely to the living true God, and each seeks all help and trust in the one God through Our Lord Jesus Christ, to call upon and recognize in worship him alone. And the goods and costs that have been laid upon these images should be turned to the poor needy human beings, who are a true image of God.[12]

By 2 July, yet another commission had been formed, with 17 members, including a representative of each guild, together with a stonemason, carpenter and three priests. Over the next 10 days, the commission moved from church to church, and behind closed doors began the work of trans-forming the worship spaces. Statues, wooden panels and altarpieces were smashed and ground up, with the stone used for cobbles and the metals melted down. The stained-glass windows were left untouched, owing to the enormous cost of replacing them.[13] When the images were gone, the walls were whitewashed. Everything of value was to be sold for poor relief, including clerical vestments.[14] The relics of Felix and Regula were removed from the Grossmünster and quietly buried in an unmarked location. Organs were to be silenced.

Even this more aggressive policy did not satisfy all. Accounts narrate that when churches were reopened, men dashed in and inflicted further damage on what little remained, including furniture and the stone altars, which on account of their weight had not yet been taken down. The Council's policy extended to the dead: on 18 November, the magistrates permitted those who wished to remove headstones from the graveyards to do so. Unclaimed headstones were taken away to be used by the city for building purposes, and bones from charnel houses were buried in common graves.[15]

By one contemporary reckoning, the value of the precious items removed or destroyed was eye-watering. The sale of silk paraments raised 1,400 gulden, while the melted silver brought almost 6,000 gulden.[16] The numbers rose to almost 9,000 gulden in gold and 10,000 gulden worth of manuscripts and books. To give a sense of proportion: Zwingli, as the most senior cleric in the city, was paid less than a hundred gulden a year. The value of the lost altar paintings and statues cannot be calculated as they perished. Apart from the pillaging of religious houses by Vikings, the Western Church had never witnessed such intentional destruction of the fabric of worship and devotion. The smashed statues and the fires that consumed paintings marked Zurich's break with a thousand years of European Christianity. The destructive force of Zwingli's reformation had been unleashed.

The stripping of churches during the summer of 1524 shocked the Confederation. The medieval Church had seen heresy come and go, but never had the Catholic faith been so desecrated. The Five States were outraged and resolutely refused to meet Zurich representatives at the federal Diet. Rumours of a military intervention once more circulated, dampened, however, by the reluctance of powerful urban Confederates in Bern and

Basel to be drawn into conflict with Zurich. Both cities contained evangelical preachers and the stirrings of popular support for the new faith. They, too, had experienced random iconoclasm. Bern permitted itself distance from the growing hostilities by arguing that there were no grounds for intervention in the religious affairs of another Confederate. In the east, where Zurich had traditionally exerted considerable influence, Appenzell, Thurgau, St Gallen and Schaffhausen gave their consent to the orderly removal of images from the churches. Bishop Hugo von Hohenlandenberg of Constance, together with Zurich's powerful Catholic neighbour Lucerne, demanded that the decision to strip the churches be reversed. The bishop's protest was largely symbolic, and Zwingli replied on behalf of the city in August, stressing divine proscription of images in the second commandment.[17]

The images were gone by the end of the summer. Next on the scaffold were the religious houses, which largely acquiesced in their demise. The houses of the Dominicans and Augustinians were seized by the Council and the monks and friars were retired, left the city or embraced the reform movement. The Dominican house ultimately became a city hospital. All who did not depart gathered in the Franciscan friary. The plan for the monks was relatively simple: they were to find gainful employment, with those who were younger given the option of studying the Bible or taking up a useful trade.[18] A number later became evangelical pastors. The older generation was treated gently, allowed to retain their incomes on the condition that no novices were recruited. A large number of monks chose to leave their vocation and marry, often taking positions serving in the hospitals into which many of the religious houses in the city were transformed. These houses occupied a large amount of property within the walls of Zurich, and their dissolution proved a windfall for the Council.

There were four convents in the city: two Dominican, one Cistercian and one Benedictine.[19] The desire that the nuns should leave their religious houses brought extreme hardship for many women. The options given were limited: they could remain in the house until their death or else leave and either marry or support themselves through work. Zwingli and the reformers thought they should marry, but many fell into poverty. Those nuns who rejected the new faith often found themselves at odds with their families, who were supporters. The last abbess of the oldest Zurich convent, Katharina von Zimmern, handed over her house with all its rights to the Council at the end of 1524; in return she received a generous living that sustained her over the next 20 years. In the spring of 1525, the Council decided that all the remaining nuns should be moved into one location, the former Dominican house at Oetenbach. The range of experiences for the nuns was considerable, and often challenging. What was clear was that they had no say in Zwingli's reformation.

Christianity had long associated heresy with moral degeneracy, and Zwingli's opponents were no exception. He had been a promiscuous priest and a coward who hid behind the walls of Zurich; his musical abilities were also derided, making him a dilettante or even effeminate. Zwingli was simply reaping what he had sown, as he had never held back from mocking opponents. Such was the outrage caused by the stripping of the churches that the Swiss Diet, meeting in Lucerne, demanded that Zurich account for its actions. At the session, Zwingli was vociferously denounced. He responded to the two principal accusations: that his false teaching had come from Jews and that he did not preach Christ as the crucified Son of God.[20] He denied both accusations and identified as his slanderers Catholic priests who lived in and near Zurich. In future, he warned, they should preach the Word of God, instead of inciting hatred and gossip. If they failed to do so, he would expose their ignorance for all to see.

The zeal in Zurich among the reformers for Hebrew, and their emphasis on the Old Testament, frequently led to accusations that they were 'Judaizers', meaning that they adopted the errors of rabbinical teaching. Late-medieval hostility to Jews intensified during the 1520s in the wake of the infamous Reuchlin affair, which had been an attempt to destroy Jewish learning.[21] Zwingli's hands were not clean, and he shared much of the standard Christian animus toward Jews. Nevertheless, a continuous stream of charges claimed that his reforms arose from rabbinical teachings that stressed the Hebrew scriptures over the New Testament. He addressed a particular story of a Jew named Moses from Winterthur, with whom he had been in contact:

> However, it is true that some time ago I talked with him [Moses] in the presence of more than ten other learned and upright men from Zurich and Winterthur about many promises in the Old Testament against their errors. [Jews] sin for not accepting the Lord Jesus as the Christ. [Moses] also came twice to us in Zurich not to teach but to

listen to our Hebrew lectures to see if we handle the Hebrew Scriptures rightly. He admitted afterwards that we did and wished he could himself do so in such a way.[22]

The accusation of consulting with Jews was closely associated with the charge that Zwingli did not preach Christ as the Son of God. The sting was deeply felt: 'All our work, who preach the Gospel at this time, consists only in preaching how we find the assurance of our salvation in the death of the living Son of God.'[23]

## PILLAGE

Zurich's precarious position was underscored over a couple of days in mid-June, when once more reform was in danger of spinning out of control. The incident was the dramatic destruction of a religious house. In mid-June, peasants stormed and destroyed the Carthusian monastery at Ittingen in Thurgau, a Mandated Territory jointly governed by the Confederates, but very much under Zurich's influence.[24] The hostility was rooted in a dispute between the monastery and peasants who owed it tithes. The volatile situation was inflamed by evangelical preachers supported by Zurich who were active in the region.[25] The crowd that turned on the wealthy abbey had demanded food and drink from the monks. Unsatisfied, they raided the cellars and seized the wine, at which point the violence broke out. By the time the Zurich troops arrived, much of the monastery had already been reduced to ruins. While negotiations were attempted, the remaining part of the building was consumed in a fire.

Catholics, already appalled by the iconoclasm in Zurich, held the city responsible for the destruction of a religious house. The Zurich magistrates, having sought to prevent acts of destruction in their own land, did not want to be associated with riotous actions at Ittingen. They sought to settle the matter by arresting some of the ringleaders, but at their trial the men were found not guilty of any capital offence. Zwingli had acted as an expert witness, expressing sympathy for the peasants and the demands, while re-iterating his conviction that the tithe should remain.[26] The ensuing Catholic outrage cowed the Council, which did not want to be seen as fomenting rural unrest, as it had to keep a wary eye on its own lands. After threats from the Swiss Diet, backed up by the Austrians, the divided magistrates consented to hand over the men to the Catholic Confederates, who were less benevolent. A number of the men were executed.[27] The Ittingen crisis underscored Zurich's perilous position. The humiliation of having to accede to the wishes of the Catholic Confederates was a harsh reminder for the magistrates of their isolation and limited ability to dictate events outside their lands.

## THE WILD GOAT

While in Zurich committed Catholics used status and power to resist change, the most significant theological assaults came from outside the city. Most notable were the attacks by Jerome Emser (1477–1527) and, in particular, Johann Eck (1486–1543), both of whom had been in the vanguard of the struggle against Luther. Turning his attention to the Swiss, Emser took up his pen in April 1524 to write 'A Defence of the Canon of the Mass against Ulrich Zwingli', which was little more than a collection of insults. It made, however, a deadly serious point: Emser provided an argument for the antiquity and continuous history of the Roman mass.[28] His arrow struck the target, and Zwingli was forced to step back from his position on the novelty of the mass. Emser took aim at Zwingli's published revision of the mass liturgy and the insertion of his own prayers, and fiercely denounced the Zurich reformer as a fraud and heretic, and, worse, a lesser version of Luther.

Zwingli only learned of Emser's pamphlet, which was printed in Dresden, when a traveller brought him a copy. He replied in August 1524, claiming to be responding 'lovingly and benignly'. In truth, he mocked Emser as a 'wild goat' – a joke first used by Luther on account of a goat on the Emser coat of arms. As a man of the mountains, Zwingli knew his opponent: 'Wild goat that you are, you brandish your horns against one who has seen so many of those animals that he does not fear their look at all.'[29]

The purpose was not mere verbal jousting. Zwingli used Emser's attack on his revision of the liturgy to offer a full account of the nature of the Church. The body of Christ is both visible and invisible, and is not formed like the hierarchical institution of Rome, with orders, laws and offices. The visible body in this world consists of all people, believers and non-believers, and is constantly in need of correction. The invisible Church is the gathering of the faithful past, present and future. It alone was the spotless body:

As many, then, as trust in Christ are built upon a rock, which no blasts of wind can shake, no inundating floods wash away. As many as are built upon this are the Church of Christ, for he himself said 'my'.[30]

Soon Zwingli was also forced to defend himself against Johann Eck, a more formidable opponent. A brilliant theologian and humanist at the University of Ingolstadt, Eck was a figure well known from his confrontation with Luther at Leipzig in 1519, and he continued in his role as a scourge of the reformers. During the years 1524–1526, Eck emerged as Zwingli's most capable enemy.[31] The theologian took considerable interest in the developing religious controversies in the Swiss Confederation, and in the summer of 1524 addressed the Swiss Diet in Baden, where he attacked Zwingli's *Exposition of the Sixty-Seven Articles*.[32] He proposed to the Diet that he and Zwingli should hold a public debate, and that a body of delegates should determine who was the true heretic. Zwingli's response was fierce. He contended that Eck was nothing more than a showman and self-promoter, adding that the Catholic professor was deeply disappointed not to have been made a bishop.[33] One performer was attacking another.

Zwingli was drawn to the possibility of a debate, but insisted that the confrontation should take place in Zurich before an open Bible, which alone should be the standard of judgement, not church hierarchy or tradition. Despite his bravado, Zwingli knew full well that he could not risk travelling to Baden, where the Diet was sitting. Reports recounted that his books, as well as an effigy of him, had been burned in public, and he had every reason to believe that if apprehended, he would suffer the same fate. Eck was the most dangerous opponent Zwingli had faced and the reformer's instinct was to attack.[34]

Eck was more than a match for Zwingli's acid tones. He knew exactly how to exasperate the reformer. In his first epistle, of 18 September 1524, he claimed that the true source of Swiss errors was Luther, and he continued to call Zwingli a 'Lutheran'. Both heretics had destroyed the unity of the Church with their specious claims for scripture alone. His own response came from Paul's words to Titus: 'After a first and second admonition, have nothing more to do with anyone who causes divisions, since you know that such a person is perverted and sinful, being self-condemned' (Titus 3:10–11). Eck was withering: Zwingli could not be serious about a debate or he would have accepted the terms.[35] The heretic would not dare debate unless he was also judge. He was a coward who believed that he alone possessed the Holy Spirit.

Although expectations rose during the late summer and autumn of 1524 of an encounter between Eck and Zwingli, for which there was support in both the Swiss Diet and the Zurich Council, each of the two combatants refused to accept the other's terms. Eck refused to enter the walls of heretical Zurich and Zwingli refused to leave. Both knew what awaited them if they ventured into hostile territory, and by 1524 there was no neutral ground.

### BAPTIZED IN THE SPIRIT

In the summer of 1524, parishioners in Witikon and Zollikon, which were under Zurich control, refused to bring their children for baptism, claiming that they had been told not to do so by their preachers. Once again, Wilhelm Reublin was in the fray, insisting that he would not baptize anyone who had not made a profession of faith. Infant baptism, he declared, was nowhere to be found in the New Testament. The response from the magistrates was uncompromising. Beyond theology, they connected this resistance with the rural unrest currently widespread in Zurich lands. All newborns, the Council thundered, must be brought to the parish church for baptism and their names duly recorded, making them subjects. The decision on baptism was the first explicit theological decision made by the magistrates without any form of disputation. By refusing to administer the sacrament to their infants, men and women were setting their faith in conflict with their civic duties, raising the question of their allegiance.

In a collective letter to Thomas Müntzer in early September 1524, the group, led by Konrad Grebel and Felix Manz, sought to outline its theological convictions and establish connections beyond the Confederation of like-minded reformers. The letter is not a dogmatic statement, but ranges across the nature of the Church, baptism, discipline and pacifism. The Church was to be reformed in conformity with scripture, and Zwingli's compromises with temporal authority were rejected. It was to be separated from the rulers as an autonomous community of believers.[36] The letter harshly indicted Zwingli and his supporters who, Grebel and his colleagues insisted, 'follow their own notions, yes, even those of Antichrist, above God and contrary to God, as is not right for ambassadors of God so to act and so to preach'.[37]

In the autumn of 1524, the debate over baptism continued to escalate. In the face of the demands of the Council, the opponents of infant baptism began to look further afield for support. In October, they made contact with Andreas Bodenstein von Karlstadt and then with Thomas Müntzer. Karlstadt's writings on baptism had been highly influential on the radicals, and his works were disseminated throughout the Swiss lands. He was a fierce opponent of infant baptism.[38]

Between October and December, the radical circle in Zurich cultivated their views on baptism, which were in conflict with Zwingli's, in a series of private debates. Felix Manz's 'Protestation to the Council' set out the case against infant baptism, and demonstrated that Zwingli was wrong. His statement formulated what would become the heart of the Anabaptist argument: scripture makes it clear that faith follows from preaching and that baptism follows from faith.[39] Manz argued that baptism should be administered 'upon one who having been converted through God's Word and having changed his heart now henceforth desires to live in newness of life'.[40] Such a person could only be an adult, for 'to apply such things as have just been related to children is without any foundation and against all Scriptures'. Particular emphasis was placed on the desire of the believer to be baptized and their conduct after the rite.

By early 1525, the debate over infant baptism was no longer confined to private discussions, but was a public controversy that unnerved the magistrates. They called for a disputation in January, which resulted in a hardening of their position: infant baptism was mandatory; private reading groups banned. Those who had not had their children baptized had eight days in which to do so. The principal antagonists, including Grebel, Manz and Castelberger were either to remain silent or be banished. Zwingli and the Council were determined to extirpate the threat to the reform movement, and as Andrea Strübind has remarked, 'the magistrates had resolved to protect their protégé by decree'.[41] The opponents of infant baptism had been made criminals.

Starting on 21 January 1525, the first adult baptisms took place in Zurich and the rural areas. In the home of Felix Manz, Konrad Grebel baptized Georg Blaurock, who then baptized the others present. Theirs was an act of enormous courage, as those gathered knew full well that their convictions would bring persecution and exile. The baptisms took place in an atmosphere created by prayer and scripture reading, within a gathering of the faithful, not a new church. To be baptized, one had to make a public profession of faith. Soon afterwards, baptisms followed in nearby Zollikon, where a celebration of baptism and the Lord's Supper took place in a private home. The communal worship was named a 'meal of unity'. Participation was open to all who demonstrated 'brotherly love', with those who received the sacraments expected to live according to the New Testament. The participants had taken the sacraments into their own hands, away from the clergy and magistrates.[42]

One of the most gifted figures in this movement was Balthasar Hubmaier (1480–1528), an educated humanist, theologian and former pupil of Johann Eck. He knew Zwingli, Oecolampadius and Vadian well, initially agreeing with them in broad outline on evangelical teaching, and had participated at the second disputation in Zurich, in 1523. In the spring of 1524, he drew up a plan for the reform of Waldshut, a town on the Swiss–German border under Austrian rule. During the autumn of 1524, when Waldshut was caught up in peasant unrest and military conflict loomed, Zurich sent a small number of soldiers to aid.

Hubmaier's rejection of infant baptism seriously strained his relations with Zwingli and Oecolampadius, and by January 1525 he was in contact with Konrad Grebel, Felix Manz and Georg Blaurock in Zurich. Their connections were enhanced with the arrival of several Anabaptists in Waldshut during that winter, after their expulsion from Zurich. Adult baptisms followed in the town, and Hubmaier himself was baptized at Easter 1525. Unlike Grebel, Manz and others, Hubmaier attempted to retain good relations with Zwingli and Oecolampadius, despite the rift. Indeed, on several occasions Hubmaier insisted that Zwingli and Oecolampadius had shared his doubts about infant baptism.

Zwingli responded to the Anabaptist challenge in May 1525 with the first of two major works on the sacrament that would appear that year. In *Baptism, Rebaptism and Infant Baptism*, he took direct aim at his opponents, accusing them of having completely distorted the sacrament. Turning their argument on its head, he claimed that, as infant baptism was not forbidden in scripture, it could not be an offence.[43] But his argument was not based on silence. He was eager to state what baptism actually is: a covenantal sign that does not in itself or as an act impart or even strengthen faith. Zwingli rejected what he saw as the pernicious Anabaptist argument that baptism was a pledge to live a sinless life, a position he claimed was a new form of legalism to bind the conscience. It would make God a liar, as such lives were not possible. For Zwingli, baptism marked the beginning of a journey of following Christ: 'baptism in water is an initiatory sign, with which we pledge ourselves to a new life'.[44] He denied that children do not possess the Spirit, arguing that God can act through whomsoever he wills.

Zwingli accused the Anabaptists of reading scripture too literally: the command to baptize made no distinction between adults and children.[45] Furthermore, the fact that infants are not mentioned was not an argument against their reception of the sacrament, for if one took that position, then women would not be permitted to receive communion, as there were no women at the Last Supper. Baptism is the rite of initiation into the covenant of Christ, as circumcision was for the Israelites. Circumcision did not bring faith: it was a covenantal sign that those who trust in God will raise their children to know and love God. Instruction follows initiation, so children are baptized and then are taught the faith. Baptism cannot save, but it is a sign or pledge of the covenant God has made with humanity. It was instituted by Christ for all.

## 'THIEF, HERETIC AND ADULTERER'

Although much of Zwingli's life was determined by the urgency of events over which he had little control and by the constant need to respond to opponents in the city and abroad, he drew strength from order and discipline. He sought to preserve a balance of life involving family, study, worship and public events. His biographer Myconius offers a window on the reformer's daily world:

> He carried on his studies standing up, setting apart certain hours for them, and nothing but dire necessity compelled him to omit them. From early morning to 10 o'clock he gave himself to reading, exegesis, theology and writing, as time and occasion required. After lunch [10 a.m.] he attended to those who wished to talk to him or hear his advice, and then strolled with friends until two o'clock. Then he returned to his study. After supper he again walked a little, then generally wrote his letters, an occupation that sometimes kept him up

till midnight. Moreover, as often as business compelled, he was at the command of the Council.[46]

Those letters often speak of physical and mental exhaustion and the failure to meet the myriad demands. Strikingly, however, Myconius had almost nothing to say about Zwingli's beloved Anna, their children or domestic life. He did not pass over, however, the assaults, verbal and physical, on Zwingli's person, and he was well informed on what was being said about the man in the taverns and civic chambers. He tells one story of an attack on the reformer's sleeping household, probably in 1525. From the street two men, filled with wine, shouted insults and smashed windows with stones:

> [They] behaved so cruelly, basely and inhumanly with their shouts and curses and blows that none of the neighbours dared to protest even through the windows. So they kept on till they used up their stones, their words, and their strength. The tumult was reported to the *Bürgermeister* in the morning and the gates were shut and armed men searched for the offenders in vain in every nook and cranny of the city until certain prostitutes who knew about their hiding places, not being adept in concealing, unintentionally betrayed one of them. The other had already escaped.[47]

The captured offender was found hiding in a wine barrel that belonged to a priest, and was taken to prison by an 'enraged crowd'. He was condemned to indefinite imprisonment and languished in the Wellenberg, the prison tower in the middle of the River Limmat, until released at the request of the city of Bern.

Zwingli was clearly rattled. On 22 September 1525 he wrote to Vadian describing the 'extremely tragic event' that had befallen him.[48] He added that Christian Fribolt, the merchant from St Gallen who carried the letter, would recount the story in greater detail. Zwingli described the situation as 'horrible', although God ('the holy Jupiter'), he was certain, would somehow use this incident to his honour. He told Vadian that the assault reflected a disease in the community and that the Council had been properly stern, acting to heal the poisoned body. The well-meaning people of the city had responded well, and Vadian was not to be unduly worried. Zwingli assured his friend that he was unfazed and back at work.

The broken windows were not the only occasion when Zwingli was personally threatened. Myconius recalled an incident of a man, reportedly from Zug, who was apprehended in Zurich carrying a large sword under his cloak with the intention, so he claimed, of running Zwingli through when the right moment presented itself. After being arrested, the would-be assassin managed to vanish from the city.[49] Such incidents, Myconius tells us, were not isolated. Zwingli was frequently called a 'thief', 'heretic' and an 'adulterer'. His being mocked in the streets of Zurich was an almost daily occurrence:

> They calumniated him, made him of no account, publicly and privately jeered at him to such a degree that the Zurichers began to consider how they might avert this evil. It would require a volume if anyone would know this affair fully or write exhaustively about it.[50]

Zwingli's volatile relations with the people and Council in Zurich were well known abroad. Thus, for example, in January 1526 Zwingli recorded that a traveller had arrived in Zurich reporting rumours circulating in Strasbourg that Zwingli had been killed, banished or gone into hiding.[51]

The controversial preacher and reformer required a security detail:

> Zwingli sometimes dined away from home with friends or enter-tainers. Therefore, returning he was almost always escorted without being aware of it by good citizens, lest evil should befall him on the way. And the Council in this time placed watchers around his house at night. See, I beseech you, what unjust accusations were brought against the man that he should have to be protected in this way![52]

Perhaps most dramatic was an abortive kidnapping. Myconius alluded to numerous 'secret plots' against Zwingli, but also recounted how a figure appeared at Zwingli's door after midnight, beseeching the preacher to tend to a dying man. Zwingli's servant replied that he would do whatever was necessary, as the reformer was not to be disturbed during the night, on account of his busy days. The man at the door objected so vehemently that the quick-witted servant became suspicious:

> The servant, therefore, going as if he was to rouse his master and tell him about it, frustrated the marauder by closing the door and leaving him outside. In the morning the facts were discovered that he [Zwingli] was to have been gagged and carried away secretly in a boat. Shortly thereafter a horse was got ready to be used for the same purpose.[53]

We read of graffiti on the city walls and bridges denouncing Zwingli as excrement and a fornicator.

### THE BODY OF CHRIST

While the debate over baptism was a defining moment for the Reformation, on the Lord's Supper, the other sacrament, Zwingli and his radical opponents were largely in agreement. Nevertheless, the question of what took place during the celebration of the meal was soon to open another fissure. In his *Exposition of the Sixty-Seven Articles* of 1523, Zwingli had attacked transubstantiation and argued that he and Luther were saying much the same thing, albeit with different words. A year later, it was evident that they held very different positions on the sacrament, and Zwingli distanced himself from Wittenberg, denying that he was a 'Lutheran', as opponents such as Eck had asserted. But his own position was by no means clear. He had repeatedly rejected the sacrificial character of the mass, and continued to claim that the Roman Church taught that Christ's once-offered sacrifice was repeated by priests at the altar. He preferred to speak of the Lord's Supper as a 'remembrance' or 'memorial', but what exactly he meant awaited further explanation.

Zwingli articulated more fully an understanding of the Lord's Supper in November 1524 in his 'Letter to Matthew Alber', addressed to a pastor in Reutlingen in Germany.[54] In the missive, Zwingli responded to a variety of criticisms, not just those of his Catholic opponents. It marked his intense engagement with the sixth chapter of the Gospel of John as central to his sacramental thought: Jesus speaks of himself as the 'bread of life', telling his disciples:

very truly I tell you, unless you eat the flesh of the Son of Man and drink his blood, you have no life in you. Whoever eats my flesh and drinks my blood has eternal life, and I will raise them up at the last day.

Zwingli drew the conclusion that it was Christ slain on the cross, not eaten in the sacramental meal, that feeds the faithful. Eating the flesh of Christ is not, therefore, a physical act, but a spiritual one. To eat the body is to believe; it means believing that Christ died to save humanity.

A significant influence on Zwingli's evolving convictions about the Lord's Supper, as found in the 'Letter to Matthew Alber', came from a somewhat unusual source. In or around 1521, the Dutch humanist and jurist Cornelius Hoen had written a letter in which he argued that Christ's words 'this is my body' actually meant 'this signifies my body'.[55] In proposing that the bread and wine do not really become the body and blood of Christ, but represent them, he articulated a rejection of both Catholic transubstantiation and Luther's teaching. Zwingli came in contact with the letter in manuscript at some point in 1524. Hoen had provided him with a crucial piece of his argument, leading the reformer to claim:

The flesh of Christ is the food and hope of the human heart, simply in that he was slain for us. For what is produced of flesh is flesh. The flesh of Christ, therefore, when it is eaten cannot produce anything but flesh. Yet, the flesh of Christ in dying for us makes that person spiritual, that is, truly a child of God who rests upon his death. I conclude, therefore, that this bread of which Christ speaks is simply this: that Christ was delivered up to death for our life.[56]

Zwingli rejected the notion that the bread was in any way the physical body of Christ, or that Christ's body was present in any 'real' sense. Although Zwingli did not name Luther in the letter to Alber, here he departed from what the German doctor was saying about the physical presence of Christ in the Supper. For Zwingli, the promises of Christ are for those who believe, those who have faith, and simply for those who consume the bread and wine:

Christ gives life to the world not because he is flesh, but because he is God and the Son of God. Again, it appears that he is life insofar as he

is believed to be the Son of God and to have died according to the
flesh he had taken on from the virgin, and that he gives life to those
who have believed in this way, not those who have eaten physically.[57]

Although it would be six more months before the mass was officially
abolished in Zurich, by November 1524 Zwingli evidently possessed a
coherent view of the sacrament. Having stripped away any sacrificial role at
the altar for the priest, he envisaged the community gathered around a table
with bread and wine to recall Christ's last meal with his disciples. Christ
would be present not physically, but in the Spirit, who fed those who partook
in faith.

## REVOLT

The tumult over religion between 1523 and 1525 took place against the
background of growing unrest among the peasants in the rural territories.[58]
In comparison to most of the lands of northern Europe, the plight of the
peasants in the Confederation was less dire – a result of the strong Swiss
communal tradition, particularly in the inner Confederates.[59] Nevertheless,
suffering was considerable, particularly as Zurich continued into economic
decline during the 1520s, through a heady mixture of bad weather, a failure
of markets and the city's isolation. A disproportionate amount of the hardship fell on the rural communities. As we have seen, the feudal bonds of
tithing remained a serious grievance. Peasants also faced payments for virtually every aspect of their lives: the marriage of a daughter, grinding corn and
inheriting, to name but a few.[60] The Church played a key role in this catalogue of customary payments, exacting money to baptize children and bury
the dead, as well as receiving tithes from crops and animals. Despite his
readiness to identify himself with the peasantry of his native Toggenburg,
Zwingli had known privilege and advantages that set him apart. His family
situation had enabled him to attend university and become a priest. Few
peasants experienced that level of social or economic advancement.

The evangelical preaching in Zurich in the autumn of 1523 had begun to
exacerbate the situation, with protests about the tithe hurled by the peasants
against the Grossmünster and the religious houses at Rüti and Bubikon.
Riots and looting took place. Inspired by what they heard from Zwingli,

pastors called for profound changes at the parish level. The grievances were both well established and radical: calls for the end of episcopal authority and for communities to both elect their own priests and control the possessions of the parish that paid for the clergy went hand in hand with demands for the end of serfdom and of feudal dues.

The Swiss Diet – alarmed by the situation to the north, in the German lands of Swabia, where unrest was becoming increasingly militant – met in April and May 1524 to draw up plans for defence against the peasant armies assembling in Germany.[61] They foresaw the Rhine as the front for the Confederation, but disturbances were soon also happening on Swiss territory, in Bernese and Basel lands, as well as in Appenzell, St Gallen, Schaffhausen and other territories in the eastern part of the Confederation. Moderate responses from the ruling magistrates were initially sufficient to avoid loss of life.

In the spring of 1525, some 4,000 peasants gathered in Töss, not far from Zurich, but they eventually disbanded after assurances from the Zurich *Bürgermeister* that their cause would be investigated. Zwingli took a direct hand in events, and advised the Zurich Council on how to respond to the combination of religious, economic and political demands.[62] In his written intervention, he argued that the government should consider the grievances, as was the tradition in Swiss lands, but his conclusions offered no radical alternative, for he held that established contractual demands must be honoured, leaving the peasants to pay tithes, rents and interest. The Bible was clear: both the Old and the New Testament told of serfs of whom obedience to their overlords was demanded.[63] Zwingli was deeply concerned with the justice of the tithes and commerce, and proposed capping interest at 5 per cent for loans in business transactions.[64] A statement from the magistrates in late June 1525 made it clear that they did not accept the Bible as the basis for economic arrangements. Some concessions were made, but the tithe was to stay.[65]

Zwingli was forced onto the defensive. Pamphlets were circulating that invoked his language of fraternal love as the basis for social reform. Additionally, the magistrates believed that the clergy were behind the unrest, no doubt thinking of the radicals in the rural parishes. Zwingli counselled compassion towards the peasants without overturning the system: rents and interest were to be charged at reasonable rates.

Zwingli's position was straightforward, if rather naïve. There was to be no economic or social reform to liberate the peasantry, but in turn it fell to the rulers to act in a godly and benevolent manner consonant with their role as God's appointed. Magistrates were to keep order, protect true religion and cultivate virtue, while subjects were to submit to the established structures of authority. Zwingli never adopted Luther's attitude, found in his direly titled *Against the Murderous, Thieving Hordes of Peasants* of May 1525. In Wittenberg, Luther recorded, 'The peasants have taken upon themselves the burden of three terrible sins against God and man; by this they have abundantly merited death in body and soul.'[66] In Zurich, the appeal was to the good will of the rulers in responding to the rural grievances. The Swiss lands suffered little, compared to the hostility and slaughter of the peasant revolts in German lands. For the most part, negotiations, rather than conflict, marked those events in the Confederation that related to the peasants; but in the end, little changed. The Reformation would do nothing for the plight of the rural populace, whose subjugation suited both magistrates and their reformers.

## FINAL BREAK

Zurich had truly broken with the Catholic Church when it purged its churches; the abolition of the mass was a delayed consequence. Zwingli's calculation was that this step would not be taken unless the magistrates were persuaded that disorder would not ensue.[67] Yet significant Catholic opposition remained in the city, and victory was not guaranteed. Anabaptism was spreading and the rural areas were restive. The growing threat from the inner Confederates and their links to Habsburg Austria suggested that military action was imminent. Bern and Basel had demonstrated that they had no appetite for war, but they were still officially Catholic.

In the early months of 1525, however, the reform party in Zurich was well placed, for – led by *Bürgermeister* Diethelm Röist (1482–1544) (son of Marx) and Heinrich Walder (1460s–1542) – the Large Council was fully behind change. On 11 April, Zwingli appeared before the Council, alongside two other priests from the Grossmünster and his friends Kaspar Megander and Oswald Myconius, to call for the abolition of the mass. It should be replaced, they proposed, by a celebration of the Lord's Supper that followed the biblical model provided by the Apostle Paul.

The Catholics were not yet done. Joachim am Grüt, deputy town clerk, addressed the Council, denouncing Zwingli and his appeal to scripture, and warning the magistrates not to be fooled by the reformer's sophistry.[68] Although he was unsuccessful, he remained a fierce defender of the Catholic faith. He was unable to prevail, and in a narrow vote the members of the Large Council mandated that the mass be abolished and replaced by a biblically based celebration of the Lord's Supper.[69] Several days before the vote, Zwingli had had printed a liturgy for the service, with the sacrifice of the mass replaced by a service of remembrance and thanksgiving.[70] The first celebration of the Lord's Supper in the Grossmünster took place the following day, on Maundy Thursday 1525.[71] The bread and wine, contained within wooden vessels, were placed on a simple table located between the choir and the nave. Some leading citizens who did not wish to be coerced into the new faith sought to have the mass permitted in other churches, but their request was denied, and it was sternly advised that they go to places outside Zurich, where the mass was still available.[72]

The houses of worship had been stripped and whitewashed, their altars eventually replaced by simple wooden tables, and music had ceased. The body of Christ was no longer physically present in the hands of the priests, and Mary and the saints had been demoted to being models of the faith. Virtually all religious symbols, including crucifixes, had been removed from public spaces, and time was reordered by the abolition of liturgical seasons, saints' days and traditional feast days, apart from Christmas and Easter. The Lutheran churches had largely preserved the medieval fabric of worship, but in Zurich there was little to remind people of the vanished faith.

Bishops, priests, monks or nuns were replaced by men in black who preached through the week and urged obedience to the state. Although beards would become one of the distinguishing features of Reformed ministers of the Reformation – notably Oecolampadius, Calvin and Bullinger – the first generation of Zurich reformers remained clean shaven. Zwingli, Jud and Konrad Pellikan retained their priestly visages.

Although the churches had been purged the previous year, the heavy stone altars proved a formidable remnant of Catholic culture. The last stage in the ritual break with Rome was their removal from the churches, which took another year to complete. Military banners that hung in the Wasserkirche on the River Limmat, which had survived cleansing, were also removed, as were organs from the city churches. Those who held to the 'old faith' were left with nothing. Zwingli's triumph was complete – at least in terms of the worship of the community.

The break with Rome in terms of religion had been made, but the relationship was not over. In the months up to the autumn of 1525, Zurich made various attempts to reach a deal with the pope for repayment of the funds owed. Finally, Joachim am Grüt was sent to Rome on behalf of Zurich, in the hope that he might gain even a portion of the money owed. One of the conditions set by Rome was a colloquy, to be held in Geneva or Lausanne, to resolve the religious dispute.[73] The Zurich Council tasked Zwingli with writing a reply, which he undertook with venomous delight.[74] His answer was full of sarcasm and faux deference. The Council tactfully set Zwingli's reply aside.

Zurich stood alone outside the Catholic Church with its hierarchy, priests and sacraments. This revolution from within had been brought about by Zwingli and his clerical and lay colleagues, who had succeeded in gathering enough support among the magistrates and guilds to upend the Latin Church. Although preaching had been crucial, and the appeal of the Bible alone was powerful, there had been no social revolution. The Reformation was a movement not of the people, but of educated men working within the system. Those who objected to Zwingli's approach were driven out and marginalized, soon to be persecuted. Dissent was not tolerated and freedom of conscience was extended only to those who accepted the new order. The Church that emerged in the spring of 1525 had no room for either Catholicism or Anabaptism.

The liturgy for the Lord's Supper, introduced on Maundy Thursday 1525, was the fullest expression of Zwingli's vision of the Christian community.[75] True religion was performed through true worship. Although he cast the liturgical reform of 1525 as a recovery of the Lord's Supper, Zwingli created a form of worship previously unknown.[76] No longer, as with his initial liturgical reforms proposed in 1523, was worship principally framed around the canon of the mass, although certain aspects were retained in the form of prayers. In 1525, Zwingli dispensed with any pretence of continuity with the Catholic sacrament, in order to place his emphasis on the sacral relationship of the Zurich Church with the ancient Israelites. A remarkable dream, he would recount, had pointed him to Exodus and the link of the Eucharist with the Passover, providing him with a usable past for his changes.[77]

The introductory letter that accompanied the liturgy for the Lord's Supper, published in 1525, drew on the biblical narrative in 2 Chronicles 34, where the young King Josiah purged the worship of the land, removing idols and cutting down the altars of Baal. Similarly, Hezekiah, in 2 Kings, 'did what was right in the eyes of the Lord' and destroyed images and altars, including the bronze serpent of Moses.[78] Zwingli linked the ancient stories of cleansing religion with the Church's sacred meal of the Easter Lamb. He would soon directly associate the Lord's Supper with the Passover meal. Zwingli's reading of the Old Testament in light of Christ formed the backbone to the practice of Reformed theological thought and the creation of liturgical drama.[79] For Zwingli in Zurich, for Oecolampadius in Basel, for Martin Bucer (1491–1551) in Strasbourg and their evangelical contemporaries, Christ was found everywhere in the Old Testament.[80]

Zwingli entitled his new liturgy 'Aktion oder Brauch', drawing a distinction between 'practice or use' and 'ceremony'. 'Practice or use' referred to the historical fact that the sacrament had been inaugurated by Christ at the Last Supper.[81] The term had the force of both divine command and historical continuity, for the Supper was a Passover meal, linking the sacrament to the salvation story of Israel. Ceremony, in contrast, possessed no divine warrant and, therefore, could be adapted to human circumstance; this ceremony was to be celebrated four times a year. Zwingli spoke of ceremony as a concession to 'human weakness', intended to ensure that the essential sacramental act was not performed 'without life and shape'.[82] The introductory letter gave expression to Zwingli's vision of the liturgy:

> we have authorized such ceremonies for the action – as appointed here – which we have deemed beneficial and appropriate to enhance in some degree the spiritual memorial of the death of Christ, the increase of faith and brotherly love, the reformation of life, and the prevention of the vices of the human heart.[83]

In the preface that followed the letter, Zwingli provided a model of the liturgy and for its performance. He did retain certain aspects of the mass – for example, the scripture readings, confession of sin, the Creed, the Gloria, the words of institution and the post-communion prayer.[84] But he opened with a bold theological statement about the nature of reform: the liturgy was distinguished by virtue of having been purged of 'everything that does not conform to the divine Word'.[85] The liturgy was also an act of recovery, for

Christ's Supper had been 'seriously abused' for 'a long time'. Reform redeemed that time, cleansing the polluted history of the Church. Crucially, at no point in the text did he refer to the Supper as a sacrament. Rather he described what was to take place as 'this memorial', as 'a thanksgiving and a rejoicing before Almighty God for the benefit which He has manifested to us through His Son'.[86]

The 1525 liturgy was marked by its relative simplicity. The bread and wine were placed on a table among the people, with the pastor facing the congregation. After opening prayers and a reading of the words of institution from 1 Corinthians 11 – 'For I received from the Lord what I also passed on to you: The Lord Jesus, on the night he was betrayed, took bread, and when he had given thanks, he broke it and said, "This is my body, which is for you; do this in remembrance of me"' – the people, following Paul's stern words, were warned against the unworthy reception of the bread and wine. The congregants then recited the Gloria antiphonally, coming together with the Amen. At the conclusion of the Gloria, the faithful heard passages from John 6, principally verses 47 ('In truth, he who believes has everlasting life') and 63 ('The Spirit gives life; the flesh counts for nothing. The words I have spoken to you are spirit, and they are life'). The pastor then kissed the Bible and proclaimed: 'Praise and thanks be to God. He will forgive all our sins according to his holy Word.'

Following the confession of sin, those present sang the Apostles' Creed antiphonally, after which the invitation and admonition to the Supper were pronounced, during which all were warned against 'anyone [who might] pretend to be a believer who is not, and so be guilty of the Lord's death'. The people knelt for the Lord's Prayer and a prayer said by the pastor beseeching God that the faithful might live 'purely as becomes the body'.

The words of institution were read at the table over unleavened bread and wine. The pastors served themselves first, before the servers took the elements to the people, who knelt to receive them. The bread and wine were passed among the people in silence, which Zwingli deemed the appropriate response to the gift of God. The drama of the liturgy was built around the interplay of words and silence, emphasizing the approach to the table as contemplation of God. Following the eating and drinking, Psalm 113 was recited, once more antiphonally. The reading of Psalm 113 linked the Supper with the Passover, where the Psalm was part of the Hallel, recited on joyous occasions in praise and thanksgiving. To conclude, the benediction was pronounced and the people departed.

The 1525 liturgy, and its slightly revised 1529 form, gave expression to Zwingli's conviction of the inseparability of thanksgiving and Christian living.[87] It was his fullest expression of his understanding of Christianity. The community was the body of Christ, not because of any liturgical action, but through the divine promises. The rituals of worship were nothing in themselves: they directed the people to higher realities. Yet Zwingli believed that liturgy was essential to memory, gratitude and contemplation. Liturgy shaped the emotions and senses; it formed the gathered community as one before God, yet still visible in its social, political and gender distinctions. Zwingli's purpose was a moving, poignant moment in which the lightness of the walls and the illumination through the windows united with the bread and wine to elevate the community into the body of Christ, the unity of the visible and invisible Church through Word and Spirit.

Worship was about being 'innocent' and 'pure', which was not to suggest any form of human perfection, but rather the realization of God's gracious gift in Christ. Through the imitation of the Son of God, the faithful were able to fulfil God's principal command, as expressed in Leviticus 20:7: 'Consecrate yourselves therefore, and be holy; for I am the Lord your God.' Zwingli rephrased the biblical text as: 'I am righteous, pure, godly, therefore if you wish to be of me you must be like me.'[88] God demands in worship, as in life, that each person be 'untainted' and 'clean'. Christ says in Matthew that 'you must be perfect as your heavenly father is perfect' (5:48), to which Zwingli responded:

> it is impossible, as long as we live, to be that pure. Therefore, we must at all times come to God through the one, righteous, innocent Jesus Christ, for he alone is the advocate and recompense for our sin unto eternity.[89]

The liturgy was the heart of a changed reckoning of time in Zurich. The abolition of days for celebrating saints and church feasts established a new rhythm to life and worship. In 1526, Zwingli proposed that the Lord's Supper was to be celebrated only four times a year: at Christmas, Easter, the

Annunciation and Michaelmas.[90] The Council found the reformer's proposal too severe, and permitted other religious holidays, such as Pentecost and certain days to mark biblical figures. The Reformation's reduction in the number of religious holidays was accompanied by an increased emphasis on Sundays, when all work was to cease, games were forbidden and taverns closed in order that the whole community might gather to hear the Word preached.

## CHURCH MUSIC

Singing was not to be part of worship in Zurich, unlike in the churches in Wittenberg, Strasbourg and Basel.[91] In 1523, in article 46 of his *Exposition of the Sixty-Seven Articles* Zwingli had quoted the prophet Amos, who declared: 'Take away from me the noise of your songs; to the melody of your harps I will not listen' (Amos 5:23). 'What would the rustic Amos say in our day,' asked Zwingli, 'if he saw and heard the horrors that were being performed and the mass priests mumbling at the altar . . . Indeed, he would cry out so that the whole world could not bear his words.'[92]

Yet Zwingli had a deep conviction that music had a power over the soul like no other force. Zwingli, the talented musician, believed passionately in the ability of the harmonious to transform.[93] In his commentary on the prophet Isaiah, he addressed the prophet's words that seemed to contrast musical ability with reverence for the Lord: 'They have harps and lyres at their banquets, pipes and timbrels and wine, but they have no regard for the deeds of the Lord, no respect for the work of his hands.' Such is the power of music that beauty and danger await:

> The *ratio* of no other discipline is so profoundly rooted and innate in the souls of all men as that of music. For no men are so stupid that they are not captivated by it, even though they are entirely ignorant of its technique. There are none, on the other hand, who are not offended by the confusion and discord of voices, even those who cannot explain what is dissonant and what is unsuitable. So powerful is the native talent of everyone to judge what is harmonious; on the other hand, in judging *ratio* and technique, such native talent is the property of the very few.[94]

Zwingli's views on music were so complex and ambiguous that simple judgements are ill advised. Although it was not part of his liturgical reforms, the singing of psalms was clearly attractive to Zwingli, who in December 1524 had expressed delight that the practice had been introduced in the Strasbourg Church.[95]

After his death, an apocryphal story circulated that one day Zwingli had appeared in Basel to demand that the Council abolish singing in church. Curiously, he had made his petition by singing to the magistrates, who thought he was mad. In response, he explained that their reaction confirmed his point that singing had no place before the rulers of the city. In the same way, he explained, it was ridiculous for the people to sing before God.[96] Basel did not follow Zurich, and the reformer Johannes Oecolampadius supported singing in worship, above all during the Lord's Supper, provoking a contemporary to remark: 'Husschin [Oecolampadius] upholds the singing of psalms, but Zwingli . . . cannot tolerate psalms.'[97]

Zwingli's objections to church music were grounded in polemic against what he had known as a boy and a priest, but also in a theological and devotional anxiety about the relationship between the outward forms of worship (prayer and music) and the inner contemplation of the heart, where the faithful meet God. His own music was composed for house gatherings. The style in which he set the Psalms to music was not designed for congregational praise, but spoke to trials of the individual and the refuge found in God. That tension between music for worship and for contemplation was ultimately left unresolved at his death. He wrote little on the subject, although he may have said more. The question of music reminds us of the reality of Zwingli's life, most of which was spent fighting battles determined by his opponents. Sudden death left much unresolved. Ironically, in the end his ambiguity on music created a silence that enabled his friends and successors to interpret him differently.

## PROPHETS OF THE WORD

The work of God's prophet was, for Zwingli, a collective labour. The varied gifts of the learned were to be shared and tested. Zwingli's vision was of a circle of humanists dedicated not only to education in the service of the Church, but also to providing interpretations of the Bible for the preaching of the pastors. In 1520, he had already gathered a sodality of learned men, whose principal interest lay in interpreting scripture in Greek; this group had been an engaged audience for his interpretation of the Psalms in 1521, for example.[98] Its members included several men who would later emerge as his fierce opponents: Konrad Grebel, Felix Manz and Simon Stumpf. Although the future Anabaptist Andreas Castelberger founded his own circle of readers two years later, for the most part it retained friendly relations with Zwingli's sodality.[99]

In the summer of 1525, Zwingli's nascent vision came to full fruition with the establishment of a regular meeting of a group of scholars who would undertake public interpretation of the Old Testament, working from the Hebrew, Greek and Latin. In *On the Preaching Office* of 1525, Zwingli declared the two roles of the prophet to be to resist evil and plant good, and to engage in the public exposition of scripture.[100] The *Prophezei*, as it was later named, was the visible, communal expression of Zwingli's ideal of Church and pastor – scholarship at prayer.[101] The sessions began on 19 June 1525 in the Grossmünster, with a clear order that they were to undertake a combination of study and worship. The symbolism was powerful. Gathering in the choir of Zurich's principal church, the scholars appropriated the authority of the medieval Church, replacing hierarchy with learning and prayer. The event was thoroughly ecclesiastical, in that the interpretation of the Bible belonged in the sacred space of the church, but was performed by the new priesthood.

The *Prophezei* began work at eight o'clock that first morning, turning to the opening of Genesis in Hebrew, Greek, Latin and German. The sessions then took place every day of the week except Fridays and Sundays, with the canons, city clergy and students of the Latin School required to attend. The plan was simple: to work through all the books of the Old Testament – and when finished, to start again.[102] This focus reversed the lack of regard for the Old Testament demonstrated by many radicals. Its line-by-line approach echoed the *lectio continua* style of Zwingli's preaching through the Bible. Zwingli opened each day with a prayer in Latin:[103]

O merciful God, heavenly Father! Because your Word is a candle to our feet and a light that should illuminate our way, we pray that through Christ, who is the true light of the whole world, you will open and enlighten our hearts that we should clearly and purely understand your Word and form our entire lives accordingly, that we do not displease your exulted majesty, through our Lord Jesus Christ.[104]

In *On the Preaching Office*, Zwingli argued that knowledge of Greek alone was insufficient: familiarity with Hebrew was needed to fulfil Paul's understanding of prophecy in 1 Corinthians 14:5:

Paul desires here that Christians should be knowledgeable in all tongues for the purpose of prophesying. He knows well, of course, that not everyone is well versed in tongues; but he shows how useful a thing it is for Christians to know the languages in which God's word is written, when he desires such knowledge for everyone.[105]

This rationale determined the shape of each gathering. Following the invocation, a student or Kaspar Megander, one of Zwingli's closest companions, read the appointed text in Latin, from the Vulgate.[106] The exegetical work then began with Jakob Ceporin (1499–1525) rising to read the Hebrew from the Masoretic text printed by the Christian Daniel Bomberg in Venice. A native of Zurich's rural lands, Ceporin had learned Hebrew at the feet of the great Johannes Reuchlin in Cologne.[107] Zwingli had supported Ceporin as a student, and had previously promoted his career by recommending him to the humanist circle in Basel, on account of his remarkable fluency in Latin, Greek and Hebrew; since 1522, he had himself been instructed by Ceporin in Hebrew. At the *Prophezei*, Ceporin first translated the Hebrew into Latin, before undertaking a meticulous philological interpretation. Zwingli would then do the same with the Septuagint, the divinely inspired Greek translation of the Old Testament begun in Alexandria in the third century BCE. Once the Latin, Hebrew and Greek texts had been fully examined, Zwingli would draw together and summarize the theological fruits. Clearly the principal theological voice of the Zurich Church, Zwingli turned the finely tuned philological work into doctrinal explanation. When he had finished, it fell to Leo Jud to prepare a sermon based on Zwingli's words, to be delivered in German for the faithful who had come to the Grossmünster for the final part of the session.

By November 1525, the members of the *Prophezei* had reached the end of Genesis. Eighteen months later, Zwingli's annotations on the first book of the Bible appeared from Froschauer's press. The achievement was cut short by tragedy: Jakob Ceporin fell ill and died, depriving the Zurich Church of its rising star. Perhaps with a sense of guilt, Zwingli lamented that Ceporin had been sent to an early grave, aged just 26, by the great burden of work placed on him by his colleagues. They had shared a humanist vision, having worked together on the poet Pindar, with Zwingli writing in the preface that no other Greek author understood scripture so well.[108] Looking for a prominent replacement for Ceporin, he turned to an older, more established scholar, Konrad Pellikan in Basel.[109] Pellikan, a former Franciscan, had produced the first printed Hebrew lexicon and belonged to the first generation of Hebrew scholars.[110] He had worked closely with Erasmus on his edition of the church fathers. Like others of his generation, he parted company with the Dutch humanist by embracing the Reformation, but unlike Zwingli the break was not acrimonious.

Across the River Limmat from the Grossmünster, an equivalent of the *Prophezei* for the New Testament was established at the Fraumünster, under the aegis of Oswald Myconius, schoolmaster and close friend of Zwingli. Myconius' lectures, in which he addressed the students and laity in German, took place in the afternoons. Once a week, Zwingli gave an oration in Latin on the New Testament text that Myconius was expounding.[111] In the summer of 1526, he began with interpretation of the First Epistle of John, before turning to 1 and 2 Thessalonians, Colossians, Philemon, Hebrews and 1 and 2 Corinthians, in that order.[112] Notes taken by colleagues at these sessions were published after Zwingli's death.

With the creation of the *Prophezei*, Zwingli had placed prophecy at the heart of the new Church.[113] For years, he had associated the prophetic office with the work of the Spirit in enlightening the hearts of believers who communally possessed the wisdom to discern the Word. By 1525, partially in response to his radical opponents, the reformer refined his understanding of the prophet and of his own role.[114] Prophecy became more closely associated with interpretation of the Bible in the original languages. He rejected the Anabaptist itinerant ministers, and in his *On the Preaching Office* of late June 1525 he declared that the people would be taught by educated pastors properly called and ordained by the Church. Preaching was the lifeblood of the godly community, and each person who truly proclaimed the Word was a prophet. In this prophetic role, the minister was responsible for society and was a defender of divine righteousness, standing together with the magistrate, who oversaw the laws of the state. This was the role of the ancient prophets of Israel, as restored in Zurich.

The *Prophezei* became the foundation for theological education in Zurich and for the preparation of a new generation of pastors for the Church. It was the fulfilment of Zwingli's reform of education in the service of the godly community. It was to create a new generation of prophetic ministers capable of instructing the faithful through their knowledge of the ancient languages. This would become one of Zwingli's enduring legacies, and a model copied by other communities across Europe. The *Prophezei* was also integral to the work of translating the Bible into the language of the people. The work on the Old and New Testaments during the 1520s led to the greatest creation of the Zurich Reformation: the Froschauer Bible of 1531.

The introduction of the Reformed liturgy at Easter 1525, together with the struggles over the sacraments of baptism and the Lord's Supper, led Zwingli to a vision of the community in light of the Bible.[115] By summer of that year, he had found a new vocabulary that enhanced his sense of continuity between ancient Israel and the Church. Zwingli came to think of God's relationship with humanity in terms of an eternal covenant, emerging from God's promises to the patriarchs. He had already drawn the analogy between circumcision and baptism, but here he went further. God's promise to Abraham was nothing less than Christ's sacrifice for humanity: the covenant with Abraham anticipated the new testament of the Son of God. What was promised long ago has been fulfilled. Christ is the absolute centre, who alone reconciled God and the world.

The new Christian Church and society that had taken shape was a covenanted community – a term with deep resonance in Swiss history. The summer of 1525 saw Zwingli deeply engaged with the first book of the Bible, Genesis. He preached on it and the study group he assembled in the Grossmünster went through it line by line. The sacraments that came to occupy his mind were increasingly seen as signs of the covenant, but they were not the covenant itself. They were signs of what God had done in the past and would remain for eternity. Zwingli stressed the continuity of the people of Israel with the Church of Christ. Those whom God has elected receive the law not as a source of terror – as condemning them for their sins – but as a transformative work of the Spirit that guides them to Christ.

Zwingli's Christian society was deeply rooted in memories. Gathered at the tables in the churches, the people re-enacted the Passover: they were God's chosen people delivered from the Egyptians. The bread and wine consumed by Christians had been shared by Christ with his disciples. Memory was the way to truth. Zwingli reminded his former friend Balthasar Hubmaier that

> as soon as we recognize by way of the covenant that God has made with Christian people that they are no less blessed or children of God than in the Old Testament, it follows that we should give them the sign of the covenant no less than in the Old Testament [circumcision was granted to the children of Israel].[116]

In the summer of 1525, the conviction that the Church is the covenanted body, so central to generations of Reformed Christians, found its first expression.

# SIX

# 'WE WISH TO LEARN OUT HIS OWN MOUTH WHO GOD IS'

## TRUE AND FALSE RELIGION

D uring the months leading up to the introduction of the Reformation in Zurich at Easter 1525, Zwingli prepared what would be his most comprehensive statement of his theological convictions. Addressed to French King Francis I, *Commentary on True and False Religion* was directed beyond Zurich to the wider European evangelical cause. By this point, Zwingli spoke not only to the Swiss; his writings were widely available in the German Empire, in France to the west, and south of the Alps in Italy. Circulated by traders and colporteurs who travelled into Catholic lands, his texts were read eagerly, alongside those of Luther and Erasmus.[1] It was in response to evangelical sympathizers in France and Italy, Zwingli claimed, that he had written a work in Latin that would provide a coherent account of the faith for a broader, international readership. His purpose, however, was also political: Zwingli increasingly looked to the old enemy France for support for the Reformation in the Swiss Confederation. He had high hopes of reports of Francis I's reforming sympathies as a counterweight to Habsburg hostility. Zwingli drew on his years of preaching, debating and writing, but the resulting work was strikingly original. Written in clear, elegant Latin, the *Commentary on True and False Religion* appeared off Froschauer's press in March 1525 as a relatively non-polemical work that moved systematically across the whole range of theology, from God to the Christian magistrates.

The volume was also a critical intervention in the most controversial debate of the day, which stemmed from the fierce disagreement between Erasmus and Martin Luther over freedom of the will.[2] Erasmus was clear that, although the Bible was often difficult to discern on the question of whether humans possess free will, he believed men and women were affirmed by scripture and the Church. Luther was unequivocal that fallen humanity is wholly enslaved to sin. The two titans were locked in combat, but Zwingli was also eager to enter the lists. The nature of the divine–human relationship was a dominant theme of his *Commentary on True and False Religion.*

Although the text is measured, didactic and pastoral, Zwingli wrote as ever at a frantic pace, deep in the maelstrom that was Zurich. The early months of 1525 was a troubled time. Above all, attempts to resolve the split with the Anabaptists – mainly by forcing them to accept Zwingli's theology and the will of the Council – failed entirely. The radicals could not acknowledge the Zurich magistrates as Christian and regarded Zwingli as lost.

## THE MOST CHRISTIAN KING

As Zwingli composed his *Commentary on True and False Religion,* all was far from well for its dedicatee, who was taken prisoner by his archenemy Emperor Charles V in February 1525, after the debacle of the battle of Pavia. Francis had known success in Italy, when he had captured Milan in 1515, after Marignano; and in 1516, he had made an 'eternal agreement' with the Swiss, by which they would provide him with soldiers. That same year, he had concluded with Pope Leo X the 'Bologna Concordat', which gave him his long-sought control over the appointment of bishops in the French Church. But having lost out in the imperial election of 1519, Francis engaged in a series of indecisive wars against Charles V, before his humiliating defeat at Pavia.

Zwingli's attitudes towards France and its king were not particularly consistent. He had been forced out of Glarus on account of his pro-papal sympathies and he had been called to Zurich by the anti-French party in the city. In 1521, he had supported the divided Zurich Council in rejecting the new military alliance with the kingdom. Yet, four years later, he optimistically dedicated his most significant theological work to the king. An expanding web of contacts had left Zwingli much more knowledgeable about France by 1525, and he was aware, through Heinrich Glarean, his mentor and friend, and others, of the humanist reformers favoured by Marguerite of Navarre, the king's sister. Zwingli was not looking for a military alliance, and he certainly did not wish to see Swiss soldiers fighting for the king. The sermon he preached on 5 March 1525 was fiercely critical of the mercenary service, and his finger pointed clearly at the French. When he climbed into the pulpit that day, he may well have known of Francis' fate as prisoner of the emperor.[3] Zwingli was hoping for diplomatic and religious support.

The theological architecture of the *Commentary on True and False Religion* took shape around Zwingli's doctrines of God, humanity and sacred history. History was crucial, for the urgency of the present moment could only be comprehended in terms of God's interaction with humanity from its creation. As for the ancient Israelites, so for contemporaries, the wheel of history was turning: God repeatedly enjoins to repentance men and women, who again and again have shown themselves deaf to his words. Insolence has incurred punishment and suffering, with three periods of imprisonment: first in Egypt, then in Babylon and now under the Roman Church. Repentance, however, brings hope, for it is absurd to imagine that God would abandon his own creation, as if a mother would forget her child.[4]

The world is an unjust place where God is neglected. Zwingli condemned not only princes and rulers, but also every part of the Church – from bishops to monks and nuns, reflecting his hatred of the religious orders. Bishops were 'wolves', the mendicants begged without shame, and the nuns had only disdain for the people; meanwhile monasteries, for which he reserved particular contempt, were nothing more than brothels. Yet although the lay people had suffered at the hands of the greedy and predatory clergy, they were not innocent victims. They drank, fornicated and flouted God's Word no less than the wretched clerics: the whole of society stood under divine judgement. Zwingli addressed the three estates (princes, clergy and the people), but his primary interest lay with the princes and the people. The clerical estate was beyond saving.

Christ will return in judgement, that is certain; but Zwingli's eyes, unlike Martin Luther's, were not fixed on that final day. Divine judgement was now. That had been his constant reminder to his fellow Swiss over their loss of virtue: 'Who can fail to see that the day of the Lord is at hand? Not that day on which the Lord will judge the whole world, but the day on which He is to correct the present condition of things.'[5] The prophet Amos had said that the lion will roar and all will be terrified, crying out: 'I will hear what the Lord God has to say to me.' The long-neglected gospel has been restored, as Deuteronomy had once been restored to the Jews, 'to cleanse the foulness of sin'. God has provided for the amendment of life before his rod falls.[6]

Zwingli established his prophetic calling, and it was personal:

> I too saw that the world overflows with the most iniquitous wars and the fiercest battles and is defiled and unsettled with rapine assault, theft and robbery. I too put my hand to the plough [Luke 9:62] and raised my voice so loudly that greedy Rome and the idol worshipped there did hear, even though its hide is very thick.[7]

The man who had been to northern Italy with troops from Glarus, had tended to the maimed and dying, and had witnessed in Zurich the public wealth of those grown rich on foreign pensions did not seek to conceal his ire. It had been given to him to speak God's words of repentance and judgement. His prophetic calling had brought him before the French king.

Francis should permit the Word of God to be heard in his lands. A major step in this direction would be to silence his scholastic theologians, who knew nothing of the biblical languages, who 'prophesy for hire and worship the belly as their only God, which has forced me and not a few others much against our will to maintain our cause with pen as well as tongue'.[8] The philosophers were even worse, for they had no clue or understanding of what Aristotle had actually written. 'So barbarous is all that they teach, so lifeless, that you would sooner think they were telling dreams than expounding philosophy'.[9] The ancient Greek god of silence, Harpocrates, was to be invoked against those men who 'blab out against Christ whatever comes into their heads'.

But the king had at his disposal 'a greater class of men', learned in languages and possessing 'simplicity of character and holiness of life'.[10] Zwingli was referring to the circle of humanists in Paris, gathered around the king's sister, Marguerite of Navarre:

> This class do you cherish, and hold nothing so valuable as these men. Nor only keep them about yourself, save a few to confer with on sacred things, but assign them posts through the length and breadth of your kingdom in which to fix not upon pillars but in men's hearts the new commands of Christ.[11]

Unlike the hated Charles V, the king of France, Zwingli hoped, might raise up true reform.

## COMPANIONS IN FAITH

Zwingli claimed that people 'on the other side of the Alps' had appealed to him. This casual and rather oblique remark conceals a great deal. By early 1525 he had an extensive network of correspondents and personal connections that extended across France, but that was found particularly in the Dauphiné and Provence and included some of the most prominent humanists of the day.[12] These notable figures included those to whom he referred when reminding Francis of 'a greater class of men'. His mentor and friend Glarean had gone to Paris in 1517 and had moved among the leading lights of the French Renaissance. Teaching in Paris, Glarean was able to provide valuable information on the religious climate in France. In 1520, he reported that Luther's books were the subject of intense discussion, far more so than any other publications.[13]

One strange twist to Zwingli's relations with the French was the rumour that he had actually travelled to the kingdom in 1524.[14] A man claimed to have witnessed Zwingli preach about his time in Paris.[15] He may, however, simply have misheard or misunderstood, for Heinrich Bullinger, who was well informed about the preacher's life, denied the suggestion.[16]

Numerous French clerics and noblemen did visit Zurich as they travelled through Swiss lands. François Lambert, a Franciscan monk who had studied the works of Luther and travelled to Wittenberg, arrived in Zurich in 1522 and debated with Zwingli on religious images.[17] The nobleman Antoine du Blet also came to Zurich and carried one of the reformer's letters to men in Lyon who moved in the innermost court circles and knew both Francis' mother, Louise of Savoy, and his sister Marguerite.[18] These sympathizers had suggested that Zwingli dedicate his *Commentary on True and False Religion* to Louise of Savoy.[19]

Perhaps the most notable humanist connection was the great Jacques Lefèvre d'Étaples (1455–1536), renowned for his work on the Psalms and his translation of and commentary on the four Gospels. He had sent greetings to Zwingli via a 1519 letter to Glarean.[20] His commentary on the Psalms had influenced Zwingli as a young priest, shaping his approach to interpreting the Bible. From 1521, d'Étaples was a central figure among the circle of reformers in the diocese of Meaux under Bishop Briçonnet. Zwingli had contact with a number of the Meaux circle, including Guillaume Farel and Gérard Roussel, to whom Farel had given some of Zwingli's works and who openly praised the Zurich reformer.

Guillaume Farel, who would become John Calvin's friend and colleague in Geneva, had visited Zwingli in early 1524, and the two men discussed the development of the evangelical faith in France.[21] Although Zwingli knew no French and Farel no German, they were easily able to communicate in Latin. They struck up an enduring friendship, and Farel was not only an essential source of information, but also did much to spread Zwingli's ideas in the kingdom, bringing with him Zwingli's *Exposition*. Before going to Zurich, Farel had been a guest of Oecolampadius in Basel. He was expelled from that city in 1524 for his vociferous evangelism. Zurich and Basel had a deep influence on his thinking.[22]

Zwingli's Italian contacts are somewhat harder to trace, but are equally intriguing. In December 1525, after the appearance of his *Commentary on True and False Religion*, Zwingli received a letter from a former Augustinian monk in Como named Aegidius a Porta, in which the sender described his lamentable life in a monastery, where he had preached without 'knowledge of Christ'.[23] God had not allowed him to be lost, however, and spoke to him in a dream, saying 'go to Huldrych Zwingli and he himself will instruct you as to what you ought to do'. A Porta expressed a desire to go with some brothers to Zurich to learn true doctrine, although he confessed that he knew neither Hebrew nor Greek, and that his Latin was poor. Zwingli evidently replied in a now-lost letter, for a year later the Augustinian wrote once more, expressing his gratitude for the kind words.[24]

Catholics, including Erasmus, had only disdain for Zwingli's *Commentary on True and False Religion*. Writing in May 1525, Glarean – once Zwingli's mentor and friend, but who had rejected the reforms in Zurich – opined: 'On all sides the most learned people wish the Swiss the best, while the Swiss themselves gnash their teeth on account of Zwingli.'[25] From Luther there was no response. The text, which made no reference to the Wittenberg reformer, appeared as the storm clouds of the Eucharistic debate were gathering. In the autumn of 1524, Luther's archenemy Karlstadt had published a series of tracts on the Lord's Supper which Zwingli and Oecolampadius had openly praised, giving Luther good cause to lump the three men together as 'fanatics'.

## TRUE RELIGION

In his *Commentary on True and False Religion*, Zwingli followed Erasmus in baptizing *religio* in antiquity as the 'whole piety of Christians', encompassing faith, life, laws, worship and the sacraments. 'Religion' concerns not only a cultic function, but also the nature of God's relationship to humanity and the proper response.[26] God alone is the initiator. After the fall, there would have been no religion if God had not reached out to humanity. Adam, who had fled from God's presence, would never have become 'religious' had it not been for God's summons, 'Adam, where are you?' 'Here,' wrote Zwingli, 'we see more clearly than day the origin of religion. It took its rise when God called a runaway man back to Himself, when otherwise he would have been a deserter forever.'[27] Religion did not spring from any natural act of humanity: God in his pleasure granted knowledge of his love and desire for relationship.

The key was 'piety', a term Zwingli took from Cicero and made synonymous with true religion. Our sense of the word retains little of its potent classical meaning. Piety was not mere sentiment, but the fullness of the Christian life, a disposition of the whole self towards God.[28] Erasmus had declared piety the goal of Christian education, but it was neither mere knowledge nor a manner of behaviour. Zwingli concurred: beyond intellectual assent, piety does more than assert the existence of one God, for even the pagans did that. It is a persuasion by which a person 'holds' to God with the gift of faith. In the world, the pious and impious cannot be easily distinguished, because that faith is an invisible matter of the heart. The righteous and reprobate are separated by the wisdom granted the elect before the moment of creation. All men and women can hear the Word proclaimed, but only those with faith respond:

It is manifest that the faithful believe that God exists, and that the world is His work, etc., just because they are taught this by God. It is from God alone, therefore, that you believe that God exists and that you have faith in him.[29]

In contrast to what he saw as the error of his radical opponents, Zwingli rejected the interpretation of piety as moral perfection. Although they respond in faith, the elect remain fallen, fully aware of their 'sinfulness, disobedience, treason and wretchedness'. Without grace, such awareness would lead only to despair; but God, as creator and father, in his goodness and bounty, rescues his chosen from this wretched state. The life of the faithful, therefore, is a continuous struggle, in which one must 'cling to God' as a drowning man holds to a plank of wood.

Zwingli associated piety with hearing and holding, and throughout the *Commentary on True and False Religion* sought to convey the 'unshaken truth' that God alone can turn the believer from destruction to service and joy. Piety is religion. It is 'an eagerness to live according to the will of God, just as, likewise, perfect devotion between parents and children requires that the son shall study to obey the father as much as the father seeks to benefit the son'.[30] True religion of Christ consists in despairing of self and in resting in the confidence of God. The pious sing out that God denies them nothing, for 'the Lord is mercy in exceeding abundance'.[31]

## GOD

Zwingli offered a succinct statement of his theological vision:

> From the foundation of the world God has manifested Himself in various ways to the human race that we might recognize Him as Father and Dispenser of all things. The first thing, therefore, in piety is that we should firmly believe that He whom we confess as our God is God, the Source and Father of all things; for unless we do so, we shall never obey His laws. The next thing is that we should know ourselves, for when we have not knowledge of ourselves also, we accept no law.[32]

But who is that God? And what can be known of him? In a sense, both very little and a great deal. God is inscrutable, in that nothing can be known of his decrees. He has revealed himself through his benevolent providence, and that, through faith, is knowable. Zwingli followed Erasmus' distaste for scholastic explorations of God's being or essence, although Duns Scotus' conception of the majesty and power of God remained imprinted on the Zurich reformer.[33] Human knowledge has been strictly circumscribed. What one is able to know is limited to what God has chosen to reveal, and that is in scripture. Employing Paul's words from Romans, knowledge of the divine 'depends not on human will or exertion, but on God who shows mercy' (9:16).

Human reason might be dismissed as irrelevant in the face of the divine, but Zwingli was not prepared to go down that path, and took particular interest in philosophy, above all the place of the great thinkers of the ancient world:

> It will perhaps not be inconsistent with my purpose to introduce here, as a sort of imported embellishment, the opinion of a most learned and eloquent man – I mean Cicero – as given in the oration in defence of Archias, in which the passage showing that man does everything from a desire for glory agrees so completely with the divine teachings that the words seem due to the direct influence of God, rather than to the unconstrained utterance of Cicero, a creature of glory.[34]

God speaks through the ancient philosophers, and their wisdom was to be heeded, but not uncritically. Zwingli did not refrain from judging harshly Cicero's call to glory as the supreme example of self-love and lust for personal glory, a folly exemplified by Julius Caesar. In contrast, love of human virtue and honour was to be found in his beloved Plato.[35] But among non-Christian authors, by which Zwingli meant the Greek and Roman, a certain God-given sense of purity existed. The philosophers had affirmed God's existence, while remaining blind to his being and attributes. The ancients knew that God was the greatest good (*summum bonum*) and that the world was governed by providence.

God alone is being and goodness, a truth revealed to Moses in the words 'I am who I am.'[36] No one has seen God, but what we know of him is no more or less than what he intends us to know. Zwingli was interested not in speculation about the nature of God's attributes, but in the knowledge that God is good – indeed that he is goodness itself.

The goodness of God informed every aspect of Zwingli's convictions, leading to his core belief that God governs the world benevolently.[37] The

*Commentary on True and False Religion* cast in sharp relief Zwingli's deep sense of divine providence, that God rules the world without chance or fortune, but through his will, which is good. That is what Christians must know, accept and commit themselves to through the vicissitudes of life. Zwingli told his 'dear reader' that the whole business of predestination, free will and merit rests upon this matter of providence, offering a hymn of praise to the God who governed all things:

> it must be, therefore, that this supreme good, which is God, is by its nature kind and bountiful . . . with a bounty that causes him to desire the profit of those to whom he gives with only this one thing in view. For he desires to impart himself freely.[38]

All things have been created to one end: that they might enjoy their creator.

What *is* given to know should fill humanity with awe and humility, and not idle curiosity that attempts to peer behind the divine curtain.[39] Referring to Psalm 104, Zwingli found an image for God's overwhelming sovereignty in the Alps of his youth:

> David portrays both the wisdom and providence of God so that you see God as creator balancing the mountains in his mighty hand, putting each in its place, drawing out the valleys between them and the cool streams in the valleys, spreading out the fields . . . then assigning settlers to each region and adding abundant provisions.[40]

Knowledge of God is only in and through Christ. We know God as Father through the incarnation of Christ. Zwingli was always at pains to stress the continuity of God throughout the history of his relationship with humanity. Christ's incarnation was not a second revelation or a jarring new divine initiative, but rather the fulfilment of what God had already revealed. God had entered human history for a period of time during the earthly life of Christ to reveal fully what had been made partially manifest in the Old Testament. The incarnation reveals God and his righteousness more completely, enabling humanity to know God as the merciful creator who cares for his people, and as the source of all trust. Where Luther stressed the difficulty of faith, Zwingli wrote of its lightness and certainty. For those to whom it is granted, faith is a work of the Spirit brought forth in the deeds of God's people in the world. For Zwingli, nothing could be clearer, nothing more fully evident.[41]

Following Erasmus, Zwingli understood reformation as the rebirth of Christianity, or, more directly, as the rebirth of Christ. Christ himself has led the restoration of the Word as the 'captain' or 'leader'. The title of 'captain' was central to Zwingli's Christology.[42] The Zurich reformer was speaking a language of Christ that the people in a militarized Swiss culture could readily grasp. This emphasis on Christ as leader was an excellent rhetorical move, rendering Christ as the man who had come to change the world, to reorder it according to God's will.[43] The authority of the son extended to all areas of human life, not just to the Church. The Son was the fearless leader who sacrificed himself for his followers. He was a hero. Zwingli gave Christ the title of Jupiter as *'optimus maximus'*,[44] the greatest leader the world had known. In pathetic contrast, the pope did not die for humanity.

Yet Zwingli's repeated emphasis on the human Christ as the obedient son who offered a model for how the faithful should live was never intended to diminish his salvific role.[45] Only Christ could guarantee the gift of God's mercy and assuage the troubled conscience.[46] His life offered humanity three precious gifts: reconciliation, the model of Christian living and the guarantee of God's mercy. Whereas Luther pointed the faithful to the theology of the cross, Zwingli's inclination was for the dynamic figure of the living Christ.

Although Zwingli's early thought was not deeply concerned with the doctrine of election, he was clear that God predestined his chosen in Christ to eternal life.[47] According to God's pleasure and will, hidden from all humans, the election of some and not others was decreed before the moment of creation. Predestination therefore preceded faith, as only those whom God chose would come to believe. Zwingli did not treat election at any length in his *Commentary on True and False Religion*, paying a great deal more attention to God's providence, which he called the 'mother of predestination'. Predestination, he wrote,

> which is only another word for foreordination, is born of providence, rather is providence (for even the theologians distinguish providence from wisdom in that the former proceeds to act and to dispose, while the

latter simply sees what should be done and how). For it would be incongruous for the Supreme Good to know all things before they took place and not to be able to dispose and to order all things . . . By the providence of God, therefore, are taken away together free will and merit.[48]

From 1526, largely in response to the Anabaptists, Zwingli began to speak more directly about election, a term he preferred to predestination.[49]

## FAITH

In his *Commentary on True and False Religion*, Zwingli sought to frame theology in terms of pastoral comfort: 'Faith leans upon one God, clings to one, trusts in one, flies to one for refuge, knows for certain it will find with that one all that it needs.'[50] There is certainty: 'we know that no one can be saved unless he is in Christ. We judge that no one can be grafted into Christ without faith.'[51] That faith is a fruit of divine election. In the *Commentary*, Zwingli reflected on Paul's words to the Romans that a remnant would be saved by grace: 'And if by grace, then it cannot be based on works. If it were, grace would no longer be grace.'

The elect hear the Word of God in preaching that empowers them to trust God and reform their lives. Zwingli made a distinction between forms of faith, identifying that which is possessed by the elect from the moment of creation (a form of prior faith) and that which bears fruit during their regenerate lives in the Spirit. In other words, the elect do not simply receive faith at a particular moment in their lives, transforming them from unbelievers into believers; they have been elected in Christ and possess faith from the very beginning. That faith may not come to fruition until later in life, but it was always present. It precedes any knowledge that the elect will develop of God or of themselves, which follows only once the seed of faith has germinated. Zwingli saw faith in three distinct, but related phases: the inner gift of faith given to the elect; the fruitful knowledge of God and self that faith engenders; and finally, the creation of a new humanity through faith, in which the person lives only for God and neighbour.[52]

The elect bring into the world an inner faith that will eventually bloom into knowledge and piety. The Spirit is encountered in the outward forms of religion, including scripture and preaching, as well as the sacraments. These external forms cannot provide faith, but are the means by which the Spirit leads God's chosen. As we shall see in the next chapter, neither baptism nor the Lord's Supper can generate or convey faith; they are symbols of what God has done in Christ, marks of his eternal promises. In a process of self-realization, the inner and outer are brought into harmony. The preaching of the Word confirms what is already present in the heart. The Christian receives faith as an inner working of God in the person, who knows that external things contribute nothing to salvation.[53] External threats, such as persecution, horrific as they are, cannot destroy faith. Faith brings security, certainty and assurance, as it arises from no created thing and cannot find aid or sustenance from the fleshly or material.

What, then, is the purpose of the life of faith? When God speaks, humans are called out of the ruck of the quotidian to know that their God is holy and demands holiness. A Christian, wrote Zwingli,

> is a man who trusts in the one true and only God; who relies upon His mercy through His Son Christ, God of God; who models himself upon His example; who dies daily [cf. I Cor. 15:31]; who daily renounces self; who is intent upon this one thing, not to do anything that can offend his God.[54]

At the centre of life stands Christ, who freed the elect from sin and provided the model for the redeemed life marked by blameless living. In extolling Christ, Zwingli turned to his favourite bywords: watchfulness, diligence and zeal. Christ's entry into the world relieved the anxiety of a Christian

> by bringing hope and an example of the godly life: when we are so terrified by the righteousness of Him to whom we are hastening and by our consciences that are driving us headlong to despair, Christ, the Son of God, comes to help our distress.[55]

Zwingli held together the bond of Christ with the Christian life, a relationship that consists of faith, righteousness, blamelessness and mercy.[56]

This promise was delivered in the keys Christ gave to his disciples, to all who acknowledge Jesus to be the Son of God, and not to Peter alone. The

Christian pastor was to proclaim this good news, but first believe it himself. 'Behold the grandeur of the Christian shepherd!' Zwingli cried. 'He feeds the flock with painstaking watchfulness, and does not constrain except as far as the Word itself constrains.'[57] The binding and loosing of which Christ spoke to his disciples had nothing to do with ecclesiastical authority: it was about relieving consciences once burdened by condemnation before the law. 'To loose, therefore, is nothing else than to raise to sure hope the heart that despairs of salvation. To bind is to abandon the obstinate heart.'[58]

The Church 'is a congregation, an assembly, the whole people, the whole multitude gathered together' and, Zwingli insists, 'nowhere in scripture do we find the Church of Christ or of God to mean a few bishops or rather mumblers.'[59] In its visible form, the Church for Zwingli is the local parish or urban church attended by all members of the community; the invisible Church is the gathering of the elect, who in their faith are united with all generations of believers. Zwingli addressed the visible Church in his evocation of the Christian life, marked by true piety in which men and women imitated the example of Christ.

## THE FREED CONSCIENCE

The justified Christian possesses a free conscience, brought by Christ and realized through the presence of the Holy Spirit. Referencing the Gospel of John – 'So if the Son makes you free, you will be free indeed' (8:36) – Zwingli wrote that Christian doctrine is nothing other than freedom of the conscience. For the conscience to be imprisoned would mean not simply that it is weighed down by a bad deed or a harmful word, but that the whole person is oppressed and enslaved. Good works cannot in any way assuage the conscience. Freedom comes only in the form of liberation from self-absorption and self-love, an awareness of the brokenness of life and an acceptance of God's forgiveness and embrace. The bound conscience is the seat of anguish and unbearable anxiety, and the place where God's saving and transformative action takes effect.[60] Right from the beginning and the sausage meal, the conscience lay at the heart of Zwingli's reformation. It was, in the end, freedom from oppressive rules arbitrarily set by the Roman Church.

The redeemed life has an order. God's illumination leads to the sinner's self-awareness of their condition, which engenders doubt, a limbo between despair and God's fearful righteousness. This path progresses to the vision of Christ and complete trust in Him, and to transformation into a new life marked by repentance and unity in Christ: 'The whole of the Christian life is penance.'[61] Zwingli's account of the tormented conscience was not far from Martin Luther's. They are distinguished, however, by Luther's insistence that what remained for the Christian was a powerful sense of darkness – perhaps accounting for his severe battles with depression – while Zwingli viewed the liberation of the conscience as movement into a wholly changed way of living.[62]

Trust manifests itself in love and works of love, although Zwingli frequently acknowledged that non-believers could seem to act virtuously, and he was unwilling to identify good works as signs of election. He was not eager to distinguish between Paul's virtues of faith, hope and love. Rather, he saw them as absolutely interchangeable:

> Whoever does not understand that faith, hope and love are the same, that is trust in God, for that person the knots of scripture will never be loosed . . . The whole trust that a human heart has for God is sometimes faith, sometimes hope and sometimes love. Whether you love, hope or believe, it is a pious emotion that is directed to God.[63]

Because God is love, those who trust in him live in love, for love of God and of neighbour remain inseparable. Liberation of the conscience is the freedom to love one another, echoing Luther's words in his *Freedom of a Christian* (1520).

The liberated Christian experiences joy, Zwingli's most cherished emotion. He once more invoked the spiritual gift of eating. The spiritual and material worlds are enfolded into one another: the faithful are fed and grow; their bodies conforming to the image of Christ:

> For as the starving stomach rejoices when food comes into it, wherewith the used-up breath and heat and strength are replenished, so the starving soul, when God discloses Himself to it, leaps for joy and daily grows and increases in strength more and more, being transformed into the likeness of God until it develops into the perfect man. It is,

therefore, spiritual food of which I am speaking, for only the Spirit gives it, since the Spirit alone draws the heart to itself and refreshes it.[64]

No contemporary reformer spoke so frequently and fervently about the joy of a Christian.[65] Certainty, a peaceful conscience, and safety from anxiety and doubt – these constituted the freedom sealed by God's Spirit, a liberation that in Zwingli's mind was inseparable from joy:

> For when our consciences are labouring amid the narrows and cliffs of despair, what tidings more joyful can be brought us than that there is at hand a Redeemer who will 'bring us forth into a broad place' [Psalm 18:19] and a deliverer and leader who can do all things, for he is God?[66]

Joy is first and foremost the work of the Holy Spirit. Zwingli enthused that Christ had said, 'who trusts in me is already saved, for he felt within himself as soon as he set all his trust on me how joyful his conscience became, how his soul was raised from despair to the sure possession of salvation.'[67] The heart becomes a musical instrument, Zwingli wrote in his commentary on Psalm 150, where David sings: 'Praise him with trumpet sound; praise him with lute and harp! Praise him with timbral and dance; praise him with strings and pipe!' The joy of the Christian life is a foretaste of heaven.

The freedom of the conscience and the joy of the Christian life were not licence to indulgence or disorder. As Zwingli preached from Jeremiah, 'Freedom is with virtue and with all righteousness, not that one can do whatever he will. Freedom is that by which one plants virtue in young and old people, uproots vice and punishes it.'[68] One is not free to give offence, harm a neighbour or create scandal. Freedom leads to the strengthening of the community, not its undermining. However righteous a cause, hatred can never be the root of religious, social or political action, which must be based instead on love of God and other. That objection to impulsive action was evident in Zwingli's opposition to violence against priests and monks and iconoclasm. Similarly, freedom is not permission to carry on with gaming, drinking, violence and love of wealth; it is not freedom from the laws, but a joyful fulfilment of them.

In many respects, Zwingli's thought did not lend itself well to system and organization. Like his beloved Pindar and Homer, he was a poet, a man with a heightened sense of the meeting of the divine and the human. The *Commentary on True and False Religion* bursts through its intellectual structures as Zwingli weaves back and forth between topics, eager to reinforce his deepest convictions: the providential God is good and seeks the salvation of his people; God governs the world with a benevolent providence; the created world is the manifestation of divine goodness and beauty; and humans are called to lives of piety, the fulfilment of having been created in the image of God. Zwingli was an astute and learned theologian, but at heart he was the preacher seeking to persuade, cajole and comfort. John Calvin would later speak of the created world as the 'theatre of God's glory', but the concept came from Zwingli, who found expression of divine goodness in the mountains, valleys and verdant fields. Zwingli gifted to Reformed Christianity its sense of anticipation, of becoming a new self, a new society. He would continue to preach and write feverishly, and usually in the fires of polemic; but in the spring of 1525, he provided the first full vision of his new form of Christianity.

# SEVEN

# BROKEN BODY

## ZWINGLI AND LUTHER

Huldrych Zwingli's relationship with Martin Luther is a story of many parts.[1] Since the nineteenth century, narratives of their antagonism have been freighted with issues of identity and confessional pride. The laser-like German focus on the person and thought of Martin Luther could only assume that Zwingli had in some form derived his theology from the Wittenberg doctor. Such an unquestioned article of faith naturally rankled with Swiss sensibilities, particularly in an age of patriotic, especially Protestant, pride. In reply, they insisted on Zwingli's independence. As we shall see, many nineteenth-century historians of the Reformation were fascinated by comparisons of the two men in thought and character, often finding in Luther the mystical monk and in Zwingli the social, communal reformer. Indisputably, the Wittenberger has remained the pre-eminent figure in the triumphal narrative of Protestantism's victory over a corrupt medieval Church. Zwingli was at best Batman's Robin. At worst, the Joker.

If we leave behind old narratives of Luther and Zwingli as the clash of the titans, it is to acknowledge that the story was more complex, involving a much larger cast of characters whose convictions and hopes were not one. Certainly, the dispute over the Lord's Supper tore the curtain of the Reformation, but that alone was not the tragedy. The Reformation had never enjoyed an arcadian age of peace and unity. As Luther had predicted, the renewal of the Word brought tumult and conflict. When Luther returned to Wittenberg after his time in the Wartburg castle, he found churches vandalized by followers who were convinced that they had faithfully followed his words. In Zurich, once-close friends felt deeply betrayed by Zwingli on several fronts, and by early 1525 some were baptizing one another against the will of the magistrates and the reformer. Zwingli's godly community had no place for them, and the response was banishment. The catastrophe of the Peasants' War threw a harsh light on the disharmony among the evangelicals, their discordant voices offering plenty of grist for Catholic mills. The house of the heretics was divided.

Optimistic, liberal and ecumenical-minded views of the Reformation that arose in the nineteenth century and retain their force cannot paper over the real differences between Luther and Zwingli. Their paths diverged intellectually, spiritually and existentially, although they shared a foundational conviction that the Word of God alone is authoritative and that men and women are saved by faith in Christ. Both had rejected the papacy and the Roman Church, abhorred the Anabaptists and held to the authority of temporal rulers in matters of religion. Christ had instituted two, not seven, sacraments. It is misleading to find some Manichean divide between the two men: their words often expressed unity of emphasis and expression.

Their story was not simply theological, but all too human. Zwingli and Luther did not have the personal relationship they had experienced with many others who became bitter opponents. They never corresponded, communicating only through their tracts and colleagues, and they possessed remarkably little knowledge or understanding of each other. Zwingli's grasp of affairs in the German lands was partial, tendentious and often determined by religious aspirations. Luther, in turn, knew little about the Swiss nation – and cared even less. The polemic and politics of the age, with doctrinal statements often forged in the heat of battle, can tempt us into essentializing differences, believing there were only polarities. We forget that Zwingli and Luther lived and worked within friendship networks that extended across the German-speaking lands, from Saxony to Strasbourg to Basel and Bern, where committed reformers such as Philipp Melanchthon, Martin Bucer and Johannes Oecolampadius crafted theological arguments that moderated, tempered and nuanced the debates.

## HERO TO FOE

Without question, Zwingli was influenced by both Luther's thought and his life story, but that reality does little justice to his formation as a reformer.[2]

The Wittenberg professor had no singular influence on the Swiss priest, whose distinctive spiritual vision arose from a scholastic education, the model of Erasmus and years of reading the church fathers, and was influenced by contemporaries such as Melanchthon and Oecolampadius, alongside Luther. To this, naturally, we must add his Swiss culture, artistic gifts and charismatic nature. Until at least 1522, Zwingli regarded Erasmus as the leading theologian and the scholar who had opened his eyes to the possibilities of a renewed Christianity. His stay at Einsiedeln, as we have seen, offered the priest an extraordinary library and time to study the church fathers, notably Augustine and Jerome, whose influence on his conception of God's justification through faith was pivotal.

Zwingli was certainly aware of Luther by the end of 1518, although he may have known of the indulgence controversy before that.[3] By 1519, he was clearly well informed about the rising tide in Germany, as the humanist epistolary network in which he was active buzzed with news, rumours and prognostications. Luther's works were printed in Basel and soon arrived in Zurich. Zwingli actively encouraged early reading circles in the city to take up Luther, emphasizing that the two men spoke in the same tones. Luther was for Zwingli proof that his own convictions about the Bible were neither isolated nor eccentric. Beatus Rhenanus, humanist friend of Erasmus, enthused to the Zurich priest that soon Luther's works should be in every Swiss household.[4] In June 1519, Zwingli wrote back that he had no fear that Luther's writing on the Lord's Prayer would not please him, adding that many copies should be purchased, particularly if the German wrote against the veneration of saints. Zwingli claimed that he had already forbidden the invocation of the blessed, and that it would be good to have a second, supportive voice, as the people were so attached to the practice.[5] Several days later, he ordered a large number of Luther's works from printers in Basel.[6]

In February 1520, Zwingli reported that Johannes Fabri, vicar general of the diocese of Constance, had been in Zurich and had encouraged him to write against Luther, which he politely declined to do.[7] An early shared concern was the vexed issue of the tithe, which Zwingli had initially declared to be without scriptural warrant. Kaspar Hedio in Strasbourg, who had procured a Luther book for Zwingli, wrote: 'you will find everything here about interest and tithes'.[8] In July 1520, the Zurich priest maintained to Myconius that he had read almost nothing by Luther – although following the 1520 condemnation of the German by the scholastic theological faculties at Louvain and Cologne, he was certainly aware of the sharp reply from Wittenberg.[9] Although it is difficult to prove, there is good reason to believe that Zwingli was reading as much Luther as he could get his hands on.

## MARTIN LUTHER THROUGH ZWINGLI'S EYES

In a rare autobiographical passage in his 1523 *Exposition of the Sixty-Seven Articles*, Zwingli retold the story of his conversion in 1516 to an Erasmian view of Christ and the gospel. His account runs to his arrival in Zurich and the beginning of his preaching in January 1519, which led to accusations that he was a 'Lutheran'. Zwingli had good reason to fear that appellation following the 1521 Edict of Worms that made Luther an outlaw. By 1523, he was still eager to claim that his enthusiasm for the Wittenberger should not make him known as a 'Lutheran', and he was eager to put some distance between them. Acknowledging Luther's decisive role in the restoration of the gospel, as a 'fearless warrior and servant of Christ', Zwingli sought to dispel any notion that the term 'Lutheran' covered anyone preaching the gospel. Ask, he continued, not whether someone is a 'Lutheran', but whether he is a Christian, 'an untiring worker towards God and people'.[10] As to Luther's influence, Zwingli was clear that it far exceeded his own, for 'through him [Luther] a far greater number of people are led to God than through me and others (whose measure God increases and diminishes as he pleases)'.[11]

Zwingli was adamant that he had never been in contact with Luther, and that they had never corresponded, although the Zurich preacher did make oblique reference to having been accused of writing letters in the name of the Wittenberg professor.[12] His purpose in maintaining a distance, Zwingli claimed, arose not out of fear of Luther, but rather to demonstrate that their similarities were the work of the Holy Spirit, which had delivered the same message through two men separated by geography and dialect. The very fact that he and Luther had preached the gospel in harmony demonstrated the verity of their calling. They were 'of one voice in teaching the doctrines of Christ without prior consultation'. Nevertheless, Zwingli made no claim to equality, and he continued to speak of Luther's lofty status: 'I am not to be compared to him,' he wrote, 'for everyone does what God directs him to do.'[13]

Matters had certainly been turned on their head within a few years. By 1527, as we shall see, the well had been poisoned by conflict over the Lord's Supper. Luther was no longer a hero, but the divider of the Church, who violated the unity of the gospel by hurling at the Swiss accusations of heresy and apostasy. Zwingli stressed how he and his colleagues had borne the assault with good will and faithfulness. The German, he noted sarcastically, would not be so 'stubborn' and 'implacable' if he had actually read what was sent to him by others. At the same time, Zwingli would not step back from a fight. Indeed, he asserted that in all their 'skirmishes' he had emerged as victor. 'For so far as I understand your position,' Zwingli addressed Luther, 'you seem to be wholly ignorant of my arguments. For those which I have brought forward are enough to demolish without any trouble, begging your pardon, all that you offer to the contrary.'[14] If Luther had intentionally not read Zwingli's work, then he could only be considered a 'deceiver of the people'.

Zwingli did not relent, pointing to Luther's reputation for having a fiery temperament. You, he told Luther, speak in the 'heat of your anger' against others, while failing to show 'good and innocent men the consideration that was due to them and worthy of yourself'.[15] In a remark likely to have enraged Luther, Zwingli advised the German reformer to remain calm and consider how 'men of piety' have refuted error without passion:

> Everyone knows how much violence has been done to the Church by greed and ambition, by guilt and hypocrisy, and are we to fancy that no harm will arise from hatred, jealousy, contention, rivalry and even bitterness, anger and impulsiveness? Are these not passions? Yes, they are fiercer ones than the others. There is no cause, then, to boast greatly of the Spirit, if we are overborne by these. Let bygones be bygones, then, and let us begin our exchange in a pleasant and light-hearted mood.[16]

Mapping the development of relations between Zwingli and Luther is challenging, for virtually all of the Zurich reformer's accounts appear later, and are coloured by their bitter feud. Zwingli clearly had a keen interest in Luther, but it was not reciprocated until the Swiss had emerged as one of the 'fanatics' – even the chief devil – who corrupted Christ's words. Luther never had anything positive to say about Zwingli.

## THE FLESH PROFITS NOTHING

The debate with Luther was never limited to the question of real presence in the Lord's Supper. The broader picture was Zwingli's interpretation of the Bible and his vision of the Christian community. His 1525 liturgy had emphasized the simplicity of the common meal, with the minister among the people, not at some distant altar. The bread and wine were taken in remembrance of the Passover meal that Jesus shared with his disciples. At heart was an unshakeable conviction that Christ could not be physically present in the bread and wine of the meal. For Zwingli, Oecolampadius and their colleagues, after his resurrection the Son ascended to the right hand of the Father, as the creeds of the Church declared. Nothing Zwingli said or wrote was more controversial, with its rejection of any physical presence of Christ, or would have such enduring influence on the history of Protestantism. He had declared the mass, the very heart of medieval worship, to be an idolatrous fabrication, in which the priest at the altar supposedly repeated Christ's sacrifice. For Zwingli, that abomination implied that the crucifixion, a once-performed act, was insufficient and required repetition in human hands. The medieval Church, in Zwingli's view, had diminished the saving work of Christ and arrogated to itself what belonged only to God.

In recasting Christ's own words 'this is my body' and 'this is my blood', Zwingli's view lacked any clear precedent. The bread and wine remained unchanged in their properties: they were symbols of the faith by which the people were transformed, lifted out of their locality by the Spirit to become the body of Christ. Zwingli emphasized the metamorphosis of the faithful, not the elements. This claim undermined not only the theology of the West, but also the devotional practices of the people, most of whom rarely received the wafer, but fell on their knees when it was consecrated in the hands of the priest. The presence of Christ in churches small and great was venerated in the host, visible to the faithful. The late-medieval world had produced the most elaborate and beautiful monstrances to display Christ's physical presence.[17] The streets of cities and towns were made sacred spaces by Corpus Christi processions.

Whatever the accusations of his opponents, Zwingli's intention was not to denigrate the sacrament, but to reclaim its place at the heart of worship. The bread and wine feed only those who believe; in 1523 he wrote:

> For the body and blood of Christ is none other than the word of faith. His body is given for us and his blood shed for us that we are redeemed and reconciled to God. If we believe that confidently, our soul has its food and drink in the flesh and blood of Christ.[18]

Without faith, Zwingli declared, one could be baptized repeatedly and gorge on the bread and wine to no effect. Rituals have no power to convey God's grace and to stir the individual to repentance and thanksgiving. Faith, following on from election, must first be present, working as the operative agent. Whether one possesses that necessary faith, however, was entirely up to God. Christ's body is given to men and women, but to receive it fully they had to believe that he had saved them because they were chosen by God.[19] Zwingli had radically shifted the sacrament away from being the objective work of priests to being the subjective experience of the people.[20]

The meal, Zwingli believed, was a memorial to Christ's passion and resurrection, to the salvation of the faithful. But what did it mean to come to the table as a memorial? To remember or commemorate was not merely an intellective act or simply observation of the event. Following Plato, Augustine and Erasmus, memory or recollection was a unitive act, in which the person is drawn to the object recalled. It was closely related to the Renaissance understanding of imitation, whereby a person is transformed into that which is imitated.[21] Remembrance for Zwingli was inseparable from becoming one with Christ and his body, which consisted of the faithful through all the ages. It was the bond of heaven and earth.

Zwingli's sacramental thought significantly developed in the summer of 1525, when he published his *Subsidiary Tract on the Eucharist*.[22] Here he began to connect the Lord's Supper with the Passover of ancient Israel, with particular reference to the command in Exodus that ran: 'This is how you shall eat it: your loins girded, your sandals on your feet, and your staff in your hand; and you shall eat it hurriedly. It is the Passover of the LORD' (Exodus 12:11). Christ's death, Zwingli was clear, was foreshadowed in the Exodus story, and Christ was the Pascal lamb.[23]

The linking of the Passover and the Lord's Supper changed everything. The Israelites had celebrated the Passover as a symbol, a sign and remembrance of their deliverance from enslavement in Egypt. Just as Jews celebrated the meal before leaving Egypt, so, too, Christ had instituted the Last

1. Huldrych Zwingli in 1531, the year of his death. The painting is by the Zurich artist Hans Asper (1499–1571), who was influenced by Hans Holbein.

2. The house in Wildhaus, Toggenburg, where Zwingli was born and lived a happy childhood that he would frequently recall. He often spoke of the virtues of those who lived in the Swiss mountains and valleys.

25. Zwingli (Max Simonischek) attends the sausage-eating at the printer Froschauer's house that broke the Lenten Fast in 1522. The flaunting of the church's prohibition of meat was the first open protest and the beginning of the reformation in Zurich.

26. Zwingli (Max Simonischek) departs Zurich for battle in 1531 with a poorly prepared army that would be overwhelmed by the Catholics. The reformer died at the Battle of Kappel and his body was quartered and burnt.

Supper before his death. The Lord's Supper, like the Passover, brought the people together to commemorate a historical act of liberation. For Christians, that moment was Christ's reconciling of humanity with God. In the same way, baptism was the sign of entry into the covenant, as circumcision had been for the Israelites. For centuries, Christian theologians had rejected the Passover as having no place in the Church. For Zwingli, it was the key to understanding Christ's meal.

Zwingli's revelation that the Lord's Supper was the Passover came to him in a most extraordinary form of theological creation. He dreamt it.[24] The claim to have received instruction in a vision was enduringly controversial. Was the truth of the sacrament of the body and blood of Christ really revealed in sleep? Long after Zwingli was dead, Catholic and Lutheran critics would continue to mock the event, claiming that a nocturnal demon had visited an inveterate heretic.[25] Nevertheless, in August 1525 the Zurich reformer made the extraordinary claim in print that during the night before the first celebration of the Reformed sacrament in the Grossmünster in Zurich, a figure had appeared to him in his sleep to exhort him to declare the true doctrine of the table.[26]

The little-known incident of Zwingli's dream, rarely mentioned in biographies, is remarkably ambiguous, sustaining multiple interpretations and fraught with the anxieties expressed by Protestants about the nature of revelation in a somnolent state. Its verity, however, was resolutely maintained by both Zwingli and those of his successors who chose to mention the incident. For the reformer, the dream was of great significance, confirmation of his prophetic state. Although he wrote of it only the once, his account in the *Subsidiary Tract* – written four months after the event – was full and carefully crafted.

Heinrich Bullinger's son-in-law, Ludwig Lavater, who had a great interest in ghosts and visions, left a comprehensive account of the dream which he may have received orally. The opening moment of the dream was a horror: it recalled an imaginary encounter between Zwingli and the Catholic Joachim am Grüt, who had fiercely argued against the reformer when the mass was to be abolished. The setting was a debate before the Council, and Zwingli recalled that in his dream he was unable to answer the questions put to him about the Lord's Supper. At a crucial moment, a mysterious figure appeared, descending from a structure, and told Zwingli off for not having cited a crucial text from Exodus: '*das ist das Phase*' ('It is the Lord's Passover') (Exodus 12:11).[27] In recalling the dream, Zwingli was unsure whether the mysterious figure was dressed in white or black. When he woke, Zwingli spoke of how he immediately flew from bed and, after his prayers, consulted the Septuagint (Greek Old Testament) to confirm the passage to which the figure had referred. A clear indication of the truth was the reference to the Septuagint, which was Zwingli's favoured version of the Hebrew scripture. He then went to the church to preach and, he wrote, all who had doubts or were unable to understand the passage comprehended.

Zwingli spoke of how, at first, he had thought the dream was a demonic manifestation of the night, but as the figure spoke to him he became increasingly aware that it was God's will.[28] He assured his readers that although he had been asleep, he could recall the details with precision. He had not wished for the dream and would gladly have ignored it, but God had spoken to him: he had been chosen to reveal the nature of the Supper as the Passover. He, as a human, had failed in the debate; only divine intervention had prevailed. Dreams had a long history in the Bible as channels through which God spoke. The fact that the mysterious figure had pointed him to the crucial text in Exodus was sufficient evidence of his divine purpose.

## THE SACRAMENTAL DEBATE

Previously largely unaware of events in the Confederation, Luther first turned his attention to Zwingli in the late summer of 1524. He had been alerted by reports that Zwingli in Zurich and Oecolampadius in Basel were following the errors of his reviled former colleague and friend Andreas Bodenstein von Karlstadt, who, to Luther's horror, had rejected the physical presence of Christ in the Lord's Supper. Although the two Swiss reformers were sympathetic to Karlstadt's position, the Saxon was not the author of their beliefs. Zwingli was explicit that his primary influence was Erasmus, who, he believed, taught a symbolic understanding of baptism and the Lord's Supper. This was of no consequence to Luther, who quickly placed the Swiss in the camp of those who had been deceived by the devil and were enemies of the gospel. However they had come to their perverse views, the Wittenberg reformer was repelled by their rejection of the truth that Christ is physically present in the bread and wine.[29]

By 1525, Luther was aware that Karlstadt, Zwingli and Oecolampadius did not always sing from the same hymn sheet. And indeed, where Zwingli emphasized that when Christ said 'this is my body' the verb *is* meant *signifies*, Oecolampadius modified that view by claiming that Christ's words meant 'this is a figure of my body'.[30] Luther was convinced that their disunity was a sure sign of error and regarded Zwingli as the prime culprit – he took a more charitable view of Oecolampadius, in whom he placed greater hope.[31] But the somewhat protective friendship between Philipp Melanchthon, Luther's colleague in Wittenberg, and Oecolampadius was soon also on the rocks.[32] The Swiss had developed an understanding of Christ's presence in the world that was fundamentally at odds with that held in Wittenberg. For the Germans, Zwingli and Oecolampadius were wrenching apart flesh and spirit – dividing Christ's two natures, as the ancient heretical Nestorians had done.[33]

The debate over the sacraments exposed a growing chasm between the Swiss and the reformers of Wittenberg. The issue of the physical presence carried with it a bundle of other problems relating to the nature and purpose of the sacraments, the divine and human natures of Christ, and the role of flesh and spirit in the human person. Those differences demonstrated that even as all the reformers looked at the Bible, they found very different things, confirming Erasmus' concern that their confidence in interpreting scripture against the consensus of the Church would only cause division – and, further, that they had betrayed him.[34] This fragmentation of the Reformation was observed with a certain satisfaction by the Catholics, for whom the house of the heretics was always divided.

Zwingli and Oecolampadius were not alone. Their teaching on the spiritual presence of Christ in the sacrament was embraced elsewhere, particularly in the German cities of the southern Empire, notably Strasbourg and Augsburg.[35] In fuelling strong anti-clerical and hierarchical sentiments, Zwingli's sacramental theology was evidently deeply embedded in the social and economic lives of the people, and not limited to rarefied debate. His symbolic interpretation of the Lord's Supper appealed to communal civic identities by moving the focus away from the priest to the people. The sacramental teaching of the Swiss reinforced the communal identity, for through baptism, a child was said to enter into the community that gathers around the table in an expression of equality.[36] The reformers in these cities were in a precarious position, perched as they were between the emerging Lutheran and Reformed camps, while threatened by Catholic opposition. Men such as Martin Bucer and Wolfgang Capito in Strasbourg, together with the leading magistrate Jakob Sturm, while largely in agreement with Zwingli, wanted to mediate.[37] 'For our lamented adversaries,' the Strasbourg preachers wrote, 'are only beginning to have some new hope, persuading themselves that we are about to destroy ourselves in empty contentions and mutual recriminations.'[38]

Luther did not calm the nerves of the Strasbourgers, chiding them instead for their support of the Swiss and defending himself against charges of provoking conflict. He had preached the gospel for many years and never sought to promote himself or seek quarrels with others. His only purpose was Christ. But he gave no ground:

> At the moment I do not intend to write against Zwingli or Oecolampadius . . . I know that they think that I do not yield because of shame. They are certainly mistaken. For there is God's Word from which I know the conquering argument.[39]

Luther and Zwingli shared the conviction that the truth should be preached and disseminated, and that God would resolve any conflict. They also both rejected all compromise, casting the other in the role of Satan's minion and breaker of the body of Christ.

By the summer of 1526, Luther was taking aim at Zwingli and Oecolampadius, writing two prefaces in which he named them as false prophets. Oecolampadius' response charged the German reformer with erring in his teaching on the Lord's Supper and with possessing an irascible temper that led him to denounce the Swiss as in league with the devil. Oecolampadius acknowledged that, as the great prophet of the Reformation, Luther was to be esteemed for his labours; but that did not put him above criticism when he behaved abysmally and without charity.[40]

During the summer of 1526, Luther became infuriated by the appearance of two works that attempted to ameliorate the growing conflict by suggesting unity where the Wittenberger saw none. First, Martin Bucer in Strasbourg produced an edition of Luther's sermons, into which he dared to introduce changes that made the Wittenberg professor sound as though he were in sympathy with the spiritual eating of the Lord's Supper advocated by the Swiss. Secondly, Leo Jud, Zwingli's friend and colleague in Zurich, managed to enrage both Luther and Erasmus when he sought to demonstrate that Erasmus had written in Latin and Luther in German, but both were in agreement with Zwingli. Like Bucer, Jud had engaged in some fancy footwork to bring the discordant voices together. Both Erasmus and Luther were persuaded that their names and reputations were being traduced to justify heresy. 'What will happen to us after we are dead,' Luther despaired, 'if such things take place while we are still alive?'[41]

During 1527, Zwingli and Luther continued to contend, with work that included the Zurich reformer's 'Friendly Exposition of the Eucharist Affair, to Martin Luther', while from Wittenberg came 'That These Words of Christ "This is My Body" Still Stand Firm against the Fanatics'. Luther was adamant that Zwingli and Oecolampadius belonged to a long tradition in which scripture was basely distorted for private means. 'So once more,' Luther attacked, 'I shall set myself against the devil and his fanatics, not for their sake, but for the sake of the weak and simple.' Zwingli, Oecolampadius and the others were lost; Luther's goal must be to save the Church.

Luther roundly rejected the Swiss argument that Christ's words 'this is my body' could be interpreted symbolically. Christ had meant what he said, he insisted. The logic of Zwingli's argument that Christ could not be in the world, because he sat at the right hand of the Father was false: such a position depended on human reason that could prove no article of faith. Christ is present in the Supper in his fullness, feeding both soul and body.[42] When Christ said that the flesh profits nothing, he was not referring to his own. The Swiss had misunderstood what was meant by spiritual: 'Thus, Spirit consists in the use, not in the object, be it seeing, hearing, speaking, touching, begetting, bearing, eating, drinking, or anything else.'[43]

Zwingli replied with his most aggressive statements about Luther to date. He denounced the way in which Luther combined his erroneous arguments with personal abuse, regarding himself as far superior to his opponents. That arrogance further combined with extreme sensitivity, which for Zwingli indicated insecurity. Although Luther had been the great warrior against the papacy, his teaching on the Lord's Supper demonstrated that he had in the end held to the doctrine of transubstantiation.

When Luther responded a year later with his 'Against the Heavenly Prophets', he once more took aim at the central arguments of Zwingli and Oecolampadius, but it was for the former that he reserved his venom. He described the Zurich reformer as 'perverted' and 'lost to Christ'. And he went on: 'I testify on my part that I regard Zwingli as un-Christian, with all his teachings, for he holds and teaches no part of the Christian faith rightly. He is seven times worse than when he was a papist.'[44] Luther continued that he had never agreed with or held any of Zwingli's positions. Significantly, when he turned to Oecolampadius, Luther was less aggressive, holding out more hope for the Basel reformer and pointing out that he disagreed with Zwingli on key points. This was Luther's last statement on the Swiss reformers before he met them in person in Marburg in 1529. When Zwingli and Oecolampadius replied in the autumn of 1528 they were met by silence.

## ENCOUNTER

The only personal encounter between Zwingli and Luther came in the autumn of 1529. It was not a success and never could have been. It was hardly conceivable, after a crescendo of vitriol, that during a short meeting the two sides would miraculously resolve a serious theological difference on which hung disparate views of God, scripture and humanity. For Luther, the stakes were not high and he expected little of Zwingli or Oecolampadius and had no interest in an alliance with the Swiss. Zwingli, however, had much to gain by even a cessation of hostilities. Zurich and the Swiss had no role in imperial religious politics, as they sat on the periphery. Yet, it had become all too clear to Zwingli that a German alliance might realize his goal of reformation in the Confederation. Zwingli believed that for him – unlike for Luther – the Rubicon had not yet been crossed and that he had a chance of finding some form of agreement.

In April 1529, following the Diet of Speyer, where evangelical principalities and cities had issued their protestation against the imposition of the Edict of Worms in the Empire, Landgrave Philipp of Hesse (1504–1567) showed himself keen to form an alliance between the evangelical states in the Empire and the Swiss, creating a union that would extend from the Alps to the Baltic Sea. He had enjoyed good relations with Zwingli and sought to bring the Zurich reformer into the discussions, but the sacramental dispute was a formidable obstacle. Luther could not imagine an alliance with 'those who strive against God and the sacraments' with their 'wickedness and blasphemy'. Such abuse of the gospel could lead only to damnation: for Luther and his followers, it ruled out any notion of conciliation. Indeed, Luther saw the creation of an alliance along the lines envisaged by Philipp as yet another of Satan's wiles. The city of Strasbourg was crucial: influential and wealthy, it was a key ally of Philipp of Hesse through the politician Jakob Sturm (1489–1553) and the reformers Martin Bucer and Wolfgang Capito. They formed the essential link between the Swiss and the Germans, although Luther remained deeply suspicious of their motives. From the spring of 1529, Zurich had formed an alliance with the city. As one historian observed, 'without Strasbourg there would have been no Marburg'.[45]

Resolution of the sacramental dispute was, however, the prerequisite for a political alliance, as Philipp of Hesse, Elector Johann of Saxony (1468–1532) and other leading political figures in the Empire recognized. Initially, the Wittenberg doctor treated Philipp of Hesse's suggestion of a personal meeting with the Swiss like the plague, but he was under considerable pressure to attend. In drawing up the Schwabach Articles in the summer of 1529, Luther and his followers stated their bottom line for agreement: the Swiss and their allies would have to concede. When Luther did agree to attend, he assumed that he would meet the more acceptable Oecolampadius, rather than Zwingli. By this point, the friendship between Oecolampadius and Melanchthon was deeply troubled by the split over the Eucharist. As Oecolampadius sought to patch up their relationship, Melanchthon warned him against the views of the Zwinglians and was eager to encourage his friend against any alliance with them.[46]

Philipp sent out the invitation to the reformers in the expectation that Luther and Melanchthon would face Zwingli and Oecolampadius. Other reformers were to be present only as spectators. The invitation was taken up enthusiastically in Zurich, although it was recognized that caution would be required. Zwingli's departure from Zurich was a secret known only to the Council, and not even to his wife, Anna. The dangers of the journey were considerable: it was perilous for Zwingli to leave the walls of the city – not that he was free of threats even within the city's limits. Catholics were only one possible adversary, for Zwingli had a reputation in the German lands as Luther's opponent. Philipp had arranged for him to travel through safe locations until he arrived at Marburg in Hesse.

Having travelled via Strasbourg, Zwingli arrived in Marburg before the party from Wittenberg. We have no written record of this relatively small and private affair, for which more intimate surroundings were deemed suitable. The discussions were held in German, not least because Latin would have excluded Philipp of Hesse and other notable participants; but the use of the vernacular did not mean that Luther and Zwingli could easily understand one another. The Wittenberger's Saxon dialect was virtually incomprehensible to a speaker of Swiss Alemannic, and Luther complained that he struggled to comprehend Zwingli.

The meeting was suffused with political consequences. Philipp of Hesse used the opportunity to announce to the Swiss his plans for a southern German alliance against the Habsburgs.[47] Accompanied by Jakob Sturm from Strasbourg and Duke Ulrich of Württemberg (1487–1550), he offered the Swiss military aid should they join the fraternity. Indeed, he would personally come to the Confederation, along with the northern German princes.

The discussions opened with Luther meeting Oecolampadius, while Zwingli met Melanchthon. Luther had, against Swiss wishes, insisted on no written record. Disagreements surfaced quickly – Oecolampadius told Zwingli that in Luther he had met another Johann Eck.[48] Debates focused on the sacrament of the Lord's Supper, and throughout the day the two sides exchanged views on the questions of spirit and flesh, the location of Christ's body and the weight of scriptural evidence. But Luther and Zwingli, together with Oecolampadius, Melanchthon and Bucer, largely restated their established views, making the level of disagreement vividly clear. There was a robust exchange on the question of whether Christ's body could be present in more than one place, with Luther rejecting the Swiss argument that it could not. Once again, Zwingli and Oecolampadius turned to John 6:63 – 'The Spirit gives life; the flesh counts for nothing.' Luther appealed to the language of 'mystery', a word that Zwingli was loath to use.[49] At one point, Luther lifted the tablecloth to read aloud the words he had written in chalk on the table: 'This is my body.' With little progress made, at the end of the day Zwingli despondently asked: 'Should, then, everything go according to your will?'

Attempts were made to reach some form of agreement. The parties could at least concur that Christ's words 'this is my body' indicate that He is present. Further, the Wittenbergers accepted that the Swiss had not fully rejected the presence of Christ, while the Swiss acknowledged that Luther had not meant that Christ's body was locally present in flesh and blood.[50] Both sides avoided the language of transubstantiation, drawing instead on

Aristotle for terms to express how the people received the body and blood in the bread and wine. But in the end, the Swiss would not agree, citing pastoral concerns about the complexity of such an agreement. They knew that much of the attraction of their arguments lay in their relative simplicity and coherence. How were they to adopt a formula consisting of contorted language?

Luther stated his scepticism about the meeting, claiming that he only attended on account of Landgrave Philipp of Hesse. He agreed to lay out the true foundations of the faith and to challenge Zwingli and Oecolampadius to respond. The Swiss were bewildered: they thought they had come to debate the Lord's Supper, not the whole of Christian doctrine. As a final gasp, Luther reworked his Schwabach Articles in a less polemical form to demonstrate the orthodoxy of the evangelical faith, its continuity with the early Church and its foundation in scripture. The screeds against the 'fanatics' were discreetly removed.

The 15 Articles of Marburg were signed by all the major figures at the meeting and printed across the German and Swiss lands. Representing the greatest achievement of the meeting, they contained agreement on the major principles of the Christian faith, including the Trinity, Christology, sin, scripture and salvation by faith alone.[51] Article 15 addressed the Lord's Supper and was deliberately vague, making a statement about receiving the sacrament in both kinds and the importance of spiritual eating:

> And although at this time, we have not reached an agreement as to whether the true body and blood of Christ are bodily present in the bread and wine, nevertheless, each side should show Christian love to the other side insofar as conscience will permit and both sides should diligently pray to Almighty God that through his Spirit he might confirm us in the right understanding. Amen.[52]

The disagreement was acknowledged and the opaque statement would later be diversely interpreted. Any real reconciliation was illusory. Famously, Zwingli broke down in tears when expressing a fervent desire for friendship.[53] Luther's judgement in a letter to his wife, Katherina, was brutal: 'We do not want them as brothers and members [of Christ], although we wish them peace and good things.'[54]

## A PROVIDENTIAL GOD

The conflict between Luther and the Swiss was never limited to whether Christ is physically present in the sacrament.[55] Their disagreement concerned nothing less than God and his Word, with Luther believing that Zwingli and Oecolampadius had wilfully denied the teaching of scripture. Luther held that God was hidden, beyond human perception and manifested in physical signs. Zwingli, in contrast, held that God is simple and evident, unable to deceive.[56] He was repeatedly optimistic: God is good and benevolent, inviting humanity into his revelation. Men and women can have absolute assurance in divine providence, which orders all things for the good and without doubt. God is absolutely provident or is not God.[57] That was Zwingli's ultimate comfort and source of hope. God is not bound to the sacraments in any way: they are symbols of his initiation, his providential care. Zwingli's thought resided in that certainty, and he never shifted.

Zwingli had arrived several days early for the meeting at Marburg, and planned to use the time to rest and prepare for the sessions with Luther and Melanchthon. On 29 October, two days after his arrival, he preached in the castle chapel, choosing as his theme not primarily the sacraments, but the providence of God.[58] Several months later, in January 1530, Philipp of Hesse wrote to Zwingli requesting that he publish the sermon.[59] The reformer, who never spoke from prepared notes, had to reconstruct his words from memory, writing a text that appeared in the summer of 1530 as 'On Providence'.

We find in the sermon Zwingli's most emphatic and poetic evocation of a God who is simple and good, and who orders all creation according to his pleasure:

> His decrees remain unalterable, because He is Himself unalterable and unchangeable. Hence, we may infer that what God once was towards His creatures, He is also today, so that if He ever showered His goodness upon the good and pursued the wicked with righteousness, He maintains the same attitude today also in the freedom of His will. Therefore, as He once was toward the elect, so He is now, and likewise toward the rejected.[60]

The ancients bore witness to God's providence:

Caesar seizes a monarchy, Brutus destroys one, the first sending headlong to ruin the Roman power already tottering to its fall, the other to tear out the tyranny of a Tarquin and make room for justice in a future democracy. Thus God uses for good all deeds both good and ill, though with the distinction that He turns to good for the elect even the evil they do, and the contrary for the rejected, while we meanwhile complain through impatience or ignorance. Thus, all things happen, because all things are done by His dispensation and command.[61]

The sermon was Zwingli's most philosophical work, drawn from the thoughts of Plato and directed against Stoic fatalism. While the ancients had glimpsed this God, he was only truly known through scripture, from which humanity knows that it has been saved by his sheer goodness.[62] As the highest good, God cares for his own. Zwingli invoked Christ's words: 'Why do you call me good? There is none good but God.' Anything else that is good is so only through participation in the divine. God foresaw the fall and even permitted it, but to humanity's ultimate benefit: to possess true knowledge of good and evil. Goodness is God's essence and the substance of his revelation: it is the source of joy.

Zwingli's reworking of his sermon at Marburg following the bitter harvest of no agreement was a full-throated prophetic declaration, a bold claim that the Swiss spoke God's Word. Zwingli had not gone to Marburg to change his mind or to find an easy path to agreement. It was evident that he and Luther shared common ground; but ultimately, they could not coexist. Their views of God and humanity, their differences as Swiss and German and their self-understandings as prophets rendered agreement impossible. Zwingli once wrote to Luther 'for if we are true prophets we shall listen to each other, and if we are in error upon any matter we shall yield the point'.[63] That never happened, and nor could it have; and neither man was either the hero or the villain. They were irreconcilable. Zwingli may have cried when he and Luther parted, but he did not beg. Providence, he believed, had put him where he was, and he led the true cause.

✦ EIGHT ✦

# EXPANSION AND CONFLICT

From his arrival in 1519 until the introduction of the Reformation with the Lord's Supper at Easter 1525, Zwingli's story was largely about his relationship with the city of Zurich. The abolition of the mass and the creation of a new order in 1525 was not an endpoint in that story, but these events mark a transition to what would prove to be the remaining six years of his life, during which time his reforming ideas would spread across the Confederation, far into the Empire and west to France. Older narratives of the Reformation tend to pigeon-hole Zwingli as an urban reformer, the creator of a godly city-state.[1] John Calvin in Geneva is generally credited with establishing a more international reach. By 1525, however, the reforms arising out of Zurich were spreading through both urban and rural territories, where they were by no means uniformly interpreted. Zwingli was not the identifiable leader of a movement, as Luther was; but he was the principal inspiration for a form of Christianity that was attracting adherents from diverse social groups.

The rapidly changing circumstances from 1525, as the Reformation moved from being focused on Zurich to becoming a Swiss and German event, were reflected in Zwingli's life. No longer concentrated alone on achieving internal reforms through the support of the magistrates, Zwingli's attention shifted to a broader canvas. The adoption of the Reformation in Zurich raised questions about the health of the Confederation. What did it mean to have a powerful Confederate depart from the Catholic Church and descend into heresy? What would religious strife mean for this loose body of states?

The Catholic states – principally the Five States of Uri, Schwyz, Unterwalden, Lucerne and Zug – together with the church hierarchy and their Austrian

182

allies, were determined to roll back the assault on the Roman Church. Zurich had to be punished. The unknown factor was the cities of Bern and Basel, which remained Catholic but had strong evangelical movements. Neither city seemed inclined to plunge the Confederation into a religious war. For his part, Zwingli was certain that Reformation was God's will for the Swiss as an elect people, and convinced that exposure to the gospel would win over the common folk. He was increasingly persuaded, however, that Catholic rulers would have to be overcome if the Word of God was to be preached to the people, and his own thinking was becoming increasingly martial.

Having seen his thought incised in the purged churches of Zurich, performed in the new liturgies by which the sacraments were administered, and printed in his *Commentary on True and False Religion*, Zwingli still had to attend to a bewildering range of challenges. The creation of a new Church required the construction of institutions, the overcoming of resistance, and the building of alliances. Zwingli experienced the period from 1525 until the first war in 1529 not as the linear story that the historian seeks out, but as a series of interlocking and coterminous events and developments that he could neither dictate nor control.

For the remaining six years of his life, Zwingli sought to balance the creation of a new order of society with unrelenting conflict with Anabaptists, Catholics and Lutherans, all within the context of efforts to create a broader Protestant alliance that would both defend the Reformation and enable its aggressive expansion. In the midst of this maelstrom, he switched from the offensive to the defensive with head-spinning rapidity. He churned out a constant flow of letters and tracts as he communicated beyond the city walls; he was deeply involved in the politics of Zurich through his connections with sympathetic magistrates; and he preached several times a week and led the efforts to interpret and translate scripture, leading to the crowning achievement of his Reformation, the Zurich Bible of 1531.

## FONT OF HISTORICAL KNOWLEDGE

As his expanding and extensive library evidenced, Zwingli continued his lifelong passion for reading and study. Books were the currency of his life.[2] As preacher at the Grossmünster, he was well remunerated and spent a good deal of money on acquiring new works and having them bound. Books also came as gifts or in exchange. By the end of his life, Zwingli had about 400 books, and at his death these were transferred to the library of the Grossmünster. The sum raised went towards care for his children.

Not only was he involved in the daily work of the *Prophezei*, but Zwingli devoured and annotated works of history, philosophy, literature and science. His collection of books, which has survived, bears witness to endless hours of study, which, as Myconius tells us, was often late into the night. His love of learning was channelled into his efforts to reform schools and create a humanist world of study for both Church and community. Erasmus was ever before him as his model, and throughout the torrid events from 1525 until the end of his life, reading was a vital and cherished part of his life.

As we have seen in his frequent evocations of the Swiss past, Zwingli was a lover of history. It was not merely nostalgia, but a conviction that the great historians of antiquity had much to teach about the contemporary world. Often in his letters he encouraged his readers to study the Greek and Roman historians, and he had a particular love of Flavius Josephus (37–100 CE). Zwingli had been reading the Roman-Jewish historian since his days in Glarus, when he acquired a set of his writings. He wrote to an unidentified person:

> I remind you of Josephus because you will find most of what he has produced in the Holy Scriptures, with the exception of the Jewish War: you should read him first and foremost, for he is the writer who demonstrates that we should never shun God's mercy and should never invoke his wrath.[3]

Greek literature, he continued, was not to be advised at this point,

> considering your age and your health, although I used to read the Greek writers in my spare time – with no other literature do I feel so comfortable – but I will make a note of what may be useful and send it to you later.

Every aspect of Zwingli's work was informed by study, whether alone or with his circle of friends. History was alive and spoke to the present: 'speaking the truth'. The great societies of the past recorded their histories, enabling them to flourish and prosper. That memory was imperative for the

Swiss. Reformation was recovery of the past, but as accurately and authentically as possible. In a summary of Josephus, Zwingli offered the moral obligation of the past for the present: 'what historians should make their chief aim is to be accurate and hold everything else of less importance than speaking the truth to those who must rely upon them in matters of which they themselves have no knowledge'.[4] The educated person who served politics and the community was a seer of the truth, an interpreter of history.

To be a prophet of the Word was to be a prophet of the wisdom of the past. Zwingli's extensive library of works mapped an expansive mental and spiritual world that formed the heart of his life. In many respects, there was no separation of library from household, Church and Council chambers. For Zwingli, books and pulpit were means by which God spoke to humanity.

## CAPTAINS AND PROPHETS

As we saw above, in the spring of 1524 Zwingli had begun to move away from Erasmian pacifism towards an increasingly aggressive stance vis-à-vis the hostile Confederates and their allies in Austria and the Empire. His resolve only deepened with the introduction of the Reformation in 1525, which isolated and endangered Zurich. Zwingli had begun to understand the wider international ramifications of the reform movement in terms of international politics. He was part of an epistolary network that spread through southern German cities such as Augsburg, Nuremberg and, crucially, Strasbourg. He was fed news of events in the Empire, including the alliances among princes and cities sympathetic to the Reformation. In Basel, his primary source was his friend Oecolampadius, who was closely connected to colleagues in his native Germany.

Looking to the Empire, Zwingli revived deep hostility towards the Habsburgs, viewing Emperor Charles V and his brother Archduke Ferdinand as the principal threat to reformation. The pope was Antichrist, but Zwingli did not share Luther's fixation on the papal abomination. In turn, growing sympathy for Swiss theology in the southern German cities, as propagated by preachers, book traders and influential laity, brought Zwingli more influence and more contacts. Sympathetic audiences were not limited to the towns. By 1525, the Zurich reformer was learning of the pro-evangelical princes in the Empire, principally the young Landgrave Philipp of Hesse.

Such connections opened up the possibility of a religious alliance that extended beyond the Rhine into the German lands. Wolfgang Capito and Martin Bucer in Strasbourg were vital links, enabling Zwingli to remain attuned to the rapidly changing circumstances. Strasbourg was a centre of evangelical sympathies in the Rhineland.[5] In August 1526, Zwingli was informed by Capito of an alliance formed by Philipp of Hesse, the elector of Saxony and the imperial cities to defend the evangelical faith against the attempts by Catholics to enforce the 1521 Edict of Worms, which condemned Luther and banned his teaching.[6]

Philipp's interest in Zwingli seems to have been piqued in the summer of 1526. The wildcard was Duke Ulrich of Württemberg (1487–1550), who had been deposed in 1519 and had engaged in a long campaign for his restoration, spending some time in exile in the Swiss Confederation.[7] In 1523, he adopted the evangelical faith, and two years later joined with peasants in their insurrection. Although Zurich was officially neutral, troops from the city travelled north to fight for Duke Ulrich. Zwingli was sympathetic to Ulrich's cause, although he had not supported his city's dispatch of military support. The duke's efforts failed and further exile followed; but by 1526, Philipp of Hesse had taken up his cause, and Württemberg was a key factor in his reaching out for Swiss support.

Possible alliances were all the more attractive for Zwingli as the situation in the Confederation deteriorated. Following the Reformation in Zurich, the Catholic Five States wanted nothing to do with the city on any diplomatic level. The gravest danger for the city lay less in the threat of attack than in its loss of influence within the Confederation.

Representatives from Zurich were not permitted at the Swiss Diet, and additionally the city risked being cut off from involvement with the eastern lands and Mandated Territories, where the evangelical faith was spreading thanks to preachers sent out by Zurich.[8] Zurich's room for manoeuvre was provided by its role in the political structures of the Confederation, but its support for heresy threatened its inclusion on the list of players.

Zwingli began to set down possible ways forward, and his 'Plan for a Campaign' ('Plan zu einem Feldzug') appeared at the end of 1525 or early 1526.[9] His plans were less a coherent strategy than a somewhat loosely conceived collection of observations on the implications of the Reformation in Zurich.[10] The text provides our first insight into Zwingli's association of religion, diplomatic relations and war (although – mindful of his extremely controversial position – he did not put his name to the work). 'The pious state of Zurich,' it declared, 'prefers to lose city, possessions, land, equipment, bodies and lives rather than depart from what it knows to be the truth.' Zwingli advocated an anti-Habsburg alliance and understood that Bern, the most powerful of the Swiss Confederates, was crucial to Zurich's survival. He sought a diplomatic strategy to isolate the Catholic states and break their resistance, arguing that Zurich's opponents could only attack if they were supported by the Austrians or Habsburgs, which was unlikely. Following the lead of Philipp of Hesse and Ulrich of Württemberg, Zwingli increasingly looked to France for aid, despite Francis I's defeat at Pavia in 1525 at the hands of Charles V. The Zurich reformer had dedicated his *Commentary on True and False Religion* to the French king, and he now believed that France, with its hostility to the Habsburgs, was needed to divert Charles V from Swiss affairs. Zwingli hoped that Bern and Basel, although still Catholic, would support Zurich if it came to war. His optimism proved a misstep, as both cities soon made it clear that they would not intervene militarily. Bern's primary interest was peace.

Zwingli's joint role as preacher and military campaigner appeared in his enumeration of their respective duties: preachers should declare the gospel and pray for its propagation; military leaders were to be courageous, decisive and cannily grasp how victory depends on good timing.[11] Zwingli, who had been trained in the use of arms in his youth, had a clear sense of what virtues made a leader in battle. To be prepared, the state must select the best military commanders and equip its soldiers with the most modern weapons. A student of ancient Roman treatises, he revealed himself remarkably well informed on military tactics, and insisted that attack was the best form of defence. Conflict to protect the faith might be necessary, but must not be sought recklessly. The most arresting conclusion we can draw from his text is that Zwingli was ready to sacrifice the Confederation for the sake of true religion.

## 'THIS HAS NEVER BEEN FULFILLED'

As Christianity had long experienced, persecution and martyrdom could be the lifeblood of the Church. After their defeat at the disputations in Zurich during 1525, the Anabaptists in Zurich were in dire straits, with most of the leading figures in prison. The more resilient refused to recant, while others took a lower road, seeking to avoid dank prisons either by retracting their words or, as would prove to have been the case in many instances, by dissembling. But the expulsion, criminalizing and persecution of the Anabaptists would not diminish their challenge to Zurich's godly community, and groups would grow up in rural areas and across the Confederation – from Appenzell and St Gallen in the east to Bern in the west.[12] Anabaptism was not a monolithic movement, for it demonstrated a spectrum of convictions about the Church, magistrates and protests in the rural communities. Its members were at one, however, in their rejection of Zwingli's defence of infant baptism as a sign of entry into the covenant.

Swiss Anabaptists largely held to a separatist ideal of the Christian community, which they understood as a gathering of the faithful, committed to an unblemished life of faith away from the political and social compromises of Zwingli's covenant. In turn, Zwingli detested their rejection of God's Church in the world, and denigrated them on every count. The radicals neglected the poor, he noted, and did not live according to the example of the Apostles in Jerusalem.[13] They were prone to slanderous gossip and 'are found to do all things without counsel for the sake of their belly and of idleness'.[14] To his interlocutors, Zwingli defended his own Christian virtue, insisting: 'I myself pray anxiously about the Anabaptists, and often I plead before the Council for them, and our prayers have accomplished this.'[15]

The situation was all the more galling – and personal for Zwingli – since he was repeatedly accused by Catholics of being the father of Anabaptism. At the same time, the Anabaptists held up before him what they saw as his failings. Felix Manz's witness before the Zurich Council on 17 January 1525 had been devastating, for in attacking his interpretation of scripture, he hit Zwingli where it hurt:

Your shepherds [the Zurich clergy] . . . have always negotiated with me on the following basis, namely that one should let scripture speak and that we should never add to it nor delete anything from it. This has never been fulfilled. They have certainly presented their opinion, but they have not based it on passages of scripture. We have not been able to come to speak, and scripture could not be heard. In addition, if the clergy thinks that someone wants to say something about the truth, they choke the speech in his throat and attack him, demanding scriptural citations, which they themselves should have presented to support the truth. This is what they do; God knows this well.[16]

His beloved Anna was likely to have been a model of female piety for Zwingli: wife and mother, keeping the holy household and raising the children in the faith. As such, his expectations of Christian domesticity were of his age. On the role of women, too, however, the Anabaptists challenged Zwingli's vision.[17] Anabaptists were hardly pro-feminist, but women often engaged in teaching and pastoral care, for which they risked their lives. One of the most prominent was Margret Hottinger, who referred to an advocate of infant baptism as 'a child of the devil'[18] and who was imprisoned in Zurich in November 1525 for almost six months.[19] Although she never recanted, Hottinger escaped death and left Zurich for St Gallen in 1526, where she earned grudging respect from Reformed chronicler Johannes Kessler:

There arose wild and arrogant error through the women of the Anabaptists, particularly one young woman from Zollikon in the land of Zurich named Margret Hottinger . . . who lived a disciplined way of life, so that she was deeply loved and respected by the Anabaptists.[20]

In late autumn 1525, Balthasar Hubmaier, now the leading Anabaptist theologian, turned up in Zurich. Hubmaier had been baptized in Waldshut at Easter 1525 by Wilhelm Reublin and had founded an Anabaptist community in the city.[21] Hubmaier left Waldshut in early December, the day before the city surrendered to the Austrians, who were the town's overlords, after an insurrection and brief independence. With the roads to Basel blocked, he arrived in Zurich and lodged with the Anabaptist widow Anna Widerker.

Hubmaier had reason to make for Zurich: as we have seen, he was once a friend of Zwingli and Oecolampadius, and he had tried to maintain cordial relations with them. He did not advocate the perfectionist separate Church, maintaining – like Zwingli – a more negative assessment of human abilities.[22] He held that the Spirit does not regenerate the faithful to lives of total moral rectitude, and that the Church therefore remains full of sinners in need of repeated reconciliation. For Hubmaier, temporal authority was justified in using legitimate force to defend the faith, while individual Christians had no right of resistance to God's appointed rulers.[23]

But too much baptismal water had flowed over the font since those earlier times, and Hubmaier's freedom in Zurich was short lived. Quickly arrested by officials, he was called upon to recant, which he did following a private disputation. The drama, however, was not over. At the end of December, Hubmaier publicly recanted his recantation, and he did so from the pulpit of the Grossmünster, Zwingli's church.[24] He had been supposed to read a scripted statement of repentance in front of the congregation, but the staged event went badly wrong. Seized by Zurich officials, he was imprisoned in the Wellenberg, the city prison in a tower in the middle of the River Limmat, and tortured. During his time in prison, Hubmaier requested a debate with Zwingli on baptism. Remarkably, his request was granted.[25] In their exchange, he reminded the reformer of his earlier remarks that infant baptism was not scriptural, poignantly commenting: 'If you do not [demonstrate infant baptism from scripture], the pastor will complain that you have used against him a sword.'[26] Zwingli emphatically countered that Hubmaier had misheard him and that he had never spoken thus. The prisoner was finally released in April 1526, having recanted one more time. Taking no chances, the Zurich magistrates had Hubmaier expelled from their lands.[27] Having travelled to Moravia, he was arrested by the Austrian authorities and burnt at the stake in Vienna in March 1528. His wife, Elsbeth, was drowned in the Danube three days later.

Polemic and persecution operated within concentric circles: just as Zwingli and Zurich were condemned by the Catholics, so they denounced the Anabaptists, as Zwingli adopted the medieval legacy of extirpating heretics from the community through banishment and, now, death.[28] The Anabaptists were not simply heretics, but were regarded by the magistrates as seditious, deserving of capital punishment. On 7 March 1526, the Council declared that denial of infant baptism was punishable by drowning.[29] The same day, 18 women and men, including Konrad Grebel, Felix Manz and Margret Hottinger, were sentenced to indefinite imprisonment on bread and water and with beds of straw until recantation or death, with the threat that any who rebaptized would be drowned 'without mercy'.[30] The persecuted had become the persecutors, and Zwingli fully supported death for the Anabaptists. 'Thus patience has endured enough and finally erupted,' he wrote to Vadian, adding ominously, 'whoever will be baptized hereafter will be submerged permanently'.[31]

Punitive decrees did not suppress the movement. In the face of their oppression, the Anabaptists took up itinerant ministry, and those who fled, including Konrad Grebel, played a key role in spreading Anabaptist ideals and in forming a powerful resistance to the church order in Zurich. Grebel himself died only six months later, in Maienfeld in Graubünden, but Manz and Georg Blaurock were active in Grüningen; Hans Pfistermeyer in the Aargau; Margret Hottinger in St Gallen and Wilhelm Reublin, Martin Weninger and Jakob Groß in various locations.[32] The former Benedictine prior Michael Sattler had returned to Zurich lands to preach in nearby Bülach. Numerous other men and women languished in prison during 1526, refusing to recant. Zwingli was relentless in condemning the Anabaptists in print and from the pulpit, backing threats from the Council that they would be put to death.

In December 1526, Manz and Blaurock were arrested in Grüningen and handed over to Zurich officials. Manz was executed on 5 January 1527, drowned in the Limmat, while Blaurock was beaten with rods and forced out of the city. He was told that, should he return, he would suffer the same fate as Manz, whose execution was an episode of ritualized high drama.[33] As he was taken from the Wellenberg to the fish market, Manz declared that he was to die for the truth. A boat then took him to the middle of the river, which ran through the centre of the city. Manz rejected the admonitions of a pastor to recant, and encouraged by his family, he called out Christ's words, 'Into your hands I commend my spirit', before being tossed into the waters with his hands bound. In the 2019 film *Zwingli*, the reformer and his wife watch the execution; while we do not in fact know where the reformer was when Manz died, we do know that he had not protested against the magistrates' decision.

In his last letter, Manz provided a damning indictment of the unnamed Zwingli:

Unfortunately, we find many people these days who exult in the gospel and teach, speak and preach much about it, yet are full of hatred and envy. They do not have the love of God in them, and their deceptions are known to everyone. For as we have experienced in these last days, there are those who have come to us in sheep's clothing, yet are ravaging wolves who hate the pious ones of this world and thwart their way of life and the true fold. This is what the false prophets and hypocrites of this world do.[34]

Zwingli found the words for his repudiation of the Anabaptists in the Gospel of John: 'They went from us but they did not really belong to us.' He was mistaken, for they had once been his friends. And they had justified their search for a purer Church with his own words. By 1532, five more Anabaptists would suffer Manz's fate.

Zwingli's condemnation of the Anabaptists coalesced in print in his *Elenchus* or *A Refutation of the Tricks of the Anabaptists*, published in late July 1527 – his last and most comprehensive effort to destroy his hated opponents. The fiercely polemical text, written in dialogue form, ran to two hundred pages and attempted a root-and-branch repudiation of their beliefs and actions in response to the Schleitheim Articles, drawn up in February 1527 by a small group led by ex-Benedictine Michael Sattler (d.1527) as a record of Anabaptist shared convictions.[35] The seven articles formed a statement on key issues rather than a full confession of faith.[36] Printed along with the account of Sattler's martyrdom – he was executed in Rottenburg in 1527 – together they created a new genre of Anabaptist literature, in which Sattler was the very embodiment of the persecuted, separated body of Christ.[37]

The godly would have no contact with either the fallen world of politics or the wider mass of the unregenerate, as the fourth article of the Schleitheim Articles starkly declared:

A separation shall be made from the evil and from the wickedness which the devil has planted in the world. We simply will not have fellowship with evil people, nor associate with them, nor participate with them in their abominations.[38]

Sattler cut away any middle ground, utterly repudiating Zwingli's concept of the mixed, visible Church where the godly and ungodly would coexist in this world, only to be separated in the next. That compromise – unacceptable to the Anabaptists – was nothing less than a deal with the devil.

Flight and martyrdom had become defining experiences of Anabaptism, reflecting a spirituality and theology of suffering that is evident in the hymn 'Lord God! To Thee Be Blessing' by Georg Blaurock:

The foe beat hard upon me
Where in the field I lay;
He fain from it would drive me,
Lord, Thou didst vict'ry stay;
With weapon sharp he on me pressed,
That all my body trembled,
From force and falsehood stressed.[39]

Zwingli only became aware of the meeting in Schleitheim in late spring 1527; but, obsessed with his opponents, he sprang into action. He provided in dialogue form a largely accurate translation of the Schleitheim Articles, although he complained that he frequently struggled with Sattler's German.[40] His systematic treatment of the articles offered refutations of his opponents and defended his own positions. Central to *A Refutation* was Zwingli's emphasis on God's grace and the renewed case for infant baptism. He concluded with the bond of election and covenant. God's election of Israel did not limit salvation to the Israelites, because God is free to choose whomsoever he will.[41] Election to the body of Christ precedes justification and faith.

His text was a heady mixture of theological and exegetical analysis, contemporary observation and ad hominem assaults. Zwingli was certainly not above mud-raking, accusing the Anabaptists of sexual immorality – 'they consummate spiritual marriage with carnal copulation' – much as his Catholic opponents continued to caricature Zwingli himself.[42]

The ferocity of Zwingli's attack was eye-watering:

for it is not sufficient for them to abuse the gospel for gain and to live at the expense of another, and to give themselves up to such base cunning for the sake of their belly, weaving plot out of plot, but they must not only assail but even destroy the faith of matrons and girls from whose husbands and parents they obtain hospitality.[43]

Doubtless referring to the executed Felix Manz, Zwingli added: 'it seems funny to strive with ghosts'.[44]

Several weeks after the appearance of the *Elenchus*, the cities of Zurich, Basel and Bern gathered to issue a common statement against the Anabaptists that made their convictions a capital offence:

> As the civil contract obliges, individuals should inform upon those favorable to Anabaptism. Whoever shall not fit his conduct to this dissuasion is liable to punishment according to the judgment of the magistracy and the circumstances of the case. Teachers, baptizing preachers, itinerants, and leaders of congregations, or those previously released from prison who had sworn to desist from such things are to be drowned.[45]

The Zurich reformer was done with these opponents: they were to be driven from the land or from this life.

## RULERS, PROPHETS AND PASTORS

From the beginning – and then robustly against the Anabaptists – Zwingli had defended the role of temporal rulers as divinely appointed to preserve the true faith. They were not, however, interpreters of God's Word. They were not prophets. The message of the Bible was conveyed to the people by the pastors of the Church, men of faith who had been trained in languages and doctrine and duly ordained. Like the kings and prophets of the Israelites, magistrates and pastors were bound together in God's service, but with distinct responsibilities. The prophetic office was to admonish rulers according to God's laws, and further, as Nathan excoriated the adulterous David, to rebuke them when they violated their duties.

Pastors were not rulers, although in Zwingli's hands the boundaries could be invisible to the naked eye, particularly when it came to his own role. Nevertheless, it fell to the magistrates, for example, to punish the Anabaptists for their rejection of both the Church and political authority. Faith and politics were not separate realms, for both are wholly rooted in the Word of God, which works to bring all things into one.[46] As aggressively as he attacked corruption and venality in the community (above all by the elites of both politics and Church), Zwingli did not wish to strip society of human righteousness, which belonged to the whole body and not just to those who would separate themselves to build alternative communities. Human righteousness refused to accept self-interest and was the manifestation in time of God's command to love.[47]

When the mass was formally abolished in April 1525, the people were given no choice in the matter. Whatever their sympathies, all were required to attend the new Reformed services. Even more dramatically, the former priests had to become preachers, an office for which most had no training whatsoever.[48] The choice was stark. Either a priest accepted the changes and swore obedience to the Council, or else he could up sticks and leave the territory. Few could afford the latter option – they might already have families, including children – and most chose to remain in their parishes with their meagre livings.

The results were predictable. In the 120 or so parishes of Zurich's urban and rural churches, from 1525 the new preachers were almost all former priests, a pattern common across the Swiss and German Reformations.[49] Theologically, most had little clue of Zwingli's teaching and little idea of how to deliver the form of sermons required of them. Furthermore, they were expected to marry and raise children (which many of them already had), becoming models of the Reformation ideal of the pious family.[50]

The task of bringing the Reformation to the villages of the Zurich territory was immense.[51] Zwingli's vision of an educated pastor in every parish, preaching the Word of God to the people, who were required to attend the services and be instructed by the sermon, was a distant prospect. This considerable ask required a major cultural shift in pastor and people. Furthermore, as the Church was in partnership with – but not subservient to – the ruling magistrates, religion had been highly politicized.[52] The pastor or parishioner attended church not only as a Christian, but also as a subject of the Zurich state, and he or she experienced constant reminders of this relationship and its attendant obligations. Parish clergy were charged with preaching and administering the two sacraments, but they were also to read from the pulpit the moral mandates of the civic government that covered all forms of behaviour, from marriage and the raising of children to the regulation of markets.

Zwingli did not delay. In May 1526, the Council mandated the creation of 'morals courts' to investigate instances of murder, adultery and prostitution (or suspicions thereof).[53] Everyone – wealthy patrician or village dayworker – was subject to the authority of such courts, and this created resentment at all social levels against this new form of intrusion.[54] Morals courts were nothing new, for they had a long history in the medieval dioceses of the German and Swiss lands, but their effectiveness and authority had been extremely patchy. Zwingli and the magistrates were essentially taking a medieval practice and giving it new life and purpose, this time with the intention that it should keep a close eye over the lives of the people.[55] He even made extensive use of canon law in the formation of positive law.[56]

Zwingli's decision to place the discipline of the Church in the hands of the magistrates spoke of his understanding of Church and rulers, whom he saw as the kings of Israel, protectors of the true faith.[57] Indeed, Zwingli viewed the visible Church not as a suffering, persecuted minority, but as God's chosen people of Israel, populated by both faithful and unfaithful, who were not distinguishable in this world. He wholly rejected the Anabaptist conception of a pure or separate body of Christ. Zwingli's Church was Israel with all its faults, yet, nevertheless, God's covenanted people. Oecolampadius in Basel saw the matter differently, arguing for the Church to hold the power of excommunication independently of the magistrates. In contrast to Zwingli, he argued that this had been the model of the early Church.[58]

Determined to exercise greater control over the clergy, the Zurich Council decreed in April 1528, when Bern finally adopted the Reformation, that a synod should be created for the clergy and laity.[59] The first meeting brought together approximately 300 participants, of whom just over a hundred were clergy. The others in attendance were members of the Large and Small Councils and lay representatives from the parishes. The disputations held in the city in 1523 provided the model, when it had been declared that the local meeting represented the whole Church. Although Zwingli spoke of the early Church, local practices in the medieval Church provided a more readily accessible foundation for his new institutional reforms. Thus, while the synod as a body of the Church went back to early Christianity, Zwingli's eyes were fixed on more recent practices. The diocese of Constance had held a number of synods in the late fifteenth and early sixteenth centuries aimed at enforcing ecclesiastical legislation and reforming the conduct and spiritual lives of priests, monks and lay people.[60]

Prophet and king, Zwingli and the *Bürgermeister* presided over the synodal meetings, which above all were intended for the reform of the ministers. The duties of the clergy were tightly scripted:[61] they were to live in their parishes, preach and administer the sacraments, care for their people and watch over their lives. Their duties to the ruling authorities were clear, and above all obedience was demanded.

These developments within the Church between 1526 and 1529 marked a new stage in Zwingli's authority in Zurich, attributable only in part to his own actions. A significant political shift in the city rendered the situation for the evangelical cause much more favourable. In 1527, the Small Council, long the seat of the most intense opposition to the Reformation, was given responsibility for church matters, a clear indication that its sympathies had shifted. A more dramatic sign of religious change came the following year, when the magistrates ruled that anyone who rejected the Reformed faith must resign his seat on the Council.[62] And there was more. Elections had brought increased numbers of Reformation sympathizers onto the benches, and in 1529 the mandate forbidding attendance at mass was reissued. A last bastion of resistance, the Constabulary, which in contrast to the guilds was made up of patricians, had its representation on the Small Council reduced from 18 to 12, further diminishing the influence of the leading families, which was good news for Zwingli and his supporters.[63]

## ADVISER

Towards the end of his life, Bullinger remembered Zwingli as a fierce preacher, polemicist and hardnose in politics, who was, nevertheless, seen by many reformers as a father figure. The somewhat beleaguered reformer was constantly implored to intercede with the Council on a broad range of matters – from errant sons and marital questions to taxes. Zwingli's disposition, Bullinger added, was to help others, and he endeavoured to comfort all those who came to him.[64] He received his petitioners with a 'friendly spirit', and when he could do no more would confess that he had done his best. Bullinger observed something of a naïvety in Zwingli: a readiness to help that was frequently exploited by others. Only experience taught Zwingli to look out for himself.[65] Above all, Bullinger described a merciful spirit, a man who neither bore grudges nor was quick to anger.

Bullinger, himself one of the most prolific correspondents of the sixteenth century, observed that Zwingli constantly wrote letters to friends and colleagues who were resident in the German lands, France, Italy and else-where.[66] A distinctive wax seal guaranteed that the letters were from his own hand, but occasionally he apologized for its absence because he was writing from the home of a friend or colleague. In March 1528, he informed Vadian that 'in my house there is only one copy of my letters. Everything goes out into the world as it comes out of my mouth, so one should refer to me as speaking rather than writing.'[67] His recipients were lay people, churchmen and magistrates, many of whom plied him with questions and sought his advice; and most of Zwingli's letters contained interpretations of biblical texts and counsel on how to deal with radicals and others in error. Many of his letters are no longer extant. Like most correspondents of his day, Zwingli was concerned about the security of epistles and feared that communications might fall into the wrong hands. Not infrequently, he asked that his recipients destroy the missives after reading them. On occasion, when writing to a humanist friend, Zwingli would write in Greek to protect his thoughts.

The surviving letters tell of Zwingli's attention to detail, his concern for the work of others committed to the gospel, and his self-awareness as an authority dispensing theological, political and practical advice. Two letters from 1527, between Zwingli and Fridolin Brunner, pastor in Glarus and a student of the Zurich reformer, are illustrative.[68] Writing on 15 January, Brunner reported that the gospel was spreading 'beautifully' in Glarus and assured Zwingli that he had abandoned all trace of papistry, although he was threatened with violence by his opponents, who supported the mercenary pensions.[69] His position, however, was challenging, for although he had preached against the abuses of the Church, the people were reluctant to abandon the belief that the Eucharist was the true body and blood of Christ. Brunner's experience was hardly novel for a reforming pastor who found himself at odds with many of his parishioners. He added that he had reached a form of compromise with the people, and, borrowing an expression often used by Zwingli, observed that they would drink milk first before receiving solid food. His plan was to proceed slowly with changes to the Lord's Supper, unless Zwingli advised otherwise. Rather ungenerously, he described his parishioners as 'imbeciles', too much influenced by Valentin Tschudi, the learned Catholic priest in Glarus and onetime friend of Zwingli.[70]

These two figures close to Zwingli in Glarus were locked in confessional strife.

The last part of the long letter was typical of much of the correspondence received by Zwingli from pastors working in the parishes. Brunner presented Zwingli with a 'knot' that the pastor could not untie. The issue sprang from two passages in scripture: John 15:5 ('I am the vine, you are the branches. He who abides in me, and I in him, he it is that bears much fruit, for apart from me you can do nothing') and Sirach 15:16 ('He has placed before you fire and water: stretch out your hand for whichever you wish'). What, he asked, is the Bible saying about the role of humans in their salvation.[71] Does God do everything? Brunner confessed that he was not sure what to teach on predestination, providence and human responsibility.

Zwingli wrote back to the pastor on 25 January that one letter was not sufficient to resolve this dilemma between Sirach and John, but that he would give a condensed reply. He asserted that divine providence governs and sets out all things, and grounded his response on an argument about God's goodness, wisdom and omnipotence. Essentially, he contended that, because of these characteristics, God always orders all things to the best possible outcome. God cannot be the author of sin, which arises from human lust and lasciviousness. This truth was the sure case against any sense of human free will in the matter of salvation.[72] However, such teaching was not easily received, and Zwingli counselled Brunner against presenting these matters to the people too directly, for 'indeed there are few who are truly pious, and only a few who can reach that height of intelligence'.[73]

In October 1526, Zwingli replied to Urbanus Rhegius, preacher in Augsburg, concerning election and damnation – a theological issue with significant pastoral implications.[74] What about children who are not able to hear the gospel and believe? Are they condemned to hell when they die? No, replied Zwingli, because they are not condemned by any law. If they come from believing parents, they are covered by the faith of the covenant. If they come from parents who do not believe, Zwingli continued, he could not say with certainty; however, if he had to speculate, he would stress the saving power of Christ, emphasizing the greater power of grace over sin. All that are born are made holy through Christ.[75]

Much of Zwingli's correspondence was with people of little social standing, who appear to have felt at liberty to write to the reformer about their concerns. Their optimism that he would be able to provide help or resolve disputes or family and financial problems is striking. Even more remarkable is the evidence from their grateful replies that he often was able to assist. The concerns were legion. Could he find accommodation for a son, help facilitate a marriage for a daughter? Frequently, he was asked to look out for the welfare of a child or student, ensuring that they had adequate provision. Heinrich Hässi from Glarus wrote asking Zwingli to help find a doctor for his dying wife, as he had no trust in the ones who were treating her.[76] Clearly, Zwingli's pastoral reputation in Glarus continued long after his departure.

Through Zwingli's vast body of written work, we find almost nothing addressed to the particular situations of female Christians. Only two surviving letters were sent by Zwingli to female recipients. One is addressed to his wife, Anna Reinhart, and says almost nothing of interest. The other dates from 1523, when he wrote to Margareta Fehr in Einsiedeln to comfort her in her evident anxieties and depression. The advice was fairly general, enjoining her to allow the tranquillity of scripture to relieve her pain. He also addressed a question she had posed about a married priest offering communion to his wife. Such a concern, Zwingli wrote, related to human regulations, not God's, and therefore she should attend more to questions of envy, bitterness, quarrelsomeness and anger.[77] He ended by complimenting her on her diligent reading of scripture.

Of greater interest are the seven surviving letters from women to Zwingli, which reveal both their various circumstances and the active role the reformer took in arranging marriages and other domestic situations. Margaretha and her sister Katherine von Wattenwyl were Poor Clares about to leave their order to marry.[78] Zwingli clearly played a part in their engagements. Margaretha became engaged to Lucius Tscharner of Chur in the summer of 1525, and by March the following year a child was on its way. Tscharner himself wrote to Zwingli asking if he knew of a woman who could tend their home during the pregnancy, as he knew nothing of kitchen duties:

As Tschudi says to me, I should go there myself and take my wife with me. I can never do that, because she is about to give birth, God give her grace! And she wrote to Frau Murerin 14 days ago begging her earnestly to inquire for a good and pious woman in good age, who shall cook and need not work in the field, however, but care for [my] wife and the children as well as cook for them. I am no landlord at all! My wife earnestly and friendly begs your pious and good wife to help Frau Murerin to look for [such a woman]. Whatever wage I shall pay her, I will.[79]

Barbara Trüllerey, abbess of the cloister of Schänis, near Glarus, wrote on 24 February 1524 to ask Zwingli whether he could offer spiritual guidance for a young relative that he might grow up well.[80] Further, she sought the reformer's interpretation of two passages in Matthew: 'The last will be first and the first last' (20:16) and 'Many are called, but few chosen' (22:14). She referred to Zwingli as 'preacher of the holy word of God in the praiseworthy city of Zurich'.[81] Two years later, Barbara Nithart from Ulm or Constance had a similar concern.[82] This time it was a wayward son, who was about to lose the financial support of his family if he did not mend his ways:

I let you know that I have a young son who studies in Zurich. His name is Hans Nithard and he is 19 years old. We have raised him since his youth to [study], which costs a fortune. And I beg you for God's sake to let me know how he behaves during studies and beyond; whether he is assiduous, or whether he is nonchalant and lazy and possesses no zeal during instruction. Further, whether he only wants to follow dancing and prostitutes and be wasteful with clothes. For he should do nothing without my consent and knowledge. I beg you for Christ our saviour's sake, that you take him in hand and chasten him and tell his teacher to punish him and to let him do nothing excessive on this earth regarding clothes, drinking or debts. For what he gives him beyond the weekly amount, I do not want to pay at all.[83]

We have no reply containing Zwingli's advice on how to deal with this 19-year-old young man. Many years later, the son's name appeared on the list of magistrates in the city of Constance, so evidently he had not turned out too badly.[84] Almost all of the letters from women to Zwingli dealt with family members, usually sons or nephews in need of assistance or patronage. They suggest that Zwingli spent considerable time acting as a paternal figure for fatherless boys in the city, arranging for their education, securing work in local trades and offering counsel when needed.

In a 1518 letter from Einsiedeln to Heinrich Utinger, he had admitted that it was extremely difficult for him to live without the intimacy of a woman, but his letters tell us almost nothing about his beloved Anna and their children.[85] Unlike Luther, Zwingli drew a curtain around his family and domestic life.

## REVENGE

One of the most dramatic confrontations between evangelicals and Catholics in the Swiss Confederation following the introduction of the Reformation was the disputation held at Baden in May–June 1526.[86] The Catholic churchman Johann Eck, Zwingli's most formidable opponent was present; but Zwingli himself, the man at the centre of the storm, was not. The episode is all the more revealing for Zwingli's biography precisely because he did *not* attend.

Disputations, so advantageous to Zwingli's cause in Zurich, took place in several locations in the Confederation between 1524 and 1526, including Basel, Appenzell and Ilanz in Graubünden, none of which were attended by Zwingli.[87] These public events were carefully stage managed and generally arrived at predetermined conclusions.[88] This pattern of disputations had served the Reformation cause well, often because of Zwingli's rhetorical gifts and his ability to maul his adversaries in theological confrontation. In 1526, however, the Catholics got their revenge on Zwingli and his supporters, and the man behind their triumph was the brilliant Eck, long-time opponent of Luther, Karlstadt and Zwingli.[89]

In March of that year, the theologian and scourge of the reformers was invited by the Swiss Diet to come to participate in a disputation with his opponents. Eck was fully prepared to ride into verbal battle. Three years earlier, he had proposed both a diocesan synod and a debate as a means of destroying the heretics, above all Zwingli. The following year, in 1524, he focused on Zwingli, seeking to lure him into a confrontation along the lines of his encounter with Luther at Leipzig in 1519.[90] Eck's intense interest in Swiss affairs was clear at a meeting in Regensburg in July 1524, when the ecclesiastical and temporal rulers of southern Germany gathered to discuss the implementation of the Edict of Worms. At Regensburg, Eck met Johannes Fabri, who had debated with Zwingli at the first disputation in Zurich, in January 1523, and was now in the service of the Habsburgs. They likely discussed a possible encounter with Zwingli.[91]

In October 1525, Eck renewed his suggestion of a disputation, and in a letter to the Swiss Confederates signalled his willingness to participate. He underscored the disruption and division caused by the Reformation in the German lands:

> So ought the blind heretics who have lost the holy faith fall into the dark abyss of all heresy so that your lords can easily see what a false and devilish faith these hardened men teach, who are full of contradictions. For earlier Zwingli and Oecolampadius doubted the sacrificial character of the mass, but at the same time taught that the sacrament of the body and blood of Christ was to be held in high honour ... that was in 1523. Not even two years later he not only madly abolished the mass, but he established a heretical form of mass and he himself deprived the people of the heavenly meal. So unstable and fickle are these heretics! They cry out that theirs is the rock of certain faith and eternal truth.[92]

Fully aware of the growing rift between Zurich and Wittenberg, Eck poured oil on the flames by making Zwingli Luther's dog:

> Zwingli forgets that he had once greatly praised Luther as an admirable and true warrior of God who with great sincerity studied the Bible as it has been on earth for the last thousand years and is in unshakeable truth. If Zwingli held such a high view of Luther as he has written, then why does he not follow and believe Luther?

The Swiss Diet determined that a debate would take place in Baden, only 14 miles from Zurich, but safely in Catholic territory. The Diet's intentions held no mystery: their enthusiasm was little less than bloodlust to destroy Zwingli, the arch-heretic. The magistrates and reformers in Zurich agonized over whether Zwingli should attend, weighing up the obvious dangers against the recognition that Baden offered a much broader stage on which to confront the Catholic Church and make their claim for a reformed Confederation. Zwingli's absence would deprive the evangelical party of its most prominent theological voice, of the man who had prevailed in 1523 against the Catholics and in 1525 against the Anabaptists. We do not know whether the reformer or the Council had the final say, but in a letter Zwingli declared that the people of Zurich were strongly against his participation.[93]

There were good reasons for not going to Baden. The Catholics would be firmly in control and their intention was clearly to humiliate the reformer and the city. Furthermore, Zwingli's life would surely be in danger, as the Council in Zurich was aware and as friends and colleagues warned. Rumours circulated of a plan to abduct Zwingli from Baden. Death threats had been issued. In the weeks leading up to the disputation, Zwingli engaged in an acidic exchange with his adversary Johannes Fabri, who had denounced the Zurich reformer as a coward. Zwingli appealed to his countrymen by reminding them that Fabri had once referred to the Swiss as 'cow buggerers'.[94]

Although he remained in Zurich, Zwingli saw himself as debating Eck from afar, and was so involved in the discussions in the weeks before the disputation that he is reported to have suffered from chronic sleep deprivation.[95] In the run-up, he also wrote to those who would attend, with advice on what to say in debate. Once the debate was under way, he was kept informed by a network of colleagues and students, whom he engaged to provide him with every detail of the proceedings. Some students carried letters from and to those participating, although missives conveying Zwingli's instructions were probably destroyed for reasons of security.[96] Such was the concern to conceal any contact between Zwingli and the participants that one letter with instructions for Oecolampadius was brought into Baden by a young man hidden in a hay wagon. Myconius observed that 'Zwingli laboured more in running about, thinking, counselling, watching, warning, writing both letters and books that he sent to Baden than he would have done had he taken part.'[97]

The Baden Disputation opened on 19 May 1526 and lasted three weeks. It was an enormous production financed by the Swiss Diet, the bishops and the participating Confederates. The invitation list had included the 13 members of the Swiss Confederation, the associated members and the bishops of Constance, Basel, Sion and Lausanne. Only a smaller number of invitees in fact chose to attend, reflecting in many cases the cost of going to Baden for three weeks.[98] Even Erasmus in Basel had been invited, but he declined, citing health reasons. Yet over two hundred delegates did assemble, with the number actually present fluctuating during the sessions. Some were lay representatives from Swiss and southern German states, but the vast majority were clerics, many of whom held university degrees. The participants were isolated from the world around them. The city walls were heavily guarded to prevent infiltration by foreign spies and messengers, although, as we have heard, Zwingli did manage to remain in contact, aided by the opening of the city gates each day to allow farmers to bring food and goods into the city.

A dramatic confrontation between Catholics and evangelicals, the event was carefully staged. Unlike the later religious colloquies in the Empire in the early 1540s, Baden was not about finding common ground. The Catholics were out for revenge and sought to demonstrate the truth of the old faith. Before the proceedings were even launched, the delegates listened to a half-hour sermon, in which the preacher inveighed against the evangelicals. Two pulpits were used for the disputation: the old pulpit was used by the Catholic party, and a second – temporary – pulpit was set up for the lead reformer Oecolampadius: the hierarchy was clear. The four men chosen to preside over the sessions were all hostile to the new faith: during the sessions, according to one evangelical witness, they applauded Eck and laughed at Oecolampadius.[99]

Eck had published seven theses for debate, on the real presence and transubstantiation, the mass, invocation of Mary and the saints, images, purgatory, original sin, and baptism.[100] The most extensive exchange concerned the presence of Christ in the Eucharist. Eck himself frequently interrupted the speaker with taunts and jibes, shouting out to the public that Oecolampadius was a liar. With his prodigious intellect, sharp tongue and fierce reputation, Eck must have been an intimidating presence. He enjoyed mocking evangelical claims that their arguments were grounded in scripture, by pointing out that a crucial point they were making was to be found in book four of Aristotle's *Metaphysics*, not in the Bible.[101] The evangelical appeal to the Word of God, he scoffed, had only led to chaos, and he pointed to the slaughter of thousands in the Peasants' War as the consequence of Luther's lies.

By the time the disputation ended, on 8 June, there had been 17 days of debate. Eck's seven theses were upheld by a vote of 84 to 24 (with three abstentions). Even the four Lutherans present voted for Eck, an act not to be forgotten by the Swiss. The Catholic victory was confirmed by decisions to suppress Zwingli's writings and the proscribed 'Lutheran' preaching. Although a final account of the proceedings was supposed to be circulated, no agreed text could be formulated, with Bern and Basel withholding their consent. The Swiss Confederation had been founded as a defensive alliance, but now it was hopelessly torn apart by religion. The disputation at Baden only confirmed that irreconcilable views of Christianity existed without any political or legal framework.

Perhaps the greatest gain for the evangelicals was ironically a product of Zwingli's absence – the emergence of Johannes Oecolampadius as a spiritual and doctrinal leader of the movement. He had courageously and ably faced Eck in the lion's den, defending his theology to a scoffing audience, patiently enduring the insults. He was by no means Zwingli's subaltern. He had relied on the Zurich reformer's advice, but he had spoken at length, with only a few notes, and had proved able to summon biblical and patristic evidence in support of his case. Indeed, it would become increasingly clear that he and Zwingli did not agree on everything. The event at Baden had been an attempt to destroy Zwingli, but Oecolampadius had acted where the Zurich reformer had hesitated. The triumph of the Catholics, however, was only partial. There had been hopes that doctrinal victory might lead to military action against Zurich to restore the old faith. The unwillingness of Bern and Basel, which were drifting towards Reformation, to participate put an end to such aspirations. The Catholic Confederates could not press home their advantage.[102]

The Catholic victory at Baden underscored Zwingli's need to bolster his own position in Zurich, where, despite reversals, the adherents of the old faith and those who continued to receive pensions posed a serious threat. The introduction of the Reformation had by no means quashed opposition.[103] Zwingli and his colleagues denounced members of distinguished families, such as the Rubli, Escher and Wellenberg, as traitors who lined their pockets with money from the king of France, the pope and the exiled duke of Württemberg.

The most infamous case in Zurich was that of Jakob Grebel, father of radical leader and former Zwingli friend Konrad Grebel. Jakob Grebel represented the Zurich elite who continued to benefit from foreign pensions, in contravention of the Council's mandates and Zwingli's preaching.[104] It was claimed that Jakob Grebel had received more than 4,000 crowns from a papal agent and was seeking more.[105] A commission of 11 men was set up by the Council to examine the claims against Grebel and others, and Zwingli was invited to submit evidence. The reformer readily obliged and presented oral testimony against a series of prominent figures. Two men, Hans Escher and Heinrich Leu, were imprisoned in the Wellenberg. On account of his status, Jakob Grebel was confined in the Rathaus. The generous treatment accorded the older man did not last long: he was tortured and then found guilty of taking pensions and committing treason. On 30 October 1526, he was executed. Death was not only for Anabaptists, but also for those who defied the Council.

## VICTORY

The efforts of the Catholic Confederates to ensure that the records of the disputation favoured their cause led to consternation in Bern and Basel, both of which were enraged by what they perceived as mendacity.[106] Zurich was encouraged by the turn of events, and in early 1527 sought to create alliances that would end its isolation in the Confederation. In January, representatives of Bern, Basel, Schaffhausen, Appenzell, St Gallen and Glarus were invited to the city to consider the precarious situation among the Swiss.[107] It was Zurich's first diplomatic initiative since the Reformation. As ever, Bern was the crucial player, its cooperation essential to any alliance against the Five States. Bern had saved the Reformation in Zurich and prevented the city from being expelled from the Confederation, but it was not willing to grant the Zurichers a free hand. The Bernese needed stability in the east in order to be able to develop their interests in the French-speaking lands of the west leading to Geneva and Savoy.

Strong evangelical impulses had sprung up in Bern during the earliest years of the Reformation, and in June 1523 the city council, like that of Zurich, had adopted gospel preaching.[108] Again like Zurich, Bern was religiously divided, but it lacked a charismatic and politically adept figure like Zwingli to advance the evangelical cause. Nevertheless, the movement grew, and in June 1526, Berchtold Haller, the principal preacher and a friend of Zwingli, was invited to speak before the 200 members of the Bernese Large Council, laying out the evangelical position on the sacraments. His address caused uproar and he immediately offered to resign his position as a canon in the main church and to leave the city; but the magistrates had other ideas. They accepted his resignation, but insisted that he remain to preach the gospel, for which he would be paid from the income of his former canonry.

To resolve the religious tensions in their city, the Bernese magistrates took a page from the Zurich playbook and summoned a disputation to be held in the city's Franciscan church, which local architects transformed into a hall for 500 observers.[109] The disputation was called for January 1528, and the bishops of Constance, Sion, Lausanne and Basel, in whose dioceses the sprawling Bernese territory fell, were invited to attend. Invitations were also sent to the other Confederates, as well as to some of the leading German imperial cities of the south. None of the bishops attended and the Catholic states refused to allow delegates to cross their lands. The Catholic parties had good reason to turn down the invitation. They could continue to ride their great victory at Baden, so why renew the debate? Furthermore, in direct contrast to Baden, at Bern, as the invitation noted, all arguments were to be on the basis of scripture alone.

Zwingli was desperate for another opportunity to take on Johann Eck, but the Catholic theologian declined to go to Bern for many of the very reasons Zwingli had used two years earlier. He knew that it would only be a public humiliation. The imperial court at Speyer responded at the last moment that the proposed disputation was illegal and that Bern should wait for the upcoming Imperial Diet at Regensburg. Further, doctrinal matters should only be debated at a legitimate council of the Church.

Zurich *Bürgermeister* Diethelm Röist gave his consent for Zwingli to attend, and after a fulsome New Year's feast in the guild hall of the skinners, the reformer set out on the three-day trip to Bern, protected by an armed guard. Zwingli and Röist rode horses, while most of the contingent travelled on foot, covering about 30 miles a day.[110] When they reached the Bernese frontier, a company of some 200 crossbowmen and halberdiers greeted them, to ensure their safe passage to the city. The journey to Bern, taking Zwingli briefly into hostile territory, was a jarring reminder that he was a hunted heretic. It was rumoured that when he passed through the village of Mellingen, a shot had been fired at him.[111] When he arrived at Bern, Zwingli refused the official quarters provided for him and chose to stay with a family member.

Whereas Oecolampadius had been left to carry the banner at Baden against Eck and Fabri, at Bern the evangelicals turned out in force. Zwingli led a large contingent from Zurich; Oecolampadius came from Basel; and

Martin Bucer and Wolfgang Capito were there from Strasbourg. Also in attendance were Zwingli's friends Joachim Vadian from St Gallen and Ambrosius Blarer from Constance. The Bernese reformers Haller and Franz Kolb took the lead, but it was Zwingli who had drafted the 10 theses for debate. The disputation then lasted almost three weeks, from 6 to 26 January, and was conducted in German so that both laity and clergy might participate. To avoid the controversy of the not impartial Baden records, the sessions were scrupulously minuted, to the extent that participants were told to speak slowly so that every word might be written down.

According to that official record, Zwingli spoke more than a hundred times. He was not alone, however: despite his commanding presence, other reformers also frequently rose to put the case for the evangelical faith. And Zwingli was careful to allow the Bern reformers Haller and Kolb to lead the debates. Delegates representing Lutheran churches in German cities such as Nuremberg were also in attendance, but rarely intervened. Catholic opposition to this array of supporters of the Reformation was rather meagre. The talented Konrad Träger from Fribourg led the opposition and offered robust objections to the reformers; but with no appeal to church authority or tradition permitted, the Catholics were hamstrung.[112] Central to the discussion was the relationship of the Church and scripture, which constituted the first three articles. The theses were upheld by an impressive majority.

The day after the disputation concluded, the Bernese Council issued an edict that the mass was to be abolished and the churches cleansed of images within eight days. During the stripping of the churches, children sang: 'We have been freed from a baked god.'[113] Following the model of Zurich, a committee was created to oversee the orderly prosecution of the decree. By no means everyone in the city was pleased with the turn of events. Fights broke out in the churches, as images, statues, vestments and liturgical vessels were removed. A member of the butcher's guild threatened to kill anyone who damaged that guild's altar and complained that the destruction made the church look like a stable. Another rode into a church on a donkey and denounced those who were participating in the desecration of the churches, expressing the hope that their hands would fall off.[114] Large bonfires burned in the Münsterplatz as centuries of devotional gifts were consumed in the flames. Objects that could not be burnt or resold were buried. The process of tearing down the fabric of the old church in Bern took over two years.

The Franciscan church was turned into a warehouse, while grain was stored in the altar space and choir of the Dominican house.

Zwingli preached twice in Bern: once during the disputation and once when it had concluded. In many respects, his sermons formed a reckoning with both his opponents and his humanist and scholastic past. From the pulpit he offered a fulsome evocation of the Christian faith, drawing on the wisdom of antiquity, his debt to Erasmus, his years of expounding the Bible, knowledge of the church fathers and his rhetorical gifts. Never before or again would he stand before such a distinguished body of reformers – men who would shape the Reformation after Zwingli was dead. His first sermon conjured up the majesty of the providential God and the glory of his creation. It was Zwingli's moment, and he relished it.

Much of the first part of the sermon focused on the credal words 'one God, Father almighty, creator of heaven and earth'. God is the source of all goodness and goodness itself. He is perfection and wisdom and thereby generative of these qualities in humanity, which possesses these qualities by participation in God. Socrates had understood that wisdom was to be shared. God is not merely a first principle or a distant creator: his immanence in the world is through his providential ordering of all things:

> With God we think of a person who in the building of a house assigns every room and corner its special purpose and use. Everything that he created has been given in advance its purpose. Further, a craftsman knows all of his tools and either uses or leaves them according to his need. He does not forget a single tool, even if for a time he allows it to rust a little . . . In the same way, God knows all His creation.[115]

To explain God's presence in the world, Zwingli turned to his beloved Swiss countryside. In the sun that streams down on a mountain valley, God reveals his presence in the world. The poet reformer saw God in the world:

> The sun is beheld by all people in the world. It illuminates and makes all fruitful while at the same time warming the earth. The smallest piece of grass, the greatest mountain and trees enjoy the sun and are refreshed by it, and yet none of them are omnipresent. To be with the sun or to walk with it is all that is needed to be warmed and to be

alive. And all things under the sun are made alive only by it. And they enjoy and see the sun not merely partially, but as a whole! Even so, God penetrates all things, is everywhere present, pleases and revives them all, and is by all things received, enjoyed and used, even by the unrighteous who do not know him.[116]

Zwingli preached for a second time on the day after the completion of the disputation. Surrounded by the debris of smashed altars and broken statues of saints, he stood in the pulpit of the Bernese Münster to address the magistrates of the city on their duties as godly rulers. Drawn from Galatians 5, his theme was perseverance and tenacity in the good. He cited Moses, who in 40 years 'never once doubted God's assistance'.[117] Then there was David, 'whom neither poverty or misery could move to lose his faith in God'. Alongside such well-known figures of the Bible, he placed Cornelius Scipio, the general and statesman of the Roman Republic, who on hearing that the surviving leadership of Rome was contemplating flight across the Mediterranean after Hannibal's victory at Cannae, burst into the chamber with his friends, brandishing their swords and swearing that they would abandon neither Italy nor Rome and would protect their homeland. 'He remained so steadfast until his death,' noted Zwingli. His example illustrated that 'virtue begets virtue'.[118]

Addressing the magistrates directly, Zwingli offered an account of how Reformation should take place. Drawing on his experiences, he claimed that true religion could only begin with the forceful destruction of the old. Crucifixes were to become firewood. Hearts must be purified by the fires that destroy objects of idolatry. In contrast to his actions in Zurich, Zwingli encouraged the Bernese rulers to act quickly and decisively. Christ had overturned the tables in the temple and warned his followers to 'keep awake therefore, for you do not know on what day your Lord is coming'. The magistrates were not to hesitate: 'this filth and dross should now be swept away in order that the huge sums that you more than others have spent on the unspeakable stupidity of the cult of saints should in future be used for the good of the living likenesses of God'.[119]

Zwingli's most commanding moment came in Bern, away from his adopted city of Zurich. For a moment, he spoke for a broad sodality of reformers and magistrates. The unity was not to last.

# NINE

# ALLIANCES AND CONFRONTATIONS

Zwingli believed passionately in the providence of God, that divine benevolence unfolded in the world, delivering humanity out of the ruck of sinfulness. Yet he would surely have struggled to identify signs of an orderly plan in his remaining years after 1528. With the Reformation – first in Bern and then in other cities, such as Basel and Schaffhausen – the attempts at alliances, the First Kappel War in 1529 and the Diet of Augsburg the following year, Zwingli was caught up in a maelstrom of events far beyond his control. Although the Reformation had been planted in Zurich and its institutional forms were slowly taking root, Zwingli's own place was never entirely secure. His influence on the ruling magistrates was significant – at moments, even decisive – but never unquestioned. The Council was equally capable of heeding his advice and ignoring his urging, giving the lie to any sense of a theocracy ruled over by a prophet. Even among the supporters of the Reformation, considerable unease was evident at Zwingli's sense that military conflict was necessary. Equally, his attempts at forming alliances in the Empire, for example with Philipp of Hesse, were seen by many as not necessarily in Zurich's best interests.

✤ ✤ ✤

By the late 1520s, the Reformation had become a fragmented movement, with few clear lines. The German territories and cities were not simply Lutheran or Reformed, for they contained a broad range of competing religious views that reflected the shifting and evolving nature of what was to become known as Protestantism. Within the Swiss Confederation, the spread and establishment of the Reformation did not, as we shall see, bring uniformity of either doctrine or goals. On almost every level, disagreement reflected particular religious, political and economic circumstances. Additionally, fierce Catholic resistance grew during the late 1520s, as Charles V became increasingly determined to staunch the flow of heresy.

Where do we find Zwingli in all of this? As we follow the story of his last years, we need to bear in mind that he was not the sole leader of a movement, but was a prominent figure within a group of reformers that extended across the Empire and Confederation. At Marburg, he shared the stage with Oecolampadius; in the period leading up to the First Kappel War, his voice was one among several, such as the Bernese reformer-politician Niklaus Manuel, a fierce opponent of military conflict. Frustrated by foes and allies alike, Zwingli moved away from compromise. His confession to the Diet of Augsburg in 1530 was his own and represented no city or other reformer. At significant moments during his last years, Zwingli was an isolated figure.

A German ballad from the late 1520s caught the mood:

> There is a noble hero, Huldrych is his name. He comes from good family, the Zwinglis, as you know. He it is who teaches in his doctrine the true honour of the living God, whose commandments we must obey. He also serves all the Swiss and labours not in vain for a Christian federation. The people, however, pride themselves on being pious folk; they give themselves to mischief and hold his plans for nought.[1]

## BEYOND THE RHINE

The Reformation in Zurich was never purely a Swiss event: it unleashed a powerful and unsettling force across the southern German lands of the Empire. Zwingli saw Charles V as a tyrant eager to restore the Roman Empire, and he had cast the new faith in terms of liberation from oppressive laws that burdened lives and consciences. In his mind, the Habsburgs posed the greatest threat to true religion, even worse than Rome, and they had to be vanquished. His calls for religious freedom were coupled with demands for liberty from tyranny, both religious and political. Yet there were limits to Zwingli's revolution: the faith had been placed in the hands of the Zurich magistrates, and the Reformation brought social reform, but not restructuring. Nevertheless, beyond his reach Zwingli's ideas fed an impulse for resistance with which his name was closely associated. Like Luther, Zwingli also found that his convictions established a life of their own, labile in nature and often at a distance from the original intentions and contexts. The appeal of 'Zwinglian' preachers in the German cities lay in their ability to hitch anti-Catholic and clerical sentiments to an idea of gospel renewal that would deliver a more just society.[2] Similarly, Zwingli's teachings were attractive to guilds that perceived a message of communal ideals dispatching patrician oligarchies. The Swiss served as a model for German cities, where hopes of reform grew from shared religious, social and political ideals. The Confederates had come together through a series of agreements. Now Zurich sought to join hands with Constance and Strasbourg, and looked to other German cities in which the Reformed faith found fertile ground.[3]

Following his triumph in Bern in 1528, Zwingli became increasingly consumed by affairs within the Empire, and with good reason. The Baden Disputation had made clear the depth of Catholic opposition within the Confederation, and the Reformation in Bern did not resolve the confessional gridlock. Although the Catholic states were not strong enough to defeat the Reformed, the Protestants possessed no unified desire to press their advantage through force. Zwingli remained the most prominent Swiss reformer, but he did not speak unequivocally for Zurich, and certainly not for Bern and Basel.

Yet the Zurich reformer was deeply involved in the unfolding drama. Friends and sympathetic preachers rapidly carried Swiss religious views through the cities of Swabia and the Upper Rhine. Zwingli's advocacy of the absolute power of God and of religion in the hands of rulers proved remarkably supple, adaptable to changing circumstances.[4] In Constance, perched on the border between the German and Swiss lands, the bishop had been displaced by a Reformation led by Johannes Zwick and Ambrosius Blarer, who were close to both Zwingli and Oecolampadius. Reformed-inspired preachers were very much in the mix in the religious tumult in wealthy Augsburg, where Zwinglians made inroads into the guilds and higher society, garnering considerable support within the ruling Council.[5] That Zwingli had not explicitly called for political change was not relevant: his influence was determined by how he was heard and read. The appeal of his message lay in its striking clarity: moral renewal, purging churches of images to benefit the poor, simplicity of worship and a doctrine of the Lord's Supper that was readily comprehensible (unlike that of the Lutherans). His ideas also found enthusiastic followers in Nuremberg, Ulm and, most significantly, Strasbourg. The close connections between the southern German cities enabled Zwingli's ideas to gain access to circles of reform-minded clerics and laity.[6] Again, we need to be careful about attributing everything to Zwingli alone, as his work was read as part of a growing body of pamphlets and texts, in particular those of his colleagues Oecolampadius, Bucer and Capito; and his ideas were declared by preachers whose influences came from Strasbourg and Basel, as well as from Zurich. Nevertheless, Zwingli's name was everywhere.

## THE LANDGRAVE

By the time of the Diet of Speyer in March 1529, more recent victories by Charles V against his long-time enemy Francis I had put the Catholics in a strong position to reverse the Reformation. Concessions to the evangelicals granted in 1525 were to be rolled back and the Edict of Worms enforced. Charles was represented by his brother Ferdinand, who was in no mood to compromise, and who demanded that the Catholic faith be restored in the Empire. The 'protest' against the recess of the Diet was signed by the leading evangelical princes, including Elector Johann of Saxony and Philipp of Hesse, together with 14 imperial cities. The Swiss were not party to the event. The signatories denounced the declarations of the Diet as contrary to the Word of God and their consciences. Little room for compromise remained, and territorial states and cities were forced to declare their hand either in support or in opposition to the emperor and the Catholic Church. Looming large in the background was the Turkish threat, as Ottoman ships sailed up the Danube and would eventually lay siege to Vienna in September 1529.

The Protestant cause, however, was politically divided. The powerful territorial princes such as Johann of Saxony and Philipp of Hesse spoke of military resistance and a refusal to pay imperial taxes. The cities, however, had traditionally enjoyed a close and profitable relationship with the Holy Roman emperors, serving as bankers and enjoying trade privileges, and were less inclined to belligerency.[7] Nevertheless, in April 1529, Strasbourg concluded a defensive alliance with Philipp of Hesse, Johann of Saxony, and the cities of Nuremberg and Ulm explicitly to defend true religion.[8]

The sacramental differences remained, however, a thorn in the side, intensified by Luther's insistence that Oecolampadius and Zwingli were literally hell bound. A broader cultural difference also separated Lutherans and Swiss Reformed. Although the Swiss still nominally belonged to the Empire, they were *de facto* independent and occupied little mental space for most Germans. Other than Germans in the south, few in the Empire knew much about the Swiss, beyond their reputation as warlike peasants. The rustic Confederates were the butt of bawdy jokes, not least about their sexual proclivities for farm animals.

Luther's association of the Swiss with the fanatics expressed his great fear that their theological errors went hand in hand with political and social disorder, an association that conjured up the Peasants' War. Luther shared the common attitude that the Swiss were insubordinate: the traditional republican and communal traditions of the Confederation might incite rebellion or insurrection in the German lands.[9] Philipp Melanchthon predicted that the Swiss would use force 'from which is to be feared not only a terrible and great butchery but also great disputes in all ecclesiastical affairs and the erosion of government, which could not be repaired in a hundred years – nay not for the rest of time.'[10] In response, Philipp of Hesse told Melanchthon that, as far as he knew, the Zwinglians were not revolutionaries.

The relationship between Philipp of Hesse and Zwingli took shape during the summer of 1529, although there had been contact for some three years. This imperial prince and the cleric with a rustic background were not equals, but their bond came with genuine respect and even fondness. Zwingli's talent lay in articulating a new faith with remarkable persuasion, and in working with those who possessed power. And although his own lands were largely Lutheran, Philipp was drawn to Zwingli's theology. At first their contact seemed to promise much, and Philipp worked hard to protect the Zurich reformer from attacks from the Lutherans. He was eager for a meeting in his own territory at Marburg to find a resolution. But he, too, had little understanding of the unique nature of the Swiss Confederation, and assumed a unity that did not exist – a miscalculation whose consequences would soon become evident. Bern, preoccupied with internal concerns and with avoiding war in the Confederation, had little interest in a grand Protestant alliance. Despite last-minute efforts to persuade them otherwise, the Bernese did not send representatives to Marburg, and their lack of engagement seriously weakened the Swiss presence. Zwingli, for his part, placed on Philipp's shoulders the weight of his expectations for the Reformation. Their exchanges were a mixture of political information and doctrinal elucidations.

After the failure to reach agreement at Marburg, Philipp revised his plans towards the possibility of two separate Protestant alliances for the north and south, in which he would play a leading role.[11] The idea was rejected out of hand by the elector of Saxony, with the result that by the end of 1529 the landgrave was becoming isolated. In the southern part of the Empire, he turned his attention to an alliance with Strasbourg and the Swiss, with Jakob Sturm in Strasbourg and Huldrych Zwingli his principal contacts. The landgrave understood his own position as pre-eminent, and while in Basel during March 1530 made clear his expectations that the Swiss would provide soldiers to aid in the restoration of Duke Ulrich of Württemberg, and possibly against the emperor. That same month, Zwingli wrote a set of brief notes in which he expressed the smug hope that Philipp would back the Reformed Swiss and secure the Reformation in the Confederation.[12] For the landgrave, however, the Swiss were to fall in line, and he paid little heed to Zwingli's opposition to the use of mercenaries.

Philipp of Hesse and Zwingli met in person only once, at Marburg. But their ongoing correspondence maintained their relationship, and their exchanges were warm and trusting – the landgrave requested that the reformer keep confidential information to himself.[13] In his letters to Zwingli, Philipp sought news, influence and ideas; for his part, Zwingli was clearly flattered by the landgrave's attention. He saw himself as a theological counsellor to the prince. Yet each man hoped for more of the other than he was able or willing to provide. Philipp believed that Zwingli might open the door to crucial political contacts that would enable the building of an alliance with the Protestant

Swiss. This sanguine assessment arose in part out of ignorance. The landgrave seemed to understand little either of the ongoing opposition to Zwingli in Zurich or of the reality that the magistrates were not always inclined to follow the preacher.[14] Yet Philipp was, in the end, shrewd enough to recognize that he needed the support of the political leaders. Zwingli likewise expected more of his influence with Philipp, whom he saw as the key to a broader alliance that would secure the Reformation among the Swiss. For the reformer, the alliance would further the spread of evangelical faith in the German lands and form a religious bond with the Confederation. The landgrave was primarily interested in imperial religious politics; Zwingli was thinking about the Swiss.

## THE FIRST KAPPEL WAR, 1529

Zwingli's instincts were for peace and negotiation, but he was also clear that the gospel must not be impeded by the agents of Antichrist. It was incumbent upon the faithful to bring the Word of God to their suffering compatriots. He did not want war, but he was willing to countenance it. And in the face of redoubtable resistance from the Catholic Five States, the reformer had a growing sense that military action would be necessary.[15] He faced an enormous challenge in rallying the magistrates to his cause, as the Council in Zurich continued to be divided over the most prudent course of action. What Zwingli perceived as havering among the magistrates increased his frustration and, ultimately, disappointment.

From January 1529, the Christian Civic Union, first formed in 1527 between Zurich, Constance and Bern, met regularly with the intention of supporting the Reformation.[16] Basel joined in March, after its successful Reformation. The Bernese were clear that the purpose was to administer matters among the Swiss, and not engage in foreign alliances with Hesse or the deposed duke of Württemberg. Although the links between the cities were a remarkable achievement of the Reformation, the individual members had differing agendas and expectations. Strasbourg was looking to bolster its position in the Empire through Swiss military and commercial support, while Bern was primarily concerned with stability in the Confederation and the avoidance of conflict with Savoy in the east. Zurich largely followed Zwingli's ambitions for an expansion of the evangelical faith, but was less certain about conflict. The admission of Basel to the union deeply unnerved the Catholics, and influenced the creation of an alliance known as the Christian Alliance between the Austrian Habsburgs, Württemberg and the Five States in the Confederation. The bond with Ferdinand of Austria brought the promise of troops, cannon and cavalry, should Zurich and its allies attack. The stated purpose of the alliance was defensive, but the Swiss Catholic states insisted on the right of legitimate conquest.[17] Ferdinand's calculations were based, however, on acknowledgement of the strength of the Reformed states of Zurich, Bern and Basel.

Within the Confederation, the Mandated Territories, jointly administered by Reformed and Catholic Confederates, were a constant flashpoint. Zurich pushed hard for the spread of the evangelical faith in Thurgau and the Freie Ämter, and for communities to be allowed to choose their religion, under the influence of evangelical preachers. Efforts to win over the villages and lands of the Mandated Territories were fiercely resisted by the Catholics, but support from the Reformed cities proved difficult to deter. Controversy also enveloped St Gallen, at the end of 1528. The city, under Zwingli's friend Vadian, who served as *Bürgermeister*, had adopted the Reformation, but its great Benedictine abbey had not. The abbey and its extensive lands had traditionally been under the joint authority of Zurich, Lucerne, Schwyz and Glarus, which would take turns to appoint a protector. Zurich attempted to impose a Reformed protector for the abbey, driving out the abbot and outraging the Catholic Confederates.[18] Zwingli was closely involved, writing briefs for the Zurich magistrates and encouraging them to stand firm for the gospel. The situation remained unresolved until the abbot was restored in 1531, after Zurich's military defeat. To this day St Gallen remains a confessionally divided city.

The burning of the evangelical preacher Jakob Kaiser in Catholic Schwyz on 29 May 1529 proved a provocation too far, and Zurich was thrown into a frenzy, with sentiments for war shouted everywhere and with Zwingli fully in the mix. Immediately he drafted his 'Advice about the War', which he seems to have done on his own initiative.[19] Zwingli regarded the execution of Kaiser as a crime, and he offered a detailed plan for an aggressive attack that involved troops liberating people in lands under the tyranny of the false religion. Whether Zwingli consulted with other military and political leaders is not clear; but remarkably, when Zurich finally mobilized in early June, it largely followed the plans set out by the reformer.[20] The proposal for the magistrates involved a three-pronged attack on Schwyz and Zug, with the bulk of the army advancing to Kappel, on the border with Zug. Bern was proving an unwilling partner, but for the reformer, the only way forward was for Zurich to act alone in forcing the true faith on the recalcitrant Confederates. Bold and confrontational, Zwingli's proposal encountered stiff resistance in Zurich from those reluctant to act without consulting Bern, and the magistrates vacillated, once more divided. The Large Council was unwilling to send its troops to war without any allies, and the preacher's martial plans were temporarily set aside.

The reversal was a harsh reminder that Zwingli served at the pleasure of his political masters. His humiliation was made all the greater in early June 1529 with the arrival in the city of the Bernese envoy Niklaus Manuel (1484–1530), who argued for the cause of peace and negotiation before the Large Council and found many sympathizers.[21] 'God's Word,' Manuel declared, 'calls only for peace and unity. You cannot really bring faith by means of spears and halberds.'[22] Zurich needed Bern, and such was the political reality that Zwingli believed he had no alternative but to resign his position and leave his adopted city, having, he reckoned, lost the confidence of Zurich's rulers. According to one report, Zwingli wept as he addressed the magistrates.[23] He was dissuaded from departing by a couple of friends. Shortly before his death in 1531, Zwingli would again declare his desire to quit the city.

Despite Manuel's words, there was a widespread presentiment of war. There was little possibility of the Catholics attacking either Zurich or Bern, but the growing sense of military conflict led to the implementation of defensive measures in the Five States.[24] Bells were ready to warn of the advance of hostile forces, while scouts were placed on mountains to light fires by which messages were conveyed and inhabitants warned as quickly as possible. Young men were forbidden from leaving to serve in foreign armies as they were needed at home. While an assault by Zurich seemed imminent, it was not known where or when the attack would come. Perhaps Lucerne, the major Catholic city, would be Zurich's focus, but there was also reason for the Zurichers to move against either Schwyz or Zug.

Zurich's vacillation ended when the city decided to go it alone. Believing its cause against the Catholics just, Zurich declared war on 8 June and was able to put 3,000 men in the field.[25] The War Council that was created by the

Zurich magistrates consisted of men with experience in the mercenary service who knew how to prosecute a campaign. Zwingli was not included in this council, which largely consisted of veterans of conflict who now wielded influence. The leading Zurich figure was Jörg Berger, who had drawn up the plans for Zurich's military action, similar to Zwingli's proposal, laid before the Large Council. Troops marched on the Catholics with the intention of driving the Five States from the Mandated Territories and the abbey of St Gallen.[26] The main force moved on Kappel, in order to engage in decisive action against Zug. But the indecision in Zurich had allowed the Catholics time to prepare, and the troops found themselves facing a well-equipped and organized force consisting of men from all of the Five States ready for combat.

Despite frantic negotiations, the Catholics received no support from Austria and were therefore woefully outmanned. A Zurich force quickly occupied Thurgau, Rheintal and St Gallen in the east.[27] Zwingli accompanied the troops on horseback with halberd in hand. He wrote to a friend that

> the peace, for which so many strive, means war. The war that we call for means peace, for we thirst for no man's blood but are determined that the effective force of the Catholic overlords shall be cut off. If that does not happen neither the truths of the Bible nor the lives of its servants are safe. Our intentions are not cruel ones, for what we seek is friendship and the true interests of our country. We hope to save it when through ignorance it is in danger of being overthrown. With all our might we strive to secure freedom.[28]

The Catholics and Reformed forces faced each other across a field prepared for a battle that did not happen. Bern had sent a force of 6,000 men but was by no means eager to support Zurich, and the troops stayed away from the prospective battlefield at Kappel. Basel and the other Reformed states were equally unwilling, and offered to negotiate. Bern counselled Zurich to lower its swords – indeed, it went beyond mere words of caution to demand that Zurich pull back, emphatically stating that the cities of the Christian Civic Union would not come to its support. The warning resonated in Zurich, where, although the Large Council was divided, the desire for peace prevailed and, at the last moment, the army at Kappel was ordered not to attack. Zwingli had wanted battle, and years later Bullinger reported his words to a mediator from Glarus:

> You shall give account of your conduct before God. While the enemy is weak and ill equipped, they speak fair words that you believe and call for peace. But if they are able to rearm, they will have no pity on us and there will be no one to make peace.[29]

Away from the calculated words of politicians and leading clerics, the soldiers facing one another at Kappel had little interest in the official declarations and bellicose sermons that had brought them to the field. Few had a clear sense of why they had taken up arms against their neighbours, with whom they regularly traded. Chroniclers on both sides of the religious divide recorded fraternizing among the putative enemies: drinking, eating and even humorous banter were perhaps the most telling signs that the Swiss soldiers had little appetite for combat. A witness from Strasbourg was reported to have said, 'You Swiss are a fine people . . . you do not forget the ancient friendships.'[30]

According to legend, at Kappel the soldiers from Schwyz, having prepared a large cauldron of soup, called out to the Zurichers that, because of the sanctions, they had no bread. Loaves were duly provided and the two armies shared the soup, each remaining on its side of the line between them. When one Zurich soldier extended his spoon too far across the pot, he had his knuckles rapped and was told to eat from his own side.[31]

## FRAGILE PEACE

Most of the Swiss Confederates remained neutral in the First Kappel War. Basel, Schaffhausen, Fribourg, Solothurn and Appenzell, as well as Glarus and Graubünden, assumed the role of peace negotiators between the Five States and Zurich and Bern.[32] Zwingli found himself in an awkward position. He had donned armour and taken up the halberd to enter possible combat. Although his role was largely as preacher, his sermons were incendiary. Now, in unequivocal language, he warned the Council not to accept a cheap peace or to be overly influenced by Bern. His voice in the Council had continued to wax and wane in the run-up to the First Kappel War, but

Zurich's position now coalesced around the condition that had always been his central demand: the Five States should agree to the free preaching of the gospel in both the Mandated Territories and, more dramatically, their own lands.[33] This non-negotiable charge was, for Zwingli, nothing less than a divine command. He retained an almost naïve optimism that should gospel preaching be permitted, reform would naturally follow. Zwingli never relinquished his conviction that false and idolatrous religion was imposed on the people by corrupt political and religious leaders. He had no doubt that God would guide the way to the triumph of the Reformed faith, working as he did through the deeds of men. If war was the only option to realize this imperative, it was no time for knees to buckle.

As Zwingli well knew, his position contravened an established principle of the Swiss Confederation – no member should intervene in the affairs of another. He saw this tradition as no obstacle, for human convention could not resist the divine will, and it was God's will for the gospel to be proclaimed. Submission to God's demands was, however, only the beginning. The hated mercenary service was once more the object of his ire, and the Five States were to be required to forswear their adherence to arrangements by which pensioners were receiving blood money. As he rode to war, Zwingli had told the Zurich *Bürgermeister* that war was necessary to break the corruption of the pensions.[34]

What Zwingli refused to reckon with, however, was the continuing popularity of mercenary service among the youth of the mountainous Confederates, where few other sources of income and adventure beckoned. What he denounced as endemic evil was nothing less than a lifeline for young men in a culture where military prowess and reputation formed the very idea of being Swiss. Zwingli refused to believe that the Reformation had been rejected for any other reason than the tyranny of Catholic rulers. It seemed to make no impression on him that the reform movement had made little progress among the people in large parts of the Confederation, or that the communes of the Five States were deeply committed to the Catholic faith.[35] The tragicomedy that was the First Kappel War unravelled during the first two weeks of June 1529, but the negotiations trundled on for a good while, as dissension plagued both parties.

For Zwingli, the First Kappel War had been a punishing reversal; but the negotiations were far worse, being nothing less than a betrayal of the

Reformation.[36] Zwingli's primary goal was to spread the gospel to the Catholic lands of the Five States, and that had been denied. Furthermore, he sought the abolition of pensions for mercenaries, and that had not come to pass. He had initially had reason to be optimistic as the Reformed conducted themselves as if they had won and set punitive terms as the price for peace. The Catholic Confederates were to pay war reparations and to remove themselves from the Mandated Territories, as well as from their alliances with the Habsburgs. But Zurich's neighbour Bern did not stick to the script and set its own conditions. It became poignantly clear that Bern, not Zurich, was calling the shots. Following the traditional Swiss arrangement, the Bernese argued for the right of each Confederate to determine its own faith. In other matters there was consensus, but on the question of religion there was no disguising the disagreement. Bern, however, did demand that the alliance with the Habsburgs be dissolved and reparations paid. Further, slanderous remarks against the Reformation were to cease and offenders punished. In the matter of mercenary service, Bern did not provide its delegates with leadership, leaving them a free hand in negotiations. Zwingli found himself unsupported on the two central questions of the gospel and pensions.

On 25 June, a peace treaty was signed at Kappel. The Catholics agreed to end their alliance with Ferdinand and allow congregations to choose their faith in the Mandated Territories. The issue of gospel preaching in the Catholic Confederates was left unresolved. The Zurichers returned to their city triumphant and full of cheer, firing their guns in the Lindenhof, the site of a Roman fort in the old town of the city.[37] Two days later, however, Zwingli, who was in no mood to celebrate, preached in the Grossmünster denouncing the abomination that was the treaty, which had thwarted God's Reformation.[38] The brutal reality for Zwingli and Zurich was that their confessional allies had not supported their primary goal – the free preaching of the gospel in Catholic lands. The principal term of the peace treaty stipulated that each Confederate should decide its own confessional status, keeping intact the founding principle of non-interference.[39]

Within the city, Zwingli's position among the magistrates was again consolidated when the military leaders, whose influence on the War Council during the conflict had been decisive, were required to step down. The Zurich Council grew once more inclined to Zwingli's argument that the

Catholic Swiss Confederates must accept the Reformation. The deal that Zwingli sought to drive, backed by the Council, concerned the amount of the reparations that the Catholic Confederates should pay the Christian Civic Union. Zwingli put forward the case that the level of payment might be lowered if free preaching of the gospel was introduced. The thirteenth article of the treaty allowed the Reformed states to impose a blockade if the Catholics did not adhere to the terms of the treaty, including free preaching of the gospel and payment of reparations.[40] Such demands, however, were tempered by rumours that Habsburg forces were gathering in support of the beleaguered Swiss Catholics. The Reformed policy was very much driven by Bern, whose primary interest was to settle its dispute with Unterwalden and create an atmosphere of stability.

Zwingli pushed the Zurich Council to insist on the first article of the peace treaty, guaranteeing religious freedom, which he regarded as ensuring the right of all Swiss to hear the gospel preached. He did not accept that it actually ensured that those who wished to remain Catholic could do so with impunity.[41] In the end, the negotiators set the sum for the Catholic states to pay at a level that the Reformed states regarded as risible.[42] Nevertheless, they chose to accept the rather modest amount because of developments occurring outside the Confederation. Rumours started to circulate that the Habsburgs were massing troops in southern Germany to come to the aid of the Catholic Confederates. Fear of war, not against the Five States, but with the old dynastic fiend, pushed the Reformed Confederates to agree to the settlement. The principal weapon that remained in the hands of the Protestants was the right granted by the treaty to impose a blockade on the Catholics if they should fail to abide by their agreement to pay. Both Bern and Zurich were insistent on this point.

By September 1529, a blockade had been imposed by the Reformed cities, with the consequence that the Catholics were unable to obtain the grain necessary to survive the winter, forcing them to supplicate and promise to pay the required sum by the end of June 1530. Bern was satisfied with their submission, but Zurich was not. Zwingli's city was disposed to force its confessional position on the Catholics, but there was insufficient support among the other Reformed states for Zurich's crusading zeal. The First Kappel War and its ensuing peace was a classic pyrrhic victory for Zurich. In truth, it had lost its pre-war pre-eminence and prestige, only to find itself isolated from its allies, while facing recalcitrant opponents who had no desire to cower.

The Catholic states were not, as the Reformed suspected, negotiating an alliance with the Austrians, but were playing for time. They were unwilling either to permit the hated evangelical faith or to pay the reparations.[43] Both sides prepared for war. Bern was eager to impose a food blockade in order to force the Catholics into compliance. At this point, in early September, Zwingli secretly left Zurich for his meeting with Luther in Marburg. In his parting words to the Council, he wrote:

> although the current situation of the wars, hostilities and price increases is all too clear to us and seeks to distract me, I have always considered first the grace of God, who neither deceives nor abandons us. He ordains all things to the good for his own and he makes all things to come about for his glory.[44]

In the summer of 1529, following the First Kappel War, Zwingli's position was unclear: as he grew more adamant about a resumption of war, the magistrates seemed less sure. The preacher was the most powerful voice outside the ruling Council calling for aggression. Yet, he struggled to create a consensus. One crucial development by 1529 was that almost no Catholic opponents were any longer on the councils, thus ending years of conflict. Nevertheless, the supporters of the Reformation in Zurich were not necessarily beholden to Zwingli; Bern's calls for moderation were favourably heard by many influential politicians. Soon after his arrival in 1519, Zwingli had stirred up controversy and opposition, and over the years had fought with Catholics, Anabaptists and Lutherans. In his last years, he increasingly struggled with his religious sympathizers, many of whom found parts of his message more compelling than others. To his way of thinking, they and Bern had opted for peace and stability, not the gospel.[45]

## CONFESSION OF FAITH (1530)

On 21 January 1530, Charles V summoned the German estates to an Imperial Diet to be held at Augsburg. It would tackle the defence of the Empire against the Turkish threat and internal mutual concerns, such as currency standardization, but it would also address the confessional ructions. The emperor announced that he was prepared to receive representations from the religious parties in the German lands – a promise that led the Christian Civic Union to meet in Basel to agree on a response to this unexpected turn of events. The cities of Zurich, Bern, Basel, Strasbourg and Constance concluded that a moderate response should be made, written by the theologians of the cities.[46] It seemed prudent to prepare several confessions, with the most suitable to be sent to Augsburg. Oecolampadius in Basel took up the task, writing to Zwingli on 30 March that the two men should exchange drafts; Zwingli, however, was unpersuaded and was slow to engage.[47] He had few expectations that the overtures from Charles, whom Zwingli saw as the great enemy of the Reformation, would yield any fruit.

Jakob Sturm in Strasbourg was the key player. An influential politician close to Philipp of Hesse, he had his own ideas about peace in the Empire, and regarded Zwingli with suspicion. Sturm had never been as close to the reformer as he was to the preachers Bucer and Capito in his own city.[48] He had visited Zurich shortly after the First Kappel War, but there was no warm relationship with Zwingli. Sturm was concerned that the Swiss, following Marburg, would scupper any possible religious settlement in the Empire. To this end, he played Zwingli. On 26 May, Sturm wrote from Augsburg to the reformer to relay the situation in the run-up to the Diet.[49] He told Zwingli that it made good sense for Strasbourg and the Swiss cities to submit a confession to the emperor, but only if the text was non-polemical and timely – both factors to be decided by the Reformed delegation.[50] Thomas Brady has suggested that 'Sturm intended to ensure that the Lutheran princes and preachers could favourably compare the moderate opinions of Strasbourg and the radically anti-Lutheran opinions of Zwingli.'[51] He sought to free Strasbourg from any charge that it was too close to Zwingli and Zurich, and he believed that an unacceptable confession from the reformer would suit his purpose. The argument is compelling, as Sturm had wanted nothing to do with Zwingli's efforts to create an anti-Habsburg alliance of the Swiss and imperial cities that would lead to the spread of his theology in the Empire. Timing was everything. In mid-June, when Charles arrived in Augsburg, Sturm wrote once more to Zwingli to say that he truly believed that the emperor wanted to hear from all parties. He was now full of encouragement for the Christian Civic Union to prepare a confession.[52] Zwingli had hoped that through the good offices of Landgrave Philipp of Hesse he might receive an invitation to appear at Augsburg, but Sturm disabused him. He would not be summoned.[53]

Sturm viewed Zwingli as a major impediment to Strasbourg's efforts to make peace with the Lutheran princes. His plans to woo them, however, were not successful, as he was rebuffed by Johann of Saxony in Augsburg. It was at that point that he wrote again to Zwingli, asking for a confession of faith. He sent the reformer the Schwabach Articles, which he knew would have the effect of pouring oil on fire. The Articles revealed to Zwingli that Luther had reneged on any agreement they had made at Marburg.[54] Sturm was exploiting Zwingli for his own ends, for while writing to the Zurich reformer he was at the same time arranging for Bucer and Capito to appear in Augsburg on behalf of Strasbourg, to provide a more moderate account of their theology. Further, he was negotiating for Strasbourg to sign the Lutheran confession. He kept both Zwingli and his own city in the dark about his plans.[55]

Realizing that he was being given no role in imperial religious negotiations, and perceiving little support from the Zurich Council for involvement, Zwingli struck out on his own. The time since Marburg had made it clear to him that reconciliation with the Lutherans was beyond hope. Luther and his supporters had betrayed the Swiss and resumed hostilities. In the city, Zwingli had worked for years with the magistrates, but had grown increasingly frustrated with their dithering. The Catholics and Anabaptists were beyond redemption. Zwingli saw himself as standing alone, and in response to Augsburg he took the extraordinary step of preparing a confession that represented no one other than himself. It was his boldest statement of his convictions, uttered as a prophet convinced of his beliefs and no longer willing to compromise. Zwingli gave himself three days to draw up a statement of faith, and the text was printed by Froschauer on 3 July. Five days later, a representative from Zurich arrived in Augsburg with his confession, entitled 'Fidei ratio' or 'Account of the Faith'.[56]

The text appeared with a preface for Emperor Charles. The confession, Zwingli wrote, was personal, as he had not had sufficient time to draw one up on behalf of the cities of the Christian Civic Union. Why had he done it? Because, he claimed, he had read the *Schwabach Articles*, which had been drawn up in the summer of 1529 by Philipp of Hesse, Luther and Justus

Jonas as a confession of faith of the Wittenberg theologians. The *Articles*, presented at a meeting following Marburg, were hostile to the Swiss. Furthermore, Zwingli had read the 404 objections to the Reformation prepared by the Catholic Johann Eck. In response, he believed it appropriate to prepare his own statement of faith, which he now submitted to the emperor and the whole Church for judgement.

Zwingli may have responded to Sturm's encouragement, but he did not listen to his advice about tone. The 'Account of the Faith' was harshly polemical and took no prisoners – or if it did, they were immediately shot. Zwingli had no more time for Luther and did not even pretend to seek conciliation. The document sought to admonish Charles and rain down judgement on the Roman Church. Zwingli stuck to his guns on all the tenets of his theology, writing in a tone both deeply personal and excoriating. His confession was presented in Augsburg at the same moment as the 'Confessio Tetrapolitana', a conciliatory text drawn up by Martin Bucer and Wolfgang Capito and intended to find something more of a middle way. While Zwingli had largely spoken for himself, the 'Confession' from Strasbourg was signed by the city's magistrates, along with the rulers of Constance, Memmingen and Lindau. Bucer's confession, however, despite its moderation, fell on stony ground. Quite simply, Luther did not trust him.

Zwingli's contribution, however, crashed into the Diet, inflaming controversy. Although the confessions were meant to be confidential, the contents were quickly leaked. Bucer was appalled by the tone of the work, and the Lutherans were incensed that their old enemy had simply restated claims that they had repudiated. Worse, he had departed from the articles on which there had been agreement at Marburg. Johannes Brenz responded that the confession had no basis in scripture, while Philipp Melanchthon was uncharacteristically harsh. In a letter of 14 July to Martin Luther, he wrote that one could consider the author of the 'Account' 'mad'.[57] Zwingli had regurgitated his errors on original sin and the sacraments, and trashed any concord at Marburg. The document was widely distributed among the princes and theologians, probably leaked by the imperial officials to divide the Protestants. The Catholics, although incensed by Zwingli's coruscating attack, must have rubbed their hands in glee at this testament to Protestant sectarianism.

Zwingli was uncompromising. All ceremonies were to be abolished and the office of bishop was fiercely attacked. Melanchthon's general assessment was that the text was 'brutal' and that Zwingli had shown himself to be more 'Swiss' than 'Christian'.[58] The reference to being Swiss was by no means a compliment: Melanchthon equated that identity with 'barbarianism'.[59] Melanchthon had sent Luther a copy of the text, and the Wittenberger was hardly more charitable, responding caustically that Zwingli had finally revealed himself. The mask he wore pretending to be a Christian theologian had slipped from his face.[60] Luther's wrath, however, was not for Zurich alone: he believed that the wily Bucer had put Zwingli up to this abomination.[61]

Zwingli's friends rallied to his support, although not without a queasy sense that he had gone too far. Oecolampadius wrote that he had read the 'Fidei ratio' approvingly. However, he commented that Zwingli was preaching to stopped-up ears.[62] Berchtold Haller reported from Bern that the text was being widely read.[63] Martin Bucer was in an impossible situation, having submitted his own confession to the Augsburg Diet. His attempts to find some path between Wittenberg and Zurich could not sustain the hit inflicted by Zwingli, with his raw polemic against the Lutherans. He informed Zwingli that many Catholics had also been particularly hurt by the ferocity of the attack from Zurich.[64] Apart from causing outrage, Zwingli's work had no influence at Augsburg.

Johann Eck, Zwingli's old adversary, thought the 'Account' worthy of a response, and in haste prepared a razor-sharp refutation that appeared on 17 July 1530. He accused Zwingli of being 'a liar' bound for hell, whose claim to the emperor that he desired peace was pure dishonesty. He applied to the Zurich reformer the words of the prophet Jeremiah:

'They have treated the wound of my people carelessly, saying, "Peace, peace", when there is no peace' [8:11]. For Zwingli is of the number of those of whom David says, 'Who speak peace with their neighbour, but evils are in their heart' [Psalm 28:3].[65]

Once more he mocked the Zurich reformer's teaching on the sacraments 'as if the holy mysteries of our faith were no more efficacious than the shadowy and figurative ceremonies of the Jews'. Another favoured theme were the radicals and Zwingli's responsibility for their raving: 'I laugh at the empty boasting of Zwingli that he was the first to teach and write against the

Anabaptists, since I am aware that it was Zwingli who by his counsel and advice really founded this lost sect.'[66]

Zwingli's submission to the Diet was a repudiation of all his opponents: Catholics, Lutherans and Anabaptists. He rejected their teachings by re-affirming those beliefs they had found so offensive. That is perhaps why we find in the 'Account' the reformer's few ventures into speaking about death, judgement and the afterlife. For those who believe in purgatory, they have no Christ. Hell, in contrast, was an eternal reality, of which Christ spoke in the Gospel of Matthew when he warned that 'then he will say to those on his left, "Depart from me, you who are cursed, into the eternal fire prepared for the devil and his angels"' (25:41). Against the Anabaptists, Zwingli was adamant that the fires of hell are eternal.[67] It is difficult not to find in his words judgement on his opponents.

Zwingli had not written on behalf of any institution, but had offered Charles a statement of his own convictions. In the text, his old enemies were assaulted with renewed ferocity, indicating that the Swiss reformer no longer felt the slightest obligation to make any concessions. Catholics were idolatrous and beyond the pale of the Church; Lutherans were committed to papist errors; and Anabaptists were a pernicious sect. There was no room in the 'Account of the Faith' for any of them, and the Swiss stood in opposition to their errors. Unless his interpretation of Christianity was accepted, the Church was a broken body. Despite the influence of his thought in the southern German cities, none was inclined to adopt his confession. In the end, it remained a statement of personal convictions that reflected Zwingli's unrelenting hostility to his enemies and confidence in his prophetic calling.

# TEN

# END

Zwingli's life did not come to a tidy conclusion. His was not the expected death following ill health that Luther and Calvin experienced. Zwingli died suddenly and without preparation. He had no obvious successor in Zurich coached to receive the baton. He was a casualty of his own willingness to use force to religious ends. At Marignano in 1515 he had seen his fellow Swiss die for a cause that was not their own. In 1531, he died in a battle that he had championed, a conflict that moderate voices had insisted could be avoided.

## PREACHER AND POLITICIAN

Zwingli's role in the events of his last years is difficult to construct with confidence.[1] His Catholic opponents declared that he was the 'colonel', but their polemic flattered the reformer.[2] Although he played a significant role in the disaster of Zurich's defeat in the Second Kappel War, through his advocacy of war, Zwingli neither acted alone nor enjoyed the unfettered support of the Council and military leaders. His fluctuating fortunes with the magistrates before the First Kappel War, and his anger at the peace they had settled for, underscored his limitations – even his vulnerability. Although he himself was clear that military action was necessary, he faced a divided Council that continued to change its mind. His convictions never wavered: the gospel should be delivered to all the Swiss, and it was the duty of political rulers to bring the divine will to fruition. Their justice must mirror God's justice. Zwingli never doubted that the power of God's Word would convert the people, even if it had to be delivered at sword point.

We can follow Zwingli as preacher and author, but the politician is harder to locate. He wrote a stream of memoranda offering his opinions on virtually every subject, but these documents could suggest that his influence was greater than it was. He was an adviser to the Council, not a decision maker.[3] He did, however, have the ear of influential figures. From 1529, the Large and Small Councils were overwhelmingly occupied by supporters of the Reformation, and although opponents remained within the city, those who resisted the new order lacked strong leadership. Zwingli often met members of the so-called 'Secret Council', an inner circle of magistrates that met on an ad hoc basis to determine foreign policy and war.[4] The political culture in which he was operating was characterized by a mutual dependence. Realization of his ideas required the support of *Bürgermeister* Diethelm Röist and other sympathetic leaders, but the magistrates for their part also needed the preacher, who commanded a great following within the city, was the most prominent voice from the pulpit, and belonged to an international network of religious and lay figures.[5]

Zwingli controlled virtually every aspect of the Church in the city and its rural territory, including the appointment of preachers sent out to evangelize the Swiss lands and the Mandated Territories. Through his work on commissions, his preaching and personal contacts, his influence in the city was considerable. His authority arose from charisma, trust and connections. Yet his step was not always sure. Zwingli was inclined to overestimate his influence and fail to understand the concerns of others. So certain was he of God's ultimate triumph that he could fail to fathom the ways of humans.

Zwingli gave himself over to spreading the evangelical message in the eastern parts of the Confederation, notably Thurgau, which was under joint Catholic and Reformed authority. Together with his colleagues, he addressed gatherings of clergy and pushed for communities to adopt the new faith.[6] He went on preaching tours through the region and debated with the considerable number of Anabaptists who had also sprung up in the rural areas. Against the protests of the Catholic authorities, Zwingli continued to insist that religious houses be dissolved and that gospel preaching be introduced – and, indeed, this was taking place.

Although deeply disappointed by the First Kappel Treaty, Zwingli continued to hold the trust of most magistrates, and his voice was heard throughout the city. The Council depended on his assessment of religious affairs, and their theological statements were prepared by the reformer's hand.[7] His impressive contacts extended even beyond church circles: he was the connection to Philipp of Hesse, to the political leaders of Milan and to agents of the French king. And yet there was always a fragility about his relations with the civic rulers, largely because his perspective was almost exclusively religious. On the whole, the Zurich magistrates were not persuaded by Zwingli's plans for grand alliances. Dramatically, in the summer of 1531, he declared once more to the Large Council a willingness to resign, on the grounds that Zurich was not sufficiently tough on the Catholic states.[8] After three days of negotiations, he withdrew his resignation. In his eyes, his calling was ultimately not to Zurich, but to his Swiss fatherland.

## FINAL CONFESSION

Actively seeking a resolution to the question of the Lord's Supper, during the autumn of 1530 Martin Bucer, reformer in Strasbourg, had met Luther in Coburg.[9] Their relationship was deeply strained as Luther believed Bucer sympathized with the Swiss. The Strasbourger then appeared in Zurich in October to provide the magistrates with a report, and to propose a reconciling confession directed towards the Lutherans, as well as Zwingli and Oecolampadius. The Basel Church was fairly receptive, but not Zwingli, who informed the Council that 'this letter will bring nothing but conflict'. He insisted that Bucer had 'fallen for Lutheran tricks and errors':

> We will maintain the opinion we agreed upon, which holds that the body of Christ is present in the Supper, neither bodily nor substantially, but sacramentally to the clear and pure mind. For you will see that any concession will be to the detriment of the truth, and that this evil cover-up will empower darkness more than light.[10]

As Bucer persisted, Zwingli denounced his efforts to mediate as worthless.[11] No hope was to be placed in the mendacious Lutherans. Compromise led to superficial statements, and Zwingli warned that further disputes might erupt at any time. The Lutherans, he claimed, held to a form of the mass more papist than that of the papists.[12] On that point, he was resolved and would never change his mind, even if the rest of the world disagreed with him.

Despite all the theological wrangling, Zurich's close relations with Strasbourg and Philipp of Hesse held out the possibility of Swiss involvement with the Protestant Schmalkaldic League, formed in February 1531, and its members, who included five electors of the Empire, eight cities from the southwest and three from the Hanseatic League.[13] Indeed, in January 1531, Zurich, Basel, Bern and Strasbourg had formed an alliance with Philipp of Hesse. The elector of Saxony declared himself prepared to receive the Swiss cities into the League, provided they accepted the Lutheran position on the sacraments. That condition was as good as dead. Zwingli was able to win over Zurich and Bern against Bucer, and the Swiss decided that the price of entering the Schmalkaldic League was too high. The isolation of Zwingli and the other Swiss from their sympathizers from the German lands was now almost complete.[14] The Schmalkaldic League would be Lutheran, not Reformed.

The vulnerability of the Swiss led Zwingli and Zurich to turn to France. That contact did not come out of thin air: the French had been active in the Confederation since 1529, seeking an alliance against the Habsburgs. A delegation led by Louis Dangerant and Lambert Maigret had had two issues in mind: the ongoing need for Swiss mercenaries for French armies and, more intriguingly, resolution of the differences between the Reformed and Catholic Confederates. In January 1530, two Swiss mercenary leaders in French service, Hans Kaltschmid and Hans Junker, came to Zwingli offering the possibility of an alliance of Zurich and other Confederates with the kingdom.[15] Those negotiations went nowhere, but in early 1531 the subject was raised once more. Out of both political and religious concerns, the Zurich Council sent the churchman and theologian Rudolf Collin to Solothurn to meet the French. Collin had led Zurich's unsuccessful mission to the doge in Venice to seek support against the Habsburgs. He had been received with kind words – and sent away empty handed. With the French, however, an alluring prospect emerged, although in the end it never materialized: the French were prepared to provide the Swiss with financial aid in the event of war with Charles V, while Zwingli was to send Francis I a confession of faith on behalf of the Christian Civic Union, the alliance of the Swiss Reformed cities.

The French, traditional allies of the Swiss, could not afford to watch the Confederation, a crucial source of mercenaries, being torn apart by civil war. They negotiated with both sides and were in frequent contact with

Zwingli through a series of letters and personal meetings.[16] Writing to the Zurich Council, they urged relief from the blockade of the Catholics and a continuation of the search for peace. To Zwingli, they made clear the dire consequences of conflict:

> [We trust] that you might consider this writing and receive it with the best will and that you will let us know how we should prepare with regard to this agreement and peaceful operation ... For if [peace] does not occur in the Confederation, in which there should be no revolt or war, [the Swiss lands] will pass away.[17]

In late May 1531, French agents arrived in Zurich to meet the Council and Zwingli, who optimistically reported to Oecolampadius that the visitors had accepted his demand for the free preaching of the gospel in Catholic lands.[18] The reformer, who held the Habsburgs to be the great nemesis of true religion, had long believed that deliverance might come from the French. His dedication of his 1525 *Commentary on True and False Religion* signalled his hopes for the kingdom, and even for Francis I as a patron of religious reform. In June 1531, he wrote a draft for an alliance between the Christian Civic Union and France.[19] He opened by praising the French as the most heroic opponents of imperial tyranny. An alliance with the kingdom would preserve the freedom of the Swiss. Although Zwingli primarily looked for financial rather than military support, in the event of attack the French should send soldiers. Zwingli was clear that support would come from Strasbourg, and that Constance was the key to the Empire. He showered unbridled praise on Philipp of Hesse: he was young but wise beyond his years, a true friend and defender of the faith. The landgrave was to be trusted in the event of an attack by the emperor. Even the exiled duke of Württemberg was a crucial ally. In addition, Zwingli expressed the hope that Milan might also be drawn into an alliance against the emperor.[20]

During this period of optimism, Zwingli composed what would prove to be his last significant theological work. His 'Exposition of Faith' was prepared for Francis I. Encouragement for the dedication to the king came in part from the Frenchman Maigret, who held pronounced evangelical sympathies and was familiar with Zwingli's writings. French connections in Strasbourg and Basel had led to repeated requests for Zwingli to provide material for evangelicals in the kingdom.[21] Despite Zwingli's hopes of aid from France, there was considerable distress among his compatriots during the early months of 1531 that a possible alliance between Francis I and Charles V might lead to war against the Reformed states. The Swiss were extremely vulnerable. Excluded from Augsburg and the Schmalkaldic League on account of their theology, they were locked in battle with the Lutherans over the sacraments, and now faced the real possibility of attack from the emperor. Furthermore, war among the Swiss Confederates remained starkly possible. All of these conditions combined to make it essential for some form of protective alliance to be found, even with a Catholic king.

The 'Exposition of Faith' was completed in time for Rudolf Collin to deliver a fair copy in Paris at the end of August 1531. As with his 1530 confession for Augsburg, Zwingli framed his confession around the Apostles' Creed, following the articles while providing extensive digressions on key theological points such as the sacraments. The text, written in Latin, would not be published until after Zwingli's death, edited in 1536 by Heinrich Bullinger. It is highly unlikely that Francis ever laid eyes on it.

The 'Exposition' was one of Zwingli's most carefully crafted works, skilfully prepared for the French context. On the whole, there was little new: Zwingli offered a vindication of his orthodoxy, defending the key points of credal Christianity on topics such as the Trinity and the two natures of Christ. At every point, he was at pains to remind Francis that scripture alone was the source of his teaching, and that he did not rely on church traditions. He rejected the pope and institutions of the Roman Church, reiterating that the true Church was made up of the elect who possess the gift of faith.

No longer worrying about agreement with the Lutherans on the Lord's Supper, Zwingli shaped his treatment of the sacrament in terms that addressed Catholics. As he had done in the 'Account of the Faith' for Augsburg, he emphasized that the bread and wine are aids to the contemplation of Christ's sacrifice that point the faithful to what is real. The material elements do not generate faith, but are the means by which an almost mystical union with Christ is achieved. Some have found in his late language a shift towards an emphasis on the efficacy of the sacraments on the inner person, and certainly his language is notable for its implications of spiritual interiority. On the whole, however, his last statements on the sacrament remained faithful to his central convictions.

As an appendix to his confession, Zwingli sent Francis a copy of the 1525 liturgy for the Lord's Supper, with an extended commentary. The Zurich reformer offered a passionate defence for the presence of Christ at the meal. 'It is no true meal,' he argued, 'if Christ is not present.'[22] Indeed, as the Gospel of Matthew witnesses, Christ assured his followers that, where two or three are gathered, He is present. When the community gathers, Christ is with the people, but not in the flesh. His presence has nothing to do with the eating of the bread or the drinking of wine. The body of Christ is received 'sacramentally' and 'spiritually' by pious, faithful and holy nature, as Chrysostom had said.[23] Francis was provided with a Latin translation of the liturgy, with the assurance that 'the words of Christ have not been altered, falsified and corrupted by false meaning'.[24]

In his dedication, Zwingli urged the king to rule well, that he might join the heavenly company of exalted monarchs:

> Then you may hope to see the whole company and assemblage of all the saints, the wise, the faithful, brave, and good who have lived since the world began. Here you will see the two Adams, the redeemed and the redeemer, Abel, Enoch, Noah, Abraham, Isaac, Jacob, Judah, Moses, Joshua, Gideon, Samuel, Phineas, Elijah, Elisha, Isaiah, and the Virgin Mother of God of whom he prophesied, David, Hezekiah, Josiah, the Baptist, Peter, Paul; here too, Hercules, Theseus, Socrates, Aristides, Antigonus, Numa, Camillus, the Catos and Scipios, here Louis the Pious, and your predecessors, the Louis, Philips, Pepins, and all your ancestors, who have gone hence in faith. In short there has not been a good man and will not be a holy heart or faithful soul from the beginning of the world to the end thereof that you will not see in heaven with God. And what can be imagined more glad, what more delightful, what, finally, more honourable than such a sight?[25]

As Luther and others quickly noted, Zwingli's words were arresting. Alongside the kings of Israel and France, the blessed included Socrates and the Catos. The virtuous pagans would find their place among the elect.[26] From Wittenberg came the caustic reply:

> Tell me, any one of you who wants to be a Christian, what need is there of baptism, the sacrament, Christ, the Gospel, or the prophets

and Holy Scripture, if such godless heathen, Socrates, Aristides, yes, the cruel Numa, who was the first to instigate every kind of idolatry at Rome by the devil's revelation, as St Augustine writes in the City of God, and Scipio the Epicurean, are saved and sanctified along with the patriarchs, prophets, and apostles in heaven, even though they knew nothing about God, Scripture, the Gospel, Christ, baptism, the sacrament, or the Christian faith? What can such an author, preacher, and teacher believe about the Christian faith except that it is no better than any other faith and that everyone can be saved by his own faith, even an idolater and an Epicurean like Numa and Scipio?[27]

The list was not the first time Zwingli had expressed himself on the salvation of non-Christians. Against his beloved Augustine, he was adamant that unbaptized infants would be saved. On the noble heathen, he had made his point most emphatically in his sermon on providence in 1530, when he claimed that Seneca was 'the unparalleled cultivator of the soul among pagans'. He was a 'theologian' and his works 'divine oracles'.[28]

Salvation was not limited to Israel or the visible Church. Zwingli's conviction was consistent: God is entirely free in election to choose whom he wills with reasons completely beyond human comprehension. Profound attachment to divine freedom led Zwingli to find God working through the deeds and thoughts of non-Christians. God was the source of all goodness, and faith and goodness were to be found among virtuous pagans as they were somehow part of God's election.[29] Unlike John Milton later, Zwingli felt no need to explain the ways of God to humanity.

## A NEW BIBLE

Alongside the 1525 liturgy of the Lord's Supper, the enduring spiritual, intellectual and artistic creation of the Reformation in Zurich was the first complete translation of the Bible into German. It was the culmination of Zwingli's effort to reform education, the daily sessions in the Grossmünster and Fraumünster to translate and expound scripture, and over 10 years of evangelical preaching. During the 1520s, Zwingli, alongside Ceporin, Jud and Pellikan, had committed himself to translating the Old and New Testaments into the Swiss German dialect of the people of Zurich. For the early versions, they relied heavily on the work of Martin Luther, but his Saxon German was not very accessible for the Swiss. Gradually they moved from adapting Luther's works to their own versions. In his 1529 preface to his translation of the Old Testament prophets, Zwingli gave a full account of the prophetic work of the Church. The prophet is one who possesses both the inner illumination of the mind and conviction. The Word is dictated to him by the Spirit, and he delivers his message with full confidence in his grasp of the truth. He must be 'inflamed and made passionate and arduous' by the Spirit of God.[30] It was Zwingli's vision of his own calling and place in the Church.

At the end of 1529, the scholars in Zurich had completed their own translations of all the books of the Bible, which the printer Christoph Froschauer released in octavo form in 1530, creating the first full German translation of the scriptures – anticipating Luther's Bible by four years. Expectations were high: Froschauer had a run of over 5,000 copies, anticipating a broad readership, which he addressed in a short preface.[31] No theologian, but a deeply pious man of business, Froschauer noted the handiness of an octavo for carrying in the pocket during travel. Other folio editions, he continued, contained elegant illustrations, but he had opted for a non-illustrated version that was affordable and practical. He may not have produced the first complete German printed Bible, but he had provided the first in the handier octavo format. His intended audience consisted of workers and merchants, preachers and lay people, who could read the bibles at home or bring them with them to church.

Appealing and practical as the octavo Bible was, the larger folio German Bible appeared in Zurich the following year, filled with scholarship, piety and woodcuts.[32] The volume, a delight to the eye, opened with a title page graced by a Hans Holbein woodcut of 12 scenes from the creation of the world. With its beautiful type, elegant marginal notes and illustrations, this Bible was unlike anything hitherto produced in Zurich. Without doubt it was Froschauer's finest work and the very summit of biblical scholarship in Zwingli's Zurich. The woodcuts were visually arresting: of the 140 in the Old Testament, 118 were by Hans Holbein the Younger. The New Testament contained six illustrations from an earlier Zurich Bible of 1524, plus 21 of Revelation prepared by Holbein for Thomas Wolf in Basel.[33] Signs of scholarship in the service of the faithful were everywhere. Each chapter began with a summary of its contents, while the subsequent text was surrounded by a forest of biblical citations and glosses to inform and instruct the reader.

The printer Froschauer played a vital role in the production of the 1531 Bible. Although a canny businessman, his commitment to the reform movement had been an act of faith. From the earliest days, he had played a central role in the evangelical movement in Zurich, providing contacts across the German-speaking lands. He had been with Zwingli from the beginning, and the production of the Bible was a profoundly devotional act. In his testament, he left a moving statement of his faith. His commitment to printing, he wrote, had been a vocation that 'all goodness might be planted'. Commissioning his cousin to take up his labours, he counselled him 'not to print anywhere anything that contests our true Christian religion and evangelical truth, nor anything sectarian, seditious, immoral, transgressing and shameful'. Zwingli concluded with the assurance that God advances only that which is useful, honourable and Christian.[34]

The extensive preface to the Zurich folio Bible of 1531 was anonymous. The mystery, however, is not great. The sheer weight of similarities of argument and style with his writings makes it clear that the preface was written by Zwingli during the early months of 1531. Why he did not name himself is also easily answered: his purpose was to divert attention away from himself and stress the collective nature of the work. The prophets of Zurich, like those of 1 Corinthians, had together produced this translation of the Bible.

The preface opened in an Erasmian spirit, reflecting on the disposition of the Christian towards scripture, which must be formed by a peaceful heart untouched by the vices of the world, a heart that mirrors the divine truth.[35] The language is almost directly from the Dutch humanist's 1518 text *Method of True Theology*, which in turn drew on Augustine's *On Christian Doctrine*. The Christian reader was exhorted to abjure the fleshly or worldly and was commended to humility, love and a yearning for 'heavenly matters'.[36] Such piety was preparation for reading and understanding God's Word correctly, attentive to the figurative language and pursuing the essential questions of who was the author and in what context did he live and write. Reflecting on a history of persecution and the banning of Luther's works in 1521, Zwingli argued that there had always been those who had sought to keep the Word of God from the people. No work is perfect, and there was always room for fraternal correction in producing editions of the Bible, but the burning of holy books could not be justified.

The argument against perfection was also a defence of the Zurich project of translating the whole Bible into German when other partial versions were available – in particular, the work from Wittenberg, although Luther's name was never mentioned. The early Church, above all in the time of Augustine, the preface noted, had had numerous translations of scripture, which was all to the good, for it demonstrated the vitality of the work of the Holy Spirit. Each was prepared as faithfully as possible, with none possessing the status of an official version. Divergent translations formed a community of texts to be consulted and compared; they were not rivals, and nor should the work of Wittenberg and Zurich be placed in opposition to one another. Rather, a spirit of fraternity should prevail in which each rejoiced at the achievements of the other. 'How,' Zwingli asked,

> should it harm the Wittenberg Church that the Old and New Testaments have been freshly translated? . . . that the servants of the Church in Zurich have prepared also a notable and unique transla-tion, as here follows, of the Prophets, Job, the Psalms, and the Wisdom of Solomon, Ecclesiastes, and the Song of Songs?[37]

In the Old Testament, God demonstrated his power, wisdom, goodness and righteousness. Taking aim at the Anabaptists' supposedly low estima-tion of the Hebrew Bible, Zwingli reminded his readers that Christ himself had encouraged his followers to study the sacred texts:

> The New Testament or Gospel is a clear witness to Christ, to how God brought about his mercy and promises in the Old Testament. The New is signalled and sealed in the Old. The Old Testament is fulfilled in the New and made true.[38]

The preface was bursting with Zwingli's undiminished conviction that the Word of God could be understood by women and men of all social rank and distinction. He passionately believed in the power of scripture to turn the heart. His doctrine of election was the unstated condition: only those to whom the gift of faith had been given might possess true understanding.

And yet the preface rang with hope for the present: in these days when the prophets spoke of impending judgement, the Word of God had been restored and spread by the divine gift of the printing press. It concluded with something of a puff for the book:

> As God has now brought us this time of grace, let us not disdain the gifts of God. Hasten and let no one delay. Let everyone purchase a copy, the cost is not too great. Great is the reward, precious is the treasure received.[39]

The liturgy of the Lord's Supper and the vernacular Bible were poignant expressions of Zwingli's Reformed Christian community. Word and worship formed a seamless robe of the Church. The expertise of languages and textual studies, the legacy of Erasmus, had been embraced in the creation of a new Bible that would endure for centuries. The sacred philology of Zwingli, Ceporin, Pellikan and Jud was produced in an edition of scripture that sang in the Swiss vernacular. It would never find the audience of Luther's translation that appeared a few years later: the Swiss dialect limited its audience. Nevertheless, from William Tyndale onwards, the legacy of the Zurich Bible would shape Reformed Christianity.

## WAR

During 1530, the rivalry between Bern and Zurich had heightened, drawing in sharp relief their different goals. Bern was largely concerned with the west, with France, Savoy and the Catholic lands of Wallis (the Valais) – all of which posed a serious threat. In 1530, the city acted to defend Geneva against the duke of Savoy, and the French-speaking lands of the Pays de Vaud came increasingly under Bern's control. The rulers of the city on the Aare were not prepared to go to war for Zurich and were not supportive of Zwingli's efforts to make an alliance with Philipp of Hesse.[40] Zwingli fully understood that without Bern, his hopes for any form of Protestant front were doomed.

The religious divide within the Confederation was accentuated in 1531 by the so-called Musso War, a curious affair involving the eccentric castellan Gian Giacomo de' Medici, known as *Il Medeghino*.[41] He had come into possession of the castle known as Musso, from which he was able to exercise considerable authority, terrorizing Graubünden and attempting to have his brother made a bishop. His various adventures put enormous strain on the Confederation, particularly after two officials from Graubünden were murdered on their return from negotiations in Milan. When Medici launched an attack on the Valtelline, which lay in Swiss territory and contained evangelicals, Reformed Confederates responded quickly with troops and arms; the Catholic Confederates did not engage. Zurich identified a confessional struggle in which co-religionists were under threat, and its artillery brought low the castle of Musso, after Gian Giacomo found that his Austrian allies had no intention of supporting him. The reluctance of the Catholics to participate was interpreted by Zurich as further evidence of their infidelity; but once again, the members of the Christian Civic Union refused to be drawn into conflict with fellow Confederates. Zwingli was persuaded that the Musso War was not an isolated event, but rather evidence that Catholic attacks were in the offing. He suspected that the Catholics had cleverly lured Zurich troops into Graubünden in order to leave the city open to attack.

On the wider Swiss front, Zwingli and his supporters in Zurich were sceptical that anything short of coercion would have any effect. The Bernese favoured, by contrast, the economic sanctions permitted under the terms of the Kappel Peace; but these could only be effective with the cooperation of all the Reformed states. When Zwingli preached at Pentecost in 1531, he rejected the blockade as immoral, on the grounds that it primarily hurt the common people, who were innocent. According to Bullinger, Zwingli declared from the pulpit: 'If a person is called a liar to their face they must defend themselves. Not to attack leads to defeat.'[42] The sermon caused a furore in Zurich, but the agreement with Bern to hold to the blockade remained intact and Zurich did contribute to enforcing it. Prices rose in Catholic lands and provisions were in short supply, creating hardships for the people, a suffering compounded by bad weather. The price of grain quadrupled, while that of wine doubled. A measure of salt cost double the wages of the average man. The situation was so dire that the Catholic Confederates created a culture of smuggling, by which goods made their way into the lands, often through Reformed territories.

During August 1531, Zwingli wrote a radical plan for the wholesale restructuring of the Confederation that would place Zurich and Bern in control and utterly exclude the Catholics from political influence.[43] The two cities were to be the 'oxen' pulling the cart. Central to Zwingli's plan was the creation of a Christian political authority that would reform the Confederation. Zwingli seemed ready to completely redesign the Confederation and forge a unified Christian state, to the alarm of many, particularly in Bern. With theological and historical arguments, he attacked the rights of the Catholic states, which he claimed had forfeited their political privileges through their failure to accept true religion.

Zwingli was clear that in the inevitable war, the godly would prevail precisely because of their justness. The blockade, he argued, was not leading to the spread of the gospel. In strikingly bellicose language, in calling for the destruction of the Reformation's enemies he cited the example of the Israelites. It was not sufficient that the Catholics merely permit preaching of the gospel: the whole order of the Swiss Confederation was to be radically altered through their vanquishment.[44] To this end, the man who had made his name by relentless opposition to mercenaries and pensions was willing to countenance the payment of money for military support.

Zwingli's outspoken advocacy of war did not appeal to many of the magistrates in Zurich, who hoped to avoid conflict, and his writing never reached Bern. Open water appeared between his advocacy of attack and the magistrates' measured caution. Zwingli used the pulpit to continue his assaults on those who received pensions or who, in his eyes, were prepared to compromise. Even his friends were unnerved by his stridency. Oecolampadius advised calmness, but Zwingli replied that there was nothing extreme about his demands.[45]

Zwingli had argued that Reformation required Zurich and Bern to put aside their differences and be led by God, even into battle. Bern, for its part, refused to adopt the reformer's assessment of the religious and political situation, and remained committed to negotiation. Its position among the Reformed Confederates was unchallenged. The situation continued to deteriorate. The blockade badly hurt the Catholics, who faced a virtual wall composed of the Reformed Confederates and their allies; but the sanctions were hardly better for traders and craftsmen in Zurich and Bern, who complained angrily that the collapse of the markets in the Five States was ruinous for them. A comet on 12 August 1531 was seen as a portent of war. A month later, a new War Council was formed in Zurich. Zwingli was persuaded that all news pointed to a planned Habsburg–papal invasion to eradicate the Reformation.

## CALAMITY AND DEATH

The First Kappel War had been caused by the demand for gospel preaching in the Mandated Territories, but now Zwingli and Zurich were determined that preaching be introduced in all the Catholic lands.[46] The desire for war was minimal – Zwingli was hardly typical – but every effort at mediation failed miserably. Bern and Zurich showed no sign of being able to reconcile their differences. In early August, Zwingli and some colleagues met representatives from Bern at Bremgarten to urge them to support Zurich; but they had no joy. Zurich's need for Bernese support was bordering on the desperate. And their disharmony emboldened the Five States, in their dire need, to plan an attack – although when and where was uncertain.

The Catholic forces began to receive reinforcements as troops arrived from Wallis and the Italian lands. Zwingli pleaded with the Zurich Council to take action, but, mindful of Bern's opposition to war, the leading magistrates wavered.[47] Basel, too, warned Zurich that the Catholics were arming.[48] The inaction saw Catholic troops move in early October into the Freie Ämter, part of the Mandated Territories, pillaging and driving the Reformed officials to flight. The quarrel, the Catholics insisted, was with Zurich alone, which had broken the terms of the peace with its blockade, and was now to be punished by God. Panicked discussions took place in Zurich on 7 and 8 October, as invasion seemed imminent. Rumours circulated that Bern had lifted the blockade, allowing the Catholics to receive food and goods. On 9 October, the Catholic states effectively declared war. Zurich's relations with Bern were at a low point, and it was doubted whether the Bernese would even respond militarily to an attack on Zurich. On 11 October, word arrived that it would.[49]

Zurich was unclear as to Catholic intentions. Some feared an attack on the city, while others believed that enemy forces would move into the Mandated Territories. The Council was divided on several key issues, such as preparations for war and relations with Bern. Despite the blockade, the borders were porous, and for months spies had moved back and forth across them, carrying news of war preparations.[50] There was plenty of false information, fuelling rumours and anxiety. Indeed, the Secret Council in Zurich misjudged the situation and did not take action to prepare the city. Zwingli had been clear that defeat of the Catholics was essential for the Reformation cause, but worthy preparations for that defeat had not been made. Experienced commanders had been dismissed in favour of men of little ability, but who were sympathetic to the magistrates' concern for true religion. The hand of the military had also been weakened in Zurich by lay rulers looking to reduce costs. As historian George Potter has wisely observed, 'they chose the wrong commander, they agreed on impracticable strategy, the tactics were deplorable and the Zurichers who took the field were few in number and unwilling to fight for survival'.[51] Fighting this reality, Zwingli preached war to stiffen the resolve of the city. We have some evidence from Konrad Pellikan and Leo Jud for Zwingli's last sermon, on 8 October 1531: marginal notes suggest that he preached in the Grossmünster a fierce attack on the papacy and offered a vigorous defence of his own interpretation of the gospel.[52]

Zurich conjectured that the attack would come in the Freie Ämter; Zurich itself was thought a step too far for the Catholics. By 9 October, however, a large force had evidently massed at Catholic Lucerne and would advance on their city. When the error was recognized, the Zurichers scrambled to assemble a force of a thousand men to advance to Kappel under the leadership of Jörg Göldi, a prominent and competent leader who had fought in Italy and at Musso.[53] Göldi, however, would make several ill-judged decisions on the field; unfounded rumours later suggested that he had swapped information with his brother Kaspar, a supporter of the mercenary service who had left Zurich in 1523 and was fighting on the opposing side. A key issue for the commanders was whether they were to attack or defend, for that question was unanswered in the instructions from the Large Council, which remained locked in debate even as the crisis unfolded. As Göldi understood the situation, he was not to attack the Catholics.

Early in the morning of 11 October, a smaller part of the Catholic forces advanced against the Zurichers, who, because they expected an ambush, had hardly slept that night. This Catholic contingent then swung to join the main Catholic force of 7,000 men. When Göldi was entreated to attack, he demurred, still uncertain of his instructions from the magistrates. He decided to await reinforcements, but his troops were now hemmed in. The reinforcements had indeed left Zurich, although the practical arrangements for calling up the men had been repeatedly botched. This contingent included Zwingli, dressed in green, and about 30 other pastors. The reinforcements arrived to join Göldi's men exhausted and ill prepared for battle. Despite his now enhanced numbers, Göldi decided to withdraw to an alternative site, which meant crossing marshland; meanwhile the Catholics appeared before them. As daylight retreated, the two sides expected the battle to commence the following day, with the Catholics holding a superior position on the field.

But the plans changed when a small party of about a hundred soldiers emerged from the woods to launch a surprise attack on the Zurichers. In the ensuing melee, which was joined by the main Catholic force, men were cut down in the dark. The Zurichers sought to withdraw from what was developing into a rout. But the situation went from bad to disastrous. The Zurichers did not possess the weapons to face the guns and long swords of the Catholic forces, and their commanders fled the field. Many Zurichers fell as they ran. Others, weighed down by armour, drowned in the marsh and stream.

Zwingli, together with other ministers, was surrounded by enemy soldiers. Precisely what happened next is uncertain. For example, his biographers are divided over whether he used his sword or simply exhorted the soldiers in battle. In any case, wearing armour he was not identifiable among the troops when they were set upon by the enemy. Eventually, he was wounded in the leg and fell to the ground. Heinrich Bullinger portrayed him as lying with his eyes to heaven; the Catholic historian Hans Salat had him face down in the mud.[54] As he lay alive among the dead, the Catholic soldiers looked for his body; they found him still conscious. He refused confession and was run through with a sword by one Vokinger from Unterwalden. The reformer's last words were reputedly: 'You may kill the body but you cannot kill the soul.' A Catholic priest who had known Zwingli in Zurich was reported to have said: 'Whatever your religious faith, I know that you were always a loyal Confederate. May God pardon your sins.'

It fell to Zwingli's close friend Oswald Myconius, the man who had brought him to Zurich, to provide an account that evoked the miracles of a medieval saint:

> After the battle, when our soldiers had retreated, the enemy got the chance to look for Zwingli's body. They found it and after condemning

it, they cut it into four and threw it into the fire and reduced it to ashes. Three days later, after the enemy had gone, Zwingli's friends came to see if they could find anything that remained of him and, miraculously, his heart emerged from the ashes, whole and unmarked. These good men were astonished, recognizing the miracle but not understanding it. Attributing this event to God, they rejoiced greatly that this miracle confirmed the sincerity of his heart.[55]

Zwingli's heart was brought to the city and Myconius was given the opportunity to view it; however, he declined, fearing that the story was untrue.

## HUMILIATION

Just before midnight on 11 October, those who had survived the battle at Kappel straggled back into the city to recount what had taken place. Anna Reinhart was told that she had lost her husband, her son, her brother and her brother-in-law. She would live another seven years under the care of Heinrich Bullinger, who provided for her children after her death. In all, about 500 Zurichers died, as against about a hundred Catholics.

Forty years after Zwingli's death, the distinguished humanist and teacher of ancient languages Thomas Platter (1499–1582), who had lived in Zurich as a student, recalled the desperate situation in the city:

The event was very lamentable, for many a worthy and honest man met his death there. Among others that eminent man, Huldrych Zwingli. I was at that time in Zurich. When the battle was lost, and the report reached Zurich, they sounded an alarm on the great bell, just about the time the candles were lighted. Then many people ran out of the town towards the Sihl bridge, lower down on the Albis. I also snatched up a halberd and sword in Myconius' house, and ran out with the others, but when we had proceeded some distance, the sight was so dreadful that I thought to myself, 'Better for you to have stayed at home', for many met us who had only one hand; others held their head with both hands, grievously wounded and bloody; others suffering still more dreadfully, and men with them who lighted them along, for it was dark.[56]

The young man joined a motley crew hastily assembled to defend the city. When it became clear that there was no immediate threat, he returned home in shock:

> My old teacher Myconius asked me, 'What is the news? Has Huldrych Zwingli been killed?' When I said 'Yes', he said, with a grieved heart, 'My God! Have mercy upon us: now I have no wish to remain any longer in Zurich', for Zwingli and Myconius had been good friends for many years.[57]

Among the dead were many from the leading families of Zurich that had supported Zwingli. The shock of Zurich's defeat unnerved her allies, and the Catholic army had taken up a strong position in Zug, just south of the city. Bern refused to attack. A force of about 4,000 troops from Zurich, Basel, Schaffhausen and St Gallen attempted an assault, but were routed at Gubel. Over a thousand were killed. There was panic in Zurich as a Catholic army made its way up the lake, stopping only a few miles from the city walls. A month later, Zurich and Bern sued for peace.

In the wake of the surprise defeat, order broke down in Zurich. Gangs moved through the city looking to lynch anyone associated with Zwingli. Leo Jud went into hiding and was only able to make his way across the city dressed as a woman. His courage did not fail him, however, and he entered the pulpit to declare Kappel the judgement of God. Divine condemnation had fallen not on Zwingli, but on the Zurichers for their lack of faith.

As Jud attempted to rally the supporters of the Reformation, the remnants of the Zurich army made their way towards the city. Their leader, Hans Escher, was a prominent opponent of Zwingli, who boasted that he had struck a peace with the Catholics and claimed that when he arrived back inside the walls of the city, he would run a sword through Jud and all the other preachers. His army was met by negotiators sent by the panicked Zurich Council, who sought to head off civil war. Escher reluctantly agreed that his forces would lay down their swords before entering the city. The situation was dire. No sooner had Escher brought home the defeated troops than an army from Schwyz appeared outside the gates of Zurich. Fortunately, the Catholics had no desire for further battle and moved off after a few days.

The mood in Zurich ranged from shock to anger. A general sentiment held that Bern and Basel had betrayed the city. Equally, Zwingli and his clerical allies were held responsible for a war that nobody but they had wanted. But there was no stomach for further conflict, and peace was desperately sought. The restoration of order was principally a result of the emergence of a moderate party that supported the Reformed Church and sought to calm the situation.[58] The Reformation was secured by the fact that those in power in Zurich had not been dislodged: they were able to restore a semblance of peace and ensure that dissent in the rural areas did not overwhelm the city. Clerics such as Leo Jud and others might decry the failure of the magistrates to support Zwingli, but they possessed no political power.

Outside the walls of the city, the rural communities of the Zurich territory were on edge, angry that they had been led into a war they did not want.[59] The villages had long resented the authority of the city and the clerical elite. The failure of the Reformation to relieve the burden of the tithe was well remembered. Furthermore, in the rural areas cross-confessional contact was much greater than in the city, as farmers and traders were in constant contact with their Catholic neighbours. Theological differences meant little to these men and women, and they had no appetite for war with those they knew well. Intense anti-clerical sentiments were directed against those urban clergy who had instigated a needless conflict.

In late November 1531, representatives of the rural communities gathered at Meilen on Lake Zurich to draft a petition to be presented to the magistrates. War was not to be undertaken without consultation, and the clergy should be drawn from 'native sons', not foreigners. In many respects, the demands were a damning indictment of Zwingli's condescending attitude towards the rural population, with his assumption that the people would receive the gospel obediently. The reformer's words were turned back on him in one article agreed at Meilen:

Let the preachers in the countryside say only that which is God's Word, expressed in both testaments. Let the clergy, as stated, not undertake or meddle in any secular matters either in the city or the countryside, in the Council or elsewhere, which they should rather allow you, our lords, to manage.[60]

251

The Catholics were able to set the terms of the agreement between Zurich and the Five States, signed in November 1531. The reparations were so punitive that the Zurich Council had to seek a loan from Augsburg. It has been reckoned that the financial burden crippled the city for at least a decade.[61] The terms of the First Kappel Treaty were abrogated, and the villages of the Mandated Territories were left to choose their faith. The conditions, however, were not equal: those areas that decided to remain Catholic were to make no provision for evangelicals, whereas in Protestant areas Catholics were to be guaranteed access to mass. Zurich was to abandon its foreign alliances and the abbot of St Gallen was to be restored.

Myconius had witnessed from Zurich the results of the defeat at Kappel, and in a letter lamented the situation. There was great sorrow in the city, he reported, and his own fate was surely either death or exile.[62] The betrayal and even the death of Zwingli were less significant than the loss of the Word. The people were stunned and the godless rejoiced. All the good people were dead and the rest simply hung their heads. What were the preachers to do? They must follow the exhortation of Paul to persevere and be courageous – although, he admitted, such strength was not given to all. The only ray of hope that Myconius could discern came from Heinrich Bullinger, who had come to the Grossmünster and preached; many had believed that Zwingli had risen like a phoenix.

# ELEVEN

# 'IT IS CERTAIN THAT ZWINGLI DIED IN GREAT SIN AND BLASPHEMY'

## REMEMBERED AND FORGOTTEN

Zwingli's sudden death confirmed the fears and expectations of friends and foes that his bellicosity could lead to disaster. No sooner had the news reached Zurich than narratives of martyrdom and blasphemy started to circulate. Had this preacher of God really wanted to wield the sword, not in the spiritual language of the Apostle Paul but on a battlefield? Had he died serving the Word that he believed would transform the world, or had blind ambition and a toxic mixture of spiritual and temporal authority laid low the ideals of the Reformation? All were certain that they had experienced that judgement of God of which Zwingli had preached. The question was what it had meant. The preacher had denounced the conscience-binding strictures of the Church, mercenary service and pensions, moral turpitude and faint-heartedness, but divine wrath had seemingly fallen on him. Leo Jud rushed to defend his friend, taking to the pulpit to blame the feckless political leaders who had never embraced gospel reform.[1] Despite the defeat, he claimed, it was a victory that men were willing to suffer and die for the truth. Such was the danger that Jud's friends suggested that he make his way to the church dressed as a woman.

The city of Zurich was in a state of disbelief and chaos. Hatred of the clergy, and Zwingli in particular, fostered violence. Demands for the restoration of the old faith were heard in the streets, and the authority of the magistrates tottered. Proud Zurich was on its knees, unable to defend itself against a hostile army outside its walls, and now a supplicant of the victorious Catholics who had played David against the supposed Goliath of Zwingli's city. Perhaps the prophet had misread his beloved Bible. His friends were worried.[2]

Zwingli's death cast a long shadow over his legacy for his immediate followers, and indeed for centuries to come. He had embraced power and force, believing it God's will, and had perished believing that propagation of the Word required the destruction of its enemies. Whether he had died a martyr or an inveterate heretic, his demise on the battlefield put a sudden end to a tumultuous life. For supporters, it was the sacrifice of a prophet who had overturned the tables in the temple. As Martin Luther had predicted, the return of God's Word would bring conflict, not peace. The forces of Antichrist would be roused to the final battle. Zwingli concurred, but – unlike his contemporary – believed that struggle might ultimately involve swords and halberds. His courage had not failed him in his willing-ness to die for his convictions. By contrast, Luther remained in the safety of Saxony, and Calvin would counsel martyrdom for others.[3] In the decades after his death, Zwingli was rarely forgotten, even when it was still unwise or imprudent to mention his name. Heinrich Bullinger, quickly summoned to rescue the Reformation, declared the fallen reformer the 'Swiss Apostle'.[4]

In many respects, Zwingli came to represent the divided soul of the Reformation: an arresting vision of the godly community, beset with the need to establish its own boundaries and cleanse itself of dissent. The godly community depended on the sword, and nearly vanished in military defeat. Zwingli's memory would be shaped and narrated around a set of contested convictions: that he had freed the Church from servitude of pope and priests; that he had returned the Church to scripture; that his controversial teachings on faith and the sacraments were biblical and faithful to early Christianity; and that he had sought to restore, not destroy, his native land. Bullinger kept alive the flame of fidelity and orthodoxy, but even Bullinger's closest allies, including John Calvin and Philipp Melanchthon could not share his convic-tion. For them, Zwingli had divided the Reformation by parting company with Luther and insisting on the exclusive rightness of his cause.

## FIRST BIOGRAPHY

Oswald Myconius, friend and colleague, had been instrumental in Zwingli's appointment to Zurich at the end of 1518, and the two remained close. Myconius wrote the first biographical account of Zwingli following Kappel, offering a carefully crafted life of his friend. The vita would become widely known across Europe, and was eventually translated into English in 1561.[5] Myconius was an educator and preacher who ultimately led the Church in Basel.[6] Unlike Zwingli, he was held in low regard by Erasmus, who once referred to him as 'homo ineptus'.

The biography took the form of a letter to one 'Agathius Beronensis', whose identity remains unknown.[7] The recipient obviously regarded Zwingli highly and was shocked by the way in which the reformer had been traduced by his opponents, including Luther. Myconius structured his biography around a series of questions to portray Zwingli's character, the origins of his reforms, his relationship to Luther and his death. The vita was a loving memorial to a friend who had been, above all, a true minister of Christ.

The reformer's youth was of particular interest to Myconius in establishing the natural virtues of a boy gifted and patriotic. His teachers and studies were recounted in considerable detail, as were the periods of intense study in Glarus and Einsiedeln. One is struck, however, by what is missing: we find little attention to Zwingli the priest. Myconius' purpose was clear: he did not want to allow that Zwingli was ever a papist. Rather, he sought to craft a narrative in which everything from Zwingli's youth had led seamlessly to his call as a reformer. The conversion at Einsiedeln, so decisive to Zwingli in his own autobiographical remarks, finds no place in Myconius. No conversion was ever necessary, as Zwingli had always taught the truth.

The leitmotiv of the biography is Zwingli's humanist learning in the service of the faith. Almost all other aspects of the life are sublimated to this image of the learned prophet. Myconius recounted with pleasure the breadth and depth of Zwingli's knowledge of the Greek and Roman classics; however, these were never an end in themselves, but rather ways of delving deeper, in the Erasmian spirit, into the Christian mysteries. It was from the ancients that he learned about the horrors of war. Strikingly, Erasmus is barely mentioned, and we gain the impression of Zwingli that he was an autodidact.

Several aspects of the life emerge in sharp relief: Zwingli's unrelenting opposition to mercenary service and pensions, his musical gifts, the endless insults and violence to which he was subjected, and his independence from Luther. There is little about the man's piety or pastoral work: rather, we find a politically astute prophet of the Word whose death revealed an unflinching obedience to God's will. Above all, Zwingli was a deeply moral and principled person – a scholar, educator and, ultimately, military leader. We read only briefly about his battle with the Anabaptists and his sanctioning of their executions. Finally, Myconius was adamant that Zwingli had not sought war, only recognizing that it could not be avoided. He was a prophet, resolute, learned and passionate. Although written shortly after Zwingli's death, the biography was not printed until 1536, and appeared to howls of protest from Lutheran and Catholic opponents.

## TROUBLED FRIENDS

News of Zwingli's death reached Zurich by midnight on 11 October, and it took little time for the rumours to spread among his friends and reformers in other cities. In Basel, Oecolampadius, who himself had only weeks to live, lamented to Martin Frecht in Ulm:

> Dearest brother, I cannot hide from you the pain that has overcome me that our Zwingli has fallen at the hands of dreadful enemies and in their fury was torn apart. Thus, I know well how the spread of this news through the world will be met with wild, rollicking joy that will scandalize the weaker brethren.[8]

Oecolampadius immediately addressed the consuming question: was death in battle justified? The Basel reformer, with some reservations, believed so:

> It pains me most that insults abound everywhere and no one defends him. The death of our brother is not dishonourable. It is nothing new among the Swiss that armed clergy should accompany the banner into battle. Our brother was not a military captain, but a good citizen, a true shepherd who wanted to die with his own people. Who among his detractors had an ounce of his high-mindedness? Also, did he not go under his own impulse onto the battlefield?[9]

Oecolampadius acknowledged that he and Zwingli had differed on how to prosecute Reformation. There were many, he wrote, who had warned the Zurich reformer against his warlike tendencies. Yet, Zwingli would have been a coward to have remained at home, and was well versed in the ways of combat. Nevertheless, Oecolampadius had counselled restraint:

Relying on our friendship, I repeatedly appealed to him not to engage in things that had little to do with the gospel. He wrote back that the morals of his people were little known to me. He had seen the sword drawn and would do the duty of a true shepherd. He would not act rashly.[10]

Those words, his Basel friend recalled, were his last to him. Oecolampadius was adamant that war had never been Zwingli's intention, but that he had been willing to employ force to further the gospel. 'He erred, which I regret to say, and I did not concur with his view. Yet, he was by no means the worst of men.'[11]

Oecolampadius' life was also memorialized in an account written by Wolfgang Capito, reformer in Strasbourg and close friend. To counter rumours that the Basel reformer had despaired and taken his own life, Capito provided a moving death scene, in which Oecolampadius committed his soul to heaven in the presence of 10 weeping friends.[12] Capito portrayed Oecolampadius (in contrast to Zwingli) as the gentle, humanist ideal of a scholar and churchman, renowned for his piety and learning. No hint of combat in this great man.

Oecolampadius' anguish, mixed with regret, was shared by others. Ambrosius Blarer in Constance wrote to Martin Bucer in Strasbourg in grief, accompanied by a clear uneasiness about what had transpired:

Oh my dear brother! The burning pain of my soul continually places before my eyes the fall of our Zwingli, that incomparable pillar of the Church of Christ. His death not only fills all pious men and friends of the gospel with deep grief, but leaves us anticipating a grievous blow to our Christian states.[13]

He shared his misgivings with Bucer:

It has always worried me, I say freely, and filled me with concern that this man with his irrepressible attitudes was ever more armed for war so as to enter battle with the foolishness of Mars. About this, however, I remained silent, as I thought it was through some unfathomable decree of God that Zwingli with word and weapons proclaimed Christ.[14]

The Augsburg medical doctor and magistrate Geryon Sailer wrote to Bucer expressing admiration for Zwingli's achievements, but casting doubt on the course of events. Had the reformers not done that of which they had always accused the Catholics? Had they not lusted for war and blood? Now they had been laid low by their own sword:

> Would it not have been better to have made concessions to the Five States [Catholic Confederates] and their officials, rather than to have set in motion a bloodbath of these unfortunate people? What madness to follow this way to make Christians! If the eternal Word and the preaching of the cross is not able to achieve this, then how can weapons? If one resorts to the sword, so does the victor cry and the defeated are vanquished. And while one might take up the sword to defend a neighbour, a preacher of God's Word should not do this. His role is to remind through word and deed. Zwingli had such a great reputation and could have done so much more.[15]

Martin Bucer, sharing these concerns, wrote back to Ambrosius Blarer in Constance:

> I feared for Zwingli. The gospel triumphs through the cross. One deceives oneself when one expects the salvation of Israel through external means with impetuosity, and triumph through weapons . . . It greatly unsettles me that our Zwingli not only recommended the war but did so incorrectly, as it appears to have been the case, and if we are rightly informed.[16]

Leo Jud, who, directly following Zwingli's death, had denounced the Council in Zurich for betraying the reformer, could not restrain his anger. In 1532, he addressed the readers of his translation of Zwingli's commentary on the Psalms:

> He lives and will live for eternity, this most virtuous hero. He leaves behind a glorious monument that no fire can destroy, no flame consume . . . Against his wishes, he took to the battlefield and his life was stolen by his enemies. For life and holiness he endured all danger

and was exposed to great hatred. What shame! What ingratitude! Neither his fame nor his memory will be lost. Against the ill-will and insults of the enemies of his memory, his memory will remain glorious and imperishable.[17]

## WITTENBERG

No tears were shed in Wittenberg. Famously, Martin Luther referenced Matthew 26: 'For all they that take the sword shall perish with the sword.' He added, 'it is certain that Zwingli died in great sin and blasphemy.'[18] On 28 December 1531, Luther wrote to his friend and fellow reformer Niklaus von Amsdorf:

> The Zwinglians have reached an accord with the other Swiss, but under the most shameful conditions, in addition to the ignominy and disaster of so unhappily losing the leader of their doctrine. But this is the end of the glory which they sought by blaspheming Christ's Supper. And they still do not repent, although they revoked practically everything in the peace conditions and justified the papists in everything. Indeed they were forced to rescind all alliances with foreign princes such as the landgrave. It says [Phil. 3:19]: 'they are the enemies of Christ's cross . . . whose glory is in confusion.'[19]

In his *Table Talk*, we find an account of Luther being asked by a student about Zwingli's eternal fate:

> I wish from my heart Zwingli could be saved, but I fear the contrary; for Christ has said that those who deny him shall be damned. God's judgment is sure and certain, and we may safely pronounce it against all the ungodly, unless God reserve unto himself a peculiar privilege and dispensation. Even so, David from his heart wished that his son Absalom might be saved, when he said: 'Absalom my son, Absalom my son'; yet he certainly believed that he was damned, and bewailed him, not only that he died corporally, but was also lost everlastingly; for he knew that he had died in rebellion, in incest, and that he had hunted his father out of the kingdom.[20]

In early January 1532, Luther mistakenly commented that Karlstadt had been appointed Zwingli's successor in Zurich, reflecting his contempt for both men. On the same day, he wrote to Wenzel Link in Nuremberg that they had seen a second judgement of God – first Thomas Müntzer (Luther's enemy, who was executed in 1525) had been struck down, and now Zwingli:

> I was a prophet when I said that God would not long tolerate these rabid and furious blasphemies of which those people were full, ridiculing our 'breaded' God, calling us carnivores and blood drinkers and bloody Thyesteans, and calling us other horrible names.[21]

Nevertheless, in 1538, during a relative lull in the ongoing hostilities between the Swiss and Wittenberg over the Lord's Supper, Luther was able to write to Bullinger: 'After I had seen and heard Zwingli in Marburg, I took him for an excellent man, so also Oecolampadius, so that news of their fates devastated me.'[22]

Luther's hostile response to Zwingli caused enormous offence in Zurich, but friends from across the German lands counselled patience, advising Bullinger and others not to respond defensively and make the situation worse. Wolfgang Capito in Strasbourg wrote to Bullinger:

> What one should do with Luther's fury I hardly know. In sum, something like this: either be silent, so that the nothingness of his anger is revealed or let one man answer who was not such a close friend of Zwingli's.[23]

The generally hostile remarks from Wittenberg were echoed in writings from other Lutherans across German lands. In 1556, the fiery preacher Georg Melhorn in Regensburg produced mocking doggerel with a harsh truth: 'Zwingli, who vacillates in the spirit, goes to war with his weapons. His enemies hear that he has fallen. They shoot him with insults and stab, quarter and burn him. So does God punish the Zwinglian.'[24]

## THE SUCCESSOR

Heinrich Bullinger, unanimously chosen as Zwingli's successor, was a respected 27-year-old minister and schoolmaster at the former monastery of Kappel.[25] He had known Zwingli since 1523 and had great respect for a man he regarded as a father figure. Taking up the office of preacher in the Grossmünster, his task was to rebuild a broken Church and society.

If the magistrates of Zurich thought they had appointed a subaltern to do their bidding, they were quickly disabused. Bullinger held a public address in January 1532 pointedly entitled 'On the Prophetic Office'.[26] The young preacher looked back and forwards. The biblical prophets had not perished at Kappel, but remained in Zurich as Zwingli's successors. The young successor did not hesitate to name Zwingli, and offered a full-blooded defence of his predecessor. There would be no turning back from the reforms of the 1520s.

Bullinger's words were the only eulogy for Zwingli, whose adopted city had not in any way commemorated his death: there was no funeral and no grave. Bullinger told the assembled magistrates and citizens that Zwingli was a true Christian, who had stood in the line of biblical prophets. By tearing down false religion, notably the idolatry of the mass and veneration of the saints, Zwingli had declared God's covenant with humanity. He had fulfilled the role of the prophets of Israel, for he had called for the restoration of true religion by destroying the false.[27] The errors of the Zurichers had not been Zwingli's: they were the sins of the descendants of Jacob, of the unfaithful Israelites of the city.

There was more to come. Zwingli was not one among the company of prophets: he was *the* true prophet. Bullinger poured forth humanist praise: 'In this man one found once and for all and absolutely what one had sought among the true prophets of God.' The Romans, he added,

> would take pleasure in their Cicero for his rhetoric, praise their Brutus for the struggle for freedom, admire the Greeks for their generals and lawgivers: to value a Themistocles, a Pericles or a Solon. With greater truth and right we extol our Zwingli, who brought about most extraordinarily the restoration of freedom and the renewal of holy studies.[28]

Bullinger's defence was robust, but subtle and also deeply political. He offered no apology for what Zwingli had actually done, and did not mention any particular theological doctrines. He made no reference to specific events or to the manner in which his predecessor had died. Bullinger's purpose was not merely to praise the dead. Like Myconius, he fashioned a memory of Zwingli that spoke to the present and future. Zwingli was not only a prophetic hero in the establishment of the Reformation, but also a form of the Church to come.

Bullinger's defence was also directed against contemporary Catholic writers who rejoiced in Zwingli's death. Most prominent was the chronicler, dramatist and mercenary Hans Salat (1498–1561), who described in detail the grisly treatment of the reformer's body, and in particular how the body had been submitted to a mock trial befitting a heretic before being dismembered.[29] Bullinger understood that he had to make the case that Zwingli was neither a heretic nor a traitor to his native Swiss Confederation. In a brief work, wittily entitled 'Salt for Salad', written in the early months of 1532, Bullinger delivered his most polemical and passionate defence of Zwingli, whose blood, like that of Abel, cried out from the ground:

> Zwingli lives however, just as scripture speaks of Abel, though dead, still being alive. He remains in his faith and in his writings, which are being read throughout the world – everyone knows what he wrote, taught, believed and preached. Therefore, with your bitter, harsh and fabricated writings you achieve nothing. Have you read his books? If so, you know perfectly well that he never contradicted piety. If you have not read them, so is it an odious offence upon you that you dare to assert what you neither know nor understand.[30]

## THE DEFENCE OF ORTHODOXY

Oswald Myconius' vita appeared in print in 1536, in an edition of the correspondence between Zwingli and Oecolampadius.[31] The collection of letters was deliberately provocative, published as a defence of the Swiss teaching on the Lord's Supper. It did not fail to rile Luther and his followers, leading to renewed hostilities. One of the editors, Theodor Bibliander (1506–1554), was a remarkable linguist who succeeded Zwingli in teaching the Old Testament in Zurich alongside Konrad Pellikan. Bibliander provided an extensive preface in which he robustly defended the memories of the two men, arguing that he sought to refute the 'false accusations and dire calumnies', as well as the 'vile prattle' directed against the persons and books of Oecolampadius and Zwingli. His purpose, Bibliander continued, was to reveal to all learned men how the two reformers had contributed to religion, restored the Church, and furthered the causes of erudition and piety.

Above all, Bibliander was devoted to ensuring that his teachers were absolved of accusations of false religion and that their books were restored to the 'community of the faithful'.[32] The two men were subjects of great calumny, derided as teachers of 'depraved doctrine':

> Therefore, now that we have made it clear enough concerning the reason of dogma that Zwingli and Oecolampadius followed, there appears no trace of impiety, no treachery to the orthodox faith, no struggle against the foundations of the Catholic faith, but rather their [teaching was] conducive to the security of pious discipline.[33]

Bibliander did not avoid the vexed question of Zwingli's death and the relationship of faith and war. In describing the Second Kappel War, he spoke of how 'necessity dictated that the city of Zurich defend by arms its own ends, its own citizens, its own fortunes, and its own head against enemies'.[34] It had essentially been a struggle for survival, not for religious hegemony:

> Zwingli did not want to be absent from the common danger. He had always truly taught piety for the fatherland, fortitude of the soul in repelling danger, obedience to the magistrate and preservation of the faith in order that no one might deny his service to his own city when it was forced into battle contrary to all right and law.[35]

Further, his actions were fully justified,

> for martial licence is included in the divine Word, as well as the responsibility of exhorting the soul to act bravely in the just and honest cause of war, such that not without a great reason did God also want the priests of the Israelite people to be in military orders.

Zwingli and Oecolampadius were 'heralds of truth', and 'to this end, he [Zwingli] understood that the place of the herald of truth was no less on the battlefield than it was at home'.[36]

Deftly, Bibliander addressed the charge that Zwingli had hypocritically condemned mercenary service and advocated war. For the author, the distinction lay in the righteousness of the cause: 'I do not ignore how execrable are mercenaries and unjust war.' He went on:

> And when unjust war brought rash and tumultuous conflict beyond expectation that they [the Catholics] fought against Zurich inauspiciously, Zwingli lay dead together with the best and strongest men, his soul returning to God from the battle line to which he had honourably come . . . And his body was treated inhumanly by the most harsh enemies, for whom he had wanted only salvation.[37]

Zwingli's death was for the salvation of his enemies, and not merely to defend his cause.

## REQUEST DECLINED

Just over 20 years after Zwingli's sudden death in 1531, the St Gallen humanist, politician and friend of the reformer, Joachim von Watt, better known as Vadian, wrote to Heinrich Bullinger in Zurich succinctly addressing the problem of Zwingli's legacy for the Reformation.[38] Zwingli had known Vadian from his early studies in Vienna, and the humanist was a significant influence on the priest's formation. Vadian had presided at the second disputation in Zurich, in 1523, and had become a leading supporter of the Reformation in his native St Gallen. His relationship to Zwingli had been somewhat problematic on account of the Zurich reformer's aggressive politics; but his status was unquestioned, and when Heinrich Bullinger came up with the idea of printing a biography of Zwingli, he turned to the eminent figure.

In 1544, following a series of vicious attacks on the Swiss by Luther and his supporters, Bullinger decided that the only effective way of defending Zwingli against charges that he had been a heretic and the destroyer of the Swiss Confederation was to produce a Latin edition of his writings to demonstrate his orthodoxy. Bullinger's sanguine view was that such an edition should include an accurate vita, defusing charges of moral improbity. What better way to defend the fallen reformer than to have an account of his life written by one who had truly known him, but was not from

Zurich? Bullinger wrote to Vadian that he alone possessed the standing to write such a biography.[39]

> At the moment, an edition of Zwingli's works is being prepared by us in four volumes. [Rudolf] Gwalther is translating the German works into Latin. A most beautiful and useful work will result. Only one thing is missing, that you, most learned Vadian, can provide. A life of Zwingli.[40]

But Vadian was not to be persuaded. Replying about six weeks after Bullinger's letter of early May 1544, the St Gallen reformer did not provide the answer the Zurichers wanted. His hesitation arose from prudence:

> I must at least say what I mean. It seems to me by no means reason-able that at this time, when so much wisdom has been lost and so many spirits thrown into confusion and afflicted with the most unjust judgements, that a life of Zwingli should be placed in the edition of his works to be soon printed.[41]

While, in principle, an edition of Zwingli was fully justified, Vadian regarded the effort in Zurich as untimely, guaranteed only to infuriate both Catholics and Lutherans – and possibly lead to the renewal of a Swiss civil war. Bullinger seems to have accepted Vadian's affirmation of their friendship that accompanied his decline of the offer, and the subject was never raised again. While Bullinger took Vadian's refusal in good part, he did not give up the idea of producing a life of Zwingli to accompany the intended edition of the reformer's works. Ambrosius Blarer, who was somewhat unnerved by the prospect of the edition and its ramifications, informed Vadian in September 1544 of Bullinger's continuing intentions. The head of the Zurich Church wrote to Blarer in October that he was busy preparing the vita, so that the truth about Zwingli might be known. He claimed that his primary purpose was not to praise, but to put the record right.[42]

Yet what happened next – or rather, what did not happen next – remains a mystery. The collected works of Zwingli were printed in 1545 by Froschauer – but without any vita.[43] Bullinger kept the reasons private, or at least his extensive correspondence offers no clues. In the end, he may have heeded Vadian's warning.

## A FINAL REMEMBRANCE

Yet Bullinger bided his time, for he never relinquished the hope of writing an account of Zwingli's person and reforming career. When he completed the task, it was in the context of a massive history of the Reformation drawn from a remarkable range of sources, written and oral.[44] Despite Bullinger's prodigious use of sources and remarkable erudition, there was never a propitious moment for publication. By the 1570s, Bullinger was an old man, having guided the Zurich Church for over 40 years, but the wounds of the Reformation had not healed. The Reformed and the Lutherans remained locked in bitter quarrels, and the visible churches of the Reformation were as divided as ever. Bullinger's 'Reformation History' was not published, remaining instead in manuscript form, to be circulated among friends, as Vadian had suggested 30 years earlier. The name of Huldrych Zwingli continued to ignite incendiary exchanges, as the Lutherans and Catholics continued to denounce him as a heretic, Nestorius come back to life.

The theme of the prophetic preacher runs through the history, and Bullinger linked Zwingli's rhetorical gifts with his natural virtue:

> In body and face, Zwingli was an attractive man, who preached repentance and amendment of life and the enhancement of Christian love, denouncing all manner of superstition, vice, and idleness, inordinate eating, drinking, clothing, sexual activity and abuse of the poor. Zwingli never ceased to rouse the people to be obedient to the city magistrates and to live as proud Swiss.[45]

The results, Bullinger freely admitted, were decidedly mixed. The reformer's sermons were seldom delivered without catcalls and whistling. He was labelled a liar. Yet he had spoken presciently, warning the Swiss against Emperor Charles V. In Bullinger's hands, Zwingli died a martyr and a true witness for the faith.

## GENEVA

John Calvin (1509–1564) tried very hard to have nothing to do with Huldrych Zwingli. In his surviving correspondence of about 1,200 letters, the Zurich reformer is mentioned eight times, and the Frenchman's voluminous theological tracts contain some six references to him. In comparison to the frequency with which Calvin mentioned or cited Luther, Melanchthon, Bullinger and Erasmus, the name of Zwingli is strikingly absent. Even the medieval Peter Lombard and Bernard of Clairvaux appear more frequently.

Yet Calvin would have been much more aware of Zwingli's works and ideas than he was prepared to admit. From the time of his flight from France, in 1534, until his death in 1564, he lived in the world of the Swiss Reformation.[46] Geneva was not part of the Confederation, but it was a supplicant of the much more powerful Bern, where Zwingli's theology was well entrenched. In the French Pays de Vaud, Calvin faced considerable opposition from pastors who regarded themselves as Zwinglian. And from the mid-1540s, Calvin developed a close friendship with Heinrich Bullinger, despite their differences, and made several visits to Zurich.[47]

So why did he fail to speak about a man whose legacy was everywhere in the culture occupied by Calvin? He had good reasons to be circumspect. Most significantly, he knew that any invocation of Zwingli's name poured blood into the shark tank of the endless confessional war between Wittenberg and Zurich. Calvin's aspirations for a unified Reformation front demanded that Zwingli not be mentioned. Much in line with Vadian's views on a possible biography, he was convinced that the efforts of Bullinger and others to honour the fallen reformer scuppered any hopes of reconciliation.

Zwingli was, in some ways, emblematic of the problem that Calvin sought to resolve: the divided house of the Reformation.[48] Although the roots of the Frenchman's theology sprang from Zurich, his influences ran from Basel, Strasbourg and Wittenberg. Calvin was fully aware of the cosmopolitan nature of his theology and how it crossed the frontiers of Reformation battles. Through his close relationship with Bullinger, he acknowledged the role of the Swiss, and he needed their backing to sustain his threatened position in Geneva. Yet it would have been disastrous to praise Zwingli as he did Luther, Bucer and Bullinger. Part of the problem was local: Calvin's opponents in the French-speaking lands invoked the name of Zwingli to attack his teaching. Calvin pointed to the example of a Latin poem composed by the pastor André Zébédée, who wrote in Zwingli's honour:

It is a sin to expect one greater. Perhaps one should pray that an equal to him might be granted to us in this century. His learned word, his earnestness, and the sharpness of his spirit all flowed together to the praise of the Lord.[49]

Calvin was enraged, declaring that Zwingli was being defended as if he was the gospel.

Calvin's issue with Zwingli was not simply political. Although his own views on the Lord's Supper shifted over the years between the Lutheran and Swiss positions, he was adamant that Zwingli was wrong in his expression of Christ's presence in the sacrament. On this subject, Calvin had not a single positive word to say about the Swiss reformer. Even in the 1549 agreement made with Bullinger in Zurich on the Lord's Supper, for which the Frenchman made significant concessions, Zwingli's name was not invoked. When Pierre Viret, reformer in the Pays de Vaud and later Calvin's cherished friend, claimed that in his last years the Zurich reformer had changed his views towards a more favourable language of Christ's presence, Calvin replied abruptly that he had not read those works. Calvin's defining judgement was that Zwingli 'was in error'.

Calvin's few published mentions of the Zurich reformer – none in the *Institutes of the Christian Religion* – focused on a selection of theological issues. He offered no judgement on Zwingli's life or death. In biblical interpretation, Calvin remarked that he had read Zwingli's interpretation of Isaiah, which he admired for its skill, but which on account of its strong philosophical nature often departed from the text. On predestination, while there was considerable agreement, Calvin found Zwingli's arguments 'paradoxical', although he did not explain why. Against these single references, he spoke more frequently about Zwingli and the sacrament, but never positively.

On a small number of occasions, however, Calvin was prepared to pay his respects. In his 'Short Treatise on the Lord's Supper', printed in 1541, he described the meeting at Marburg. Although there was no agreement, he said of Luther, Zwingli and Oecolampadius:

For if we are not ungrateful and forgetful of what we owe them, we shall be well able to pardon that [their disagreement] and much more without blaming or defaming them. In short, since we see that they were, and still are, distinguished for holiness of life, excellent knowledge, and ardent zeal to edify the Church, we are always to speak and judge of them with modesty, and even reverence; since at last God, after having humbled them, has in mercy been pleased to put an end to this unhappy disputation, or at least to calm it preparatory to its final settlement.[50]

Calvin understood that the Zurichers did not trust him on the subject of Zwingli, and that he had offended their feelings on various occasions. But away from the theological difficulties, he was prepared to honour the man as a true reformer of the Church and a voice for the gospel. Zwingli was no Luther, but he was worthy of praise. This view in Geneva found expression in the *Icones* of Théodore Beza (1519–1605), Calvin's friend and successor. The *Icones* was a tribute to the leaders of the Reformation, pairing portraits with encomia.[51] Zwingli was placed together with his friend Oecolampadius.

Beza described the two men as 'the greatest athletes of Christ' who 'excelled in doctrine' and were 'by far the best of the Alpine peoples'.[52] For Zwingli's death, there were words of praise:

And in the war stirred up by those who could not bear the brilliance of the gospel, a hostile hand caused Zwingli's fall while he was serving in the army for his own ministry, such that God crowned the death of his servant with a double honour. For what could be a more holy or honourable death, than to die for both the glory of God and for the patria?

Zwingli was not only a faithful servant of the gospel, but a great patriot, as the accompanying verse praised him:

Because blessed Zwingli burned with twin loves,
First of God, then of his country,
It is said that he devoted himself to both,
First to God, then to his country.
How well he paid his offerings to both,
His spirit for the fatherland, his ashes for piety![53]

Beyond Swiss lands, the memory of Zwingli became part of the historical identity of the Protestant Reformation. The most influential chronicler of his fate was Johannes Sleidanus (1506–1556), who was appointed by the Schmalkaldic League to write a history of the Reformation.[54] Sleidanus, who had long had access to the most significant documents of the age, completed his first volume in 1545, finishing his work in 1554. During that time, he served in various diplomatic roles on behalf of the French and Strasbourg, at one point travelling to England, where he obtained numerous sources. He was also a Protestant representative at the Council of Trent.

In Sleidanus' account, Zwingli was a martyr to the faith and his country. In describing his death at Kappel, Sleidanus' words echo those of Oecolampadius. The following is from the Bohun translation:

> Among the number of the slain *Zuinglius* was found. For the custom of *Zurich* is such, that upon any Expedition, the principal Minister of their Church goes out along with them. Now *Zuinglius* who was in his own nature a very stout and couragious Man, consider'd likewise with himself, that if he should stay at home, and the battel should go against them, he must needs draw upon himself a great Odium for animating other Men by his Preaching, and yet shrinking back himself in the time of danger, he therefore resolv'd to run the common risque.[55]

Sleidanus' account found its way into the greatest Protestant martyrology of the century, John Foxe's *Acts and Monuments*. In the 1576 edition, Foxe provided an account of Zwingli's death taken largely from Sleidanus, but with slight embellishments that gave the reformer a more Christ-like character of self-sacrifice. Foxe emphasized the manner in which Zwingli was betrayed. Citing Oecolampadius, he portrayed Zwingli as a man knowingly meeting his fate and reluctant to go into battle, but ultimately making the honourable decision.[56] Through Foxe, Zwingli the betrayed prophet became part of the Protestant narrative of martyrdom.

## 'THE GREAT RABBI OF ZURICH'

In the dedication of a work written at the time of the disputation at Baden in 1526, so during Zwingli's lifetime, his one-time friend and early opponent Johannes Fabri offered an assessment of Zwingli, expressing views that were widely held by contemporary Catholics.[57] 'The same Luther,' he wrote, 'had a follower in Zurich with the name Huldrych Zwingli, who also five years ago began to spread the new learning among the common people. In the beginning he had greatly praised Luther.'[58] However, in certain doctrines Zwingli had departed from the Wittenberger, especially on the Lord's Supper and images, and given birth to a whole number of sects. One of the most frequent accusations levelled against Zwingli was that he was the father of Anabaptism.

Fabri sketched the Catholic portrait of Zwingli as a heretic. The Zurich priest was both a supporter and an opponent of Luther; he was the founder of Anabaptist and other splinter groups; and he destroyed images in the Church. Worst of all, he denigrated the Holy Eucharist with his heretical teaching and destroyed the worship of the Church. Fabri, as Johann Eck had done at Baden, stressed the innumerable contradictions in Zwingli's theology. In the second chapter of this work, he enumerated 150 points that demonstrated that the Zwinglians and Lutherans were at odds.

Equally repulsive as his theology was the reformer's character, and Fabri wrote that 'Zwingli had in Zurich [together with Leo Jud] turned himself into a bishop.'[59] He was a tyrant, who repeatedly committed acts of indecency. Referring to the imprisonment of the Anabaptists, who had been Zwingli's brothers in Christ, Fabri called the reformer a modern-day persecutor, a Decius, Maxentius and Valerian. Even Zwingli's musical talents were derided. Yes, he played instruments, danced and sang, but he did so as if he alone possessed the Holy Spirit. Further, it was well known that he had violated young women.[60]

The formidable Johann Eck, who had led the Catholic triumph at Baden in 1526, was Zwingli's fiercest contemporary critic, a master of polemic and concise theological argument. Like Fabri, Eck focused on Zwingli as archheretic and moral reprobate, with an emphasis on his sacramental errors. Central to Eck's polemic was the claim that became a pillar of Catholic assaults on Zwingli: the division between Wittenberg and Zurich over the Lord's Supper. If the two sides could not agree on the interpretation of scripture, then clearly the Holy Spirit was not present. By casting away tradition and rejecting the authority of the Church in interpreting scripture, Zwingli had opened the door to chaos, which he had delighted to enter.

Eck was not finished. Not only was Zwingli a heretic and not Christian, but as a scholar he was a fraud. He was no philosopher and was poor in

Greek and Hebrew. Invoking the anti-Semitism of his day, he styled Zwingli 'the great rabbi of Zurich', while deriding the reformer's ability to read Hebrew. In other words, he was not even a good Jew. Zwingli, he added, puffed himself up with his knowledge of the language, but did not know even the most elementary principles. Once more, Zwingli had only protested against celibacy because he could not control himself and entered into a relationship with a woman that was not marriage, but whoredom. Finally, Eck attacked Zwingli as a politician, accusing him of having brought the Swiss Confederation to the brink of war. He seized on a phrase often used by Zwingli – 'the gospel demands blood'. Although Zwingli had meant that one should be prepared to be martyred for Christ, Eck presented the statement as evidence of the bloodlust of the Swiss reformer.

The Franciscan poet and polemicist Thomas Murner (1475–1537), priest in Lucerne from 1525 to 1528, labelled Zwingli a 'church thief' – a tag that would stick. Murner's latent admiration for Luther was entirely absent from his judgement of Zwingli. The reformer of Zurich was a thief in that he had robbed the Church in violation of both ecclesiastical and divine laws. He was also a coward, who had not shown up at the disputation at Baden, even though he had been assured of safe passage.

Fierce words came from among the Swiss themselves, and above all from the aforementioned chronicler Hans Salat of Lucerne, who had been active in the Italian campaigns. His chronicle, which covered the years 1517–1534, is a vital source for Catholic attitudes and deeds during the early Reformation in the Confederation. Salat described in detail Zwingli's years in Glarus and Einsiedeln, and then his arrival in Zurich. There, wrote Salat, under the influence of Luther, Zwingli began to voice criticism of the Church. Particular emphasis was placed on Zwingli's opposition to pensions. The chronicler's portrayal of Zwingli touched on elements found in other Catholic writers, but he offered his own perspective. Following the disputation in Zurich in January 1523, Zwingli had become a 'furious lion', a 'crafty fox' and allegedly the military commander and governor. He was a prophet and bishop, a teacher and a god-like figure for the magistrates.[61] It was he who had determined that Zurich would not be represented at Baden.

Zwingli was responsible for everything evil that had taken place. The wretched blockade of the Catholic Confederates and the resulting misery were his doing. With his bellicose nature, he had led the Swiss to armed conflict and was responsible for the Kappel wars. His ambitions were without limit: he wanted to be dictator not only in Zurich, but also in the Confederation and over all the Reformation.[62] To that end, Zwingli had devised a plan to defeat the Catholics and the Habsburgs. Salat did give Zwingli some credit: the reformer had been successful because he was such a canny politician, well able to employ the weapons of fury, tact and flattery. Salat was much more interested in Zwingli the political operator than Zwingli the theologian, whose thinking he attributed largely to Luther. In the end, he rejoiced, in verse, at Zwingli's death, which was a great Catholic victory.

The stream of polemic continued to vilify Zwingli as a heretic, but it largely followed the agenda set by his Catholic contemporaries, with old charges repeated. A novel contribution was made, however, by German humanist and controversialist Johann Cochläus (1479–1552). His own position was not particularly original: indeed, he drew most of his information from Fabri, Eck and Murner in recounting the disputations at Baden and Bern, the Kappel wars and Zwingli's death. This humanist did, however, gather a vast body of sources, both Catholic and Protestant, which became the foundation for later accounts of the Reformation.[63] Once more, the Eucharist lay at the centre of what divided Zwingli's Reformation from the Catholic Church; however, to emphasize the true depravity of the reformers, Cochläus played Luther and Zwingli off against one another, taking great pleasure in citing Protestant sources in support of the Catholic position politically and theologically, ever attentive to contradictions.

With his death, Huldrych Zwingli passed into the memory culture of the Reformation. In the sixteenth century, the death of a reformer might be followed by struggles among his disciples to claim the leader's mantle – such was certainly the case with Luther and Calvin. Zwingli's death was otherwise. For no other figure of the Reformation do we find such simultaneous zeal to remember and to forget. For Heinrich Bullinger and Zurich, and for Lutherans and Catholics, there was good reason to recall Zwingli. For the former, he was the prophet and martyr; for the latter, the embodiment the embodiment of the sure fate of heresiarchs. For diametrically opposed reasons, his supporters and his enemies clung to his memory. But for the wider Reformation, there needed to be a selective forgetting – a way of holding to his theological and spiritual inheritance, uncoupled from hegemony and blood. Zwingli could not be a model for the future. He could be remembered only in light of a legacy now reworked by others.

Heinrich Bullinger was the perfect heir. He resolutely defended Zwingli, while gently revising and remoulding the form of Christianity he had come to lead. No longer were opponents Hittites to be eradicated. The marginal authority of the Swiss within the Reformation was acknowledged. Bullinger was indeed a leader of Protestantism, but through the circulation of his works, his extensive correspondence, and his support for Zurich as a refuge for religious exiles. Zwingli's heir turned a Swiss story into a European and ultimately transatlantic one. He and his colleagues – Konrad Pellikan, Theodor Bibliander, Konrad Gesner and Rudolf Gwalther – belonged to a Confederation in which there would be little territorial expansion of their faith. Zurich was finished as a belligerent force for the gospel. Their work was as counsellors and teachers in an expanding network of Protestantism, in which they were but one part of a community of beliefs, not a sole authority.

Zwingli's successors' world of tense religious coexistence could never have been comprehended by him – or indeed Luther, both of whom had battled for absolutes. Conflict, violence and persecution continued; but Zwingli was now a symbol of the origins of a movement, a founding father, not an authoritative voice. He would be remembered for virtues and principles that said more about his descendants than they did about the realities of the 1520s.

# TWELVE

# LEGACIES

M artin Luther and John Calvin died in their beds, surrounded by mourning friends who quickly declared the passing of saints. Zwingli has always been a far more problematic figure to commemorate. Certainly, he was the originator of a new form of Christianity that became the Reformed tradition. Many of its most fundamental concepts, such as covenantal theology, the nature of the Church and the character of the sacraments came from him and from those with whom he was closely connected, notably Leo Jud, Johannes Oecolampadius and Martin Bucer. Triumphal Protestantism has always found in the Swiss reformer a warrior against a benighted medieval Church, a humanist who saw beyond Erasmus, the founder of Reformed thought, and the warm-up act to John Calvin. When the Genevan reformer took the stage, Zwingli was able to bow out gracefully. There was gratitude for his services, but the real show had begun. Yet, a problem endured. Whereas narratives of Luther have, until recently, stepped lightly over his indefensible views of peasants and Jews, it has remained deeply problematic to commemorate the Zwingli who died sword in hand.[1]

One way of treating Zwingli has been to see him as a provincial, Swiss reformer, in contrast to the later Calvinists, with their more 'international' perspective. Luther appealed to German-speaking audiences across and beyond the Holy Roman Empire. Calvin the refugee became the voice of Reformed Protestantism in his native France, but he spoke also to the nascent movements in the Netherlands, Britain, Eastern Europe and the new colonies. Zwingli's place is less easily located: he thought in terms of an elect Swiss people and dreamt of the conversion of the Confederation to the gospel, but few of his countrymen saw him in that light. Bern and Basel adopted the Reformation, but never believed themselves to be in the shadow of the Zurich reformer. Curiously, his enormous influence was almost completely devoid of any particular image or persona. He was not the Hercules or Elijah of Wittenberg or the Moses of Geneva. His opponents, from Luther to Felix Manz and Johann Eck, were far more effective in creating the image of a fanatic, betrayer or heretic. From the earliest insults scrawled on the walls of the city, Zwingli's opponents have had the upper hand in sealing his identity for posterity.

Yet the Zurich reformer has never been wholly forgotten beyond the walls of his adopted city. Nor could he be, given his formative role in the early Reformation. But memory and commemoration have been both troubled and labile. As for John Calvin, narratives of Zwingli's life have repeatedly attempted to make him part of a pantheon of Reformation heroes or a harbinger of modernity.[2] He could be a symbol of nineteenth-century patriotism, a warrior against a benighted medieval Church, an advocate for freedom of the conscience, a proto-liberal theologian and the prophet of an expansive Christianity prepared to find salvation beyond the strict boundaries of the Church. Others have cast him in an entirely different role. For Catholics and Anabaptist communities, he remained an arch-heresiarch and the Judas of the gospel. The issue of the drownings in the Reformation remained sensitive in Zurich: in 1952, an attempt to place a plaque on the Limmat to remember the executed Anabaptists was stymied by the city. Permission was finally given in 2004 and a simple memorial was created.

For modern secular society, Zwingli poses a particular conundrum. It is a challenge to see past what appears to be no more than religious bigotry, coercion of ideas and 'puritanical' morality. What could fit more neatly with contemporary discourses of religious fanaticism and illiberalism than death in battle attempting to promulgate faith? The 2019 marking of Zwingli's arrival in Zurich and the commencement of his preaching demonstrated the deep ambivalence among many towards the Reformation and its inherent violence. Not surprisingly, in the public sphere the most prominent response was irony and somewhat dark humour.

The language of commemoration is parsed only with difficulty. Does remembrance necessarily mean honouring, or should it require a reckoning with the past? Commemoration has been, and remains, central to the formation of identities, of asking who we are and how we have arrived where we are. History and memory were crucial to the Reformation: the reformers imagined a golden age of the early Church, when the gospel was purely preached and Antichrist had not yet unleashed his power. Such a vision, which retains its force in many circles, also required a good deal of forgetting. One of Zwingli's principal challenges was to convince women and men to abandon and erase their memories of devotion to saints, Mary and the Eucharist. The suffering Jesus on the cross, so central to late-medieval piety, was replaced by the living Christ, the model for a new society. Zwingli evoked the traditional virtues of the Swiss, once faithful to God and heroic in the defence of their liberties. It was hopeful nostalgia for a non-existent age of manly virtue. The Anabaptists, in turn, looked to the community of the Apostles, while the Catholics sought to preserve an arcadian unity of the medieval Church.

## 'HE LIVES'

Commemoration of Huldrych Zwingli in the eighteenth century had remained sporadic, but matters changed significantly in the nineteenth century, as Zwingli emerged as central to Swiss cultures of memorialization. This renewal owed much to the creation of Protestant Switzerland as a nation after the Napoleonic period. But there were other issues at stake, such as the enormous influence of the Enlightenment on religion. Zwingli, the learned, social renewer lent himself as a symbol for hegemonic Swiss Protestantism against backward Catholicism. Further, his seemingly rational, philosophical thought formed a bulwark against sectarian spiritualism that flourished in the eighteenth century and was perceived as a challenge to the established state Church. As widespread religious sentiments saw in the state Church an ossified institution, Zwingli could be recovered by its defenders as a founding father of the Reformation ideal of the Christian society, with the marriage of temporal and spiritual authority, the coexistence of Church and society.

In 1811, the author Joseph August Eckschlager produced a dramatic account of Zwingli's life and death for public performance. Towards the end of the story, he addressed the spectral theme that occupied virtually all nineteenth-century Protestant and Catholic accounts of Zwingli: his culpability for a religious war. The playwright allowed the dead reformer to reveal his blessedness:

The war brought me to my end. I am hated as the author of this war, and all misfortune is attributed to me. I am not guilty, and that heaven knows! Can I speak against my own conscience? I cannot. The war was necessary, and it was better than the peace we have. I am hated for my words. Can I, the hated one, further instruct? Woe is me when my teaching does not plant love in the hearts of my brothers. One rarely wishes to hear the truth, particularly from the mouth of the despised.[3]

The play concluded apocryphally with Zwingli's friends Oswald Myconius and Thomas Platter walking on the battlefield of Kappel, looking for the reformer's body.

MYCONIUS. Is he truly dead?
PLATTER. Dead!
MYCONIUS, *throwing himself into Platter's arms*. Dead! My Zwingli!
PLATTER. Look there, do you not see something? My hair is
    standing on end!
MYCONIUS. He hovers closer, do you not see him?
*Zwingli's shadow floats above the ground.*
MYCONIUS, *looking at the shadow*. Dead, he is dead!
A VOICE (GOD). He lives!
*The shadow disappears into the light.*
MYCONIUS. He lives in me, in you!
THE VOICE. His teaching is through you! A blessing to posterity.[4]

Zwingli was a hero who was not confined to religion: rather, he embraced a mythological manifestation of an aspiring Protestant land. The drama of his shadow vanishing into the light was not out of place with other celebrations, as festive gatherings were held in the city and on the Kappel battlefield to mark a 'hero's death', the sacrifice of a martyr and an 'apostle'. Speakers stressed that the dead Zwingli lived on in those who held to pure religion and love of fatherland.

The first major anniversary of the century came in 1819, 300 years after the priest's arrival in Zurich. We find a complex web of memories that constituted the commemoration. In addition to being a patriot and defender of the gospel, Zwingli the moderate emerged, the rational humanist and follower of Erasmus who stood for the solidity of the establishment of Church and state.[5] This image of the reformer was of more than local or only Swiss interest, for it served a broader agenda of uniting Protestantism. That meant a long-overdue reconciliation with Lutherans. The inspiration was the 1817 union of the Lutherans and Reformed in Prussia. The Enlightenment shift away from the stricter Protestant doctrines, such as predestination, created hopes that a broader basis for union might be found. Central to this aspiration was an obsession with the relationship between the embattled founders, Zwingli and Luther. Harmony required looking past seemingly irreconcilable differences and leaving their debate in the world of the sixteenth century. The rise of liberal theology created an opening for a more flexible approach to doctrine.

Ecumenical hopes by no means deafened the rhetoric of heroism. A crucial step in Zwingli's return to prominence was the preparation and publication of a critical edition of his works, which appeared in eight volumes between 1828 and 1842.[6] Nevertheless, much remained unresolved, notably the death: had it been a righteous deed or delusional act? Swiss Reformed patriots insisted that it was martyrdom to religious freedom, democracy and independence. We find such sentiments expressed by a fraternity of students assembled at the field of Kappel in 1831 to celebrate their 'hero of the faith':

> We gathered at the place where Zwingli fell, not only in order that we might offer to him with fleeting emotion due payment of our grati-tude, our admiration, our love, even if it would be from still so sincere hearts, but also as it were to invoke his heroic spirit in order that he might speak to us like an immortal, like an angel from beyond to a brother in this world, and that he might consecrate us as warriors in the same battle that was and remains his.[7]

Salomon Hess, the head of the Zurich Church, who had taken the lead in organizing the commemorations of 1819, published a number of sermons and tracts. Perhaps most remarkable was an 1820 account of Anna Reinhart, Zwingli's wife, about whom we know so little.[8] Hess' intention was not only to demonstrate that the Reformation was a time of pious females, but also to offer Anna as a model for 'Christian women'. The author's view of what those virtues entailed is very evident, for the reader is not to view Anna merely as a tragic figure, as Zwingli's widow: she was a source of encouragement through her faith and trust in providence. The text fell comfortably into the established Protestant tradition of exemplary literature. Anna embodied nineteenth-century gender stereotypes: a 'beautiful, great character' who reaches out to our time from the obscurity of the past. A role model for contemporary women, she possessed a 'noble soul', and her love of her husband, family and friends sustained her through adversity and 'the storms of fate', remaining her comfort in life and death.

## HISTORICAL VISIONS

Zwingli was sympathetically treated by the most influential historian of the century, the towering figure of the Berlin historian Leopold von Ranke (1795–1886), whose six-volume history of the German Reformation (1839–1847) became a model of research-based scholarship and elegant prose.[9] Von Ranke devoted considerable attention to the Zurich reformer.[10] He explored in detail the political contexts of the Swiss Reformation, sharing the judgement of others that in contrast to Luther's profound interior spirituality, Zwingli was a prophet of the transformation of Church and society. Von Ranke played a crucial role in bringing Zwingli into the wider story of European history.

In the sacramental quarrel, Zwingli had revealed considerable courage, together with intellectual rigour and spiritual profundity, offering in many respects not only an alternative vision to that of Luther, but also an important corrective. 'With a view to the progressive development of religious ideas,' Ranke observed,

> it was not, I think, to be wished that Zwingli should have given up his theory [of the sacrament], which by continually referring to the original and historical character of the institution of the great Mystery was of such immense importance to the whole of Christianity, independently of the church as actually constituted.[11]

Enthusiasm for finding the true Zwingli through historical research similarly informed the roughly contemporary biography written by Johann

Jakob Hottinger in 1842. The highly sympathetic portrait, which appeared in English just over a decade later, had a pronounced impact and continues to be printed in our time. For Hottinger, historical research confirmed the truths of Christian piety. He concluded his author's preface:

> If we regard [Zwingli] merely as a reformer of the Church, he may perhaps appear to us surrounded by a brighter glory; but history demands a full representation, and such a representation exhibits him as a man possessed of like passions with ourselves. Yet, just in the acknowledgement of his own infirmities by Zwingli, and in his submission with humble faith to a Higher Power, do the unmistakable features of true religion shine victoriously above that worship of self which springs only from vain conceit. May the following work produce the same conviction in the mind of the reader![12]

Twenty-five years after Hottinger, another influential Zwingli biography appeared, from the hand of the Swiss author and historian Johann Kaspar Mörikofer (1799–1877), who dedicated himself to tracing the original sources.[13] His work resulted in an exponential expansion of materials relating to the life of the reformer. Mörikofer observed that previous biographies had made too little use of Zwingli's writings, in particular his letters. Further, his intention was to give more weight to the social and political circumstances of the reformer's life.[14] Through his archival labours, Mörikofer claimed to have discovered sources from the hand of Zwingli himself that offered precious insights on the man.[15] Zwingli, he warned, posed a unique challenge in comparison to Luther, as the Zurich reformer was more reticent in revealing his inner world.[16] The best witness, he argued, was Heinrich Bullinger, who was a great historian and had been close to Zwingli.[17]

## CHANGING WINDS

By the middle of the nineteenth century, the Protestant world was embroiled in conflict over the nature of the Church and its faith. Old doctrinal verities were under siege from scholarship that questioned the authority of the Bible.[18] The growth of historical research and liberal theology encouraged a move away from traditional Reformed Protestant teachings. The Swiss churches were no exception, and a particularly fierce row erupted in Zurich, with parties roughly divided into conservatives, liberals and moderates.[19] The political atmosphere remained tense, and in 1868 a referendum overwhelmingly supported a new, more autonomous constitution for the Church, with greater freedom from the state.[20] Conservatives were alarmed that the symbiotic relationship of political rule and the Church founded in the Reformation was about to be dissolved.

The struggles for the Church against the backdrop of declining attendance at services and increasing criticism of established religion led to the most visible image of Huldrych Zwingli in the nineteenth century. When Georg Finsler (1819–1899) became chief pastor in the Grossmünster in 1871, he began a campaign to have a Zwingli monument erected in the city. The proposal was highly controversial, not least on account of the troubled reputation of the reformer and his close association with a state Church. Finsler was clear in articulating his purpose: 'We certainly want to erect a monument to honour Zwingli, but not in any manner to idolize him, but rather to express our gratitude and joy for that which God gave in this man.'[21] After much discussion and numerous proposals, the commission went to an Austrian Catholic, Heinrich Natter. His design raised further objections, especially on account of the large sword Zwingli was to carry. Many then – and today – regarded it as a commemoration of the reformer's bellicose spirit, death on a battlefield and religious coercion. Facing southwards, towards the Catholic states, Zwingli appeared an image of aggressive Protestantism. Christian Moser, however, has persuasively argued otherwise, demonstrating that Natter's intention, following Albrecht Dürer's diptych *The Four Apostles*, was to present Zwingli as St Paul, whom a longstanding iconography had carrying a sword, recalling his words to the Ephesians: 'Take the helmet of salvation, and the sword of the Spirit, which is the word of God' (6:17). The sword indicated not war or politics, but martyrdom.[22] Zwingli the warrior-preacher was to be reimagined as the Pauline soldier of Christ.

Finsler was determined. The leading pastor of the Zurich Church believed that Zwingli could serve as a figure of reconciliation among the warring theological and church parties. Each faction, he claimed, had its own Zwingli: the liberals, the conservatives, the supporters of free and state churches. Finsler's drive to commemorate the reformer thus went hand in hand with efforts to forestall further splintering among the Reformed churches in Switzerland. In a lecture held in support of the monument, for which he was actively raising money, he appealed to Zwingli as a figure who could unite the divided Zurich, Swiss and international churches:

> Personally, Zwingli will remain a model of a robust faith and trust in God in a troubled age . . . With Zwingli, we do not want today a church that is a narrow religious circle, but one that stands in the middle of the people and works with them, serves its morals and social problems. [A church] that shares its joys and sorrows. Indeed, out of the gospel the Church exercises on the whole population a sanctifying and consecrating influence . . . This is what Zwingli desired.[23]

Enthusiasm for Zwingli in the late nineteenth and early twentieth centuries shaped an emerging scholarly narrative of the Swiss Reformation, supported by source collections that provided greater knowledge of the period leading to the reformer's death in 1531. There was marriage of a desire for greater historical detail with a residual need to retain Zwingli's nobility of character and patriotism. Notable was a source collection from the Zurich archives for the years 1519–1531 assembled and edited by the pastor and professor Emil Egli (1848–1908), who would also take the lead in creating a new critical edition of Zwingli's works.[24] Adding to the earlier work of Mörikofer, Egli's volume opened new perspectives on both Zwingli and the political and social dimensions of the Zurich Reformation. The liberal-minded professor was a passionate advocate of the enduring significance of the Reformation for contemporary society, dedicating himself to enabling interested pastors and lay people to access Zwingli as a powerful force for church and social renewal.[25]

In our selective tour, reference must be made to the distinguished Basel professor Rudolf Staehelin (1841–1900), a liberal Protestant who shared Egli's enthusiasm for bringing the Reformation to a broader public. For the 400th anniversary of Zwingli's birth in 1884, he prepared a short, source-based account of Zwingli's life as a reformer that had a deep ecumenical purpose. The time was past, he opined, for partisan accounts of Zwingli directed against Luther.[26] Luther was the great figure of the Reformation, the man who brought the Church back to the Word of God; but Zwingli was a towering prophet in his own right, with his own path to the gospel and reform of the Church. The Lutheran and Reformed churches were both grounded in the Bible, but had their distinctive characters, reflecting the differences between their founders. Ten years later, and shortly before his death, Staehelin published in two volumes the most extensive biography of Zwingli yet – an extraordinary piece of scholarship, made possible by the publication of a large body of primary sources, Protestant and Catholic, over the previous 20 years.[27] The biography, with its attention to detail and judicious, liberal assessment of Zwingli, remains essential reading. Staehelin sought to free Zwingli from the Zurich tradition of insisting on his total independence from Luther, and demonstrate the reliance of the Swiss reformer on the Wittenberger.[28]

The thirst for the sources of the reformers led to ambitious endeavours to produce critical editions of their writings. Most famous was the Weimar Edition, begun in 1883 for the 400th anniversary of Martin Luther's birth. In Germany, the *Corpus Reformatorum* was a massive undertaking to publish the works of Philipp Melanchthon, John Calvin and Huldrych Zwingli. The first volumes of Melanchthon's works had appeared in 1834. Following a decision in Zurich by the newly formed Zwingliverein (Zwingli Society), led by Emil Egli, the third part of the series would comprise the works of Zwingli.[29] The first volume appeared in 1904, and the series was completed recently, after more than 100 years of scholarship. Decisions about whose works to edit and include in the *Corpus Reformatorum*, and whose to omit, greatly shaped the narrative of the Reformation in the late nineteenth and twentieth centuries. For the Swiss Reformation in particular, those choices meant that Zwingli became widely known, while his successor Heinrich Bullinger was consigned to oblivion.

The 1919 Zwingli anniversary was the high-water mark of the liberal interpretation of the reformer, who was celebrated with public events and commemorative volumes. Representative of the publications was a collection which contained essays by the leading scholars of the day, including Walther Köhler (1870–1946), Oskar Farner (1884–1958) and Wilhelm Oechsli (1851–1919).[30] Köhler would remain one of the most prominent authorities on Zwingli in the interwar period, publishing extensively on the reformer's theological and institutional labours. In 1920, he produced an influential study of the role of humanism in the Zurich Reformation.[31] Among his numerous achievements was a detailed reconstruction of the Marburg Colloquy between Luther and Zwingli.[32] The nineteenth century had sought to find the essential Zwingli, asking what qualities defined the man. That search, Köhler responded, should not seek to identify him with one particular aspect or context; rather, it is in the nature of biography to find the complexity of the subject.[33] Köhler's magisterial 1943 biography placed Zwingli the theologian above Zwingli the politician. More than any previous work, this biography explored the depths of the reformer's character.[34]

Köhler found in Zwingli the direct forerunner for Calvin and Calvinism, with the Zurich reformer's vision of God and the state. But most distinctive of the Zurich reformer was the impulse of the Christian and classical, not in the elegant and learned manner of Erasmus, but as the real means of restoring the Church through learning and the propagation of the Word of God. Zwingli was not Luther's equal, but he was original and brought a vision to the Reformation that did not arise from Wittenberg.[35]

The young Karl Barth (1896–1968), who had written on Zwingli during his student years at Bern, and whose father had taught seminars on the reformer's theology, returned to the subject in 1922/1923 for a number of lectures to students in Göttingen.[36] Barth quickly discovered that his lectures on Zwingli received a hostile reception from German Luther scholars, including from his later nemesis and Nazi supporter Emanuel Hirsch, who denounced him as 'Swiss, foreigner, agitator, and disrupter'.[37] Barth's lectures were part of a series on Reformed theology, and his treatment of Zwingli followed Calvin and the Heidelberg Confession. Barth was fully aware that for liberal Protestants of the nineteenth century, Zwingli was something of a hero, on account of his supposed emphasis on the ethical nature of Christianity and his favourable view, as Köhler had remarked, of the relationship between antiquity and Christianity. Barth, in contrast, was not inclined to defend Zwingli against Luther, but he did seek to demonstrate the distinctiveness of the Swiss reformer's thought.[38] He argued that Luther and Zwingli were different manifestations of the central Reformation doctrine of God's address to humanity. While the Wittenberger focused on the inner nature of faith, Zwingli looked to its application in the world.[39] Barth's formulation of Zwingli's thought was clearly part of his own developing theology of social and political action.

What did not appeal to Barth, however, was Zwingli's emphasis on the role of reason – found, for example, in his argument that Luther's teaching on real presence contradicted what was reasonable. Barth rejected earlier interpretations that saw Zwingli as a forerunner of Enlightenment and liberal theology, a most unfortunate legacy. In this respect, Calvin far surpassed Zwingli by developing a theology of the Holy Spirit that spoke of the mystery of Christ's presence in the Lord's Supper and not of a rational distinction between sign and what is signified.

Barth's assessment of Zwingli was one of disappointment. He had hoped to find in the reformer an inspiration for his own Christian ethical thought; but in the end, he encountered a humanist rationalist whom he regarded as a secondary figure of the Reformation, far behind Luther and Calvin. Barth made virtually no use of Zwingli in his later writings, referring to him as a spiritualist and enthusiast, an activist in the world.[40] Nevertheless, attentive readers of Barth have noted Zwinglian themes in his later work, including the Barmen Declaration of 1934, namely in his writing on divine and human righteousness and the sacraments. Although for Barth, Calvin was the major figure of the Reformed tradition, he continued to read and engage with the Swiss reformer.

## ZWINGLI IN ENGLISH

Two very different, contrasting perspectives on the Reformation in Zurich:

> The death of Zwingli is a heroic tragedy. He died for God and his country. He was a martyr of religious liberty and of the independence of Switzerland. He was right in his aim to secure the freedom of preaching in all the Cantons and bailiwicks, and to abolish the military pensions which made the Swiss tributary to foreign masters.[41]

And:

> If God was with Luther, He was not with Zuingle [sic]; if he was with Zuingle, He certainly could not be with Luther. God is the God of order, and not of confusion; and truth is one and indivisible, not manifold and contradictory.[42]

The first comes from the Swiss-born church historian and churchman Philip Schaff (1819–1893), whose history of the Reformation was of enormous influence on Protestant writers of the late nineteenth and early twentieth centuries, and continues to be read today. The second, distinctly less positive, was by Martin John Spalding (1810–1872), the Catholic ultramontane archbishop of Baltimore, who, in the early 1860s, wrote a multivolume refutation of the history of the Reformation by another great Swiss historian, Jean-Henri Merle d'Aubigné, published in French and translated into English in the 1860s.[43] D'Aubigné's highly sympathetic portrayal of Huldrych Zwingli built on the success of another Swiss author, Johann Jakob Hottinger, whose popular biography of the Zurich reformer appeared in 1856. Hottinger and D'Aubigné introduced English-speaking audiences to Zwingli, and crafted the narrative of the courageous reformer. Hottinger gave Anglo-American readers Zwingli the patriot and martyr, and left an enduring impression in the Anglo-American world. Here, the reformer's heroic journey to his end:

> he acknowledged the duty of abiding by his Zurichers, whose temporal and eternal welfare he desired from the bottom of his heart, in the defense of their native soil, even unto death; of proving by his own blood, that it was no mere selfish ambition or love of revolution, which had prompted him to speak and act, as in their blindness, his raging enemies had asserted.

Zwingli was no fanatic, but a true martyr for the faith:

> Not in sullen stupefaction, not in a fit of frenzy or of recklessness did he march forth, but with the earnestness of a man, who knows what may happen, and, not girding himself with his own hands, relies on the arm of Him, who is best acquainted with the human heart, and pardons the multitude of our errors, if only redeemed by faith, love, and a spirit of self-sacrifice.[44]

Although he regarded Zwingli as a modern spirit, Philip Schaff took a more American view of the reformer's activities:

It is dangerous to involve religion in entangling political alliances. Christ and the Apostles kept aloof from secular complications, and confined themselves to preaching the ethics of politics. Zwingli, with the best intentions, overstepped the line of his proper calling, and was doomed to bitter disappointment.[45]

Indeed, for Schaff, Zwingli's close bond to the magistrates, in contrast to Luther, brought only misery and regret. As if to stress the difficulties of such a close alliance of Church and rulers, Schaff described in detail Zwingli's sense of betrayal at the hands of the magistrates, as if entrusting the Council with religion had been an error.[46]

Despite erring in placing religion in the hands of secular rulers, Zwingli was to be admired for his moderation and reasonableness. Philip Schaff shared a conviction with his nineteenth-century contemporaries that Zwingli was a founder of liberal theology, more satisfyingly modern than other reformers:

Zwingli was trained in the school of Erasmus, and passed from the heathen classics directly to the New Testament. He represents more than any other Reformer, except Melanchthon, the spirit of the Renaissance in harmony with the Reformation. He was a forerunner of modern liberal theology.[47]

Zwingli's humanism, in Schaff's mind, made him more tolerant and open minded, as in his willingness to extend salvation to the virtuous heathen:

In this direction Zwingli was more liberal than any Reformer and opened a new path. St Augustine moderated the rigor of the doctrine of predestination by the doctrine of baptismal regeneration and the hypothesis of future purification. Zwingli moderated it by extending the divine revelation and the working of the Holy Spirit beyond the boundaries of the visible Church and the ordinary means of grace.[48]

This moderation, and the reformer's emphasis on a gospel-centred renewal of society with which it was paired, became the markers of the liberal Zwingli.

The contentious nature of Zwingli's death was taken up by one of the most prominent British authors on the Zurich reformer's theology during the nineteenth century, William Cunningham (1805–1861), professor of church history and later principal of New College, Edinburgh, and an eager defender of Calvinism.[49] In a collection of essays printed after his death, in 1862, Cunningham wrote at length on Zwingli and provided an account of the reformer's death that simultaneously exonerated his subject and engaged a contemporary debate: 'It is well known,' wrote Cunningham,

> that he [Zwingli] disapproved, and did what he could to prevent the steps that led to the war in which he lost his life; and it was in obedience to the express orders of the civil authorities and in the discharge of his duties as a pastor, that, not without some melancholy forebodings, he accompanied his countrymen to the fatal field of Cappell.[50]

Historical circumstances are key to deciphering Cunningham's account. His *Reformers and the Theology of the Reformation* appeared in 1862, and his inclinations were deeply informed by the major crisis in the Scottish Church known as the Disruption, which began in 1843. The core of that debate was the relationship of the Church to the state, and the involvement of the Church in the political affairs of the nation. Cunningham saw in Zwingli a prophet who had advocated the close bond between the Church and temporal authority: he both claimed the reformer's death to have been a heroic act and defended his controversial role in politics.

Cunningham's British defence of the state Church continued to find ambivalent responses in America, where it tended to be seen as one of the less desirable parts of the Reformation legacy. Perhaps one of the most extreme cases is found in a popular author of the turn of the twentieth century. During the First World War, the American Presbyterian cleric and author James Isaac Good wrote a chapter in his book *The Reformed Reformation* entitled 'The Contribution of Zwingli to the Spirit of the Reformation'.[51]

This characteristic of the Zwinglian Reformation, Good maintained, in which Church and magistrates were closely bound, jarred with American sensibilities and damaged the reformer's reputation:

And this prejudice against Zwingli thus cultivated, has been helped on here by the spirit of America. For we in the United States have so strongly emphasized the separation of Church and state that any political activity has seemed objectionable to many.[52]

Writing at a time when America was about to become directly involved in the First World War, Good held up Zwingli not as a man of conflict, but as one of peace. In fact, he was a visionary of state diplomacy, and his efforts were directly applicable to the present day. Far from being the advocate of a disastrous religious war, he was a herald of peace:

> Zwingli thus becomes the prophet of the 'League of Nations to enforce Peace', of which we hear so much now. He like Erasmus was an ardent advocate of peace but he also believed in thorough preparedness for war. Zwingli thus assumes a new importance in the light of present events. The great political reformer was the harbinger of these great international Reforms, in which the Church must nobly bear her part if they are ever to be carried through successfully – of that millennial day.[53]

George Park Fisher (1827–1909), the first to hold the newly created chair of ecclesiastical history at Yale, had studied for several years in Germany and sought to bring historical *Wissenschaft* to the subject of church history. He saw Zwingli and Luther as two distinctly different characters. Luther was troubled in spirit and defined by his discovery of justification by faith alone. Zwingli had no inclinations to be a monk; he was cheerful by disposition and fond of the ancient classics:

> He came out of the Erasmian school. The authority of the Church never had a strong hold upon him, even before he explicitly questioned the validity of it. As he studied the scriptures and felt their power, he easily gave to them the allegiance of his mind and heart. It cost him little inward effort to cast off whatever in the doctrinal or ecclesiastical system of the Latin church appeared to him at variance with the Bible or with common sense. In the mind there was no hard conflict with an established prejudice.

He was not, however, Luther:

> It would be very unjust to deny to Zwingli religious earnestness; but
> the course of his inward life was such that, although he heartily
> accepted the principle of justification by faith, he had not the same
> vivid idea of its transcendent importance that Luther had. Zwingli, a
> bold and independent student, took the Bible for his chart, and was
> deterred by no scruples of latent reverence for abruptly discarding
> usages which the Bible did not sanction.[54]

Fisher's assessment found further expression in the work of the most
influential American church historian of the early twentieth century,
Williston Walker (1860–1922), who succeeded to the chair of church history
at Yale in 1901. In his 1900 *The Reformation*, Walker added to the nineteenth-
century fascination with comparing Zwingli and Luther:

> Both reformers reached similar results in many – but by no means all
> – things; but their methods of approach were somewhat unlike, owing
> to diversities of natural genius and training. This want of tempes-
> tuous personal experience such as Luther had, has often been treated
> as if it were a reproach to Zwingli, but most unjustly. It is true that his
> early ministry had not the moral earnestness or the moral purity that
> Luther showed; but no one can question his sincerity, his zeal, or his
> spiritual power from the time that his real work as a reformer began.[55]

Walker's admiration for Zwingli was not mere ancestor worship. Echoing
Schaff, he argued that Zwingli was a forerunner of the liberal theology at
Yale and in New England. Zwingli's communal spirit was said to be found in
American congregationalism, sowing the seeds of democracy and freedom
of worship. New England was the cradle from which American history
demonstrated a reassuring 'steady trend toward democracy'. Zwingli played
a crucial role in this development, but his role was something of a John the
Baptist. Zwingli had 'planted deep' and was cultivated by Heinrich Bullinger,
but all would be reaped by a later hero: 'And the Swiss movement as a whole
was soon given a world-wide significance by the master-hand of the reformer
of French Switzerland, John Calvin.'[56]

The honouring of Zwingli did not escape the eyes of Catholic polemicists, and we return to Archbishop Spalding's acid judgement of what transpired in Zurich, which presaged the errors in his own land:

> The 'enlightened' council of Zurich decided in favor of the reformed doctrines, and resorted to force in order to suppress the ancient worship. Only think of a town council, composed of fat aldermen and stupid burgomasters, pronouncing definitely on articles of faith! . . . They of Zurich . . . were perhaps too well satisfied with their superior wisdom and knowledge to entertain a doubt![57]

## UNKNOWN FIGURE

The most influential modern interpreter of Zwingli was the Swiss pastor and theologian Gottfried W. Locher (1911–1996), who sought to bring Zwingli into the twentieth century. The influence of his teachers Karl Barth and Emil Brunner is evident in his presentation of the reformer, but Locher was more than a student.[58] He was the major voice in seeking to recover Zwingli as a distinctive mind, not to be seen only in comparison with Luther and Calvin. Locher authored the most comprehensive study of Zwingli's thought, historical contexts and influence.[59] His Zwingli was a reformer who was distinctive through his theological engagement with social issues.[60] Not merely a political figure, Zwingli for Locher transformed sixteenth-century religion through a thoroughly Christological approach to the Christian community. Locher rejected Köhler's interpretation of Zwingli as a man of two minds, classical and Christian, preferring to see in him the tension between the two resolved in his commitment to education and reform. Although Locher's Zwingli was distinctively Swiss, his importance for the development of theology and the Reformed tradition was the theologian's principal concern. 'Zwingli is an unknown figure,' Locher wrote, largely because he had only been placed unfavourably alongside Luther and Calvin. Locher saw his task as being to examine the reformer on his own terrain, 'to understand Zwingli in terms of his own presuppositions, and not merely by comparing him with the other reformers and the humanists.'[61]

Locher inherited the decidedly mixed legacy of the nineteenth and early twentieth centuries, which represented Zwingli as caught between his striving for orthodox theology and the disastrous course of his politics. Locher proposed an interpretation of Zwingli that emphasized the community as the source of Reformation through the actualization of the Holy Spirit. Politics and theology were not separate aspects of Zwingli's life, Locher argued, but lay at the heart of his understanding of divine–human relations; he thus distanced the reformer from his earlier image as a Platonist and humanist who was brought to the Reformation by Luther's ideas.[62] Zwingli's distinctive turn to the Reformation, Locher argues, grew out of his deep concern for the social and political conditions of the Swiss. 'For Zwingli,' Locher has written, '"belief in the Gospel" means not only a personal laying hold of the gracious promise of eternal salvation, but also a decision to make a total change in the whole social and political spheres of life.'[63]

## 'NO LONGER ZWINGLI'S ZURICH'

The dominance of the Grossmünster in the centre of old Zurich, rising above Zwingliplatz and the nearby monument to the reformer, has ensured that Zwingli and his legacy remain prominent in the public space of the city. His name and, to a lesser extent, his life are known, but his reputation is controversial.[64] Zurich is a modern, secular city that now has more Catholics than Reformed Protestants, and very low church attendance. The cultural life of the city is deeply ambivalent about Zwingli. In 2003, for example, the Swiss author, dramatist and theatre director Lukas Bärfuss, who grew up in the Protestant Church, reflected on his image of the Swiss reformer:

The Zurich in which I live is no longer Zwingli's Zurich. Life in my neighbourhood is colourful and wild, by no means Protestant. Here one finds more confessions than I could not have imagined in my childhood, and few of them are Christian. There are Jews, Muslims, Hindus, Christians and Buddhists. There are also heathens and tribalists. The shades run from ultraorthodox to extreme liberals. My quarter is close to an ideal in which each has their own religion and possesses their own book, and in each book there is at least one prayer for the poor Zwingli and his dreadful fate on some field in the Zurich hinterland.[65]

Bärfüss' perspective resonated with those more closely attached to the Church. Recently, in an essay entitled 'Nobody Wants to Return to Zwingli', the politician Markus Notter, once responsible for Church–state relations, recorded:

> Zwingli stands for hatred of enjoyment, music, theatre, images and entertainment. He stands for morals mandates, proscriptions, early curfews and even earlier starting of the workday, few breaks, strong work ethic, elderberry juice, verbena tea, decaffeinated coffee, alcohol-free beer and vegan bratwurst.[66]

Much like in contemporary Scotland, where Calvinism is widely regarded as having been what was wrong with the country, liberal Zurich had, by the late twentieth century, come to regard its reformer as the founder of the city's puritanical tendencies.

Disagreement about Zwingli has featured prominently in the press. In an interview published online in 2015, Thomas Maissen, director of the German Historical Institute in Paris, robustly argued of Zwingli that

> He is the most important contribution of the Swiss to world history. He was a humanist thinker, he had a religious vision, a conviction for which he was prepared to die. No other reformer died on the battle-field. The other reformers worked in their church rooms. The Swiss Reformation came first from Zurich and later became a successful worldwide export through Calvin's Geneva.[67]

Yet in February 2019, in a guest essay in the *Neue Zürcher Zeitung*, Zurich's principal broadsheet, Maissen's peer André Holenstein, a professor in Bern, portrayed Zwingli's Reformation as 'a fundamentalist revolution'.[68] Holenstein argues that 'like most revolutions, the Reformation released an enormous potential for violence', which polarized society and politics, and soon provoked not only 'vile insults', but also 'material violence, whether in assaults on altars and sacred images, or in attacks against dissidents up to the point of their exclusion, or in the incitement of wars'. Although Holenstein also addressed positive outcomes from the Swiss Reformation movement, the contrast between his and Maissen's perspectives speaks to an unresolved and uneasy relationship between Zwingli and contemporary culture.

Zurich's tourist office, attempting to find a more upbeat way of presenting the Reformation, asked 'Affluent Switzerland Thanks to the Reformation?'. Among his numerous achievements, this intervention continued, Zwingli brought strict moral laws to the city. Striking a remarkably confessional tone, the tourist office offered the following interpretation:

> At first sight, this seems very strict and disagreeable, but at the same time these rules and regulations laid the foundations for the affluent Switzerland that we know today. Zwingli advocated a new work ethic – diligence, discipline, thrift and frugality – and introduced a social welfare system to look after the poorest and most disadvantaged people. And while subsequently the first factories, new commercial enterprises and international trade established themselves in the Protestant areas, the Catholic cantons continued to be characterized by impoverished farming communities, which had to give their already meagre income to the all the more [sic] ostentatious Catholic churches.[69]

A related combination of irony, public-relations work and historical distance characterized many of the public art projects surrounding the commemorations, in 2019, of the 500th anniversary of Zwingli's arrival in the city – commemorations which, in characteristic Swiss style, were carried out with energy, precision and a great deal of public funding. An illuminating example appears in the city tour undertaken by Natter's 1885 statue discussed above, a pilgrimage that began when the original bronze was removed from its pedestal at the Wasserkirche so that it could stand at ground level during the annual Züri Fäscht (Zurich Festival) – accompanied by a pop-up Zwingli bar serving Zwingli beer and Zwingli sausages – and be readily available for selfies.[70] The dismounting was followed by a tour around the city and canton of 12 full-size polyester replicas, which followed a path pioneered by life-size fibreglass cows in the city.[71] Each travelling Zwingli was decorated to highlight some aspect of the city and its reformers, and presented at a public discussion – or Zwingli-Gsprööch – with figures from city politics, the economy and the Reformed Church. The versions included a silver 'climate Zwingli', who helped inaugurate the annual techno-music Street Parade in August; a 'housing Zwingli', standing with a giant Monopoly board; and a 'worker Zwingli', who had apparently stepped out of a locomotive factory to stand in a square in the Oerlikon quarter.[72]

The most visible and far-reaching public event associated with the commemorations of 2019 was the generously funded new film *Zwingli*, which opened on 17 January 2019.[73] Directed by Stefan Haupt (b. 1961), presented primarily in Swiss dialect, and produced with enormous efforts to remain historically accurate and authentic, the film reached a wide audience, immediately becoming one of the top 20 Swiss films of all time in terms of box-office takings. As a commercial production heavily subsidized by public and church resources, the film inevitably faced multiple – and largely incompatible – expectations from its audiences. The priority given to historical accuracy did not necessarily square with the hope that the film could help rehabilitate Zwingli as an individual and rescue him from his modern reputation as a puritanical prig. The film received a special prize for costume design at the annual Swiss film awards, although, somewhat controversially, it was not nominated for best picture.

For the film, the production team sought to build a narrative arc that would retain the viewer's attention and provide appropriate tension and catharsis around its hero's struggles and fate. This it achieved largely by narrating much of the film as a love story, seen from the perspective of Zwingli's wife, Anna Reinhart – even though we know almost nothing about their relationship. In one of the opening scenes, Anna is portrayed as being tormented before images of damnation; her experience with Zwingli then leads her to liberation of conscience and the freedom of the gospel. She is the everywoman of the Reformation.

The final product demonstrated a laudable and very modern desire to avoid covering up or apologizing for Zwingli's participation in the execution of Felix Manz and the persecution of other early Zurich Anabaptists, or for Zwingli's encouragement of, and participation in, a holy war against the Catholic Confederates in 1529 and 1531. These issues, however, are touched on rather than explored. Zwingli remains a man of single purpose, and little attention is given to his moral complexity, whether his sexual activity or his advocacy of conflict. The battle at Kappel and Zwingli's violent death are not portrayed. Given the effort made to ensure historical fidelity, the absence of the death can only have been a very deliberate directorial decision.[74] The moral ambiguity of dying in battle for the faith, which even Zwingli's friends felt deeply, is not a question the film wants to touch. Zwingli's ambivalences do not lend themselves to the constraints of narrative filmmaking nearly as well as Luther's. Whereas the elements of the Saxon reformer's life that most trouble modern audiences, such as his denunciation of the rebelling peasants and his virulent anti-Semitism, have rarely (if ever) appeared in film, Zwingli's prophetic zeal and support for religious violence were central to his most active years and to his dramatic death.

The visuals are stunning, the costumes striking and the dialogue remarkably authentic – as Haupt has said, in effect a language had to be invented to convey sixteenth-century Swiss discourse for a modern audience, but the filmmakers were clear that they would not use High German. The violence of the age is stressed, with Anabaptists and Jakob Kaiser put to death. The radical presence is portrayed by iconoclasm and the drowning of Felix Manz. Apart from the role created for Anna, the Zwingli story has little place for women, and so Haupt devotes considerable attention to the abbess of the Fraumünster, whose handing over of her religious house is presented at a crucial moment of the Reformation. Catholics come off very badly: leading members of the ecclesiastical hierarchy are unsympathetic figures, and often gluttonous, with no effort made to understand the perspectives of Bishop Hugo von Hohenlandenberg and Johannes Fabri, who debated with Zwingli. Lutherans are absent from the script. Luther is irrelevant to the story and Marburg is not mentioned.

Violence and confrontation run through the film, but so, too, does a message which contemporary audiences might embrace: Zwingli's powerful concern for the poor, sick and outcasts, in effect as a founder of the modern welfare state. His compassion for those in need is presented alongside a crusade against corruption. He is a whistle-blower, a role that speaks to a modern generation alienated from contemporary politics. Haupt is clear that the Bible is the source of Zwingli's powerful convictions, but those principles come across as strikingly modern. In a historically inaccurate scene – a rare accusation for this film – Zwingli is portrayed as having been involved in a translation of the Koran. In fact, the translation came long after his death, but the idea aligns with a modern aura of religious tolerance.

A film about Zwingli as a remote, unsympathetic figure would hardly connect with modern audiences. Stefan Haupt has endeavoured to put the past in conversation with contemporary society, even if that required historical licence. Zwingli's story is powerful and uncomfortable, and after 500 years we remain unsettled by its questions.

# AFTERWORD

T he Reformation was never one thing or person. It was not even a set of doctrines or institutional reforms. It was born in revolution and remained a convulsive force until domesticated, at which point it frequently ossified and became another form of institutionalized religion. Luther, Zwingli, the radicals and the spiritualists won people over not to theological ideas, but to a visceral belief that God was present in the world through a life of faith, and that faith was a gift. No less than the Catholics they sought to replace or the radicals they despised, the reformers had to demonstrate the immediacy of the sacred and provide ministrations for the journey from birth to death. The reformers, including Zwingli, constructed a theological scaffold that expressed those central convictions; but these arguments were never the lifeblood of a movement that, in many respects, was oppositional, a torrent of reform ideas and visions that arose from multiple sources. Nothing was inevitable, and coherence, particularly for the first generation, was provided by those who saw the hand of God in the unfolding of events.

All commemorations of Protestant reformers – from the Luther monument in Worms and the Calvin of the Reformation Wall in Geneva, to the shifting Zwingli statues in 2019 Zurich – invite consideration of the individual and his (usually) lasting contribution. We endeavour to find some way, however tangential, to relate their lives to our own, to demonstrate that their beliefs were not utterly foreign or entirely unattractive. We seek to find a Zwingli who was not a Zwinglian, a person of his time, but somehow acceptable to ours. The usual trick is to make the reformer a progenitor of ideas or values that we embrace or find palatable: social reform, welfare, anti-corruption or freedom of thought. Famously, in *A Man for All Seasons*, Thomas More is portrayed by Robert Bolt less as a religious figure than as a man of conscience, who spoke to secular post-war society. Stefan Haupt takes something of this approach with his film *Zwingli*. What are modern, contemporary and highly secular societies to make of a profoundly religious and divisive moment?

With their emphasis on the power of one person to conceive, initiate and prosecute, biographies are complicit in the attempt to make reformers part of our story. The early Reformation continues to be the lives of Luther, Zwingli and Calvin, as recent anniversaries have underscored. Their worlds are interpreted as offering straightforward narratives not overly cluttered by others, such as those of Anabaptists, Catholics, peasants and Jews. In the end, accounts of Luther's opponents are often really about Luther, not Karlstadt: the same tenet holds for Zwingli and the Anabaptists, and for Calvin and Michael Servetus. The perspective remains firmly that of the dominant reformer.

Huldrych Zwingli dreamt of reform, of a purified Church and a godly society; but he was never alone. His story was one of many possible outcomes of the early Reformation. Erasmus' friend Bishop Hugo von Hohenlandenberg had sought to reform the late-medieval Church; Johannes Fabri and Johann Eck were not simply heretic hunters, but visionaries of a changed Catholic Church, in which the priesthood and the sacraments would be restored and the devotions of the people enriched. Anabaptists Konrad Grebel, Felix Manz and Michael Sattler strove for Christ's Church as a body of the faithful, untouched by dirty compromises. The latter two died for their beliefs, executed by those who claimed the mantle of true reform. Their convictions were deemed sedition. Luther hated Zwingli not because he could not bear competition, but because he believed that the Swiss had misunderstood and even twisted God's Word. For the Wittenberger, Christ truly meant what he said: the bread and wine are His body and blood.

In the end, all these characters parted ways, usually acrimoniously; but none relinquished their resolute belief that they sought the restoration of Christ's body and the extirpation of error. In other words, religion mattered deeply, and the desire to purify had many voices. In the early modern world, such pluriformity led not to mutual understanding or tolerance, but to persecution, exile and death. Neither Zwingli nor any of his contemporaries could contemplate a multiplicity or diversity of truths.

And that reality is sufficient to make the Reformation a tough sell in the modern world.

The origins of spiritual and theological conversions were as diverse as the people who experienced them. Luther's transformation was a deeply personal moment that was only later made exemplary in order to mould a religious culture. Most men and women came to their religious convictions through local, frequently changing and quotidian encounters. Preachers, priests, monks and teachers played an undeniable role; but as the diverse crowd of characters from the 1520s demonstrates, there was no single path. For many, personal experience and spiritual crises were catalysts. Some were deeply moved by hearing the words of the Bible; others were appalled by the venality and corruption of the Church. Still others were passionately committed to the spiritual and theological worlds of the late-medieval Church, and sought their cultivation. As the turn to scripture alone in the early 1520s quickly demonstrated, the same words of the Bible were pregnant with multiple and contradictory meanings. In Reformation Zurich, as in all the cities and rural villages, the reform movements played out amidst local circumstances and specific personalities, leading to very different outcomes.

Our story has focused on a man of inspiring imagination, of poignant artistic and literary gifts, and of arresting limitations. He held an unshakeable conviction, carried with him onto the battlefield at Kappel, that if men and women were exposed to the Word of God, they would be converted. The implication was not that they should be coerced into belief, but rather that they could be entirely sure that God works through the gospel. In a way, everything about Zwingli boiled down to that persuasion. The belief rooted his understanding of God as good and providential – all things work to his glory. Education and preaching are tools of God's kingdom; he himself had learned from his mentor Erasmus and was trained in the late-medieval tradition of sermons.

Zwingli saw himself and the world around him through religion. He was not alone. So, too, did those companions who became Anabaptists. They parted company on how that religion would be lived in the world. Although he is often thought of as a political reformer, the case for that label is not compelling. Certainly, through his closeness to the Röist family and others he occupied a place among the rulers of the city, but he never held political office. In the last years of his life, he often sat on commissions that addressed particular issues and advised the magistrates, but his views never went unchallenged and his word frequently did not carry the day. In his last months, he was a dispirited figure, who feared that he had lost the confidence of the politicians and would have to leave his adopted city. Zwingli was no theocrat and no Cardinal Richelieu. His place was secured by his powerful preaching and his status within the larger Reformation. However, his unrelenting hostility to Catholicism and Anabaptism, and his ultimate willingness to sacrifice the Swiss Confederation to the gospel, strongly circumscribed his authority. Bern, Basel, Schaffhausen and St Gallen adopted the Reformation, but they did not adopt Zwingli. The reformer showed a limited grasp of foreign affairs, over-estimating his influence, misjudging the Holy Roman Empire and France, and seeing in Landgrave Philipp of Hesse a man who was never there.

Zwingli was a visionary of what became Reformed Christianity. The pursuit of the godly community came from his pulpit and his pen, but not evenly. He believed that divine justice could form the foundation of Church and society (which were one) and human life was one of transformation into Christ. Most of his writings and ideas were formed in fierce conflict, and frequently the fights were not of his choosing. Against the Catholics, he battled over the Church; against the Lutherans, over the Lord's Supper; and against the Anabaptists, over baptism and the covenant. His thought was not consistent, and was constantly in a state of becoming. He relied heavily on others, notably Oecolampadius, who was more than his theological equal. The speed with which he had to write left much unsaid and incomplete, such as his views on church music. Although he was a musician and a poet, he wrote almost no works of consolation or devotion. Many of his ideas were broadcast as seeds, to be cultivated by later authors who drew both on him and on his colleagues. He was not a systematician: he wrote for particular moments. He was neither hero nor martyr. We must see him for what he was – an embattled prophet.

Zwingli is a crucial part of Swiss history. But globally, he is also the founder of a form of Christianity that flourishes from Korea (Kim Il-sung's father was a Presbyterian elder!) and California to South Africa. The faith that his beliefs shaped has a long history of change in innumerable historical and cultural contexts. While much remains, much has also gone. He died in an unnecessary battle that he had advocated out of that deep faith, pushing an impossible situation to a disastrous conclusion, in the belief that God would prevail. What he could never accept was that God might have viewed matters differently.

✢

# NOTES

| | |
|---|---|
| Bullinger, *Reformationsgeschichte* | *Heinrich Bullingers Reformationsgeschichte* [. . .] 3 vols, ed. Johann Jakob Hottinger and Hans Heinrich Vögeli (Frauenfeld, Beyel, 1838). |
| CR | *Corpus Reformatorum. Philippi Melanchthonis Opera Quae Supersunt Omnia*, ed. C.G. Bretschneider and H.E. Bindseil (Halle, 1834–1860) |
| EA | *Amtliche Sammlung der ältern eidgenössischen Abschiede*, 3 vols (Bern, K.J. Wyss'sche Buchdruckerei, 1874–1886) |
| Egli, *Actensammlung* | Emil Egli, *Actensammlung zur Geschichte der Zürcher Reformation in den Jahren 1519-1533* (Zurich, J. Schabelitz, 1879) |
| Latin Works | *The Latin Works and the Correspondence of Huldreich Zwingli*, 3 vols, ed. Samuel Macauley Jackson and trans. Henry Preble, Walter Lichtenstein and Lawrence A. McLouth (New York and London, G.P. Putnam's Sons, 1912–1929) |
| LW | *Luther's Works*, ed. Jaroslav Pelikan and Helmut T. Lehmann (St Louis, Concord and Philadelphia, Fortress, 1956–) |
| Myconius, *Briefwechsel* | Oswald Myconius, *Briefwechsel 1515-1552*, ed. Rainer Henrich, 2 vols (Zurich, Theologischer Verlag, 2017) |
| *Selected Writings* | *Selected Writings of Huldrych Zwingli*, 2 vols, trans. E.J. Furcha (Allison Park, PA, Pickwick Publications, 1984) |
| Z | *Huldreich Zwinglis sämtliche Werke* in *Corpus Reformatorum*, 88–, ed. Emil Egli et al. (Berlin, Schwettschke and Zurich, Theologischer Verlag, 1905–) |
| *Zwingli Schriften* | *Huldrych Zwingli Schriften*, 4 vols, ed. Thomas Brunnschweiler and Samuel Lutz (Zurich, Theologischer Verlag, 1995) |

## CHAPTER 1

1. Clive H. Church and Randolph C. Head, *A Concise History of Switzerland* (Cambridge, Cambridge University Press, 2013), 40–72. Also, Bernhard Stettler, *Eidgenossenschaft im 15. Jahrhundert: die Suche nach einem gemeinsamen Nenner* (Zurich, Widmer-Dean, 2004).
2. Latin Works, vol. 1, 2 (altered).

3. Andreas Zwingli to Huldrych Zwingli, 13 October 1519, Z VII, 211.
4. Z I, 392.
5. Rudolf Staehelin, *Huldreich Zwingli: Sein Leben und Wirken nach den Quellen dargestellt*, 2 vols (Basel, B. Schwabe, 1895–1897), vol. 1, 21.
6. Zwingli to Vadian, 17 September 1531, Z XI, 620–621.
7. Staehelin, *Huldreich Zwingli*, vol. 1, 22.
8. Fritz Büsser, 'Das Bild der Natur bei Zwingli', *Zwingliana*, 11 (1960), 241–256.
9. Z III, 648, 29–35; Latin Works, vol. 3, 68 (altered).
10. Z I, 55; Latin Works, vol. 1, 52–53.
11. Staehelin, *Huldreich Zwingli*, vol. 1, 25.
12. Johann Kaspar Mörikofer, *Ulrich Zwingli: Nach den urkundlichen Quellen* (Leipzig, S. Hirzel, 1867–1869), 344.
13. Zwingli to Gregor Bünzli, 30 December 1522, Z VII, 649.
14. Latin Works, vol. 1, 2–3 (altered).
15. Anna Rapp Buri and Monica Stucky-Schürer, 'Der Berner Chorherr Heinrich Wölfli (1470–1532)', *Zwingliana*, 25 (1998), 65–105.
16. David J. Collins, *Reforming Saints: Saints' lives and their authors in Germany, 1470–1530* (Oxford, Oxford University Press, 2008), 99–122; Robert Durer (ed.), *Bruder Klaus: Die ältesten Quellen über den seligen Nikolaus von Flüe, sein Leben und seinen Einfluss*, 2 vols (Sarnen, Buch- und Kunstdruck-Verlag I. Ehrli, 1917–1921).
17. Staehelin, *Huldreich Zwingli*, vol. 1, 28.
18. Bullinger, *Reformationsgeschichte*, vol. 1, 6.
19. Ferdinand Rüegg, 'Zwingli in Wien', *Zeitschrift für Schweizerische Kirchengeschichte*, 2 (1908), 214–219.
20. Conrad Bonorand, 'Die Bedeutung der Universität Wien für Humanismus und Reformation, insbesondere in der Ostschweiz', *Zwingliana*, 12 (1965), 162–180.
21. See Rudolf Gamper, *Joachim Vadian, 1483/84–1551: Humanist, Arzt, Reformator, Politiker* (Zurich, Chronos, 2017); Conrad Bonorand, *Aus Vadians Freundes- und Schülerkreis in Wien* (St Gallen, Fehr, 1965).
22. Lewis W. Spitz, *Conrad Celtis, the German Arch-Humanist* (Oxford, Oxford University Press, 1958); Kurt Stadtwald, 'Patriotism and antipapalism in the politics of Conrad Celtis's "Vienna Circle"', *Archiv für Reformationsgeschichte/Archive for Reformation History*, 84 (1993), 83–102.
23. Christopher B. Krebs, *Negotiatio Germaniae: Tacitus' Germania und Enea Silvio Piccolomini, Giannantonio Campano, Conrad Celtis und Heinrich Bebel* (Göttingen, Vandenhoeck & Ruprecht, 2005).
24. Marc Sieber, *Die Universität Basel und die Eidgenossenschaft 1460 bis 1529; eidgenössische Studenten in Basel* (Basel, Helbing & Lichtenhahn, 1960).
25. Staehelin, *Huldreich Zwingli*, vol. 1, 32.
26. Latin Works, vol. 1, 4 (altered).
27. Bullinger, *Reformationsgeschichte*, vol. 1, 7.
28. A. Claudin, *The First Paris Press: An account of the books printed for G. Fichet and J. Heynlin in the Sorbonne, 1470–1472* (London, Printed for the Bibliographical Society at the Chiswick Press, 1898).
29. Edwin H. Zeydel, 'Johann Reuchlin and Sebastian Brant: A study in early German humanism', *Studies in Philology*, 67 (1970), 117–138; William Gilbert, 'Sebastian Brant: Conservative humanist', *Archiv für Reformationsgeschichte/Archive for Reformation History*, 46 (1955), 145–166.
30. Ulrich Gaier, 'Sebastian Brant's "Narrenschiff" and the humanists', *PMLA*, 83 (1968), 266–270.
31. See *Die Hauschronik Konrad Pellikans von Rufach: ein Lebensbild aus der Reformationszeit* (Strassburg, J.H. Ed. Heitz (Heitz und Mündel), 1892).
32. Valentina Sebastiani, *Johann Froben, Printer of Basel: A biographical profile and catalogue of his editions* (Leiden and Boston, MA, Brill, 2018); Earle Hilgert, 'Johann Froben and the Basel

university scholars, 1513–1523', *Library Quarterly*, 41 (1971), 141–169; David H. Price, 'Hans Holbein the Younger and Reformation Bible production', *Church History*, 86 (2017), 1001.

33. Daniel Bolliger, *Infiniti Contemplatio: Grundzüge der Scotus- und Scotismusrezeption im Werk Huldrych Zwinglis. Mit ausführlicher Edition bisher unpublizierter Annotationen Zwinglis* (Leiden, Brill, 2003).

34. Fritz Schmidt-Clausing, 'Johann Ulrich Surgant: Ein Wegweiser des jungen Zwingli', *Zwingliana*, 11 (1961), 289–290.

35. Schmidt-Clausing, 'Johann Ulrich Surgant', 295.

36. Schmidt-Clausing, 'Johann Ulrich Surgant', 298–299.

37. Erich Wenneker, 'Thomas Wyttenbach', *Biographisch-Bibliographisches Kirchenlexikon*, 14, 264–266.

38. Bullinger, *Reformationsgeschichte*, vol. 1, 7.

39. Quoted in Staehelin, *Huldreich Zwingli*, vol. 1, 39.

40. Zwingli to Thomas Wyttenbach, 15 June 1523, Z VIII, 84–89.

41. See the essays in Katharina Koller-Weiss and Christian Sieber (eds), *Aegidius Tschudi und seine Zeit* (Basel, Krebs, 2002). For the text, see Peter Stadler and Bernhard Stettler (eds), *Chronicon Helveticum* (Bern, Selbstverlag der Allgemeinen Geschichtsforschenden Gesellschaft der Schweiz: Stadt- und Universitätsbibliothek Bern, 1968–2000).

42. See Randolph C. Head, 'William Tell and his comrades: Association and fraternity in the propaganda of fifteenth and sixteenth-century Switzerland', *Journal of Modern History*, 67 (1995), 527–557.

43. Guy P. Marchal, 'Zum Verlauf der Schlacht bei Sempach', *Schweizerische Zeitschrift für Geschichte*, 37 (1987), 428–436.

44. Heinrich Thommen, *Die Schlacht von Sempach im Bild der Nachwelt* (Lucerne, Kantonaler Lehrmittelverlag, 1986).

45. Susan Marti, Till-Holger Borchert and Gabrielle Keck (eds), *Splendour of the Burgundian Court: Charles the Bold, 1433–1477* (Brussels, Mercatorfonds, 2009); Richard Vaughan, *Charles the Bold, the Last Valois Duke of Burgundy* (London, Longman, 1973).

46. See Tom Scott, *The Swiss and their Neighbours, 1460–1560: Between accommodation and aggression* (Oxford, Oxford University Press, 2017), 30–33; François de Capitani, *Adel, Bürger und Zünfte im Bern des 15. Jahrhunderts* (Bern, Stämpfli, 1982).

47. See the exhibition catalogue *Le butin des guerres de Bourgogne et œuvres d'art de la cour de Bourgogne, Mai–Septembre, 1969 / The Burgundian Booty and Works of Burgundian Court Art, May–September, 1969* (Bern, Musée d'Histoire de Berne, 1969).

48. For contemporary accounts, see Georges Grosjean (ed.), *Die Schlacht bei Murten in drei altschweizerischen Chronikbildern*, 3 vols (Dietikon Zurich, Bibliophile Druck, 1975).

49. John McCormack, *One Million Mercenaries: Swiss soldiers in the armies of the world* (London, L. Cooper, 1993); Hans Rudolf Fuhrer and Robert-Peter Eyer, *Schweizer in 'Fremden Diensten': verherrlicht und verurteilt* (Zurich, Neue Zürcher Zeitung, 2006).

50. Thomas Maissen, *Geschichte der Schweiz* (Baden, Hier und Jetzt, 2010), 61–62.

51. Ernst Walder, *Das Stanser Verkommnis: Ein Kapitel eidgenössischer Geschichte neu untersucht: die Entstehung des Verkommnisses von Stans in den Jahren 1477 bis 1481* (Nidwalden, Stans, Historischer Verein, 1994).

52. Maissen, *Geschichte der Schweiz*, 65.

53. Maissen, *Geschichte der Schweiz*, 65.

54. Ulrich Vonrufs, *Die politische Führungsgruppe Zürichs zur Zeit von Hans Waldmann (1450–1489): Struktur, politische Networks und die sozialen Beziehungstypen, Verwandschaft, Freundschaft und Patron-Klient-Beziehung* (Bern and New York, P. Lang, 2002); Hans Morf, *Zunftverfassung, Obrigkeit und Kirche in Zürich von Waldmann bis Zwingli* (Zurich, Leemann, 1968).

55. Thomas A. Brady, Jr., *Turning Swiss: Cities and Empire, 1450–1550* (Cambridge and New York, Cambridge University Press, 1985); Peter Niederhäuser and Werner Fischer (eds), *Vom "Freiheitskrieg" zum Geschichtsmythos: 500 Jahre Schweizer- oder Schwabenkrieg* (Zurich, Chronos, 2000).

56. Maissen, *Geschichte der Schweiz*, 69.
57. Thomas Maissen, 'Inventing the sovereign republic: Imperial structures, French chal-lenges, Dutch models and the early modern Swiss Confederation' in André Holenstein, Thomas Maissen and Maarten Prak (eds), *The Republican Alternative: The Netherlands and Switzerland compared* (Amsterdam, Amsterdam University Press, 2008), 126.
58. Andreas Würgler, *Die Tagsatzung der Eidgenossen. Politik, Kommunikation und Symbolik einer repräsentativen Institution im europäischen Kontext 1470-1798* (Epfendorf, Verlag Bibliotheca Academica, 2014).
59. Maissen, 'Inventing the sovereign republic', 125.
60. Thomas Maissen, *Schweizer Heldengeschichten – und was dahintersteckt* (Baden, Hier und Jetzt, 2015), 27; see also, Regula, 'Albrecht of Bonstetten' in Graeme Dunphy (ed.), *Encyclopedia of the Medieval Chronicle* (Leiden, Brill, 2010), 27.
61. Claudius Sieber-Lehmann, 'Albrecht von Bonstettens geographische Darstellung der Schweiz von 1479', *Cartographica Helvetica*, 16 (1997), 39–46; Maissen, *Schweizer Heldengeschichten*, 25.
62. Heinrich Glarean, *Beschreibung der Schweiz: Lob der dreizehn Orte (Helvetiae descriptio Panegyricum)*, ed. and trans. Werner Näf (St Gallen, St Gallen Tschudy, 1948).
63. M. Huber-Ravazzi, *Die Darstellung der Umwelt der Eidgenossenschaft in der Zeit von 1477 bis 1499 in der Berner Chronik des Valerius Anshelm, der Schweizerchronik des Heinrich Brennwald, der Luzerner Chronik des Diebold Schilling und in der Chronik 'Eydgnoschafft' des Johannes Stumpf* (Zurich, Juris Druck, 1976).
64. Eduard Jakob Kobelt, *Die Bedeutung der Eidgenossenschaft für Huldrych Zwingli* (Zurich, Leemann, 1970), 21–22.
65. Scott, *The Swiss and their Neighbours*, 55–56.
66. Kobelt, *Die Bedeutung der Eidgenossenschaft*, 5.
67. Z III, 103, 8 – 104, 113.
68. Z III, 103, 8 – 104, 113.
69. Ulrich Gäbler, 'Die Schweizer – ein "Auserwähltes Volk"', *Zwingliana*, 19 (1992), 146–147.
70. Fritz Blanke, Oskar Farner and Rudolf Pfister (eds), *Zwingli Hauptschriften* (Zurich, Zwingli-Verlag, 1948), vol. 2, 8.

## CHAPTER 2

1. Hans Schneider, 'Zwinglis Anfänge als Priester' in Martin Sallmann and Martin Wallraff (eds), *Schweizer Kirchengeschichte – neu reflektiert* (Bern, Peter Lang, 2010), 38–39.
2. George Potter, *Zwingli* (Cambridge, Cambridge University Press, 1976), 22; Oskar Vasella, 'Die Wahl Zwinglis als Leutpriester von Glarus', *Zeitschrift für schweizerische Kirchengeschichte*, 51 (1957), 27–35. It has been plausibly suggested that Göldi's claims might not have been resolved until 1507, a year after the traditional dating of Zwingli's arrival in Glarus. Schneider, 'Zwinglis Anfänge', 60.
3. On Hugo, see Schneider, 'Zwinglis Anfänge', 40.
4. See Peter Niederhäuser (ed.), *Ein feiner Fürst in einer rauen Zeit: Der Konstanzer Bischof Hugo von Hohenlandenberg* (Zurich, Chronos, 2011). The standard biography of Bishop Hugo remains August Willburger, *Die Konstanzer Bischöfe: Hugo von Landenberg, Balthasar Merklin, Johann von Lupfen (1496–1537) und die Glaubensspaltung* (Münster i.W., Aschendorff, 1917), 32–76.
5. Z IV, 60, 6–15.
6. See Christopher M. Bellitto, *The General Councils: A history of the twenty-one church councils from Nicaea to Vatican II* (New York, Paulist Press, 2002), 68.
7. Schneider, 'Zwinglis Anfänge', 41.
8. Bullinger, *Reformationsgeschichte*, vol. 1, 7.
9. Cited in Schneider, 'Zwinglis Anfänge', 51.
10. Schneider, 'Zwinglis Anfänge', 52.

11. Urs B. Leu and Sandra Weidmann, *Huldrych Zwingli's Private Library* (Leiden, Brill, 2019), 10.
12. Leu and Weidmann, *Private Library*, 1.
13. Z I, 10, 4–7; Latin Works, vol. 1, 28.
14. Z I, 18, 6–11.
15. See McCormack, *One Million Mercenaries*, 6–60.
16. Thomas Maissen, 'Why did the Swiss miss the Machiavellian moment? History, myth, imperial and constitutional law in the early modern Swiss Confederation', *Republics of Letters: A Journal for the Study of Knowledge, Politics, and the Arts*, 2 (2010), 105.
17. Marc Lienhard, 'Guerre et paix dans les écrits de Zwingli et de Luther: Une comparaison' in Christopher Ocker, Michael Printy, Peter Sterenko and Peter Wallace (eds), *Politics and Reformations: Histories and reformations. Essays in Honor of Thomas A. Brady, Jr.* (Leiden, Brill, 2007), 219.
18. Latin Works, vol. 1, 42.
19. Robert Durrer, 'Die Geschenke Papst Julius II. an die Eidgenossen', *Wissen und Leben*, 1 (1907/08), 288–289.
20. Z VII, 540 n1; Emil Egli, 'Zwingli in Monza', *Zwingliana*, 1 (1904), 387–392.
21. Thomas Maissen, 'An den Grenzen der Söldnerkühnheit', *Neue Zürcher Zeitung*, 12 September 2015.
22. Maissen, 'An den Grenzen der Söldnerkühnheit'.
23. Peter Jankovsky, 'Mythos Marignano', *Neue Zürcher Zeitung*, 13 September 2015.
24. Z I, 10, 15–17; Latin Works, vol. 1, 54.
25. Leu and Weidmann, *Private Library*, 35.
26. Leu and Weidmann, *Private Library*, 25.
27. Zwingli to Glarean, 13 July 1510, Z VII, 3.
28. Zwingli to Vadian, 23 February 1513, Z VII, 22, 8–12. Translation from Leu and Weidmann, *Private Library*, 27.
29. Cornelis Augustijn, 'Zwingli als Humanist', *Nederlands Archief voor Kerkgeschiedenis/Dutch Review of Church History*, 67 (1987),123.
30. Augustijn, 'Zwingli als Humanist', 123.
31. Quoted in G.W. Bromiley, *Zwingli and Bullinger* (Louisville, KY, Westminster Press, 1953), 89.
32. Martin Wallraff, Silvana Seidel Menchi and Kaspar von Greyerz (eds), *Basel 1516: Erasmus' edition of the New Testament* (Tübingen, Mohr Siebeck, 2016); Robert D. Sider (ed.), *The New Testament Scholarship of Erasmus: An introduction with Erasmus' prefaces and ancillary writings* (Toronto, University of Toronto Press, 2019), 25–84; Jerry H. Bentley, *Humanists and Holy Writ: New Testament scholarship in the Renaissance* (Princeton, NJ, Princeton University Press, 1983), 112–193; Henk Jan de Jonge, 'Novum Testamentum a nobis versum: The essence of Erasmus' edition of the New Testament', *Journal of Theological Studies*, 35 (1984), 394–413; Albert Rabil, Jr., *Erasmus and the New Testament: The mind of a Christian humanist* (San Antonio, TX, Trinity University Press, 1972).
33. Traudel Himmighöfer, *Die Zürcher Bibel bis zum Tode Zwinglis, 1531: Darstellung und Bibliographie* (Mainz, P. von Zabern, 1995), 10.
34. Augustijn, 'Zwingli als Humanist', 125.
35. Z II, 217, 19–21; Gottfried W. Locher, 'Zwingli and Erasmus' in his *Zwingli's Thought: New perspectives* (Leiden, Brill, 1981), 233–255; Joachim Rogge, *Zwingli und Erasmus: Die Friedensgedanken des jungen Zwingli* (Stuttgart, Calwer, 1962).
36. Cited in Jeremy S. Begbie, *Resounding Truth: Christian wisdom in the world of music* (Grand Rapids, MI, Baker Academic, 2007).
37. Christine Christ-von Wedel, 'Erasmus und die Zürcher Reformatoren: Huldrich Zwingli, Leo Jud, Konrad Pellikan, Heinrich Bullinger und Theodor Bibliander', in Christine Christ-von Wedel and Urs B. Leu (eds), *Erasmus in Zürich: Eine verschwiegene Autorität* (Zurich, Verlag Neue Zürcher Zeitung, 2007), 78.
38. Cited from Leu and Weidmann, *Private Library*, 39.

39. Zwingli to Erasmus, 29 June 1516, Z VII, 36, 9–14.
40. Locher, 'Zwingli and Erasmus', 233–255.
41. Erasmus to Zwingli, 1516, Z VII, 37–38.
42. Erasmus to Zwingli, 1516, Z VII, 37, 9–14.
43. Erasmus to Zwingli, 1516, Z VII, 38, 3–5.
44. John F. D'Amico, *Theory and Practice in Renaissance Textual Criticism: Beatus Rhenanus between conjecture and history* (Berkeley, University of California Press, 1988).
45. Iain Fenlon and Inga Mai (eds), *Heinrich Glarean's Books: The intellectual world of a sixteenth-century musical humanist* (Cambridge, Cambridge University Press, 2013), 1.
46. Zwingli to Erasmus, 29 April 1516, Z VII, 35, 8.
47. Glarean to Zwingli, 25 October 1516, Z VII, 48, 4–5.
48. Augustijn, 'Zwingli als Humanist', 130.
49. Glarean to Zwingli, 25 October 1516, Z VII, 48, 3–4.
50. Zwingli to Vadian, 23 February 1513, Z VII, 22, 8–12.
51. Vadian to Zwingli, 7 May 1513, Z VII, 26, 8.
52. Valentin Tschudi to Zwingli, 31 July 1514, Z VII, 27–29.
53. Valentin Tschudi to Zwingli, 31 July 1514, Z VII, 27, 7–28, 6.
54. Valentin Tschudi to Zwingli, 31 July 1514, Z VII, 28, 7–12.
55. Valentin Tschudi to Zwingli, 31 July 1514, Z VII, 28, 29–32.
56. Peter Tschudi to Zwingli, 8 November 1516, Z VII, 49–50.
57. Aegidius Tschudi to Zwingli, Easter 1517, Z VII, 53, 5–7.
58. Aegidius Tschudi to Zwingli, 12 July 1517, 56, 3–11.
59. Bullinger, *Reformationsgeschichte*, vol. 1, 8.
60. Zwingli to Vadian, 13 June 1517, Z VII, 54–55.
61. See note on 'Leutpriester' in Potter, *Zwingli*, 41.
62. Leu and Weidmann, *Private Library*, 15.
63. Leu and Weidmann, *Private Library*, 28.
64. Z V, 713, 2–714, 1; *Selected Writings*, vol. 2, 344.
65. Z II, 144, 32–145, 4.
66. Himmighöfer, *Die Zürcher Bibel*, 17.
67. Z VII, 213, 9–21, cited in Augustijn, 'Zwingli als Humanist', 126.
68. Z II, 226, 10–11; *Selected Writings*, vol. 1, 180.
69. Z II, 226, 12–16.
70. Bullinger, *Reformationsgeschichte*, vol. 1, 8.
71. Zwingli to Heinrich Utinger, 5 December 1518, Z VII, 110–113.
72. Zwingli to Heinrich Utinger, 5 December 1518, Z VII, 111, 2–5.
73. Z I, 395, 22–26.
74. Latin Works, vol. 1, 156.
75. *Bürgermeister* and Council in Winterthur to Zwingli, 30 October 1517, Z VII, 70–71.
76. Antonio Pucci to Zwingli, 1 September 1518, Z VII, 107, 7.
77. Staehelin, *Huldreich Zwingli*, vol. 1, 109.
78. Myconius to Zwingli, 29 October 1518, Z VII, 101, 12–102, 8.
79. Zwingli to Myconius, 2 December 1518, Z VII, 105–106.
80. Staehelin, *Huldreich Zwingli*, vol. 1, 114.

## CHAPTER 3

1. Hans Morf, 'Obrigkeit und Kirche in Zürich bis zu Beginn der Reformation', *Zwingliana*, 13 (1970), 164–205.
2. Walter Jacob, *Politische Führungsschicht und Reformation: Untersuchungen zur Reformation in Zürich 1519–1528* (Zurich, Juris Druck + Verlag, 1969); Morf, 'Obrigkeit und Kirche'.
3. Jacob, *Politische Führungsschicht*, 39–40.
4. Jacob, *Politische Führungsschicht*, 59.

5. Otto Sigg, 'Bevölkerungs-, agrar-, und sozialgeschichtliche Probleme des 16. Jahrhunderts am Beispiel der Zürcher Landschaft', *Schweizerische Zeitschrift für Geschichte*, 24 (1974), 1–25.

6. Ernst Gagliardi, Hans Müller and Fritz Büsser (eds), *Johannes Stumpfs Schweizer- und Reformationschronik* (Basel, Verlag Birkhäuser, 1952–1955), vol. 5, 137–138.

7. Lee Palmer Wandel, *Always Among Us: Images of the poor in Zwingli's Zurich* (Cambridge and New York, Cambridge University Press, 1990), 26.

8. Gerald Dörner, *Kirche, Klerus und Kirchliches Leben in Zürich von der Brunschen Revolution (1336) bis zur Reformation (1523)* (Würzburg, Könighausen und Neumann, 1996), 129.

9. Lee Palmer Wandel, 'Switzerland' in Larissa Taylor (ed.), *Preachers and People in the Reformation and Early Modern World* (Leiden, Brill, 2001), 91–124. Also, Charlotte Steenbrugge, *Drama and Sermon in Late Medieval England: Performance, authority, devotion* (Kalamazoo, MI, Medieval Institute Publications, 2017); Larissa Taylor, *Soldiers of Christ: Preaching in late medieval and reformation France* (Toronto, University of Toronto Press, 2002).

10. Andrew Pettegree, *Reformation and the Culture of Persuasion* (Cambridge, Cambridge University Press, 2005), 14.

11. Zwingli to Myconius, 2 December 1518, Z VII, 106, 3–4.

12. Hans-Christoph Rublack, 'Zwingli und Zürich', *Zwingliana*, 16 (1985), 394–395.

13. Christ-von Wedel, 'Erasmus und die Zürcher Reformatoren', 84.

14. Christ-von Wedel, 'Erasmus und die Zürcher Reformatoren', 88.

15. Z I, 285, 29–30; Latin Works, vol. 1, 239.

16. Z I, 286, 11–14; Latin Works, vol. 1, 239.

17. Pamela Biel, 'Personal conviction and pastoral care: Zwingli and the cult of saints 1522–1530', *Zwingliana*, 16 (1985), 442–469.

18. Z VII, 250, 10–15.

19. Ludwig Rochus Schmidlin, *Bernhardin Sanson, der Ablassprediger in der Schweiz, 1518/1519; eine historische, dogmatische und kirchenrechtliche Erörterung* (Solothurn, Buch- und Kunstdruckerei Union, 1898).

20. Potter, *Zwingli*, 67.

21. Alfred Schindler, 'Die Anliegen des Chorherrn Hofmann', *Zwingliana*, 23 (1996), 63–82.

22. Ulrich Gäbler, 'Huldrych Zwingli and his City of Zurich', *St Andrews University Seminary Studies*, 23 (1985), 148.

23. Schindler, 'Die Anliegen des Chorherrn Hofmann', 74.

24. Josephine Steffen-Zehnder, *Das Verhältnis von Staat und Kirche im spätmittelalterlichen Zürich* (Zurich, Calendaria, 1935), 42–43.

25. Bullinger, *Reformationsgeschichte*, vol. 1, 48.

26. René Hauswirth, *Landgraf Philipp von Hessen und Zwingli* (Tübingen, Osiander (Kommisionsverlag), 1968), 69.

27. Lee Palmer Wandel, 'Brothers and neighbors: The language of community in Zwingli's preaching', *Zwingliana*, 17 (1988), 361–374.

28. Hauswirth, *Philipp von Hessen*, 70.

29. Z VII, 231, 2–3.

30. Zwingli to Myconius, 26 November 1519, Z VII, 280–281; Myconius, *Briefwechsel*, vol. 1, 128.

31. Z VII, 245, 13–17, cited in Robert C. Walton, *Zwingli's Theocracy* (Toronto, University of Toronto Press, 1968), 41 (altered).

32. Walton, *Zwingli's Theocracy*, 48–49.

33. Walton, *Zwingli's Theocracy*, 42.

34. Gagliardi, Müller and Büsser (eds), *Johannes Stumpfs Schweizer- und Reformationschronik*, vol. 1, 163.

35. Kaspar Hedio to Zwingli, 6 September 1519, Z VII, 214, 9–12.

36. Latin Works, vol. 1, 56–57 (altered).

37. See Thomas Martin Schneider, 'Der Mensch als "Gefäß Gottes": Huldrych Zwinglis Gebetslied in der Pest und die Frage nach seiner reformatorischen Wende', *Zwingliana*, 35 (2008), 5–21.
38. Myconius to Zwingli, 26 May 1520, Z VII, 317; Myconius, *Briefwechsel*, vol. 1, 143.
39. Scott H. Hendrix, *Early Protestant Spirituality* (New York, Paulist Press, 2009), 12.
40. Ulrich Gäbler, 'Huldrych Zwinglis "reformatorische Wende"', *Zeitschrift für Kirchengeschichte*, 89 (1978), 120–121.
41. Gäbler, 'Huldrych Zwinglis "reformatorische Wende"', 128.
42. Zwingli to Myconius, 24 July 1520, Z VII, 341–345; Myconius, *Briefwechsel*, vol. 1, 147.
43. Egli, *Actensammlung*, 8 September 1520, 132, 25–31.
44. Wandel, *Always Among Us*, 128.
45. James Muldoon, *Bridging the Medieval–Modern Divide: Medieval themes in the world of the Reformation* (London and New York, Routledge, 2013), 165.
46. Christian Moser and Hans Rudolf Fuhrer, *Der lange Schatten Zwinglis: Zürich, das französische Soldbündnis und eidgenössische Bündnispolitik, 1500–1650* (Zurich, Verlag Neue Zürcher Zeitung, 2009), 25.
47. Egli, *Actensammlung*, 11 January 1522, 215.
48. Moser and Fuhrer, *Der lange Schatten Zwinglis*, 44–45.
49. Walton, *Zwingli's Theocracy*, 59.
50. Andrea Strübind, *Eifriger als Zwingli: Die frühe Täuferbewegung in der Schweiz* (Berlin, Duncker & Humblot, 2003), 125–129. Also, Andrea Strübind, 'The Swiss Anabaptists' in Amy Nelson Burnett and Emidio Campi (eds), *A Companion to the Swiss Reformation* (Leiden, Brill, 2016), 391–395.
51. Strübind, 'The Swiss Anabaptists', 393.
52. Paul Leemann-van Elck, *Die Offizin Froschauer, Zürichs berühmte Druckerei im 16. Jahrhundert; ein Beitrag zur Geschichte der Buchdruckerkunst anlässlich der Halbjahrtausendfeier ihrer Erfindung* (Zurich and Leipzig, Orell Füssli Verlag, 1940); Urs B. Leu, 'Die Zürcher Buch-und Lesekultur 1520 bis 1575', *Zwingliana*, 31 (2004), 61–90; Iren L. Snavely, 'Zwingli, Froschauer, and the Word of God in print', *Journal of Religious and Theological Reformation*, 3 (2000), 65–87.
53. Helmut Meyer, '"Uns sind die Fastengebote Wurst!" Das "Wurstessen" von 1522 als Auslöser der Zürcher Reformation', *Zürcher Taschenbuch* (2019), 16.
54. Egli, *Actensammlung*, April 1522, 234, 74.
55. Christopher Kissane, *Food, Religion and Communities in Early Modern Europe* (London, Bloomsbury Academic, 2018), 64.
56. Z I, 98, 16–20; Latin Works, vol. 1, 79–80.
57. Z I, 88–136.
58. Meyer, '"Uns sind die Fastengebote Wurst!"', 24.
59. Egli, *Actensammlung*, April 1522, 235, 75–76.
60. Z I, 134–157.
61. Kissane, *Food*, 70.
62. Latin Works, vol. 1, 114.
63. Z I, 263, 32–264, 3.
64. Z I, 269, 31–270, 4; Latin Works, vol. 1, 216–217.
65. Kissane, *Food*, 69.
66. Walton, *Zwingli's Theocracy*, 62–63.
67. Egli, *Actensammlung*, September 1522, 269, 94.
68. Zwingli to Beatus Rhenanus, 30 July 1522, Z VII, 548, 5–11.
69. Potter, *Zwingli*, 82 n3.
70. Oskar Farner, 'Anna Reinhart: die Gattin Ulrich Zwinglis', *Zwingliana*, 3 (1916), 197–212.
71. Marjorie Elizabeth Plummer, *From Priest's Whore to Pastor's Wife: Clerical marriage and the process of reform in the early German Reformation* (Aldershot, Ashgate, 2012).
72. Oskar Vasella, *Reform und Reformation in der Schweiz* (Münster, Aschendorff, 1958), 28.
73. Potter, *Zwingli*, 80.

74. Z I, 197–209.
75. Z I, 210–248.
76. Latin Works, vol. 1, 158.
77. Latin Works, vol. 1, 158.
78. Maurizio Arfaioli, *The Black Bands of Giovanni: Infantry and diplomacy during the Italian Wars (1526–1528)* (Pisa, Pisa University Press, Edizioni Plus, 2005).
79. Z I, 165–188.
80. Z I, 186, 2.
81. Moser and Fuhrer, *Der lange Schatten Zwinglis*, 36–37.
82. Z I, 187, 5–14.
83. Bullinger, *Reformationsgeschichte*, vol. 1, 30–31.
84. Z I, 327, 4–6; Latin Works, vol. 1, 291–292.
85. Z I, 263, 8–10; Latin Works, vol. 1, 207.
86. Z I, 283, 6–8.
87. Z I, 284, 24–25; Latin Works, vol. 1, 237.
88. Z I, 287, 31–32; Latin Works, vol. 1, 242.
89. Z I, 318, 9–11; Latin Works, vol. 1, 279.
90. Cited in Christine Christ-von Wedel, *Erasmus of Rotterdam: Advocate of a new Christianity* (Toronto, University of Toronto Press, 2013), 187.
91. Zwingli to Oswald Myconius, 23 August 1522, Z VII, 565, 3 – 566, 4.
92. Zwingli to Oecolampadius, 19 April 1523, Z VIII, 67, 15 – 68, 2.
93. Zwingli to Berchtold Haller, 29 December 1521, Z VII, 485, 6–9.
94. Oskar Farner, 'Huldrych Zwingli als Persönlichkeit', *Zwingliana*, 5 (1931), 229–242.
95. Z III, 681, 26–27; Latin Works, vol. 3, 106.
96. Z II, 472, 9–16; *Selected Writings*, vol. 2, 3–4.
97. Zwingli to Ambrosius Blarer, 10 December 1525, Z VIII, 458, 17 – 459, 4.
98. The standard biography is Karl-Heinz Wyss, *Leo Jud: seine Entwicklung zum Reformator, 1519–1523* (Bern and Frankfurt am Main, Peter Lang, 1976).
99. Christine Christ-von Wedel, 'The vernacular paraphrases of Erasmus in Zurich', *Erasmus Studies*, 24 (2004), 71–88.
100. On Jud as translator of medieval spiritual works, see Maximilian von Habsburg, *Catholic and Protestant Translations of the Imitatio Christi, 1425–1650: From late medieval classic to early modern bestseller* (Aldershot, Ashgate, 2011), 111–113, 154–155.
101. Zwingli to Leo Jud, 5 May 1522, Z VII, 520, 1–5.
102. Zwingli to Oswald Myconius, 23 August 1522, Z VII, 568, 14–16.
103. Christian Hild, *Die Reformatoren übersetzen: theologisch-politische Dimensionen bei Leo Juds (1482–1542) Übersetzungen von Zwinglis und Bullingers Schriften ins Lateinische* (Zurich, TVZ, 2016).
104. Zwingli to Werner Steiner, 19 February 1523, Z VII, 31, 1–6.
105. Walther Köhler, *Zwingli und Luther: Ihr Streit über das Abendmahl nach seinen politischen und religiösen Beziehungen*, 2 vols (Leipzig, Verein für Reformationsgeschichte, 1924), vol. 2, 414.
106. Quoted in Wyss, *Leo Jud*, 122.
107. Gordon Rupp, 'Johannes Oecolampadius: The reformer as scholar', *Patterns of Reformation* (London, Epworth, 1969), 3–46. Essential on Oecolampadius is Amy Nelson Burnett's *Teaching the Reformation: Ministers and their message in Basel, 1529–1629* (Oxford and New York, Oxford University Press, 2006). For Oecolampadius' theological development, see Jeff Fisher, *A Christoscopic Reading of Scripture: Johannes Oecolampadius on Hebrews* (Göttingen, Vandenhoeck & Ruprecht, 2016).
108. K.R. Hagenbach, *Johann Oekolampad und Oswald Myconius: Die Reformatoren Basels* (Siberfeld, R.L. Fridrichs, 1859).
109. Jeff Fisher, 'The breakdown of a Reformation friendship: John Oecolampadius and Philip Melanchthon', *Westminster Journal of Theology*, 77 (2015), 265–291; E.A. De Boer, *John Calvin on the Visions of Ezekiel: Historical and hermeneutical studies in John Calvin's*

'sermons inédits', especially on Ezek. 36–48 (Leiden and Boston, Brill, 2004), 83; Paul Wernle, *Calvin und Basel bis zum Tode des Myconius, 1535–1552* (Basel, F. Reinhardt Universitäts-Buchdruckerei, 1909); Uwe Plath, *Calvin und Basel in den Jahren 1552–1556* (Zürich, Theologischer Verlag, 1974).

110. Andres Moser, 'Die Anfänge der Freundschaft zwischen Zwingli und Ökolampad', *Zwingliana*, 10 (1958), 614–620.

111. Quoted in K.R. Hagenbach, *Leben und ausgewählte Schriften der Väter und Begründer der reformierten Kirche* (Elberfeld, R.L. Friderichs, 1859), 26.

112. Oskar Farner, *Huldrych Zwinglis Briefe* (Zurich, Rascher, 1918–1920), vol. 1, 166.

113. Leu and Weidmann, *Private Library*, 42–43.

114. Leu and Weidmann, *Private Library*, 42.

115. Z I, 350, 7–9; Bromiley, *Zwingli and Bullinger*, 65.

116. Z I, 361, 12–16; Bromiley, *Zwingli and Bullinger*, 75.

117. Peter Opitz, 'The authority of scripture in the early Zurich Reformation (1522–1540)', *Journal of Reformed Theology*, 5 (2011), 298–303.

118. Bromiley, *Zwingli and Bullinger*, 73.

119. Z I, 367, 23–27; Bromiley, *Zwingli and Bullinger*, 80.

120. Z I, 379, 21–25; Bromiley, *Zwingli and Bullinger*, 90.

121. Christ-von Wedel, 'Erasmus und die Zürcher Reformatoren', 89.

122. Z I, 379, 25–32; Bromiley, *Zwingli and Bullinger*, 90–91.

123. Z I, 391–428.

124. Z I, 392, 5–20.

125. Hans Schneider, 'Zwinglis Marienpredigt und Luthers Magnifikat-Auslegung: Ein Beitrag zum Verhältnis Zwinglis zu Luther', *Zwingliana*, 23 (1996), 105–141; Emidio Campi, *Zwingli und Maria: Eine reformationsgeschichtliche Studie* (Zurich, Theologischer Verlag, 1997).

126. Z I, 404, 18–25.

127. Potter, *Zwingli*, 89 n6.

128. Z I, 405, 1–7.

129. Eamon Duffy, *Saints and Sinners: A history of the popes* (New Haven, CT, and London: Yale University Press, 1997), 157.

130. Suggestio deliberandi super propositione Hadriani Nerobergae facta, November 1522, Z I, 434–441.

131. Z I, 14–24.

132. EA IV, 1b, 247–250.

133. Ulrich Gäbler, *Huldrych Zwingli: His Life and work*, trans. Ruth C.L. Gritsch (Philadelphia, PA, Fortress Press, 1986), 64.

## CHAPTER 4

1. Rainer Henrich, 'Bischof Hugo und die Zürcher Reformation' in Peter Niederhäuser (ed.), *Ein feiner Fürst in einer rauen Zeit: Der Konstanzer Bischof Hugo von Hohenlandenberg* (Zurich, Chronos, 2011), 81–91.

2. See the discussion in Fabrice Flückiger, *Dire le vrai. Une Histoire de la dispute religieuse au début du XVIe siècle Ancienne Confédération Helvétique, 1523–1536* (Neuchâtel, Éditions Alphil-Presses universitaires suisses, 2018), 29f.

3. Flückiger, *Dire le vrai*, 59–62.

4. Henrich, 'Bischof Hugo', 85.

5. The existing record of the debate is largely favourable to Zwingli. Erhard Hegenwald produced his account subsequently as an eyewitness, although not as official secretary. 'Handlung der Versammlung in der Stadt Zürich auf den 29. Januar 1523', Z I, 479–569.

6. Rublack, 'Zwingli und Zürich', 400.

7. Flückiger, *Dire le vrai*, 64–65.

8. Rublack, 'Zwingli und Zürich', 401.

9. Henrich, 'Bischof Hugo', 89.
10. Z I, 552, 11–13.
11. Rublack, 'Zwingli und Zürich', 401.
12. Egli, *Actensammlung*, 29 January 1523, 327, 114–115.
13. Flückiger, *Dire le vrai*, 66.
14. Egli, *Actensammlung*, 29 January 1523, 327, 114–115.
15. W. Peter Stephens, *The Theology of Huldrych Zwingli* (Oxford, Clarendon Press, 1986), 33–35.
16. Zwingli to Johannes Xylotectus and Jodocus Kilchmeyer, 1 March 1523, Z VIII, 38, 2 – 39, 2.
17. Zwingli to Werner Steiner, 19 February 1523, Z VIII, 31, 5–6.
18. Z II, 15, 9–10.
19. Z II, 16, 5–6.
20. Z II, 3, 2–3.
21. Z II, 37, 19–25.
22. Z II, 51, 13–15.
23. Z II 96, 8–16.
24. Quoted in James M. Stayer, *Anabaptists and the Sword* (reprinted Eugene, OR, Wipf and Stock, 2002), 97.
25. Werner Packull, 'The origins of Swiss Anabaptism in the context of the Reformation of the common man', *Journal of Mennonite Studies*, 3 (1985), 38–39.
26. Kissane, *Food*, 59.
27. Gäbler, *Huldrych Zwingli*, 50.
28. Arnold Snyder, 'Word and power in Reformation Zurich', *Archiv für Reformationsgeschichte/Archive for Reformation History*, 81 (1990), 272–273.
29. James M. Stayer, 'Reublin and Brötli: The revolutionary beginnings of Swiss Anabaptism' in Marc Leinhard (ed.), *The Origins and Characteristics of Anabaptism* (The Hague, Nijhoff, 1977), 83–102.
30. Egli, *Actensammlung*, 29 September 1523, 426, 168–171.
31. Jacques Figi, *Die innere Reorganisation des Grossmünsterstiftes in Zürich von 1519 bis 1531* (Zurich, Affoltern am Albis, 1951), 111–113.
32. Snyder, 'Word and power', 269.
33. Z II, 471–525.
34. Z II, 485, 17–25; *Selected Writings*, vol. 2, 13.
35. Z II, 502, 23–25; *Selected Writings*, vol. 2, 25.
36. Z II, 493, 27 – 494, 3; *Selected Writings*, vol. 2, 19.
37. The small tithe was owed to the parish and the large tithe to the patron (which could be a monastery, the magistrates or a church, such as the Grossmünster in Zurich).
38. Z II, 513, 10–15; *Selected Writings*, vol. 2, 32.
39. Cited in Arnold C. Snyder, 'The birth and evolution of Swiss Anabaptism (1520–1530)', *Mennonite Quarterly Review*, 80 (2006), 512.
40. Z II, 542, 23–26.
41. Z II, 549, 15–22.
42. Z II, 536–551.
43. Hughes Oliphant Old, *The Shaping of the Reformed Baptismal Rite in the Sixteenth Century* (Grand Rapids, MI, Eerdmans, 1992), 40–44.
44. Old, *Shaping of the Reformed Baptismal Rite*, 35–40.
45. Timothy George, 'The presuppositions of Zwingli's baptismal theology' in Edward J. Furcha and H. Wayne Pipkin (eds), *Prophet, Pastor, Protestant: The work of Huldrych Zwingli after five hundred years* (Eugene, OR, Wipf and Stock), 72.
46. Z II, 620–625.
47. Z I, 539.
48. Z I, 566, 4–9.
49. Z II, 600, 7–11.

50. Quoted in Charles Garside, *Zwingli and the Arts* (New Haven, CT, Yale University Press, 1966), 138.
51. Peter Jezler, 'Bildersturm in Zürich: Vom Angriff auf die Kunstwerke zur Säkularisierung des Kirchenguts' in Peter Niederhäuser (ed.), *Verfolgt, Verdrängt, Vergessen: Schatten der Reformation* (Zurich, Chronos, 2018), 42.
52. Peter Jezler, 'Bildersturm in Zürich,' 42.
53. Lee Palmer Wandel, *Voracious Idols and Violent Hands: Iconoclasm in Reformation Zurich, Strasbourg, and Basel* (Cambridge, Cambridge University Press, 1995), 75.
54. Cécile Dupeux, Peter Jezler and Jean Wirth (eds), *Bildersturm: Wahnsinn oder Gottes Wille?* (Zurich, NZZ Verlag, 2000), 77.
55. Katharina Heyden, 'Aureola, Hätzer und Buchstab: Drei Protagonisten des reformatorischen Bilderstreits in der Schweiz zwischen Umbruch und Transformation', *Schweizerische Zeitschrift für Religions- und Kulturgeschichte*, 111 (2017), 65–86.
56. The classic study remains Wandel, *Always Among Us*.
57. See Nicholas Paul Smiar, 'Poor law and outdoor poor relief in Zurich, 1520–1529: A case study in social welfare history and social welfare policy implementation', PhD thesis, University of Illinois at Chicago, 1986.
58. Egli, *Actensammlung*, 29 September 1523, 424, 167.
59. Quoted in Wandel, *Voracious Idols*, 80.
60. Emidio Campi, 'The Reformation in Zurich' in Amy Nelson Burnett and Emidio Campi (eds), *A Companion to the Swiss Reformation* (Leiden, Brill, 2016), 75.
61. Flückiger, *Dire le vrai*, 69–70.
62. Quoted in Wandel, *Voracious Idols*, 81.
63. Flückiger, *Dire le vrai*, 72–73.
64. John L. Ruth, *Conrad Grebel: Son of Zurich* (Scottdale, PA, Herald Press, 1975), 79.
65. Erich Bryner, 'The Reformation in Schaffhausen' in Amy Nelson Burnett and Emidio Campi (eds), *A Companion to the Swiss Reformation* (Leiden, Brill, 2016), 219.
66. Strübind, 'The Swiss Anabaptists', 396.
67. Snyder, 'Birth and evolution', 520–521.
68. Snyder, 'Birth and evolution', 521.
69. Leland Harder, *The Sources of Swiss Anabaptism: The Grebel letters and related documents* (Scottdale, PA, Herald Press, 1985), 278.
70. Harder, *Sources of Swiss Anabaptism*, 276.
71. Gagliardi, Müller and Büsser (eds), *Johannes Stumpfs Schweizer- und Reformationschronik*, vol. 2, 214.
72. Z II, 663, 12–20; *Selected Writings*, vol. 2, 74.
73. Egli, *Actensammlung*, 10 December 1523, 456, 182.
74. Egli, *Actensammlung*, 13 December 1523, 458, 183.
75. The report is found in Egli, *Actensammlung*, 19 December 1523, 460, 183–189.
76. Egli, *Actensammlung*, 23 December 1523, 464, 190.
77. Egli, *Actensammlung*, 23 December 1523, 465, 190–191.
78. Egli, *Actensammlung*, 19 January 1524, 483, 197; 486, 208; 489, 213.
79. Potter, *Zwingli*, 138.
80. Z III, 5–68. For a detailed discussion of the text and its form of ministry, see below, pp. 194–197.
81. British Library English Short Title Catalogue, 26143.
82. *Selected Writings*, vol. 2, 84.
83. Z II, 23, 12–19; *Selected Writings*, vol. 2, 93.
84. Bullinger, *Reformationsgeschichte*, vol. 1, 148.
85. *Die Chronik des Bernhard Wyss, 1519–1530*, ed. Georg Finsler (Basel, Basler Buch- und Antiquariats-Handlung, 1901), 4–7.
86. Bullinger, *Reformationsgeschichte*, vol. 1, 31.
87. Cited from Ernst Götzinger, *Zwei Kalender vom Jahre 1527* (Schaffhausen, Carl Schoch, 1865), 42.

88. Z V, 54, 16 – 55, 12.
89. Hannes Reimann, 'Zwingli als Musiker', *Archiv für Musikwissenschaft*, 17 (1960), 131.
90. Wolfgang Capito to Zwingli, 27 September 1530, Z XI, 163.
91. Markus Jenny, *Zwinglis Stellung zur Musik im Gottesdienst* (Zürich, Zwingli-Verlag, 1966), 77.
92. Bullinger, *Reformationsgeschichte*, vol. 2, 309.
93. Christ-von Wedel, *Erasmus of Rotterdam*, 189.
94. Christ-von Wedel, *Erasmus of Rotterdam*, 189.
95. Christ-von Wedel, *Erasmus of Rotterdam*, 190.
96. Quoted in Christ-von Wedel, *Erasmus of Rotterdam*, 190.

## CHAPTER 5

1. Hauswirth, *Philipp von Hessen*, 72.
2. 'Eine treue und ernstliche Vermahnung an die Eidgenossen', 2 May 1524, Z III, 103–113.
3. Z III, 103, 20 – 104, 10.
4. Z III, 111, 9–12.
5. Z III, 111, 17–26.
6. Jezler, 'Bildersturm in Zurich', 46.
7. Egli, *Actensammlung*, 14 May 1524, 530, 231.
8. 'Vorschlag wegen der Bilder und der Messe', Z III, 115–131.
9. Cited in Wandel, *Voracious Idols*, 94.
10. Wandel, *Voracious Idols*, 95.
11. Peter Jezler, 'Der Bildersturm in Zürich 1523–1530' in Cécile Dupeux, Peter Jezler and Jean Wirth (eds), *Bildersturm: Wahnsinn oder Gottes Wille?* (Zurich, NZZ Verlag, 2000), 78.
12. Quoted in Wandel, *Voracious Idols*, 96–97.
13. Jezler, 'Der Bildersturm in Zürich 1523–1530', 79.
14. Wandel, *Voracious Idols*, 97.
15. Wandel, *Voracious Idols*, 98.
16. Jezler, 'Der Bildersturm in Zürich 1523–1530', 47.
17. 'Christliche Antwort Burgermeisters und Rats zu Zürich an Bischof Hugo', Z III, 153–229.
18. Bullinger, *Reformationsgeschichte*, vol. 1, 228–229.
19. Sybille Knecht, 'Wohin mit den Nonnen? Zürcher Frauenklöster im Brennpunkt der Reformation' in Peter Niederhäuser (ed.), *Verfolgt, Verdrängt, Vergessen: Schatten der Reformation* (Zurich, Chronos, 2018), 27–40.
20. 'Eine Unterrichtung, wie man sich vor Lügen hüten soll', 25 June 1524, Z III, 136–145.
21. On the Reuchlin affair, see above all David H. Price, *Johannes Reuchlin and the Campaign to Destroy Jewish Books* (Oxford and New York, Oxford University Press, 2011). On Zwingli and Jews, see Hans-Martin Kirn, 'Ulrich Zwingli, the Jews, and Judaism' in Dean Phillip Bell and Stephen G. Burnet (eds), *Jews, Judaism, and the Reformation in Sixteenth-Century Germany* (Leiden, Brill, 2006), 171–196; Achim Detmers, *Reformation und Judentum: Israel-Lehren und Einstellungen zum Judentum von Luther bis zum frühen Calvin* (Stuttgart, Kohlhammer, 2001); Peter Niederhäuser, 'Fremd- und Feindbilder? Juden in der Zürcher Reformation' in Peter Niederhäuser (ed.), *Verfolgt, Verdrängt, Vergessen: Schatten der Reformation* (Zurich, Chronos, 2018), 121–132.
22. Z III, 139, 4–10.
23. Z III, 140, 12–24.
24. John P. Maarbjerg, 'Iconoclasm in the Thurgau: Two related incidents in the summer of 1524', *Sixteenth Century Journal*, 24 (1993), 577–593.
25. Maarbjerg, 'Iconoclasm in the Thurgau', 584.
26. Z III, 511–538.
27. Maarbjerg, 'Iconoclasm in the Thurgau', 584.
28. Susan Schreiner, *Are You Alone Wise?: The search for certainty in the early modern era* (Oxford, Oxford University Press, 2011), 177.

29. Latin Works, vol. 2, 361.
30. Latin Works, vol. 2, 370–371.
31. Z III, 304–312.
32. EA IV, 1a, 473.
33. Potter, *Zwingli*, 155.
34. 'Antwort auf Johannes Ecks Missiv und Entbieten', Z III, 304–312.
35. Potter, *Zwingli*, 155.
36. Strübind, 'The Swiss Anabaptists', 400.
37. Konrad Grebel to Thomas Müntzer, 5 September 1524, German History in Documents and Images, http://ghdi.ghi-dc.org/document.cfm?document_id=4313
38. Strübind, *Eifriger als Zwingli*, 296–305.
39. Strübind, 'The Swiss Anabaptists', 403.
40. Harder, *Sources of Swiss Anabaptism*, 313.
41. Strübind, 'The Swiss Anabaptists', 404
42. Strübind, 'The Swiss Anabaptists', 407.
43. Z IV, 211, 8 – 212, 4.
44. Z IV 228, 1–5.
45. Stephens, *Theology of Huldrych Zwingli*, 203–204.
46. Latin Works, vol. 1, 11.
47. Latin Works, vol. 1, 18.
48. Zwingli to Vadian, 22 September 1525, Z VIII, 370, 3–5.
49. Latin Works, vol. 1, 18.
50. Latin Works, vol. 1, 19.
51. Zwingli to Wolfgang Capito, 1 January 1526; Erika Rummerl (ed.), *The Correspondence of Wolfgang Capito* (Toronto, University of Toronto Press, 2005), 271, 178–179.
52. Latin Works, vol. 1, 18.
53. Latin Works, vol. 1, 18.
54. Z III, 335–354.
55. B.J. Spruyt, *Cornelius Henrici Hoen (Honius) and his Epistle on the Eucharist (1525)* (Leiden, Brill, 2006).
56. Z III, 238, 23–28; *Selected Writings*, vol. 2, 133.
57. Z III, 340, 21–24; *Selected Writings*, vol. 2, 135.
58. Christian Dietrich, *Die Stadt Zürich und ihre Landgemeinden während der Bauernunruhen von 1489 bis 1525* (Frankfurt, Europäischen Hochschulschriften, 1985), 216–224. Also, Brady, *Turning Swiss*, 29–33.
59. Peter Blickle, *The Communal Reformation: The quest for salvation in sixteenth-century Germany* (reprinted Leiden, Brill, 1992).
60. Potter, *Zwingli*, 198.
61. EA IV, 1a, 625.
62. 'Erstes Gutachten betreffend Zehnten', Z IV, 352–360.
63. Z IV, 355, 20 – 356, 3.
64. See discussion in Peter Opitz, *Ulrich Zwingli: Prophet, Ketzer, Pionier des Protestantismus* (Zurich, Theologischer Verlag, 2015), 48–54.
65. Bruce Gordon, *The Swiss Reformation* (Manchester, Manchester University Press, 2002), 66.
66. 'Against the Murderous, Thieving Hordes of Peasants', LW, 46, 46.
67. Staehelin, *Huldreich Zwingli*, vol. 1, 442.
68. Bullinger, *Reformationsgeschichte*, vol. 1, 264.
69. Egli, *Actensammlung*, 19 April 1525, 684, 306.
70. 'Aktion oder Brauch des Nachtmahls', Z IV, 13–24.
71. On the liturgy of the Lord's Supper, see below.
72. Bullinger, *Reformationsgeschichte*, vol. 1, 264–265.
73. Staehelin, *Huldreich Zwingli*, vol. 1, 450.
74. 'Entwurf zur Antwort auf des Papsts Schreiben vom 11. December 1525', Z IV, 734–739.

75. 'Aktion oder Brauch des Nachtmahls', Z IV, 13–24; Bruce Gordon, '"It is the Lord's Passover": History, theology, and memory in the liturgy of the Lord's Supper in Reformation Zurich' in Teresa Berger and Bryan D. Spinks (eds), *Liturgy's Imagined Past/s: Methodologies and materials in the writing of liturgical history today* (Collegeville, MN, Liturgical Press, 2016), 172–200; Lee Palmer Wandel, 'Envisioning God: Image and liturgy in Reformation Zurich', *Sixteenth Century Journal*, 24 (1993), 21–40.

76. Z IV, 15, 10–17.

77. On Zwingli's dream of the Lord's Supper, see chapter 7.

78. Z IV, 13, 13–17.

79. Peter Opitz, 'Huldrych Zwingli' in Magne Sæbø (ed.), *Hebrew Bible/Old Testament: The history of its interpretation*, vol. 2: *From the Renaissance to the Enlightenment* (Göttingen, Vandenhoeck & Ruprecht, 2008).

80. R. Gerald Hobbs, 'Pluriformity of early Reformation scriptural interpretation' in Magne Sæbø (ed.), *Hebrew Bible/Old Testament: The history of its interpretation*, vol. 2: *From the Renaissance to the Enlightenment* (Göttingen, Vandenhoeck & Ruprecht, 2008).

81. Bard Thompson, *Liturgies of the Western Church* (New York and Scarborough, ON, Meridian Books, 1961), 149.

82. Thompson, *Liturgies*, 149.

83. Thompson, *Liturgies*, 149.

84. Alfred Ehrensperger, *Geschichte des Gottesdienstes in Zürich Stadt und Land im Spätmittelalter und in der frühen Reformation bis 1531* (Zurich, Theologischer Verlag, 2018), 648.

85. Thompson, *Liturgies*, 150.

86. Thompson, *Liturgies*, 150.

87. Johannes Voigtländer, *Ein Fest der Befreiung: Huldrych Zwingli Abendmahlslehre* (Neukirchener-Vluyn, Neukirchener Verlag, 2013), 205–206.

88. *Selected Writings*, vol. 2, 7.

89. *Selected Writings*, vol. 2, 7–8.

90. Philip Benedict, *Christ's Churches Purely Reformed* (New Haven, CT, Yale University Press, 2004), 31.

91. See Jenny, *Zwinglis Stellung zur Musik im Gottesdienst*; Gerhard Aeschbacher, 'Zwingli und die Musik in Gottesdienst', *Zwingliana*, 19 (1992), 1–11; Julius Schweizer, *Reformierte Abendmahlsgestaltung in der Schau Zwinglis* (Basel, Reinhart, 1954); Gottfried Wilhelm Locher, *Die Zwinglische Reformation im Rahmen der europäischen Kirchengeschichte* (Göttingen, Vandenhoeck & Ruprecht, 1979), 212.

92. Z II, 352, 22 – 353, 3.

93. Markus Jenny, 'Zwingli als Liedschöpfer', *Jahrbuch für Liturgie und Hymnologie*, 36 (1997), 227–234.

94. Cited in Garside, *Zwingli and the Arts*, 74.

95. Zwingli to Franz Lambert, 16 December 1524, Z VIII, 276, 17–19.

96. Reimann, 'Zwingli als Musiker', 140.

97. Cited in Kenneth H. Marcus, 'Hymnody and hymnals in Basel, 1526–1606', *Sixteenth Century Journal*, 32 (2001), 740.

98. Hans Rudolf Lavater, 'Die Froschauer-Bibel 1531' in Christoph Sigrist (ed.), *Die Zürcher Bibel von 1531: Entstehung, Verbreitung und Wirkung* (Zurich, Theologischer Verlag, 2011), 105; Daniël Timmerman, *Heinrich Bullinger on Prophecy and the Prophetic Office (1523–1538)* (Göttingen, Vandenhoeck & Ruprecht, 2015), 112.

99. Strübind, *Eifriger als Zwingli*, 129–146.

100. *Selected Writings*, vol. 2, 156.

101. Opitz, 'Huldrych Zwingli', 420–421; Gordon, *Swiss Reformation*, 232–239; Locher, *Zwinglische Reformation*, 161–163; Christoph Riedweg, 'Ein Philologe an Zwinglis Seite', *Museum Helveticum*, 57 (2000), 209–210.

102. Bullinger, *Reformationsgeschichte*, vol. 1, 290.

103. Bullinger, *Reformationsgeschichte*, vol. 1, 290. For Bullinger's account of the *Prophezei*, see 289–291.

104. Z IV, 365, 4f.

105. *Selected Writings*, vol. 2, 173.

106. On the role of the Vulgate in the Zurich Church, see Hobbs, 'Pluriformity of early Reformation scriptural interpretation', 485.

107. On Ceporin in Zurich, see Emil Egli, 'Ceporins Leben und Schriften', *Analecta Reformatoria 2* (Zurich, Zürcher und Furrer, 1901), 145–160; Riedweg, 'Ein Philologe', 201–219.

108. Riedweg, 'Ein Philologe', 211.

109. See Christoph Zürcher, *Konrad Pellikans Wirken in Zürich, 1526–1556* (Zurich, Theologischer Verlag, 1975).

110. R. Gerald Hobbs, 'Conrad Pellican and the Psalms: The ambivalent legacy of a pioneer Hebraist', *Reformation and Renaissance Review*, 1 (1999), 72–99. Also, Hobbs, 'Pluriformity of early Reformation scriptural interpretation', 482–484.

111. Lavater, 'Die Froschauer-Bibel 1531', 108.

112. Walter E. Meyer, 'Die Entstehung von Huldrych Zwinglis neutestamentlischen Kommentaren und Predigtnachschriften', *Zwingliana*, 14 (1976), 330–331.

113. Timmerman, *Heinrich Bullinger on Prophecy*, 111–124.

114. Timmerman, *Heinrich Bullinger on Prophecy*, 96–102.

115. For the following, I make use of Pierrick Hildebrand's 2019 Zurich dissertation, 'The Zurich origins of reformed covenant theology.'

116. Cited in Hildebrand, 'Zurich origins', 72.

## CHAPTER 6

1. Helpful are Jonathan A. Reid, 'France' in Andrew Pettegree (ed.), *The Reformation World* (London and New York, Routledge, 2002), 211–224; Jason Zuidema and Theodore van Raalte, *Early French Reform: The theology and spirituality of Guillaume Farel* (Aldershot, Ashgate, 2011); Mack P. Holt, *Renaissance and Reformation in France, 1500–1648* (Oxford, Oxford University Press, 2002); Denis Crouzet, *La genèse de la Réforme française 1520–1562* (Paris, SEDES, 1996); Janine Garrisson, *Les protestants au XVIᵉ siècle* (Paris, Fayard, 1988); and Francis Higman, *La diffusion de la Réforme en France* (Geneva, Labor et Fides, 1992).

2. See Marjory O'Rourke Boyle, *Rhetoric and Reform: Erasmus' civil dispute with Luther* (Cambridge, MA, Harvard University Press, 1983); Christ-von Wedel, *Erasmus of Rotterdam*, 167–182.

3. Martin Sallmann, *Zwischen Gott und Mensch: Huldrych Zwinglis theologischer Denkweg im De vera et falsa religione commentarius (1525)* (Tübingen, Mohr Siebeck, 1999), 16.

4. Z III, 630, 18–29.

5. Z III, 633, 16–18; Latin Works, vol. 3, 49.

6. Z III, 633, 24; Latin Works, vol. 3, 50.

7. Z III, 634, 14–17; Latin Works, vol. 3, 51.

8. Z III, 634, 17–20; Latin Works, vol. 3, 51.

9. Z III, 635, 10–12; Latin Works, vol. 3, 51.

10. Z III, 635, 19–21; Latin Works, vol. 3, 52.

11. Z III, 635, 23–26; Latin Works, vol. 3, 52.

12. Sallmann, *Zwischen Gott und Mensch*, 24–30.

13. Glarean to Zwingli, 1 November 1520, Z VII, 362, 7–12.

14. Walter Köhler, 'Zwingli Student in Paris?', *Zwingliana*, 12 (1918), 414–417.

15. Sallmann, *Zwischen Gott und Mensch*, 22–23.

16. Walther Köhler, 'Zu Zwinglis (angeblichen?) Pariser Studienaufenthalt', *Zwingliana*, 4 (1921), 46–51.

17. Richard Stauffer, 'Einfluß und Kritik des Humanismus in Zwinglis "Commentarius de vera et falsa religione"', *Zwingliana*, 16 (1983), 101.

18. Sallmann, *Zwischen Gott und Mensch*, 26.
19. Antonius Papilio 7 October 1524, Z VIII, 225, 5–8.
20. Jan R. Veenstra, 'Jacques Lefèvre Détaples: Humanism and Hermeticism in the *De Magia Naturali*' in Alasdair A. MacDonald, Zweder R.W.M. von Martels and Jan Riepke Veenstra (eds), *Christian Humanism: Essays in honour of Arjo Vanderjagt* (Leiden, Brill, 2009), 353–362.
21. Rudolf Pfister, 'Die Freundschaft zwischen Guillaume Farel und Huldrych Zwingli', *Zwingliana*, 8 (1947), 377–378.
22. Zuidema and van Raalte, *Early French Reform*.
23. Aegidius a Porto, 11 December 1525, Z VIII, 460–461.
24. Aegidius a Porto, 15 December 1526, Z VIII, 801–804.
25. Zwingli to Vadian, 28 May 1525, Z VIII, 334, 13–14.
26. Stephens, *Theology of Huldrych Zwingli*, 80–81; James D. Tracy, *Erasmus of the Low Countries* (Berkeley, University of California Press, 1997), 66–67; Manfred Hoffmann, 'Faith and piety in Erasmus' thought', *Sixteenth Century Journal*, 20 (1989), 241–258; Brian A. Gerrish, 'De Libero Arbitrio (1524): Erasmus on piety, theology, and the Lutheran dogma' in Richard L. DeMolen (ed.), *Essays on the Work of Erasmus* (New Haven, CT, Yale University Press, 1978), 187–209.
27. Z III, 667, 30.
28. Görge K. Hasselhoff, 'Huldrych Zwinglis Verständnis von religio', *Zeitschrift für Religions- und Geistesgeschichte*, 67 (2015), 132.
29. Z III, 642, 30–37; Latin Works, vol. 3, 61.
30. Z III, 668, 36 – 669, 3; Latin Works, vol. 3, 91.
31. Z III, 669, 10–12; Latin Works, vol. 3, 91.
32. Z III, 908, 17–23; Latin Works, vol. 3, 339.
33. See Bolliger, *Infiniti contemplatio*.
34. Z III, 662, 3–10; Latin Works, vol. 3, 83–84.
35. Z III, 664, 18–22.
36. Christoph Burger, 'Die Entwicklung von Zwinglis Reden über Gottes Güte, Barmherzigkeit und Gerechtigkeit', *Zwingliana*, 19 (1992), 71–76.
37. See the discussion in Stephens, *Theology of Huldrych Zwingli*, 81–86.
38. Z III, 650, 24–29; Latin Works, vol. 3, 70.
39. Sallmann, *Zwischen Gott und Mensch*, 105.
40. Z III, 648, 30–35; Latin Works, vol. 3, 68.
41. Z III, 639, 4–5.
42. Gottfried W. Locher, '"Christ our Captain": An example of Huldrych Zwingli's preaching in its cultural setting' in his *Zwingli's Thought: New perspectives* (Leiden, Brill, 1981), 72–86.
43. Volker Leppin, 'Adams Wille und Gottes Provenienz: Die Bestreitung des freien Willens in Zwinglis "Commentarius"', *Zwingliana*, 22 (1995), 37–43.
44. Z II, 560, 20.
45. Stephens, *Theology of Huldrych Zwingli*, 111–118.
46. Z II, 381, 9.
47. Stephens, *Theology of Huldrych Zwingli*, 102–106.
48. Z III, 843, 15–19; Latin Works, vol. 2, 272–273.
49. Peter Stephens, 'The place of predestination in Zwingli and Bucer', *Zwingliana*, 19 (1992), 393–410.
50. Z III, 841, 30–32; Latin Works, vol. 3, 271.
51. Z VIII, 726–727.
52. Christof Gestrich, *Zwingli als Theologe: Glaube und Geist beim Zürcher Reformator* (Zurich, Zwingli-Verlag, 1967), 93.
53. Z V, 787, 27–30.
54. Z III, 910, 14–21; Latin Works, vol. 3, 341.
55. Z III, 695, 7–9; Latin Works, vol. 3, 123.

56. Sallmann, *Zwischen Gott und Mensch*, 232–233.
57. Z III, 728, 28–32; Latin Works, vol. 3, 162.
58. Z III, 734, 7–9; Latin Works, vol. 3, 167.
59. Z III, 742, 23–28; Latin Works, vol. 3, 178.
60. Berndt Hamm, *Zwinglis Reformation der Freiheit* (Neukirchen-Vluyn, Neukirchener Verlag, 1988), 64.
61. Z II, 695, 13–21.
62. Hamm, *Zwinglis Reformation*, 67.
63. Z III, 848, 37 – 849, 3.
64. Z III, 782, 11–17; Latin Works, vol. 3, 208.
65. Hamm, *Zwinglis Reformation*, 97.
66. Z III, 697, 9–12; Latin Works, vol. 3, 125.
67. Z III, 784, 27–30; Latin Works, vol. 3, 211.
68. Cited in Hamm, *Zwinglis Reformation*, 100.

## CHAPTER 7

1. Lyndal Roper, *Martin Luther: Renegade and prophet* (London, Bodley Head, 2016); Heinz Schilling, *Martin Luther: Rebel in an age of upheaval*, trans. Rona Johnston (New York, Oxford University Press, 2017).
2. See Bruce Gordon, '"For if we are true prophets": Huldrych Zwingli on Martin Luther', *Reformation*, 22 (2017), 102–119; See Potter, *Zwingli*, 287–315; Martin Brecht, 'Zwingli als Schüler Luthers: Zu seiner theologischen Entwicklung 1518–22', *Zeitschrift für Kirchengeschichte*, 96 (1985), 301–319; Wilhelm H. Neuser, *Die reformatorische Wende bei Zwingli* (Neukirchen-Vluyn, Neukirchener Verlag, 1977); Fritz Blanke, 'Zwinglis Urteile über sich selbst', *Furche-Jahrbuch*, 22 (1936), 31–39; Köhler, *Zwingli und Luther*; Stephens, *Theology of Huldrych Zwingli*, 45–49; Arthur Rich, *Die Anfänge der Theologie Huldrych Zwinglis* (Zurich, Zwingli-Verlag, 1949); Locher, *Die Zwinglische Reformation*, 87–90; Gottfried W. Locher, 'The characteristic features of Zwingli's theology in comparison with Luther and Calvin' in his *Zwingli's Thought: New perspectives* (Leiden, Brill, 1981), 142–232; Joachim Rogge, 'Die Initia Zwinglis und Luthers: Ein Einführung in die Probleme', *Luther-Jahrbuch*, 30 (1963), 107–133; Schneider, 'Zwinglis Marienpredigt'; August Pieper, 'What makes up the "different spirit" of which Luther accused the Zwinglians?', *Wisconsin Lutheran Quarterly*, 107 (2010), 166–190.
3. Leu and Weidmann, *Private Library*, 66.
4. Beatus Rhenanus to Zwingli, 24 May 1519, Z VII, 175.
5. Zwingli to Beatus Rhenanus, 7 June 1519, Z VII, 181, 6–9.
6. Leu and Weidmann, *Private Library*, 68.
7. Zwingli to Myconius, 16 February 1520, Z VII, 271–273; Myconius, *Briefwechsel*, vol. 1, 134.
8. Kaspar Hedio to Zwingli, 10 June 1520, Z VII, 320, 2–5.
9. Zwingli to Oswald Myconius, 24 July 1520, Z VII, 344, 23–24; Arthur Rich, 'Zwinglis Weg zur Reformation', *Zwingliana*, 8 (1948), 516.
10. Z II 149, 19–22.
11. Z II 149, 36 – 150, 3; *Selected Writings*, vol. 1, 119.
12. Z II 150, 7–11; *Selected Writings*, vol. 1, 120.
13. Z II, 150, 15–16.
14. Z V 565, 12–15; *Selected Writings*, vol. 2, 240.
15. Z V 566, 6–8; *Selected Writings*, vol. 2, 240.
16. Z V 566, 17–22; *Selected Writings*, vol. 2, 240–241.
17. Kristen van Ausdall, 'Art and Eucharist in the late middle ages' in Ian Levy, Gary Macy and Kristen Van Ausdall (eds), *Companion to the Eucharist* (Leiden, Brill, 2011), 541–618.
18. *Selected Writings*, vol. 1, 115.
19. Stephens, *Theology of Huldrych Zwingli*, 221.

20. Voigtländer, *Ein Fest der Befreiung*, 31.
21. G.W. Pigman III, 'Versions of imitation in the Renaissance', *Renaissance Quarterly*, 33 (1980), 29–31.
22. *Subsidium sive coronis de eucharistia* (17 August 1525), Z IV 458–504.
23. Z IV 484, 3–9.
24. Bruce Gordon, 'Zwingli's dream of the Lord's Supper' in Maria-Christina Pitassi and Solfaroli Camillocci (eds), *Crossing Traditions: Essays on the Reformation and intellectual history in honour of Irena Backus* (Leiden, Brill, 2017), 298–310.
25. Fritz Büsser, *Das katholische Zwinglibild: Von der Reformation bis zur Gegenwart* (Zurich and Stuttgart, Zwingli-Verlag, 1968), 197f.
26. Z IV, 483, 2–8.
27. Ludwig Lavater, *Historia, Oder Gschicht, Von dem ursprung und fürgang der grossen zwyspaltung, so sich zwüschen D. Martin Luthern . . ., und Huldrychen Zwinglio . . ., auch zwüschend anderen Gelehrten, Von wägen dess Herren Nachtmals gehalten hat . . . Von . . . 1524 an, bisz uff das 1563* (Zurich, Froschauer, 1564), sig. Biiiv.
28. Gordon, 'Zwingli's dream', 305.
29. LW 49, 88–90.
30. On Oecolampadius' key sacramental ideas, see Amy Nelson Burnett, *Debating the Sacraments: Print and authority in the early Reformation* (Oxford, Oxford University Press, 2019), 154f.
31. Burnett, *Debating the Sacraments*, 151.
32. Fisher, 'The breakdown of a Reformation friendship', 280–285.
33. Stephens, *Theology of Huldrych Zwingli*, 127.
34. Christ-von Wedel, *Erasmus of Rotterdam*, 189f.
35. See the essential works on the broader reach of the sacramental debate: Amy Nelson Burnett, *Karlstadt and the Origins of the Eucharistic Controversy: A study in the circulation of ideas* (Oxford, Oxford University Press, 2011), and her *Debating the Sacraments*. Also, Martin Greschat, *Martin Bucer: A reformer and his times*, trans. Stephen E. Buckwalter (Louisville, KY, Westminster John Knox Press, 2004); Amy Nelson Burnett, 'The development of Martin Bucer's thinking on the sacrament of the Lord's Supper in its historical and theological context 1523–1534', *Zwingliana*, 32 (2005), 45–70; Wilhelm H. Neuser, 'Martin Bucer als Mittler im Abendmahlsstreit (1530/31)' in A. Lexutt and V. von Bülow (eds), *Kaum zu glauben: Von der Häresie und dem Umgang mit ihr* (Rheinbach, 1998), 140–161.
36. See Joel van Amberg, *A Real Presence: Religious and social dynamics of the eucharistic conflicts in early modern Augsburg 1520–1530* (Leiden, Brill, 2011).
37. Thomas A. Brady, Jr., *Protestant Politics: Jacob Sturm (1489–1553)* (Atlantic Highlands, NJ, Humanities Press, 1995), 69–70.
38. Cited in Mark U. Edwards, Jr., *Luther and the False Brethren* (Stanford, CA, Stanford University Press, 1975), 86.
39. Edwards, *Luther*, 88.
40. Edwards, *Luther*, 90.
41. Christ-von Wedel, 'Erasmus und die Zürcher Reformatoren', 125.
42. Edwards, *Luther*, 96.
43. Edwards, *Luther*, 97.
44. Edwards, *Luther*, 103.
45. Walter Köhler cited in Hauswirth, *Philipp von Hessen*, 534.
46. Cited in Fisher, 'The breakdown of a Reformation friendship', 286.
47. Brady, *Protestant Politics*, 71.
48. Edwards, *Luther*, 107.
49. Burnett, *Debating the Sacraments*, 577.
50. Burnett, *Debating the Sacraments*, 578.
51. Burnett, *Debating the Sacraments*, 580.
52. LW 38, 85–89.

53. Burnett, *Debating the Sacraments*, 577.
54. Cited in Burnett, *Debating the Sacraments*, 582.
55. Carl M. Leth, 'Signs and providence: A study of Ulrich Zwingli's sacramental theology', PhD thesis, Duke University, 1992, 30.
56. Ulrich Gäbler, 'Luther und Zwingli: eine Skizze', *Luther*, 55 (1984), 105–112.
57. Leth, 'Signs and providence', 203–204.
58. W. Peter Stephens, 'Election in Zwingli and Bullinger: A comparison of Zwingli's *Sermonis de providentia dei anamnema* (1530) and Bullinger's *Oratio de moderatione servanda in negotio Providentiae, Praedestinationis, gratiae et liberi arbitrii* (1536)', *Reformation and Renaissance Review*, 7 (2005), 42–56.
59. Philipp of Hesse to Zwingli, 25 January 1530, Z X 422, 8–10.
60. Latin Works, vol. 3, 208.
61. Latin Works, vol. 3, 224.
62. Aurelio A. Garcia, '"Summum Bonum" in the Zurich Reformation: Zwingli and Bullinger', *Zwingliana*, 44 (2017), 183–188.
63. Z V 563; *Selected Writings*, vol. 2, 239.

## CHAPTER 8

1. See the fascinating and provocative essay on Zwingli by Heiko A. Oberman, *Reformation: Roots and ramifications*, trans. Andrew Colin Gow (London and New York, T&T Clark, 1994), 183–200. The classic work on Zwingli and the urban Reformation is Bernd Moeller, *Reichsstadt und Reformation: Neue Ausgabe* (Tübingen, Mohr Siebeck, 1994).
2. Essential is Leu and Weidmann, *Private Library*, and I draw heavily on their work.
3. Quoted in Leu and Weidmann, *Private Library*, 70.
4. Leu and Weidmann, *Private Library*, 73.
5. See Thomas A. Brady, Jr., *Ruling Class, Regime and Reformation at Strasbourg 1520–1555* (Leiden, Brill, 1978); Laura Jane Abray, *The People's Reformation: Magistrates, clergy, and commons in Strassburg, 1500–1598* (Oxford, Oxford University Press, 1985); William S. Stafford, *Domesticating the Clergy: The inception of the Reformation in Strasbourg, 1522–1524* (Missoula, MO, Scholars' Press, 1976). On Bucer, see Greschat, *Martin Bucer*; on Capito, James M. Kittleson, *Wolfgang Capito: From humanist to reformer* (Leiden, Brill, 1997).
6. Wolfgang Capito to Zwingli, 18 August 1526, Z VIII, 3–7, 687.
7. See, Scott, *The Swiss and their Neighbours*, 48–50. The classic work is Bernhard Kugler, *Ulrich, Herzog zu Württemberg* (Stuttgart, Ebner und Seubert, 1865).
8. Hauswirth, *Philipp von Hessen*, 81.
9. 'Plan zu einem Feldzug', Z III, 551–583. See Lienhard, 'Guerre et paix', 217–240.
10. Hauswirth, *Philipp von Hessen*, 76–77.
11. Z III, 581, 3–9.
12. See James M. Stayer, 'Swiss South German Anabaptism, 1526–1540' in John D. Roth and James M. Stayer (eds), *A Companion to Anabaptism and Spiritualism* (Leiden and Boston, MA, Brill, 2007), 83–118.
13. Zwingli to Berchtold Haller and Franz Kolb, 28 April 1527, Z IX, 114, 3–18.
14. Zwingli to Capito, 8 August, 1527, Z IX, 182, 9–11.
15. Zwingli to Konrad Sam, 1 September 1527, Z IX, 210, 21–23.
16. Felix Manz, 'Protest and defense' in Michael G. Baylor (ed. and trans.), *The Radical Reformation* (Cambridge, Cambridge University Press, 1991), 96.
17. On Margret Hottinger from Zollikon, see C. Arnold Snyder and Linda A. Hueberg Hecht (eds), *Profiles of Anabaptist Women: Sixteenth-century reforming pioneers* (Waterloo, ON, Wilfred Laurier Press, 1996), 43–53; Wes Harrison, 'The role of women in Anabaptist thought and practice: The Hutterite experience of the sixteenth and seventeenth centuries', *Sixteenth Century Journal*, 23 (1992), 49–69.
18. Snyder, 'Birth and evolution', 592.
19. Snyder and Hueberg, *Profiles of Anabaptist Women*, 49.

20. Snyder, 'Birth and evolution', 592.
21. Andrew P. Klager, 'The early influence of humanism on Balthasar Hubmaier (1485–1528) during his university studies', *Reformation and Renaissance Review*, 22 (2020), 4–24; Kirk R. MacGregor, 'Hubmaier's death and the threat of a free state church', *Church History and Religious Culture*, 91 (2011), 321–348.
22. David Funk, 'The relation of Church and state in the thought of Balthasar Hubmaier', *Didaskalia*, 17 (2006), 37–50.
23. Simon Victor Goncharenko, *Wounds that Heal: The importance of church discipline within Balthasar Hubmaier's theology* (Eugene, OR, Pickwick Publications, 2012).
24. Graeme R. Chatfield, *Balthasar Hubmaier and the Clarity of Scripture: A critical reformation issue* (Cambridge, James Clarke & Co., 2013), 156–157.
25. Catherine Deieument, 'Dialogue du Docteur Balthasar Hubmaier, de Friedberg, à propos du livret sur le baptême de Maître Zwingli de Zurich, au sujet du baptême des enfants (1526)', *Études théologiques et religieuses*, 92 (2017), 53–133.
26. Cited in Henry Clay Vedder, *Balthasar Hubmaier: Leader of the Anabaptists* (1905, rpt. La Vergne, TN, Kessinger, 2010), 119.
27. Torsten Bergsten, *Balthasar Hubmaier: Anabaptist theologian* (King of Prussia, PA, Judson Press, 1978), 305.
28. Akira Demura offers a helpful comparison of Zwingli's views of the Anabaptists with those of John Calvin in 'From Zwingli to Calvin: A comparative study of Zwingli's Elenchus and Calvin's Brière Instruction' in Alfred Schindler and Hans Stickelberger (eds), *Die Zürcher Reformation: Ausstrahlungen und Rückwirkungen* (Zurich, Peter Lang, 2001), 87–99.
29. Egli, *Actensammlung*, 7 March 1526, 935, 445.
30. Egli, *Actensammlung*, 7 March 1526, 934, 444–445.
31. Zwingli to Vadian, 7 March 1526, Z VIII, 542. See Leland Harder, 'Zwingli's reaction to the Schleitheim Confession of Faith of the Anabaptists', *Sixteenth Century Journal*, 11 (1980), 54.
32. Snyder, 'Birth and evolution', 584.
33. Gottfried W. Locher, 'Felix Manz' Abschiedsworte an seine Mitbrüder vor der Hinrichtung 1527: Spiritualität und Theologie. Die Echtheit des Liedes "Bey Christo will ich bleiben" Andreas Lindt zum Gedenken', *Zwingliana*, 17 (1986), 25–26.
34. Daniel Liechty, *Early Anabaptist Spirituality. Selected Writings* (New York, Paulist Press, 1994), 18.
35. C. Arnold Snyder, *The Life and Thought of Michael Sattler* (Scottsdale, PA, Herald Press, 1984); C. Arnold Snyder, 'Revolution and the Swiss Brethren: The case of Michael Sattler', *Church History*, 50 (1981), 276–287; C. Arnold Snyder, 'The Schleitheim Articles in light of the revolution of the common man: Continuation or departure?', *Sixteenth Century Journal*, 16 (1985), 419–430; James M. Stayer, 'The Swiss Brethren: An exercise in self-definition', *Church History*, 47 (1978), 174–195; Walter Klaassen, 'The "Schleitheim Articles" and the "New Transformation of Christian Living"', *Historical Reflections/ Réflexions Historiques*, 14 (1987), 95–111.
36. Snyder, 'The Schleitheim Articles', 421–422.
37. See Brad S. Gregory, 'Anabaptist martyrdom: Imperatives, experience and memorialization' in D. Roth and James M. Stayer (eds), *Companion to Anabaptism and Spiritualism* (Leiden and Boston, MA, Brill, 2007), 467–506.
38. Michael G. Baylor (ed. and trans.), *The Radical Reformation* (Cambridge, Cambridge University Press, 1991), 175.
39. Preston Lee Atwood, 'The Martyrs' Song: The hymnody of the early Swiss Brethren Anabaptists', *The Artistic Theologian*, 2 (2013), 85.
40. Harder, 'Zwingli's reaction', 55.
41. Stephens, *Theology of Huldrych Zwingli*, 100.
42. Cited in Harder, 'Zwingli's reaction', 55.

43. Z VI.1, 25, 3–7; *Selected works of Huldreich Zwingli, 1484–1531*, trans. Lawrence A. McLouth, Henry Preble and George W. Gilmore (Philadelphia, University of Pennsylvania, 1901), 127.

44. Z VI.1, 65, 15 – 66, 1.

45. Harder, 'Zwingli's reaction', 66.

46. Z I, 35, 10–11.

47. Arthur Rich, 'Zwingli als sozialpolitischer Denker', *Zwingliana*, 13 (1969), 79–80.

48. See Bruce Gordon, 'The Protestant clergy and the culture of rule: The reformed Zurich clergy of the sixteenth century' in C. Scott Dixon and Luise Schorn-Schütte (eds), *The Protestant Clergy of Early Modern Europe* (London, Palgrave, 2003), 137–155.

49. Jay Goodale, 'Pastors, privation and the process of Reformation in Saxony', *Sixteenth Century Journal*, 33 (2002), 71–92.

50. The classic work on the family in the Reformation remains Lyndal Roper, *The Holy Household: Women and morals in Reformation Augsburg* (Oxford, Oxford University Press, 1989).

51. Bruce Gordon, 'Polity and reform in the Swiss Reformed churches' in Amy Nelson Burnett and Emidio Campi (eds), *A Companion to the Swiss Reformation* (Leiden, Brill, 2016), 489–519.

52. Jacques Vincent Pollet, 'Zwingli und die Kirche: Scholastik und Humanismus im Kirchenbegriff Zwinglis', *Zwingliana*, 16 (1985), 489–499.

53. Egli, *Actensammlung*, 10 May 1526, 711, 326–329.

54. Küngolt Kilchenmann, *Die Organisation des zürcherischen Ehegerichts zur Zeit Zwinglis* (Zurich, Zwingli-Verlag, 1946).

55. Martin Hauser, *Prophet und Bischof: Huldrych Zwinglis Amtsverständnis im Rahmen der Zürcher Reformation* (Fribourg, Schweiz, Universitätsverlag, 1994), 164.

56. F. Schmidt-Clausing, 'Das Corpus Juris Canonici als reformatorisches Mittel Zwinglis', *Zeitschrift für Kirchengeschichte*, 80 (1969), 14–21.

57. Roger Ley, *Kirchenzucht bei Zwingli* (Zurich, Zwingli-Verlag, 1948).

58. Benedict, *Christ's Churches*, 40.

59. See Bruce Gordon, *Clerical Discipline and the Rural Reformation: The synod in Zurich, 1532–1580* (Bern, Peter Lang, 1992).

60. Kurt Maier, 'Die Konstanzer Diözesansynoden im Mittelalter und in der Neuzeit', *Rottenburger Jahrbuch für Kirchengeschichte*, 5 (1986), 53–70.

61. Gordon, *Clerical Discipline*, 36–41.

62. Hauser, *Prophet und Bischof*, 170.

63. Jacob, *Politische Führungsschicht*, 63.

64. Bullinger, *Reformationsgeschichte*, vol. 1, 308.

65. Bullinger, *Reformationsgeschichte*, vol. 1, 308.

66. Bullinger, *Reformationsgeschichte*, vol. 1, 307.

67. Zwingli to Vadian, 28 March 1524, Z VIII, 167, 6–7.

68. Brunner wrote to Zwingli on 15 January 1527 (Z IX, 18–20) and Zwingli replied on 25 January (Z IX, 29–32).

69. Z IX, 18, 3 – 19, 1.

70. Z IX, 19, 13–14.

71. Z IX, 20, 1–8.

72. Z IX, 30, 7–14.

73. Z IX, 31, 3–11.

74. Zwingli to Urbanus Rhegius, 16 October 1526, Z VIII, 737–739.

75. Z VIII, 738, 9–17.

76. Heinrich Hässi to Zwingli, 19 February 1527, Z IX, 54–55.

77. Edward J. Furcha, 'Women in Zwingli's world', *Zwingliana*, 19 (1992), 132.

78. Katharina von Wattenwyl to Zwingli, 1524–1525, Z VIII, 284–285.

79. Luis Tscharner to Zwingli, 31 March 1526, Z VIII, 550, 8–17.

80. Barbara Trüllerey to Zwingli, 24 February 1524, Z VIII, 154–155.

81. Furcha, 'Women', 133.
82. Barbara Nithart to Zwingli, 13 September 1526, Z VIII, 711–714.
83. Z VIII, 711, 3 – 712, 10.
84. Furcha, 'Women', 132.
85. Zwingli to Heinrich Utinger, 5 December 1518, Z VII, 110–113.
86. See the excellent discussion in Flückiger, *Dire le vrai*, 77–82.
87. See above all, Flückiger, *Dire le vrai*. Also, Ulrich Pfister, 'Konfessionskonflikte in der frühneuzeitlichen Schweiz: Eine strukturalistische Interpretation', *Schweizerische Zeitschrift für Religions- und Kulturgeschichte*, 101 (2007), 257–312. On the Ilanz disputation and articles, Jan-Andrea Bernhard, 'The Reformation in the Three Leagues (Grisons)' in Amy Nelson Burnett and Emidio Campi (eds), *A Companion to the Swiss Reformation* (Leiden, Brill, 2016), 295–297.
88. Susan Schuster, *Dialogflugschriften der frühen Reformationszeit: Literarische Fortführung der Disputation und Resonanzräume reformatorischen Denkens* (Göttingen, Vandenhoeck & Ruprecht, 2019), 27–28.
89. Jürgen Bärsch and Konstantin Maier (eds), *Johannes Eck (1486–1543): Scholastiker – Humanist – Kontroverstheologe* (Regensburg, Friedrich Pustet, 2014).
90. Martin H. Jung, 'Historische Einleitung. Gründe, Verlauf und Folgen der Disputation' in Alfred Schindler and Wolfram Schneider-Lastin (eds), *Die Badener Disputation von 1526: Kommentierte Edition des Protokolls* (Zurich, Theologischer Verlag, 2015), 70.
91. Jung, 'Historische Einleitung', 71.
92. http://ivv7srv15.uni-muenster.de/mnkg/pfnuer/Eckbriefe/N194.html (accessed 19 June 2019).
93. Zwingli to Vadian, 22 April 1526, Z VIII, 573, 9.
94. The term used was *kůghyer*. See C. Sieber-Lehmann and T. Wilhelmi, *In Helvetios - Wider die Kuhschweizer: Fremd- und Feindbilder von den Schweizern in antieidgenössischen Texten aus der Zeit von 1386 bis 1532* (Bern, Haupt, 1998), 49ff.
95. Jung, 'Historische Einleitung', 111.
96. Oecolampadius to Zwingli, 12 June 1526, Z VIII, 626, 7–9.
97. Latin Works, vol. 1, 16.
98. Jung, 'Historische Einleitung', 115.
99. Jung, 'Historische Einleitung', 140.
100. Flückiger, *Dire le vrai*, 79.
101. Jung, 'Historische Einleitung', 148.
102. Flückiger, *Dire le vrai*, 82.
103. Jacob, *Politische Führungsschicht*, 63.
104. Leo Schelbert, 'Jacob Grebel's trial revised', *Archiv für Reformationsgeschichte/Archive for Reformation History*, 60 (1969), 32–64; Jacob, *Politische Führungsschicht*, 62–66.
105. Potter, *Zwingli*, 242.
106. Flückiger, *Dire le vrai*, 85.
107. Hauswirth, *Philipp von Hessen*, 81.
108. Martin Sallmann, 'The Reformation in Bern' in Amy Nelson Burnett and Emidio Campi (eds), *A Companion to the Swiss Reformation* (Leiden, Brill, 2016), 142; Ernst Koch, 'Zwingli und die Berner Reformation', *Theologische Rundschau*, 60 (1995), 131–151.
109. Flückiger, *Dire le vrai*, 85–88.
110. Potter, *Zwingli*, 256–257.
111. Oskar Farner, *Huldrych Zwingli* (Zurich, Zwingli-Verlag, 1943–1960), vol. 4, 268.
112. Flückiger, *Dire le vrai*, 87.
113. Benedict, *Christ's Churches*, 39.
114. Sallmann, 'Reformation in Bern', 146.
115. *Zwingli Schriften*, vol. 4, 45.
116. *Zwingli Schriften*, vol. 4, 62.
117. *Zwingli Schriften*, vol. 4, 86.

118. *Zwingli Schriften*, vol. 4, 87.
119. *Zwingli Schriften*, vol. 4, 89.

## CHAPTER 9

1. Cited in Brady, *Turning Swiss*, 203.
2. Heinrich Richard Schmidt, *Reichstädte, Reich und Reformation* (Stuttgart, Franz Steiner Verlag, 1986), 666–681.
3. Brady, *Turning Swiss*, 203f.
4. Schmidt, *Reichstädte*, 324–326.
5. Benedict, *Christ's Churches*, 43; Philip Broadhead, 'Guildsmen, religious reform and the search for the common good: The role of the guilds in the early Reformation in Augsburg', *Historical Journal*, 39 (1996), 577–597.
6. Gordon, *Swiss Reformation*, 285–296.
7. Brady, *Turning Swiss*, 193–201.
8. Brady, *Protestant Politics*, 68.
9. Hauswirth, 'Landgraf Philipp von Hessen und Zwingli: Ihre politischen Beziehungen 1529/1530', *Zwingliana*, 11 (1962), 503.
10. Cited in Brady, *Protestant Politics*, 69.
11. Hauswirth, 'Landgraf Philipp von Hessen', 515.
12. Z VI.2, 739, 2–10.
13. Hauswirth, 'Landgraf Philipp von Hessen', 521.
14. Hauswirth, 'Landgraf Philipp von Hessen', 520.
15. I have made extensive use of Martin Haas, 'Zwingli und der Erste Kappelerkrieg', *Zwingliana*, 12 (1964), 93–136.
16. Heinzpeter Stucki, 'Christliches Burgrecht' in *Historisches Lexikon der Schweiz*, https://hls-dhs-dss.ch/de/articles/017174/2003-12-17/
17. Hauswirth, 'Landgraf Philipp von Hessen', 518.
18. Kurt Spillmann, 'Zwinglis politische Pläne in der Ostschweiz', *Rorschacher Neujahrsblatt*, 52 (1962), 64–66. Much of the following comes from Spillmann.
19. Z VI.2, 426.
20. Z VI.2, 431.
21. Jean-Paul Tardent, *Niklaus Manuel als Staatsmann* (Bern, Archiv des historischen Vereins des Kantons Bern, 1967), 242–255.
22. Cited in Potter, *Zwingli*, 364.
23. Martin Haas, *Zwingli und der Erste Kappelerkrieg* (Zurich, Verlag Berichthaus, 1965), 230.
24. Rudolf Braun, 'Zur Militärpolitik Zürichs im Zeitalter der Kappeler Krieg', *Zwingliana*, 10 (1958), 537–573.
25. Haas, *Zwingli und der Erste Kappelerkrieg*, 147.
26. Haas, *Zwingli und der Erste Kappelerkrieg*, 144.
27. Haas, *Zwingli und der Erste Kappelerkrieg*, 153.
28. Z X, 147–148, cited in Potter, *Zwingli*, 366.
29. Bullinger, *Reformationsgeschichte*, vol. 2, 170; Potter, *Zwingli*, 367.
30. Bullinger, *Reformationsgeschichte*, vol. 2, 182–183.
31. Georg Kreis, 'Die Kappeler Milchsuppe: Kernstück der schweizerischen Versöhnungsikonographie', *Schweizer Zeitschrift für Geschichte*, 44 (1994), 288–310.
32. Z VI.2, 457–459.
33. Haas, *Zwingli und der Erste Kappelerkrieg*, 160.
34. Kurt Spillmann, 'Zwingli und Zürich nach dem Ersten Landfrieden', *Zwingliana*, 12 (1965), 255.
35. Sundar Henny, 'Failed reformations,' in Amy Nelson Burnett and Emidio Campi (eds), *A Companion to the Swiss Reformation* (Leiden, Brill, 2016), 264–290.
36. Spillmann, 'Zwingli und Zürich nach dem Ersten Landfrieden', 254.

37. Spillmann, 'Zwingli und Zürich nach dem Ersten Landfrieden', 257.
38. Gagliardi, Müller and Büsser (eds), *Johannes Stumpfs Schweizer- und Reformationschronik*, vol. 2, 64.
39. Spillmann, 'Zwingli und Zürich nach dem Ersten Landfrieden', 261.
40. Haas, *Zwingli und der Erste Kappelerkrieg*, 247.
41. Spillmann, 'Zwingli und Zürich nach dem Ersten Landfrieden', 262.
42. Spillmann, 'Zwingli und Zürich nach dem Ersten Landfrieden', 268.
43. Spillmann, 'Zwingli und Zürich nach dem Ersten Landfrieden', 275.
44. Z X, 293, 9–14.
45. Hauswirth, *Landgrave Philipp*, 523.
46. Oecolampadius to Zwingli, 4 May 1530, EA IV, 1b, 563–564.
47. Oecolampadius to Zwingli, 30 March 1530, Z X, 588, 15.
48. Thomas A. Brady, *Communities, Politics, and Reformation in Early Modern Europe* (Leiden, Brill, 1998), 66.
49. Jakob Sturm to Zwingli, 26 May 1530, Z X, 602.
50. Z X, 604, 3–7.
51. Brady, *Communities, Politics, and Reformation*, 66.
52. Z X, 634.
53. Z X, 629, 7.
54. Brady, *Communities, Politics, and Reformation*, 67.
55. Brady, *Communities, Politics, and Reformation*, 70.
56. Z XI, 5.
57. CR II, 193.
58. CR II, 221.
59. CR II, 193.
60. Z VI.2, 783.
61. Brady, *Communities, Politics, and Reformation*, 70.
62. Oecolampadius to Zwingli, 14 July 1530, Z XI, 23, 12–13.
63. Berchtold Haller to Zwingli, Z XI, 45, 9.
64. Z XI, 41.
65. Latin Works, vol. 2, 68.
66. Latin Works, vol. 2, 83.
67. Z VI.2, 779.

## CHAPTER 10

1. The crucial work remains Helmut Meyer, *Der Zweite Kappeler Krieg: Die Krise der schweizerischen Reformation* (Zurich, Hans Rohr, 1976).
2. L. Weisz, 'Die Geschichte der schweizerischen Glaubenskämpfe nach Ludwig Edlibach', *Neue Heidelberger Jahrbücher*, (1932), 69.
3. Kurt Spillmann, 'Zwingli und Zürich nach dem Ersten Landfrieden, (Schluß)', *Zwingliana*, 12 (1966), 309.
4. Martin Haas, 'Zwingli und die "Heimlichen Räte"', *Zwingliana*, 12 (1964), 35–68.
5. Meyer, *Der Zweite Kappeler Krieg*, 81.
6. George R. Potter, 'Zwinglian synods in Eastern Switzerland', *Journal of Ecclesiastical History*, 16 (1975), 261–266.
7. Meyer, *Der Zweite Kappeler Krieg*, 83.
8. Meyer, *Der Zweite Kappeler Krieg*, 84.
9. Greschat, *Martin Bucer*, 96.
10. Z XI, 251, 12–19.
11. Z XI, 251.
12. Z XI, 343, 9–12.
13. Peter Handy and Karl-Heinz Schmöger, *Fürsten, Stände, Reformatoren: Schmalkalden und der Schmalkaldische Bund* (Gotha, Perthes, 1996); Gabriele Haug-Moritz, *Der*

*Schmalkaldische Bund, 1530–1541/42: eine Studie zu den genossenschaftlichen Strukturelementen der politischen Ordnung des Heiligen Römischen Reiches Deutscher Nation* (Leinfelden-Echterdingen, DRW-Verlag, 2002).

14. Meyer, *Der Zweite Kappeler Krieg*, 53–56.
15. Hauswirth, *Philipp von Hessen*, 184–193.
16. Z VI.5, 6.
17. Z XI, 448, 16–20.
18. Zwingli to Oecolampadius, 4 June 1531, Z XI, 460, 4 – 461, 9.
19. Walther Köhler, *Das Buch der Reformation Huldrych Zwinglis von ihm selbst und gleichzeitigen Quellen erzählt* (Munich, Ernst Reinhardt, 1926), 313–316.
20. Meyer, *Der Zweite Kappeler Krieg*, 63.
21. Z VI.5, 8–9.
22. Z VI.5, 14.
23. Z VI.5, 17–21.
24. Z VI.5, 23.
25. Z VI.5, 130, 2 – 132, 11.
26. See W. Peter Stephens, 'Bullinger and Zwingli on the salvation of the heathen', *Reformation & Renaissance Review*, 7 (2005), 283–300; also Rudolf Pfister, *Die Seligkeit erwählter Heiden bei Zwingli* (Zurich, Theologischer Verlag, 1952).
27. LW 38, 289–291. Cited in Stephens, 'Bullinger and Zwingli', 284–285.
28. Melchior Schuler and Johannes Schultheiß (eds), *Sämtliche Werke: Opera omnia*, 8 vols (Zurich, 1828–1842), vol. 4, 95.
29. Stephens, 'Bullinger and Zwingli', 299.
30. Timmerman, *Heinrich Bullinger on Prophecy*, 107.
31. *Die gantze Bibel / der ursprünglichen ebraischen und griechischen Waarheyt nach auffs aller treüwlichest verteütschet: bey Christoffel Froschouer* [Zurich, 1531].
32. Above all, see Himmighöfer, *Die Zürcher Bibel*. Also, Sigrist, *Die Zürcher Bibel von 1531*; Wilfried Kettler, *Die Zürcher Bibel von 1531: philologische Studien zu ihrer Übersetzungstechnik und den Beziehungen zu ihren Vorlagen* (Bern and New York, Peter Lang, 2001).
33. Himmighöfer, *Die Zürcher Bibel*, 369.
34. Cited in Lavater, 'Die Froschauer-Bibel 1531', 115.
35. *Die gantze Bibel*, sig. Bl 2r.
36. Himmighöfer, *Die Zürcher Bibel*, 373.
37. *Die gantze Bibel*, sig. Bl 3v.
38. *Die gantze Bibel*, sig. Bl 5r.
39. *Die gantze Bibel*, sig. Bl 6v.
40. Hauswirth, *Philipp von Hessen*, 208.
41. Potter, *Zwingli*, 396.
42. Bullinger, *Reformationsgeschichte*, vol. 2, 388.
43. 'Was Zürich und Bernn not ze betrachten sye in dem fünförtischen Handel', 17–22 August 1531, Z VI.V, 222–253.
44. Meyer, *Der Zweite Kappeler Krieg*, 87.
45. Meyer, *Der Zweite Kappeler Krieg*, 88.
46. Meyer, *Der Zweite Kappeler Krieg*, 17.
47. Bullinger, *Reformationsgeschichte*, vol. 2, 388.
48. Staehelin, *Huldreich Zwingli*, vol. 2, 484.
49. Meyer, *Der Zweite Kappeler Krieg*, 140.
50. Meyer, *Der Zweite Kappeler Krieg*, 142–143.
51. Potter, *Zwingli*, 407.
52. Walther Köhler, 'Zwinglis letzte Predigten', *Zwingliana*, 16 (1912), 506–508.
53. Potter, *Zwingli*, 409.
54. Hans Salat, *Reformationschronik 1517–1534*, vol. 2, ed. Ruth Jörg (Bern, Allgemeine Geschichtforschende Gesellschaft der Schweiz, 1986), 771–772.

55. Latin Works, vol. 1, 23; Gottfried W. Locher, 'Die Legende vom Herzen Zwinglis neu untersucht: ein Beitrag zur Geistesgeschichte der Zürcher Reformation', Zwingliana, 10 (1953), 563–576.
56. Thomas Platter, *Thomas Platter Lebensbeschreibung*, ed. Alfred Hartmann, 3rd edn (Basel, Schwabe Verlag, 2006), 105–106.
57. Platter, *Lebensbeschreibung*, 108.
58. Helmut Meyer, 'Krisenmanagement in Zürich nach dem Zweiten Kappeler Krieg', Zwingliana, 14 (1977), 349–369.
59. Kurt Maeder, 'Die Unruhe der Zürcher Landschaft nach Kappel (1531/32) oder: Aspekte einer Herrschaftskrise', Zwingliana, 14 (1974/1975), 109–144.
60. Egli, *Actensammlung*, 1797, 28 November 1531, 789.
61. Meyer, *Der Zweiter Kappeler Krieg*, 306.
62. Myconius, *Briefwechsel*, vol. 1, 127, 193–194.

## CHAPTER 11

1. Oskar Farner, 'Leo Jud: Zwinglis treuster Helfer', Zwingliana, 10 (1955), 202.
2. Jacques Courvoisier, 'Zwinglis Tod im Urteil der Zeitgenossen', Zwingliana, 15 (1982), 607–620.
3. Bruce Gordon, 'Holy and problematic deaths: Heinrich Bullinger on Zwingli and Luther' in Marion Kobelt-Groch and Cornelia Niekus Moore (eds), *Tod und Jenseitsvorstellungen in der Schriftkultur der Frühen Neuzeit* (Wolfenbüttel, Harrassowitz, 2008), 47–62.
4. Luca Baschera, '"Apostel Helvetiens" Aspekte der Zwingli-Rezeption in Heinrich Bullingers Kommentaren zu den neutestamentlichen Briefen', paper presented at the conference 'Die Zürcher Reformation und ihre Rolle in den europäischen Reformationsbewegungen', Zurich, 6–8 February 2019. I am grateful to the author for allowing me to see the pre-publication essay.
5. *A famous and godly history contayning the lyves and Actes of three renowned reformers of the Christian churche, Martin Luther, John Oecolampadius and Huldericke Zwinglius*, trans. Henry Bennet (London, John Awdley, 1561).
6. For the fullest biography of Myconius, see Myconius, *Briefwechsel*, vol. 1, 9–71.
7. Irena Backus, *Life Writing in Reformation Europe: Lives of the reformers by friends, disciples and foes* (Aldershot, Ashgate, 2008), 47–52.
8. Alfred Erichson, *Zwingli's Tod und dessen Beurtheilung durch Zeitgenossen: Zumeist nach ungedruckten Strassburger und Zürcher Urkunden. Ein Beitrag zur 350. Todesfeier Zwingli's* (Strassburg, C.F. Schmidt, 1883), 21.
9. Erichson, *Zwingli's Tod*, 22.
10. Erichson, *Zwingli's Tod*, 23.
11. Erichson, *Zwingli's Tod*, 23.
12. Backus, *Life Writing*, 53-54.
13. Erichson, *Zwingli's Tod*, 18.
14. Erichson, *Zwingli's Tod*, 18.
15. Erichson, *Zwingli's Tod*, 19.
16. Erichson, *Zwingli's Tod*, 20.
17. Erichson, *Zwingli's Tod*, 17.
18. Erichson, *Zwingli's Tod*, 37.
19. Cited in Edwards, *Luther and the False Brethren*, 140.
20. Martin Luther, *The Table Talk of Martin Luther*, ed. Thomas S. Kepler (New York, World Publishing Company, 1952), 271.
21. Edwards, *Luther and the False Brethren*, 141.
22. Hans Ulrich Bächtold and Rainer Henrich (eds), *Heinrich Bullinger Briefwechseledition*, vol. 8 (Zurich, Theologischer Verlag Zürich, 2000), 129–130.
23. Erichson, *Zwingli's Tod*, 32.
24. J. Kammerer, 'Ein Spottlied auf Zwingli', Zwingliana, 6 (1936), 281.

25. Fritz Büsser, *Heinrich Bullinger (1504–1575): Leben, Werk und Wirkung*, 2 vols (Zurich, Theologischer Verlag, 2004–2005); Bruce Gordon and Emidio Campi (eds), *Architect of Reformation: An introduction to Heinrich Bullinger, 1504–1575* (Grand Rapids, MI, Baker Academic, 2004); Emidio Campi and Peter Opitz (eds), *Heinrich Bullinger: Life, thought, influence – Zurich, Aug. 25–29, 2004, International Congress Heinrich Bullinger (1504–1575)* (Zurich, Theologischer Verlag, 2007).

26. Fritz Büsser, 'De prophetae officio. Eine Gedenkrede Bullingers auf Zwingli' in Fritz Büsser (ed.), *Wurzeln der Reformation in Zürich. Zum 500. Geburtstag des Reformators Huldrych Zwingli* (Leiden, Brill, 1985), 106–124.

27. Daniel Bolliger, 'Bullinger on church authority: The transformation of the prophetic role in Christian ministry' in Bruce Gordon and Emidio Campi (eds), *Architect of Reformation: An introduction to Heinrich Bullinger, 1504–1575* (Grand Rapids, MI, Baker Academic, 2004), 167.

28. Emidio Campi, Detlef Roth and Peter Stolz (eds), *Bullinger Schriften*, vol. 1 (Zurich, Theologischer Verlag, 2004), 45.

29. Hans Salat, *Reformationsgeschichte*, ed. Friedrich Fiala and Peter Bannwart (Solothurn, n.p., 1868), 122.

30. Carl Pestalozzi (ed.), *Heinrich Bullinger: Leben und ausgewählte Schriften* (Eberfeld, R.L. Friedrichs, 1858), 86.

31. *Ioannis Oecolampadii et Huldrichi Zvingli Epistolarum libri quatuor: Utriusque vita et obitus Simone Grynaeo, Wolfgango Capitone, et Osvaldo Mynconio autoribus* (Basel, Thomas Platter, Balthasar Lasius, 1536); Christian Moser, *Theodor Bibliander (1505–1564, Annotierte Bibliographie der gedruckten Werke* (Zurich, Theologischer Verlag, 2009), n. B-5.I, 45–47.

32. *Ioannis Oecolampadii*, fols 2–3.

33. *Ioannis Oecolampadii*, fol. 38.

34. *Ioannis Oecolampadii*, fol. 55.

35. *Ioannis Oecolampadii*, fol. 56.

36. *Ioannis Oecolampadii*, fol. 56.

37. *Ioannis Oecolampadii*, fol. 56.

38. Ernst Gerhard Rüsch, 'Vadians Gutachten für eine Zwingli-Vita, 1544', *Zwingliana*, 15 (1979), 40–49.

39. Heinrich Bullinger to Joachim Vadian, 8 May 1544 in Heinrich Bullinger, *Heinrich Bullinger Werke*, Part II: *Briefwechsel*, vol. 14: *Briefe des Jahres 1544*, ed. Reinhard Bodenmann, Rainer Henrich, Alexandra Kess and Judith Steiniger (Zurich, TVZ, 2011), 233.

40. Quoted from Joachim von Watt, *Deutsche historische Schriften*, ed. Ernst Götzinger (St Gallen, Auf Veranstaltung des Historischen Vereins des Kantons St Gallen, 1879), vol. 3, 41–42.

41. Ernst Gerhard Rüsch (ed.), *Joachim Vadian: Ausgewählte Briefe* (St Gallen, Verlagsgemeinschaft St Gallen, 1983), 78–79.

42. Traugott Schieß (ed.), *Briefwechsel der Brüder Ambrosius und Thomas Blaurer*, vol. 2 (Freiburg im Breisgau, 1910), 307.

43. *Opera D. Huldrychi Zvinglii, vigilantissimi Tigurinae ecclesiae antistitis, partim quidem ab ipso latine conscripta, partim vero e vernaculo sermone in latinum translata: omnia novissime recognita & multis adiectis, quae hactenus visa non sunt ...* [ed. Rudolf Gwalther] (Zurich, Christoph Froschauer the Elder, 1544–1545).

44. The essential work on Bullinger's history is Christian Moser, *Die Dignität des Ereignisses: Studien zu Heinrich Bullingers Reformationsgeschichtsschreibung*, 2 vols (Leiden, Brill, 2012).

45. Bullinger, *Reformationsgeschichte*, vol. 2, 168.

46. Bruce Gordon, 'The Swiss Confederation in the age of John Calvin' in R. Ward Holder (ed.), *John Calvin in Context* (Cambridge, Cambridge University Press, 2020), 61–69.

47. Bruce Gordon, *Calvin* (New Haven, CT, and London, Yale University Press, 2009), 105–106, 180–186.

48. Gordon, *Calvin*, 164, 167, 207.

49. Cited in Fritz Blanke, 'Calvins Urteile über Zwingli', *Zwingliana*, 11 (1959), 68.

50. John Calvin, *Selections from his Writings*, ed. John Dillenberger (New York, Anchor Books, 1971), 540.

51. Théodore Beza, *Icones, id est verae imagines virorum doctrina simul et pietate illustrium, quorum praecipuè ministerio partim bonarum literarum studia sunt restituta, partim vera religio in variis orbis christiani regionibus, nostra patrúmque memoria fuit instaurata : additis eorundem vitae et operae descriptionibus, quibus adjectae sunt nonnullae picturae quas emblemata vocant. Theodoro Beza auctore* [Geneva, Jean de Laon, 1580].

52. Beza, *Icones*, mii verso.

53. Beza, *Icones*, mii recto.

54. Alexandra Kess, *Johann Sleidan and the Protestant Vision of History* (Aldershot, Ashgate, 2008).

55. Johannes Sleidanus, *The General History of the Reformation of the Church, From the Errors and Corruptions of the Church of Rome: Begun in Germany By Martin Luther, With the Progress thereof in all Parts of Christendom, From the Year 1517, to the Year 1556* (London, Printed by Edw. Jones for Abel Swall at the Unicorn, and Henry Bonwicke at the Red Lion in St Pauls Church-Yard, 1689), 156.

56. John Foxe, *Acts and Monuments* (1576), 870. Quoted from *The Unabridged Acts and Monuments Online* (Digital Humanities Institute, Sheffield, 2011), www.dhi.ac.uk/foxe

57. The discussion of the views of Zwingli's Catholic contemporaries that follows is indebted to Fritz Büsser, *Das katholische Zwinglibild*; see, in particular, 1–78.

58. Cited in Büsser, *Das katholische Zwinglibild*, 9.

59. Cited in Büsser, *Das katholische Zwinglibild*, 21.

60. Büsser, *Das katholische Zwinglibild*, 21.

61. Büsser, *Das katholische Zwinglibild*, 63.

62. Büsser, *Das katholische Zwinglibild*, 64.

63. Büsser, *Das katholische Zwinglibild*, 159.

## CHAPTER 12

1. On Luther's character and reputation, see Roper, *Martin Luther*.

2. Bruce Gordon, *John Calvin's Institutes of the Christian Religion: A biography* (Princeton, NJ, Princeton University Press, 2016).

3. Joseph August Eckschlager, *Ulrich Zwingli von Zürich* (Zurich, Orell, Füssli und Compagnie, 1811), 74–75.

4. Eckschlager, *Ulrich Zwingli von Zürich*, 96.

5. Helen Wild, 'Das Zürcher Reformationsjubiläum von 1819', *Zwingliana*, 12–13 (1918), 441–460.

6. Schuler and Schultheiß, *Sämtliche Werke*.

7. *Todtenfeier: U. Zwinglis Todtenfeyer gehalten auf dem Schlachtfeld zu Kappelden 11. Weinmonat 1831* (Zurich, 1831), 22.

8. Salomon Hess, *Anna Reinhard, Gattinn und Wittwe von Ulrich Zwingli, Reformator: Denk-Stück allernächst für Zürichs christliche Frauen, Töchter und ihre Freundinnen aus Archiven und Familienschriften bearbeitet* (Zurich, Johannes Caspar Näf, 1820).

9. Leopold von Ranke, *Deutsche Geschichte im Zeitalter der Reformation*, 6 vols (Berlin, Duncker und Humblot, 1839–1845).

10. Fritz Schmidt-Clausing, 'Das Zwingli-Bild Leopold von Rankes', *Zwingliana*, 14 (1974–1975), 145–153.

11. Leopold von Ranke, *History of the Reformation in Germany*, trans. Sarah Austin (London, George Routledge and Sons, 1905), 568.

12. J.J. Hottinger, *The Life and Times of Ulric Zwingli*, trans. T.C. Porter (Harrisburg, PA, Theo F. Scheffer, 1856), iv.

13. Johann Kaspar Mörikofer, *Ulrich Zwingli: Nach den urkundlichen Quellen* (Leipzig, S. Hirzel, 1867–1869).

14. Mörikofer, *Ulrich Zwingli*, iii.

15. Mörikofer, *Ulrich Zwingli*, vi.

16. Mörikofer, *Ulrich Zwingli*, vi.

17. Mörikofer, *Ulrich Zwingli*, vii.

18. For more information, see Konrad Schmid, *Die Theologische Fakultät der Universität Zürich: Ihre Geschichte von 1833 bis 2015* (Zurich, Theologischer Verlag, 2016).

19. Hedy Tschumi-Haefliger, 'Reformatoren-Denkmäler in der Schweiz', *Zwingliana*, 17 (1987), 219.

20. Tschumi-Haefliger, 'Reformatoren-Denkmäler', 219.

21. Cited in Tschumi-Haefliger, 'Reformatoren-Denkmäler', 22.

22. Christian Moser, 'Das Zwinglibild in der Schweiz im 19. Jahrhundert', paper presented at the conference 'Die Zürcher Reformation und ihre Rolle in den europäischen Reformationsbewegungen', Zurich, 6–8 February 2019. I am grateful to the author for allowing me to see his paper in advance of its publication. A video of the presentation is to be found at https://www.youtube.com/watch?v=hey4nk9onWA

23. Georg Finsler, *Drei Vorträge gehalten und herausgegeben zu Gunsten des Zwingli-Denkmals* (Zurich, Meyer and Zeller, 1873), 93–94.

24. Egli, *Actensammlung*.

25. Bernd Moeller, 'Der Zwingliverein und die reformationsgeschichtliche Forschung', *Zwingliana*, 25 (1998), 5–20.

26. Rudolf Staehelin, *Huldreich Zwingli und sein Reformationswerk* (Halle, Verein für Reformationsgeschichte, 1883), 1–7.

27. Staehelin, *Huldreich Zwingli*.

28. Ulrich Gäbler, *Huldrych Zwingli im 20. Jahrhundert: Forschungsbericht und annotierte Bibliographie 1897–1972* (Zurich, Theologischer Verlag, 1975), 28.

29. All issues of *Zwingliana*, the Zwingliverein's journal, from its inception are available at http://zwingliana.ch/index.php/zwa/issue/archive

30. *Ulrich Zwingli, 1519-1919, Zum Gedächtnis der Zürcher Reformation* (Zurich, Berichthaus, 1919).

31. Walther Köhler, *Die Geisteswelt Ulrich Zwinglis: Christentum und Antike* (Gotha, F.A. Perthes, 1920).

32. Köhler, *Zwingli und Luther*.

33. Walther Köhler, 'Zwingli als Theologe' in Herman Escher (ed.), *Ulrich Zwingli: zum Gedächtnis der Zürcher Reformation, 1519–1919* (Zurich, Buchdruckerei Berichthaus, 1919), 12–13.

34. Gäbler, *Huldrych Zwingli im 20. Jahrhundert*, 35.

35. Köhler, 'Zwingli als Theologe', 70.

36. Matthias Freudenberg, '". . . und Zwingli vor mir wie eine überhängende Wand" Karl Barths Wahrnehmung der Theologie Huldrych Zwinglis in seiner Göttinger Vorlesung von 1922/23', *Zwingliana*, 33 (2006), 5–27.

37. Peter Winzler, 'Zwingli und Karl Barth', *Zwingliana*, 17 (1987), 299.

38. Winzler, 'Zwingli und Karl Barth', 298–314.

39. Freudenberg, '". . . und Zwingli vor mir wie eine überhängende Wand"', 16.

40. Freudenberg, '". . . und Zwingli vor mir wie eine überhängende Wand"', 23.

41. Philip Schaff, *History of the Christian Church*, vol. 7: *Modern Christianity, the Swiss Reformation* (New York, Charles Scribner's Sons, 1892), 189.

42. Martin John Spalding, *The History of the Protestant Reformation, in Germany and Switzerland; and in England, Ireland, Scotland, the Netherlands, France and Northern Europe*, vol. 1: *Reformation in Germany and Switzerland*, 2nd edn (Louisville, KY, 1861), 170.

43. The first English translation was J.H. Merle d'Aubigné, *History of the Great Reformation of the Sixteenth Century in Germany, Switzerland, etc.*, trans. H. White, 5 vols (Hartford, CT, S. Andrus and Son, 1853–1854).

44. Hottinger, *Life and Times of Ulric Zwingli*, 404.

45. Schaff, *History of the Christian Church*, vol. 7, 175.
46. Schaff, *History of the Christian Church*, vol. 7, 181.
47. Schaff, *History of the Christian Church*, vol. 7, 34.
48. Schaff, *History of the Christian Church*, vol. 7, 93.
49. William Cunningham (1805–1861), *Oxford Dictionary of National Biography*, https://doi.org/10.1093/ref:odnb/6937
50. William Cunningham, *The Reformers and the Theology of the Reformation*, vol. 1 (Edinburgh, T. and T. Clark, 1862), 216.
51. James Isaac Good, *The Reformed Reformation* (Philadelphia, Berger Brothers, 1916).
52. Good, *The Reformed Reformation*, 125.
53. Good, *The Reformed Reformation*, 128.
54. George Park Fisher, *The Reformation* (New York, Charles Scribner's Sons, 1912), 126–127.
55. Williston Walker, *The Reformation* (New York, Charles Scribner's Sons, 1900), 150.
56. Walker, *The Reformation*, 180.
57. Spalding, *History of the Protestant Reformation*, 172.
58. Peter Winzeler, '"Losend dem Gotzwort!": Gottfried W. Lochers Bedeutung für die Zwingliforschung', *Zwingliana*, 25 (1998), 43–63.
59. Locher, *Die Zwinglische Reformation*. More handbook than monograph, it remains an indispensable resource.
60. Winzeler, '"Losend dem Gotzwort!"', 43–63.
61. Locher, *Zwingli's Thought*, 91.
62. Winzeler, '"Losend dem Gotzwort!"', 48.
63. Locher, *Zwingli's Thought*, 148.
64. Much of the discussion that follows appears also in Bruce Gordon and Randolph C. Head, 'Zwingli's ambivalent anniversary 2019: An *Ereignisbericht*', *Archiv für Reformationsgeschichte*, 111 (2020), 7–30. I am grateful to my co-author for consenting to the publication of this material here.
65. Lukas Bärfuss, 'Deshalb muss ich Huldrych Zwingli noch nicht mögen', *Du: die Zeitschrift der Kultur*, 7 (July/August 2003), 119.
66. Markus Notter, 'Nobody wants to return to Zwingli' in Peter Niederhäuser (ed.), *Verfolgt, Verdrängt, Vergessen: Schatten der Reformation* (Zurich, Chronos, 2018), 16.
67. https://www.ref.ch/news/zwingli-ist-der-wichtigste-beitrag-der-schweiz-zur-weltge-schichte/. See also Thomas Maissen, 'Der einzige Schweizer Beitrag zur Weltgeschichte', *Neue Zürcher Zeitung*, 13 May 2015.
68. André Holenstein, 'Zwinglis Reformation – eine fundamentalistische Revolution im frühen 16. Jahrhundert', *Neue Zürcher Zeitung*, 4 February 2019. https://www.nzz.ch/meinung/zwinglis-reformation-eine-fundamentalistische-revolution-im-fruehen-16-jahrhundert-ld.1451268?reduced=true
69. https://www.zuerich.com/en/visit/500-years-of-reformation
70. *Tages Anzeiger*, 3 July 2019, https://www.tagesanzeiger.ch/zuerich/stadt/zwingli-hebt-ab/story/24224349
71. See Walter Baumann and Marcel Warren, *Zürcher Kuh-Kultur* (Interlaken, Neptun, 1998).
72. All 12 versions are pictured in action at www.zhref.ch/zwinglistadt
73. *Zwingli*, directed by Stefan Haupt, C-Films, 2019. The film's funders included the Reformed Church in Zurich, Julius Bär Bank, and numerous foundations.
74. See Jan-Friedrich Missfelder, 'Ueli der Reformator', *Traverse*, 2 (2019), 163–177.

# ✤

# SELECT BIBLIOGRAPHY

## GENERAL WORKS

In English, the enduring biography of Zwingli remains George R. Potter, *Zwingli* (Cambridge, Cambridge University Press, 1976), a dense but thoroughly researched and elegantly written account of the reformer. There are a number of classic German biographies that greatly reward reading: Rudolf Staehelin's two-volume *Huldreich Zwingli: Sein Leben und Wirken nach den Quellen dargestellt* (Basel, B. Schwabe, 1895–97); Walther Köhler, *Huldreich Zwingli* (Leipzig, H. Haessel, 1923); Oskar Farner's four-volume *Huldrych Zwingli* (Zurich, Zwingli-Verlag, 1943–1960); Martin Haas, *Huldrych Zwingli und seine Zeit: Leben und Werk des Zürcher Reformators* (Zurich, Zwingli-Verlag, 1969).

The best short introduction to Zwingli remains Ulrich Gäbler, *Huldrych Zwingli: His life and work*, trans. Ruth C.L. Gritsch (Philadelphia, Fortress Press, 1986). One of the most engaging and theologically informed introductions to Zwingli's life and work is Peter Opitz's *Ulrich Zwingli: Prophet, Ketzer, Pionier des Protestantismus* (Zurich, Theologischer Verlag, 2015). The reader will also find useful W.P. Stephen's short summary, *Zwingli: An introduction to his thought* (Oxford, Clarendon, 1992). We have a number of helpful overviews of Zwingli's theology, notably Gottfried W. Locher, *Zwingli's Thought: New perspectives* (Leiden, Brill, 1981) and Peter Stephen's classic, *The Theology of Huldrych Zwingli* (Oxford, Clarendon Press, 1986). The most compendious work on Zwingli and his Reformation is Gottfried W. Locher, *Die Zwinglische Reformation im Rahmen der europäischen Kirchengeschichte* (Göttingen, Vandenhoeck & Ruprecht, 1979). The journal *Zwingliana*, produced in Zurich for the Zwingliverein, publishes in German and English the most extensive and wide-ranging work on Zwingli and the Zurich Reformation. It also provides a yearly bibliography of recently published material.

On the background to Zwingli and the Swiss Reformation, see Bruce Gordon, *The Swiss Reformation* (Manchester, Manchester University Press, 2002) and the invaluable recent collection, Amy Nelson Burnett and Emidio Campi (eds), *A Companion to the Swiss Reformation* (Leiden, Brill, 2016). Highly recommended is the treatment of the Swiss Reformation in Philip Benedict's *Christ's Churches Purely Reformed* (New Haven, CT, Yale University Press, 2004). Recent research is also expertly covered in Randolph C. Head's essay, 'The Swiss Reformations' in Ulinka Rublack (ed.), *The Oxford Handbook of the Protestant Reformations* (Oxford, Oxford University Press, 2017), 167–189. For an extremely accessible account of Swiss history, see Clive H. Church and Randolph C. Head, *A Concise History of Switzerland* (Cambridge, Cambridge University Press, 2013). Indispensable is Thomas Maissen, *Geschichte der Schweiz* (Baden, Hier und Jetzt, 2010).

## CHAPTER 1

On Swiss culture in the late Middle Ages, see David J. Collins, 'Turning Swiss: The patriotism of the holy hermit Nicholas' in his *Reforming Saints: Saint's lives and their authors in Germany, 1470-1530* (Oxford, Oxford University Press, 2008), 99–122; Tom Scott, *The Swiss and their Neighbours, 1460-1560: Between accommodation and aggression* (Oxford, Oxford University Press, 2017); Ulrich Gäbler, 'Die Schweizer – ein "Auserwähltes Volk"', *Zwingliana*, 19 (1992), 143–155; Randolph C. Head, 'William Tell and his comrades: Association and fraternity in the propaganda of fifteenth- and sixteenth-century Switzerland', *Journal of Modern History*, 67 (1995), 527–557; Eduard Jakob Kobelt, *Die Bedeutung der Eidgenossenschaft für Huldrych Zwingli* (Zurich, Leemann, 1970); Thomas Maissen, 'Inventing the sovereign republic: Imperial structures, French challenges, Dutch models and the early modern Swiss Confederation' in André Holenstein, Thomas Maissen and Maarten Prak (eds), *The Republican Alternative: The Netherlands and Switzerland compared* (Amsterdam, Amsterdam University Press, 2008), 125–155; Thomas Maissen, *Schweizer Heldengeschichten – und was dahintersteckt* (Baden, Hier und Jetzt, 2015); Peter Niederhäuser and Werner Fischer (eds), *Vom "Freiheitskrieg" zum Geschichtsmythos: 500 Jahre Schweizer- oder Schwabenkrieg* (Zurich, Chronos, 2000). On the mercenary service, see John McCormack, *One Million Mercenaries: Swiss soldiers in the armies of the world* (London, L. Cooper, 1993). On intellectual and humanist culture, see Rudolf Gamper, *Joachim Vadian, 1483/84-1551: Humanist, Arzt, Reformator, Politiker* (Zurich, Chronos, 2017); David H. Price, *Johannes Reuchlin and the Campaign to Destroy Jewish Books* (Oxford and New York, Oxford University Press, 2011); Conrad Bonorand, 'Die Bedeutung der Universität Wien für Humanismus und Reformation, insbesondere in der Ostschweiz', *Zwingliana*, 12 (1965), 162–180; Daniel Bolliger, *Infiniti Contemplatio: Grundzüge der Scotus- und Scotismusrezeption im Werk Huldrych Zwinglis. Mit ausführlicher Edition bisher unpublizierter Annotationen Zwinglis* (Leiden, Brill, 2003). On Swiss relations with France, see Christian Moser and Hans Rudolf Fuhrer, *Der lange Schatten Zwinglis: Zürich, das französische Soldbündnis und eidgenössische Bündnispolitik, 1500-1650* (Zurich, Verlag Neue Zürcher Zeitung, 2009).

## CHAPTER 2

Crucial to Zwingli's early development in Glarus is Hans Schneider, 'Zwinglis Anfänge als Priester' in Martin Sallmann and Martin Wallraff (eds), *Schweizer Kirchengeschichte – neu reflektiert* (Bern, Peter Lang, 2010), 37–62. His intellectual development through books is traced in Urs B. Leu and Sandra Weidmann, *Huldrych Zwingli's Private Library* (Leiden, Brill, 2019). On Hugo of Hohenlandenberg and his culture, Peter Niederhäuser (ed.), *Ein feiner Fürst in einer rauen Zeit: Der Konstanzer Bischof Hugo von Hohenlandenberg* (Zurich, Chronos, 2011). The literature on Erasmus is vast, but best on the Swiss connections is Christine Christ-von Wedel and Urs B. Leu (eds), *Erasmus in Zürich: Eine verschwiegene Autorität* (Zurich, Verlag Neue Zürcher Zeitung, 2007); a magisterial work is Christine Christ-von Wedel, *Erasmus of Rotterdam: Advocate of a new Christianity* (Toronto, University of Toronto Press, 2013). See also Cornelis Augustijn, 'Zwingli als Humanist', *Nederlands Archief voor Kerkgeschiedenis/Dutch Review of Church History*, 67 (1987), 120–142. There is an enormous body of literature on Erasmus' New Testament, but see Henk Jan de Jonge, 'Novum Testamentum a nobis versum: The essence of Erasmus' edition of the New Testament', *Journal of Theological Studies*, 35 (1984), 394–413. On Zwingli and the Bible from earliest times to his death: Traudel Himmighöfer, *Die Zürcher Bibel bis zum Tode Zwinglis, 1531: Darstellung und Bibliographie* (Mainz, P. von Zabern, 1995).

## CHAPTER 3

Crucial on the political and economic structure of Zurich is Walter Jacob, *Politische Führungsschicht und Reformation: Untersuchungen zur Reformation in Zürich 1519-1528*

SELECT BIBLIOGRAPHY

(Zurich, Juris Druck + Verlag, 1969); Hans Morf, 'Obrigkeit und Kirche in Zürich bis zu Beginn der Reformation', *Zwingliana*, 13 (1970), 164–205. Also seminal on Zwingli's political relations: René Hauswirth, *Landgraf Philipp von Hessen und Zwingli; Voraussetzungen und Geschichte der politischen Beziehungen zwischen Hessen, Strassburg, Konstanz, Ulrich von Württemberg und reformierten Eidgenossen, 1526–1531* (Tübingen, Osiander (Kommisionsverlag), 1968); also, Hans-Christoph Rublack, 'Zwingli und Zürich', *Zwingliana*, 16 (1985), 393–426. On the social and political conditions in Zurich, see Lee Palmer Wandel, *Always Among Us: Images of the poor in Zwingli's Zurich* (Cambridge and New York, Cambridge University Press, 1990). An older, but still very helpful work on the Zurich background is Robert C. Walton, *Zwingli's Theocracy* (Toronto, University of Toronto Press, 1968). The most authoritative work on the pre-Reformation and Reformation Church in Zurich is Gerald Dörner, *Kirche, Klerus und Kirchliches Leben in Zürich von der Brunschen Revolution (1336) bis zur Reformation (1523)* (Würzburg, Könighausen und Neumann, 1996). On Zwingli's conversion and the plague song, see Thomas Martin Schneider, 'Der Mensch als "Gefäß Gottes": Huldrych Zwinglis Gebetslied in der Pest und die Frage nach seiner reformatorischen Wende', *Zwingliana*, 35 (2008), 5–21. The crucial work on the origins of radicalism is by Andrea Strübind – above all *Eifriger als Zwingli: Die frühe Täuferbewegung in der Schweiz* (Berlin, Duncker & Humblot, 2003), 125–129, but also 'The Swiss Anabaptists' in Amy Nelson Burnett and Emidio Campi (eds), *A Companion to the Swiss Reformation* (Leiden, Brill, 2016), 391–395. On the wider cultural implications of the fast breaking, see Christopher Kissane, *Food, Religion and Communities in Early Modern Europe* (London, Bloomsbury Academic, 2018). On clerical marriage, Marjorie Elizabeth Plummer, *From Priest's Whore to Pastor's Wife: Clerical marriage and the process of reform in the early German Reformation* (Aldershot, Ashgate, 2012). On Leo Jud and Johannes Oecolampadius, see Karl-Heinz Wyss, *Leo Jud: seine Entwicklung zum Reformator, 1519–1523* (Bern and Frankfurt am Main, Peter Lang, 1976) and Jeff Fisher, 'The breakdown of a Reformation friendship: John Oecolampadius and Philip Melanchthon', *Westminster Journal of Theology*, 77 (2015), 265–291. The classic study of Oecolampadius is Rudolf Staehelin, *Das theologische Lebenswerk Johannes Oekolampads* (reprinted New York and London, Johnson, 1971).

CHAPTER 4

On disputations in the Swiss Reformation, see Fabrice Flückiger, *Dire le vrai. Une Histoire de la dispute religieuse au début du XVIe siècle Ancienne Confédération Helvétique, 1523–1536* (Neuchâtel, Éditions Alphil-Presses universitaires suisses, 2018). The literature on the emergence of the radical movement in Zurich and the Swiss lands is extremely rich. A selection includes: James M. Stayer, *Anabaptists and the Sword* (reprinted Eugene, OR, Wipf & Stock, 2002); Harold S. Bender, *Conrad Grebel: The founder of the Swiss Brethren* (reprinted Eugene, OR, Wipf & Stock, 1998); Arnold Snyder, 'Word and power in Reformation Zurich', *Archiv für Reformationsgeschichte/Archive for Reformation History*, 81 (1990), 263–285; James M. Stayer, 'Reublin and Brötli: The revolutionary beginnings of Swiss Anabaptism' in Marc Leinhard (ed.), *The Origins and Characteristics of Anabaptism* (The Hague, Nijhoff, 1977), 83–102; Arnold C. Snyder, 'The birth and evolution of Swiss Anabaptism (1520–1530)', *Mennonite Quarterly Review*, 80 (2006), 501–645. On Zwingli's baptismal theology, see Timothy George, 'The presuppositions of Zwingli's baptismal theology' in Edward J. Furcha and H. Wayne Pipkin (eds), *Prophet, Pastor, Protestant: The work of Huldrych Zwingli after five hundred years* (Eugene, OR, Wipf & Stock); Hughes Oliphant Old, *The Shaping of the Reformed Baptismal Rite in the Sixteenth Century* (Grand Rapids, MI, Eerdmans, 1992). On the development of iconoclasm in Zurich, see above all Cécile Dupeux, Peter Jezler and Jean Wirth (eds), *Bildersturm: Wahnsinn oder Gottes Wille?* (Zurich, NZZ Verlag, 2000); also, Lee Palmer Wandel, *Voracious Images and Violent Hands: Iconoclasm in Reformation Zurich, Strasbourg and Basel* (Cambridge, Cambridge University Press, 1995) and Peter Jezler, 'Bildersturm in Zürich: Vom Angriff auf die Kunstwerke zur Säkularisierung des Kirchenguts' in Peter Niederhäuser (ed.), *Verfolgt, Verdrängt, Vergessen: Schatten der Reformation* (Zurich,

336

Chronos, 2018), 41–56. Further, Katherina Heyden, 'Aureola, Hätzer und Buchstab: Drei Protagonisten des reformatorischen Bilderstreits in der Schweiz zwischen Umbruch und Transformation', *Schweizerische Zeitschrift für Religions- und Kulturgeschichte*, 111 (2017), 65–86. Also, Nicholas Paul Smiar, 'Poor law and outdoor poor relief in Zurich, 1520–1529: A case study in social welfare history and social welfare policy implementation', PhD thesis, University of Illinois at Chicago, 1986.

## CHAPTER 5

On reformation of the female religious houses, Sybille Knecht, 'Wohin mit den Nonnen? Zürcher Frauenklöster im Brennpunkt der Reformation' in Peter Niederhäuser (ed.), *Verfolgt, Verdrängt, Vergessen: Schatten der Reformation* (Zurich, Chronos, 2018), 27–40; John P. Maarbjerg, 'Iconoclasm in the Thurgau: Two related incidents in the summer of 1524', *Sixteenth Century Journal*, 24 (1993), 577–593. On Zwingli and Jews, Hans-Martin Kirn, 'Ulrich Zwingli, the Jews, and Judaism' in Dean Phillip Bell and Stephen G. Burnet (eds), *Jews, Judaism, and the Reformation in Sixteenth-Century Germany* (Leiden, Brill, 2006), 171–196; Achim Detmers, *Reformation und Judentum: Israel-Lehren und Einstellungen zum Judentum von Luther bis zum frühen Calvin* (Stuttgart, Kohlhammer, 2001); Peter Niederhäuser, 'Fremd- und Feindbilder? Juden in der Zürcher Reformation' in Peter Niederhäuser (ed.), *Verfolgt, Verdrängt, Vergessen: Schatten der Reformation* (Zurich, Chronos, 2018), 121–132. Concerning the early influences on Zwingli's eucharistic thought: B.J. Spruyt, *Cornelius Henrici Hoen (Honius) and his Epistle on the Eucharist (1525)* (Leiden, Brill, 2006). Essential reading on the early years is Amy Nelson Burnett, *Karlstadt and the Origins of the Eucharistic Controversy: A study in the circulation of ideas* (Oxford, Oxford University Press, 2011). On the development of the Peasants' War in the Swiss lands, Peter Blickle, *The Communal Reformation: The quest for salvation in sixteenth-century Germany* (reprinted Leiden, Brill, 1992). On the liturgy of the Lord's Supper, Alfred Ehrensperger, *Geschichte des Gottesdienstes in Zürich Stadt und Land im Spätmittelalter und in der frühen Reformation bis 1531* (Zurich, Theologischer Verlag, 2018); Bruce Gordon, ' "It is the Lord's Passover": History, theology, and memory in the liturgy of the Lord's Supper in Reformation Zurich' in Teresa Berger and Bryan D. Spinks (eds), *Liturgy's Imagined Past/s: Methodologies and materials in the writing of liturgical history today* (Collegeville, MN, Liturgical Press, 2016), 172–200; Lee Palmer Wandel, 'Envisioning God: Image and liturgy in Reformation Zurich', *Sixteenth Century Journal*, 24 (1993), 21–40. On Zwingli and music, Markus Jenny, *Zwinglis Stellung zur Musik im Gottesdienst* (Zürich, Zwingli-Verlag, 1966); Hannes Reimann, 'Zwingli als Musiker', *Archiv für Musikwissenschaft*, 17 (1960), 126–141; Gerhard Aeschbacher, 'Zwingli und die Musik in Gottesdienst', *Zwingliana*, 19 (1992), 1–11; Charles Garside, *Zwingli and the Arts* (New Haven, CT, Yale University Press, 1966). The work on Zwingli and Zurich biblical scholarship is extensive: helpful are Peter Opitz, 'Huldrych Zwingli' in Magne Sæbø (ed.), *Hebrew Bible/Old Testament: The history of its interpretation*, vol. 2: *From the Renaissance to the Enlightenment* (Göttingen, Vandenhoeck & Ruprecht, 2008), 413–428; Daniël Timmerman, *Heinrich Bullinger on Prophecy and the Prophetic Office (1523–1538)* (Göttingen, Vandenhoeck & Ruprecht, 2015); Christoph Zürcher, *Konrad Pellikans Wirken in Zürich, 1526–1556* (Zurich, Theologischer Verlag, 1975); R. Gerald Hobbs, 'Pluriformity of early Reformation scriptural interpretation' in Magne Sæbø (ed.), *Hebrew Bible/Old Testament: The history of its interpretation*, vol. 2: *From the Renaissance to the Enlightenment* (Göttingen, Vandenhoeck & Ruprecht, 2008), 452–487; Walter E. Meyer, 'Die Entstehung von Huldrych Zwinglis neutestamentlichen Kommentaren und Predigtnachschriften', *Zwingliana*, 14 (1976), 285–331. On Zwingli's understanding of providence, see Aurelio A. Garcia, ' "Summum Bonum" in the Zurich Reformation: Zwingli and Bullinger', *Zwingliana*, 44 (2017), 183–188. On Zwingli and the covenant, the classic work is Wayne J. Baker, *Heinrich Bullinger and the Covenant: The other reformed tradition* (Athens, OH, Ohio University Press, 1980). Baker's views on Zwingli have been significantly and persuasively revised by Pierrick Hildebrand, 'The Zurich origins of reformed covenantal theology', PhD thesis, Zurich University, 2019 (to be published by Oxford University Press).

## CHAPTER 6

On the French religious background in the 1520s, see Jonathan A. Reid, 'France' in Andrew Pettegree (ed.), *The Reformation World* (London and New York, Routledge, 2002), 211–224; Jason Zuidema and Theodore van Raalte, *Early French Reform: The theology and spirituality of Guillaume Farel* (Aldershot, Ashgate, 2011); Mack P. Holt, *Renaissance and Reformation in France, 1500–1648* (Oxford, Oxford University Press, 2002); Denis Crouzet, *La genèse de la Réforme française 1520–1562* (Paris, SEDES, 1996); Janine Garrisson, *Les protestants au XVI^e siècle* (Paris, Fayard, 1988); and Francis Higman, *La diffusion de la Réforme en France* (Geneva, Labor et Fides, 1992). Zwingli's theological work is thoroughly treated in Martin Sallmann, *Zwischen Gott und Mensch: Huldrych Zwinglis theologischer Denkweg im De vera et falsa religione commentarius (1525)* (Tübingen, Mohr Siebeck, 1999); Christof Gestrich, *Zwingli als Theologe: Glaube und Geist beim Zürcher Reformator* (Zurich, Zwingli-Verlag, 1967); Richard Stauffer, 'Einfluß und Kritik des Humanismus in Zwinglis "Commentarius de vera et falsa religione"', *Zwingliana*, 16 (1983). On Zwingli's understanding of religion, Görge K. Hasselhoff, 'Huldrych Zwinglis Verständnis von religio', *Zeitschrift für Religions- und Geistesgeschichte*, 67 (2015), 120–131. Concerning his understanding of free will, Volker Leppin, 'Adams Wille und Gottes Provenienz: Die Bestreitung des freien Willens in Zwinglis "Commentarius"', *Zwingliana*, 22 (1995), 37–43. A helpful treatment of providence and predestination is to be found in Peter Stephens, 'The place of predestination in Zwingli and Bucer', *Zwingliana*, 19 (1992), 393–410. On Zwingli's concept of freedom, see Berndt Hamm, *Zwinglis Reformation der Freiheit* (Neukirchen-Vluyn, Neukirchener Verlag, 1988).

## CHAPTER 7

A helpful source-based account of Zwingli's eucharistic theology is Johannes Voigtländer, *Ein Fest der Befreiung: Huldrych Zwingli Abendmahlslehre* (Neukirchener-Vluyn, Neukirchener Verlag, 2013). On Zwingli's relationship to Luther, the literature is vast. A selection includes: Mark U. Edwards, Jr., *Luther and the False Brethren* (Stanford, CA, Stanford University Press, 1975); Bruce Gordon, ' "For if we are true prophets": Huldrych Zwingli on Martin Luther', *Reformation*, 22 (2017), 102–119; Martin Brecht, 'Zwingli als Schüler Luthers: Zu seiner theologischen Entwicklung 1518–22', *Zeitschrift für Kirchengeschichte*, 96 (1985), 301–319; Wilhelm H. Neuser, *Die reformatorische Wende bei Zwingli* (Neukirchen-Vluyn, Neukirchener Verlag, 1977); Fritz Blanke, 'Zwinglis Urteile über sich selbst', *Furche-Jahrbuch*, 22 (1936), 31–39; Walther Köhler, *Zwingli und Luther: Ihr Streit über das Abendmahl nach seinen politischen und religiösen Beziehungen* (Leipzig and Gütersloh, Vermittlungsverlag von M. Heinsius Nachfolger, 1924, reprinted 1953); Arthur Rich, *Die Anfänge der Theologie Huldrych Zwinglis* (Zurich, Zwingli-Verlag, 1949); Gottfried W. Locher, 'The characteristic features of Zwingli's theology in comparison with Luther and Calvin' in his *Zwingli's Thought: New perspectives* (Leiden, Brill, 1981), 142–232; Joachim Rogge, 'Die Initia Zwinglis und Luthers: Ein Einführung in die Probleme', *Luther-Jahrbuch*, 30 (1963), 107–133; Hans Schneider, 'Zwinglis Marienpredigt und Luthers Magnifikat-Auslegung: Ein Beitrag zum Verhältnis Zwinglis zu Luther', *Zwingliana*, 23 (1996), 105–141; August Pieper, 'What makes up the "different spirit" of which Luther accused the Zwinglians?', *Wisconsin Lutheran Quarterly*, 107 (2010), 166–190. On Zwingli's dream of the Eucharist: Bruce Gordon, 'Zwingli's dream of the Lord's Supper' in Maria-Christina Pitassi and Solfaroli Camillocci (eds), *Crossing Traditions: Essays on the Reformation and intellectual history in honour of Irena Backus* (Leiden, Brill, 2017), 298–310.

The essential works on the sacramental debate are: Amy Nelson Burnett, *Karlstadt and the Origins of the Eucharistic Controversy: A study in the circulation of ideas* (Oxford, Oxford University Press, 2011) and her *Debating the Sacraments: Print and authority in the early Reformation* (Oxford, Oxford University Press, 2019). On the detailed political and religious negotiations: Thomas A. Brady, Jr., *Protestant Politics: Jacob Sturm (1489–1553)* (Atlantic Highlands, NJ, Humanities Press, 1995). On the spread of Zwingli's thought in the southern

Empire: Joel van Amberg, *A Real Presence: Religious and social dynamics of the eucharistic conflicts in early modern Augsburg 1520–1530* (Leiden, Brill, 2011). On Zwingli's sermon on providence: Iren Snavely, ' "The evidence of things unseen": Zwingli's sermon on providence and the colloquy of Marburg', *Westminster Theological Journal*, 56 (1994), 399–407.

## CHAPTER 8

The classic work on the Reformation in the cities is Heinrich Richard Schmidt, *Reichstädte, Reich und Reformation* (Stuttgart, Franz Steiner Verlag, 1986). On the ongoing Anabaptist threat: James M. Stayer, 'Swiss South German Anabaptism, 1526–1540' in John D. Roth and James M. Stayer (eds), *A Companion to Anabaptism and Spiritualism* (Leiden and Boston, Brill, 2007), 83–118; Akira Demura, 'From Zwingli to Calvin: A comparative study of Zwingli's Elenchus and Calvin's Briève Instruction' in Alfred Schindler and Hans Stickelberger (eds), *Die Zürcher Reformation: Ausstrahlungen und Rückwirkungen* (Zurich, Peter Lang, 2001), 87–99. On Anabaptist women: C. Arnold Snyder and Linda A. Hueberg Hecht (eds), *Profiles of Anabaptist Women: Sixteenth century reforming pioneers* (Waterloo, ON, Wilfred Laurier Press, 1996); Wes Harrison, 'The role of women in Anabaptist thought and practice: The Hutterite experience of the sixteenth and seventeenth centuries', *Sixteenth Century Journal*, 23 (1992), 49–69. On Balthasar Hubmaier, see Andrew P. Klager, 'The early influence of humanism on Balthasar Hubmaier (1485–1528) during his university studies', *Reformation and Renaissance Review*, 22 (2020), 4–24; Kirk R. MacGregor, 'Hubmaier's death and the threat of a free state church', *Church History and Religious Culture*, 91 (2011), 321–348; Graeme R. Chatfield, *Balthasar Hubmaier and the Clarity of Scripture: A critical reformation issue* (Cambridge, James Clarke & Co., 2013), 156–157; Torsten Bergsten, *Balthasar Hubmaier: Anabaptist theologian* (King of Prussia, PA, Judson Press, 1978); on Sattler and the Schleitheim Articles, see C. Arnold Snyder, *The Life and Thought of Michael Sattler* (Scottsdale, PA, Herald Press, 1984); also his 'Revolution and the Swiss Brethren: The case of Michael Sattler', *Church History*, 50 (1981), 276–287, and 'The Schleitheim Articles in light of the revolution of the common man: Continuation or departure?', *Sixteenth Century Journal*, 16 (1985), 419–430; James M. Stayer, 'The Swiss Brethren: An exercise in self-definition', *Church History*, 47 (1978), 174–195; Walter Klaassen, 'The "Schleitheim Articles" and the "New Transformation of Christian Living" ', *Historical Reflections/Réflexions Historiques*, 14 (1987), 95–111; Brad S. Gregory, 'Anabaptist martyrdom: Imperatives, experience and memorialization' in D. Roth and James M. Stayer (eds), *Companion to Anabaptism and Spiritualism* (Leiden and Boston, Brill, 2007), 467–506; Preston Lee Atwood, 'The Martyrs' Song: The hymnody of the early Swiss Brethren Anabaptists', *The Artistic Theologian*, 2 (2013), 85. On Zwingli and society: Arthur Rich, 'Zwingli als sozialpolitischer Denker', *Zwingliana*, 13 (1969), 79–80. Concerning the formation of the clergy: Bruce Gordon, *Clerical Discipline and the Rural Reformation: The synod in Zurich, 1532–1580* (Bern, Peter Lang, 1992); Bruce Gordon, 'The Protestant clergy and the culture of rule: The reformed Zurich clergy of the sixteenth century' in C. Scott Dixon and Luise Schorn-Schütte (eds), *The Protestant Clergy of Early Modern Europe* (London, Palgrave, 2003), 137–155; Martin Hauser, *Prophet und Bischof: Huldrych Zwinglis Amtsverständnis im Rahmen der Zürcher Reformation* (Fribourg, Schweiz, Universitätsverlag, 1994); Bruce Gordon, 'Polity and reform in the Swiss Reformed churches' in Amy Nelson Burnett and Emidio Campi (eds), *A Companion to the Swiss Reformation* (Leiden, Brill, 2016), 489–519; Küngolt Kilchenmann, *Die Organisation des zürcherischen Ehegerichts zur Zeit Zwinglis* (Zurich, Zwingli-Verlag, 1946). On Zwingli's correspondence with women: Edward J. Furcha, 'Women in Zwingli's world', *Zwingliana*, 19 (1992), 131–142. Background to the disputations is found in Ulrich Pfister, 'Konfessionskonflikte in der frühneuzeitlichen Schweiz: Eine strukturalistische Interpretation', *Schweizerische Zeitschrift für Religions- und Kulturgeschichte*, 101 (2007), 257–312. The protocols, with rich historical and theological interpretation, are to be found in Alfred Schindler and Wolfram Schneider-Lastin (eds), *Die Badener Disputation von 1526: Kommentierte Edition des Protokolls* (Zurich, Theologischer Verlag, 2015). On Eck, essential is Jürgen Bärsch and Konstantin Maier (eds), *Johannes Eck (1486–1543): Scholastiker – Humanist – Kontroverstheologe* (Regensburg, Friedrich Pustet, 2014).

## CHAPTER 9

On the situation for Zwinglians in southern Germany: Philip Broadhead, 'Guildsmen, religious reform and the search for the common good: The role of the guilds in the early Reformation in Augsburg', *Historical Journal*, 39 (1996), 577–597. The politics and religion of Zwingli's relationship to Philipp of Hesse are thoroughly treated in René Hauswirth, *Landgraf Philipp von Hessen und Zwingli; Voraussetzungen und Geschichte der politischen Beziehungen zwischen Hessen, Strassburg, Konstanz, Ulrich von Württemberg und reformierten Eidgenossen, 1526–1531* (Tübingen, Osiander (Kommisionsverlag), 1968). Also, Hauswirth, 'Landgraf Philipp von Hessen und Zwingli: Ihre politischen Beziehungen 1529/1530', *Zwingliana*, 11 (1962), 499–552. Crucial on the First Kappel War: Martin Haas, 'Zwingli und der Erste Kappelerkrieg', *Zwingliana*, 12 (1964), 93–136; Kurt Spillmann, 'Zwinglis politische Pläne in der Ostschweiz', *Rorschacher Neujahrsblatt*, 52 (1962), 61–74; Rudolf Braun, 'Zur Militärpolitik Zürichs im Zeitalter der Kappeler Krieg', *Zwingliana*, 10 (1958), 537–573; and Kurt Spillmann, 'Zwingli und Zürich nach dem Ersten Landfrieden', *Zwingliana*, 12 (1965), 254–280. Further, Thomas A. Brady, *Communities, Politics, and Reformation in Early Modern Europe* (Leiden, Brill, 1998).

## CHAPTER 10

The essential work on the lead-up to the Kappel War remains Helmut Meyer, *Der Zweite Kappeler Krieg: Die Krise der schweizerischen Reformation* (Zurich: Hans Rohr, 1976). On Zwingli's position in Zurich: Martin Haas, 'Zwingli und die "Heimlichen Räte"', *Zwingliana*, 12 (1964), 35–68. On the final confessions, W. Peter Stephens, 'Bullinger and Zwingli on the salvation of the heathen', *Reformation & Renaissance Review*, 7 (2005), 283–300; also, Rudolf Pfister, *Die Seligkeit erwählter Heiden bei Zwingli* (Zurich, Theologischer Verlag, 1952). On the Zurich Bible: Christoph Sigrist (ed.), *Die Zürcher Bibel von 1531: Entstehung, Verbreitung und Wirkung* (Zurich, Theologischer Verlag, 2011); Wilfried Kettler, *Die Zürcher Bibel von 1531: philologische Studien zu ihrer Übersetzungstechnik und den Beziehungen zu ihren Vorlagen* (Bern and New York, Peter Lang, 2001).

## CHAPTER 11

On the response of Zwingli's contemporaries to his death, see Jacques Courvoisier, 'Zwinglis Tod im Urteil der Zeitgenossen', *Zwingliana*, 15 (1982), 607–620; Bruce Gordon, 'Holy and problematic deaths: Heinrich Bullinger on Zwingli and Luther' in Marion Kobelt-Groch and Cornelia Niekus Moore (eds), *Tod und Jenseitsvorstellungen in der Schriftkultur der Frühen Neuzeit* (Wolfenbüttel, Harrassowitz, 2008); Alfred Erichson, *Zwingli's Tod und dessen Beurtheilung durch Zeitgenossen: Zumeist nach ungedruckten Strassburger und Züricher Urkunden. Ein Beitrag zur 350. Todesfeier Zwingli's* (Strassburg, C.F. Schmidt, 1883), 47–62. Irena Backus has studied Myconius' life of Zwingli in her *Life Writing in Reformation Europe: Lives of the reformers by friends, disciples and foes* (Aldershot, Ashgate, 2008). Luther on Zwingli's death: Mark U. Edwards, Jr., *Luther and the False Brethren* (Stanford, CA, Stanford University Press, 1975). The standard biography of Heinrich Bullinger is Fritz Büsser, *Heinrich Bullinger (1504–1575): Leben, Werk und Wirkung*, 2 vols (Zurich, Theologischer Verlag, 2004–2005). See also: Bruce Gordon and Emidio Campi (eds), *Architect of Reformation: An introduction to Heinrich Bullinger, 1504–1575* (Grand Rapids, MI, Baker Academic, 2004); Emidio Campi and Peter Opitz (eds), *Heinrich Bullinger: Life, thought, influence – Zurich, Aug. 25–29, 2004, International Congress Heinrich Bullinger (1504–1575)* (Zurich, Theologischer Verlag, 2007). Vadian's possible biography is discussed in Ernst Gerhard Rüsch, 'Vadians Gutachten für eine Zwingli-Vita, 1544', *Zwingliana*, 15 (1979), 40–49. Calvin on Zwingli is treated in

Fritz Blanke, 'Calvins Urteile über Zwingli', *Zwingliana*, 11 (1959), 66–92. The crucial study of Catholic responses to Zwingli is Fritz Büsser, *Das katholische Zwinglibild: Von der Reformation bis zur Gegenwart* (Zurich and Stuttgart, Zwingli-Verlag, 1968).

## CHAPTER 12

Much of this chapter is covered in Bruce Gordon and Randolph C. Head, 'Zwingli's ambivalent anniversary 2019: An *Ereignisbericht*', *Archiv für Reformationsgeschichte*, 111 (2020), 7–30. On the early anniversaries of Zwingli, see Helen Wild, 'Das Zürcher Reformationsjubiläum von 1819', *Zwingliana*, 12–13 (1918), 441–460; and Hedy Tschumi-Haefliger, 'Reformatoren-Denkmäler in der Schweiz', *Zwingliana*, 17 (1987), 195–262. The founding of the Zwingliverein is discussed in Bernd Moeller, 'Der Zwingliverein und die reformationsgeschichtliche Forschung', *Zwingliana*, 25 (1998), 5–20. Barth's complex relationship to Zwingli is found in Peter Winzeler, 'Zwingli und Karl Barth', *Zwingliana*, 17 (1987), 298–314, and Matthias Freudenberg, '"... und Zwingli vor mir wie eine überhängende Wand" – Karl Barths Wahrnehmung der Theologie Huldrych Zwinglis in seiner Göttinger Vorlesung von 1922/23', *Zwingliana*, 33 (2006), 5–27. On Gottfried Locher, see Peter Winzeler, '"Losend dem Gotzwort!": Gottfried W. Lochers Bedeutung für die Zwingliforschung', *Zwingliana*, 25 (1998), 43–63.

# INDEX